Cultural Change and the Market Revolution in America, 1789–1860

Cultural Change and the Market Revolution in America, 1789–1860

EDITED BY SCOTT C. MARTIN

A MADISON HOUSE BOOK
ROWMAN & LITTLEFIELD PUBLISHERS, INC.
Lanham • Boulder • New York • Toronto • Oxford

ROWMAN & LITTLEFIELD PUBLISHERS, INC.

Published in the United States of America
by Rowman & Littlefield Publishers, Inc.
A wholly owned subsidiary of The Rowman & Littlefield Publishing Group, Inc.
4501 Forbes Boulevard, Suite 200, Lanham, Maryland 20706
www.rowmanlittlefield.com

PO Box 317
Oxford
OX2 9RU, UK

British Library Cataloguing in Publication Information Available

Library of Congress Cataloging-in-Publication Data

Cultural change and the market revolution in America, 1789–1860 / edited by Scott C.
Martin.
    p. cm.
    Includes bibliographical references and index.
    ISBN 0-7425-2770-0 (hardcover : alk. paper) — ISBN 0-7425-2771-9 (pbk. : alk.
paper)
        1. Capitalism—Social aspects—United States—History. 2. Capitalism—Political
aspects—United States—History. 3. Capitalism—Religious aspects—History.
4. Democracy—United States—History. I. Martin, Scott C., 1959– II. Title.

    HC110.C3C85 2004
    306.3'42—dc22   2004010459

Printed in the United States of America

∞™ The paper used in this publication meets the minimum requirements of American
National Standard for Information Sciences—Permanence of Paper for Printed Library
Materials, ANSI/NISO Z39.48-1992.

Contents

1

Introduction: Toward a Cultural History of the Market Revolution

SCOTT C. MARTIN

In a lecture delivered more than thirty years ago, the cultural historian Neil Harris reflected on the state of urban history. Though much progress had been made in sketching the political and economic development of cities, Harris noted, the "noneconomic appeals" of urban areas—the "motives and effects of urban institutions concerned primarily with . . . people's habits, values, and diversions" (or, put another way, their cultural history)—remained elusive. To frame his discussion of that history, Harris differentiated three distinct meanings of "culture." Until the nineteenth century, culture was "more an activity than a state of being; it represented growth or nourishment, and could be applied to almost anything." The Victorians transformed culture into a noun that signified the "highest and most valued human activities." During the twentieth century, culture acquired another meaning, more "comprehensive and catholic": a "pattern of value structures, mores, and institutions" possessed by every social group.[1]

With some modification, Harris's diagnosis of the state of urban cultural history in the early 1970s, as well as his genealogy of the meaning of culture, offers an interesting analogy to trends in the study of the cultural history of the market revolution in America. As was the case with urban history thirty years ago, historians of the market revolution know a great deal about the political and economic results of market expansion during the years between the ratification of the Constitution and the outbreak of the Civil War.

Monographs, edited volumes, and journal articles have addressed the development of capitalism during the early republic, the character of market expansion, and the impact of market revolution on Jacksonian politics. Indeed, the most recent collection of articles on the market revolution, edited by Melvyn Stokes and Stephen Conway, devoted eight of twelve chapters exclusively to economic and political topics.[2] For all of this excellent work, however, our knowledge of the cultural implications and ramifications of the penetration of market relations into most of the United States during this period remains much hazier. Moreover, Harris's account of the changing meanings of culture mirrors, after a fashion, the genesis of research into the cultural impact of the market revolution. Beginning during the mid-twentieth century, early work on market expansion and related topics focused on the sheer growth of markets, along with the territorial expansion, the enlarged and improved transportation network, and the changing economic patterns that supported and underpinned them. By the 1970s and 1980s, historians had turned their attention to the market's impact on what, for historians, had traditionally been regarded as the most significant human activity: politics. Only in the past decade or so, since the publication of Charles Sellers's magisterial *The Market Revolution: Jacksonian America, 1815–1846*, have historians begun, in any sustained or systematic way, to explore the impact of early nineteenth-century market expansion on ethnic and racial identity, popular entertainment, patterns of leisure and sociability, and other topics that fall under the purview of cultural history.[3]

This is not to argue, of course, that no pertinent or useful cultural history of the market revolution has appeared until the past few years. Indeed, one of the primary tasks for cultural historians seeking to construct a solid foundation for future work will be gleaning existing scholarship for insights into the market's impact on American cultural patterns. Many classic and lesser-known studies contain important material germane to this topic, and doubtless many historians will have personal favorites. My discussion of existing scholarship here is meant to be suggestive rather than exhaustive: a starting point from which to begin reconstructing the cultural history of the market revolution in America. In this vein, the pioneering work on preindustrial *mentalité* by scholars such as Michael Merrill, James Henretta, Christopher Clark, and Allan Kulikoff provides an excellent beginning for understanding the cultural values and social practices of many Americans at the onset of market expansion.[4] Similarly, articles and books written decades ago on the development of distinctive class cultures during the early nineteenth century might be reread profitably. For the working class, important studies by Alan Dawley, Paul Faler, Bruce Laurie, and, more recently, Sean Wilentz and Christine Stansell provide vantage points from which to begin assessing the cultural impact of the market revolution on American workers.[5] For the middle class, works by Nancy Cott, Mary Ryan, Karen Haltunnen, Stuart Blumin, and others remain invaluable resources.[6] Though histories of the early nineteenth-century American upper class have not been quite so numerous as those examining other parts of the socioeconomic spectrum, important studies by E. Digby Baltzell and Ronald Story illuminate the impact of dramatic economic change on the culture of American elites.[7]

Other classic works of social and cultural history also offer materials useful for constructing a cultural history of the market revolution. Paul Johnson's study of revivals and reform along the Erie Canal, for instance, demonstrates how rapid economic expansion influenced mores, reform activity, and class identity. William Rorabaugh's delineation of the "alcoholic republic" presents the intriguing possibility that individual and cultural anxiety resulting from rapid social and economic change, as much as greater access to spirituous liquors, produced the spike in American alcohol consumption during the early nineteenth century. In his elaboration of what he termed the "operational aesthetic," Neil Harris offers cultural historians a valuable perspective on the emerging market in popular entertainment and its linkage to Americans notions of democratic culture and identity. Certainly, no adequate cultural history of the market revolution could afford to ignore Joseph J. Ellis's classic study of postrevolutionary American cultural nationalism or Lawrence Levine's account of hierarchization and sacralization in nineteenth-century American art and entertainment. In addition to these more focused monographs, general cultural histories of the early and mid-nineteenth century, such as those by Anne C. Rose and Lewis Perry, also have much to offer.[8]

In one area that sometimes falls under the rubric of cultural history—religious life and practice—the impact of market expansion has received more attention. Though published somewhat before the present upsurge in historical interest in the market revolution, Nathan Hatch's *The Democratization of American Christianity* provides a sound basis for investigating the relationship between market forces and the religious experience of nineteenth-century Americans. It was Charles Sellers's intriguing discussion of religion in *The Market Revolution*, however, that piqued historians' interest and ensured that religious issues would receive continued attention. Sellers employed theological categories to limn two divergent reactions to the market: "Protestantism's antipodal heresies" of Arminianism and antinomianism. Arminian moralism, Sellers explained, "sanctioned competitive individualism and the market's rewards of wealth and status," while antinomian "new birth recharged rural America's communal egalitarianism in resistance." Sellers's distinctive reading of this spiritual divide certainly had the salutary effect of sparking interest among other scholars in exploring the religious dimensions of the market revolution, if only to critique or modify what Richard Ellis termed his "dense . . . jargon-ridden," and "idiosyncratic" argument. On the downside, however, it seems that the centrality of Sellers's work has pushed much of the new research on religion and the market in the direction of reevaluations of his position. Daniel Walker Howe's and Richard Carwardine's fine contributions to *The Market Revolution in America*, for example, take Sellers's terminology and argument as their starting point.[9]

This is only a troubling sign, of course, if it limits the nature and scope of future research, and there are already signs that this is not the case. Historians have begun to explore the religious dimensions of market expansion with concerns and approaches not tied directly to Sellers's formulation. Surveys of antebellum religion and reform by Steven Mintz and Robert Abzug have incorporated themes related to the market revolution into their analysis, as has Stephen L. Longenecker in his fine study of religion in the Shenandoah Valley. Nathan Hatch has expanded on his previous work to address the relationship between market forces and the Second Great Awakening. Critiquing the influence of E. P. Thompson on American historians such as Bruce Laurie, Paul Johnson, and Charles Sellers, Hatch notes that they accord religion "little autonomous causal efficacy" and view revivals as merely "one more tool of elites to discipline the vagrant and unruly impulses of the working class." In contrast, Hatch emphasized the rejection of religious hierarchy by evangelical preachers and common people as a source of support for free markets:

> If capitalism is defined as the avid pursuit of improved circumstances through market exchange, then these evangelical preachers were eager capitalists—like

so many of their constituents throughout rural America. A society of contractual individualism was not merely foisted on the country by great merchants and aristocrats. A liberal social order percolated up from the convictions of ordinary people who were convinced that gospel liberty was the very meaning of America.[10]

In another promising line of research, historians have examined the expanding communications networks by which religious ideas circulated during the market revolution. David Paul Nord and Mark S. Schantz, for example, have focused on religious tracts as significant indicators of market influence, noting both their extensive distribution through expanding communications networks and their ambivalence toward the growing influence of the market on American life. In his study of the American Tract Society, Schantz notes that the "technological innovations of the kind that propelled the market revolution also drove, quite literally, the machines of the Tract Society," putting it on "the cutting edge of the publishing business." Moreover, the society relied on the systematic distribution of tracts in cities and town, along with "colporteurs," agents resembling "commercial peddlers" who handed out literature in rural areas. Still, Schantz cautions, in presenting an "alternative universe of spiritual values against which the real world could be judged and found inadequate," tracts expressed grave doubts about the spiritual cost of market revolution.[11]

If religion has garnered much attention, other areas of culture influenced by the market revolution, notably leisure and popular entertainment, have also received some notice. As part of a growing interest in the history of leisure activities, tourism, and sociability, historians of the early nineteenth-century United States have examined the ways in which expanding access to goods, services, and transportation shaped American patterns of recreation. Cultural historians have paid particular heed to the emergence of resorts, pleasure gardens, and tourist destinations as part of an expanding market in leisure. Dona Brown's *Inventing New England: Regional Tourism in the Nineteenth Century*, for instance, chronicles the creation of a tourist landscape in New England to serve the needs of the emerging middle class. My own *Killing Time: Leisure and Culture in Southwestern Pennsylvania, 1800–1850* examined both the emergence of local and regional leisure venues around Pittsburgh and the impact of the market-driven commercialization of leisure on social interaction and cultural values. Recently, several fine studies of spas and summer resorts have provided, either explicitly or implicitly, insights into the cultural significance of market expansion. These include Jon Sterngass's examination of Saratoga Springs, Newport, and Coney Island; Charlene M. Boyer Lewis's study of the Virginia Springs; and Thomas Chambers's work on mineral springs. Also of note are the early chapters of Cindy S. Aron's history of vacations in the United States.[12]

The market revolution's impact on the forms, genres, and conventions of popular entertainment has also received scrutiny. A prominent example is Eric Lott's *Love and Theft*, which examined blackface minstrelsy, perhaps Americans' favorite form of popular entertainment at midcentury. Lott deftly showed how minstrelsy helped white Americans navigate (not always successfully) the racial, social, and political rapids produced by the economic transformation and class development associated with the market revolution. James W. Cook has examined the American fascination with fraud and humbug as aspects of popular entertainment that emerged forcefully during the early nineteenth century. In an intriguing chapter that discusses P. T. Barnum's exhibition of the infamous Feejee Mermaid in the context of the market revolution, Cook likens the showman's trickery to business practices that became standard procedure during the nineteenth century. Barnum's greatest trick, Cook observed, was to convince "his new middle-class peers that humbug in the exhibition room was merely market capitalism by another name." These and other inquiries into such topics as newspapers, southern humor, middle-class literary enthusiasm for the California gold rush, and the soundscape of antebellum America constitute a promising beginning to a cultural history of the market revolution.[13]

Despite this promising start, however, our knowledge of the cultural aspects of the market expansion is far from complete, and much work remains before we will have anything like a satisfactory cultural history. In terms of Neil Harris's genealogy of the meaning of culture, with which this introduction began, scholarship has only begun to address concerns and issue characteristic of the most recent understanding of culture: as the values, practices, and institutions created by every social group. We still know relatively little, for example, about the contributions, actions, and responses of women, African Americans, Native Americans, and other ethnic groups to market change. How did participating in widening financial networks, choosing from an ever-increasing array of consumer goods and services, and struggling against the vagaries of impersonal and unfamiliar economic forces influence family life, class identity, gender roles, ethnic and racial identification, and so-cial interaction? And conversely, how did the cultural values and social prac-tices with which Americans responded to economic change shape the evolution of the market?[14]

This volume brings together essays, some previously published and some appearing here for the first time, that provide a solid basis for elaborating the cultural impact of the market revolution. Though they cover a wide range of topics, all focus on the impact of the market on one or more broad areas of concern to cultural historians: racial, ethnic, and regional identity; gender; middle-class culture; and popular entertainment. Three examine explicitly how market forces and ideologies influenced the experiences of racial or eth-nic groups. Patrick Rael investigates how market ideology provided free blacks in the antebellum North a way of articulating and responding to the racial prejudice with which whites regarded the African American community. African American leaders, Rael argues forcefully, viewed reputation as a com-modity in the marketplace of ideas. The growth of the market and of new me-dia for disseminating ideas and information made possible the circulation of racial prejudice, which both injured blacks and perverted the free market by denying meritocracy. African American thinkers came to believe that if they could intervene in the ideological marketplace to make slavery and racial prej-udice discreditable, they might begin to remove the obstacles to their self-elevation imposed by white society.

Kevin Thornton's contribution explores another group disadvantaged by the market revolution: French Canadians who settled across the border in Ver-mont. Though the market revolution had transformed this region during the first half of the nineteenth century, Thornton finds, French-speaking Cana-dian émigrés such as Antoine Lorain, the subject of his study, still lived in con-ditions that more closely resembled the frontier than the settled, market-driven society Vermont had become. Complicating the notion that winners and losers in the new economy were divided by a willingness to em-brace the imperatives of the expanding market, Thornton finds that language, ethnicity, religion, and culture shaped prospects for success in Vermont. Many of these variables also figure prominently in James Taylor Carson's account of the impact of the market revolution on the culture and cattle economy of the

Choctaws of the lower Mississippi valley. Choctaws adopted cattle raising by
the early nineteenth century in response to developments in their regional
economy, Carson discovers, but also incorporated cattle into existing cultural
patterns and practices. Rather than arguing that the encroaching market completely transformed Choctaw culture, Carson employs linguistic evidence to
demonstrate that both Choctaw men and women reconceived their participation in cattle raising to make it consonant with established cultural patterns.

Joseph Rainer's study of Yankee peddlers in the South raises issues of consumerism, market penetration of areas beyond the Northeast, and regional
identity. Some southerners resented Yankee encroachment on their section,
characterizing northern foot soldiers of the market revolution as "Commercial Scythians." Others, however, eager for consumer goods such as tinware
and clocks, allowed themselves to be drawn into the market. Sometimes their
interaction with Yankee vendors produced hostility, especially when dishon-
esty or shoddy goods were involved. Rainer shows how market expansion contributed to regional identity, intensifying and expanding the image of the
crafty Yankee that had already taken shape in New England.

Gender and class appear peripherally in the chapters by Rael, Thornton,
Carson, and Rainer but occupy center stage in those by Catherine Kelly and
Jeffrey Mullins. Though the market revolution is not the central focus of
Kelly's prize-winning essay, the impact of market forces on rural New England's middle-class culture is an implicit concern. Middle-class New Englanders, Kelly argues, used patterns of rural sociability to differentiate themselves
from the social practices of the urban bourgeoisie that arose with the development of capitalism and market expansion. New Englanders created discourses surrounding sociability that contrasted the simple, respectable leisure
of small towns to the class-based, market-driven recreation of cities. Moreover, the discourse of "provincial sociability" contained deeply gendered elements, especially as women assumed, over the course of the antebellum era, a
larger share of the responsibility for organizing parties, festivals, and outings.
In a very different context, Jeffrey Mullins's examination of the manual labor
movement also highlights middle-class concerns surrounding class and gender. The constellation of economic changes we call the market revolution,
Mullins contends, evoked concern among middle-class educators and reformers. On the one hand, they feared that inadequate access to education would
produce a permanent underclass of laborers who would be unable to take ad-

vantage of new economic opportunities. On the other, they worried that too much book learning would undermine the health and masculinity of middle-class men. Educational reformers proposed colleges that required manual labor of their students, Mullins explained, to enable poor students to pay for their tuition and wealthier students to preserve their manliness while defusing a potential course of class conflict.

The three chapters on popular entertainment during the market revolution also engage many of the previously mentioned issues, but in the context of their packaging and dissemination to a mass audience. Brett Mizelle's chapter on animal shows and exhibitions demonstrates how improved transportation and an enlarged market for amusement reshaped a traditional form of entertainment. In an era characterized by the love of novelty, unfamiliar animals from far-off places became a staple of popular entertainment. At the same time, many exhibitors of animals, as well as their critics, fretted that the market for novelty and amusement might result in entrepreneurial pandering to debased or unrefined tastes. In the resulting debates, Mizelle urges, Americans used exhibitions of exotic animals to discuss and negotiate their changing relationship to a market dominated society. Graham Warder's study of T. S. Arthur's *Ten Nights in a Bar-Room* also takes anxieties about the future of a market-driven society as its focus. Temperance fiction, and particularly his Arthur's works, Warder contends, condemned drink, one evil of market society, while extolling another, mass-produced moral literature. *Ten Nights* evoked nostalgia for the kind of close-knit communities that market forces undermined. For Warder, moral literature such as temperance fiction helped both "readers and writers to work their way through the disturbing cultural upheavals of the Market Revolution." Finally, my own chapter on the theatrical star Edwin Forrest and his Indian play *Metamora* examines how historians and literary scholars have interpreted one of the most popular American plays of the nineteenth century. Most commentators have interpreted *Metamora* as a cultural prop for the Democratic Party's Indian removal agenda. In my view, the play reveals more about American feelings of cultural inferiority to England and Europe than about an alliance between culture and politics in the service of expropriating Indian land. Though obviously racist in many particulars, *Metamora* reflects Forrest's recognition of the possibilities of cultural entrepreneurship in an expanding market for "American" entertainment rather than specific political motives.

Taken together, the chapters presented here address many of the issues central to enhancing our understanding of the cultural dimensions, ramifications, and reactions to market expansion during the early nineteenth century. While they constitute only a beginning, it is hoped that they will motivate other scholars to examine further the cultural history of the market revolution, enlarging, in Neil Harris's words, our knowledge of "people's habits, values, and diversions" during this critical period of U.S. history.

NOTES

1. Neil Harris, "Four Stages of Cultural Growth: The American City," in *Indiana Historical Society Lectures, 1971–1972: History and the Role of the City in American Life* (Indianapolis: Indiana Historical Society, 1972), 26, 27.

2. See, for example, Harry Watson, *Liberty and Power: The Politics of Jacksonian American* (New York: Noonday Press, 1990); Daniel Feller, "Politics and Society: Toward a Jacksonian Synthesis," *Journal of the Early Republic* 10, no. 2 (1990): 135–61; Paul Goodman, "The Manual Labor Movement and the Origins of Abolitionism," *Journal of the Early Republic* 13, no. 3 (1993): 355–88, and "The Emergence of Homestead Exemption in the United States: Accommodation and Resistance to the Market Revolution, 1840–1880," *Journal of American History* 80, no. 2 (1993): 470–98; Paul Gilje, ed., *Wages of Independence: Capitalism in the Early American Republic* (Madison, Wis.: Madison House, 1997); James Henretta, "The 'Market' in the Early Republic," *Journal of the Early Republic* 18, no. 2 (1998): 289–304; Andrew C. Isenberg, "The Market Revolution in the Borderlands: George Champlin Sibley in Missouri and New Mexico, 1808–1826," *Journal of the Early Republic* 21, no. 3 (2001): 445–65; and Melvyn Stokes and Stephen Conway, eds., *The Market Revolution in America: Social, Political, and Religious Expressions, 1800–1860* (Charlottesville: University Press of Virginia, 1996).

3. I will not reprise here existing discussions of the historiography of the market revolution in America. Rather, I would like to highlight scholarship that has contributed to our understanding of its cultural dimensions. For an excellent overview of market revolution historiography, consult Melvyn Stokes, "Introduction," to Stokes and Conway, *The Market Revolution in America.* For a symposium on Charles Sellers's *The Market Revolution: Jacksonian America, 1815–1846* (New York: Oxford University Press, 1991), see the special issue of the *Journal of the Early Republic* 12 (1992).

4. Michael Merrill, "Cash Is Good to Eat: Self-Sufficiency and Exchange in the Rural Economy of the United States," *Radical History Review* 4 (1977): 42–71; James Henretta, "Families and Farms: *Mentalité* in Pre-Industrial America," *William and Mary Quarterly* 35 (1978): 3–32; Christopher Clark, "Household Economy, Market Exchange, and the Rise of Capitalism in the Connecticut River Valley, 1800–1860," *Journal of Social History* 13 (1979): 169–90, and *The Roots of Rural Capitalism: Western Massachusetts, 1780–1860* (Ithaca, N.Y.: Cornell University Press, 1990). On this point, see also Daniel Vickers, "Competency and Competition: Economic Culture in Early America," *William and Mary Quarterly* 47, no. 1 (1990): 3–29; Winifred B. Rothenberg,

From Market-Places to a Market Economy: The Transformation of Rural Massachusetts, 1750–1850 (Chicago: University of Chicago Press, 1992); and Allan Kulikoff, *The Agrarian Origins of American Capitalism* (Charlottesville: University Press of Virginia, 1992).

5. Alan Dawley, *Class and Community: The Industrial Revolution in Lynn* (Cambridge, Mass.: Harvard University Press, 1976); Paul Faler, "Cultural Aspects of the Industrial Revolution: Lynn, Massachusetts Shoemakers and Industrial Morality, 1826–1860," *Labor History* 15, no. 3 (1974): 367–94; Alan Dawley and Paul Faler, "Working Class Culture and Politics in the Industrial Revolution: Sources of Loyalism and Revolution," *Journal of Social History* 9, no. 4 (1976): 466–80; Bruce Laurie, "Nothing on Compulsion: Lifestyles of Philadelphia Artisans, 1820–1850," *Labor History* 15, no. 3 (1974): 337–66; Sean Wilentz, *Chants Democratic: New York City and the Rise of the American Working Class* (New York: Oxford University Press, 1984); Christine Stansell, *City of Women: Sex and Class in New York, 1789–1860* (New York: Knopf, 1986).

6. Nancy F. Cott, *The Bonds of Womanhood: "Woman's Sphere" in New England, 1780–1835* (New Haven, Conn.: Yale University Press, 1977); Mary Ryan, *Cradle of the Middle Class: The Family in Oneida County, New York, 1790–1865* (Cambridge: Cambridge University Press, 1981); Karen Haltunnen, *Confidence Men and Painted Women: A Study of Middle Class Culture in America, 1830–1870* (New Haven, Conn.: Yale University Press, 1982); Stuart Blumin, *The Emergence of the Middle Class: Social Experience in the American City, 1760–1900* (Cambridge: Cambridge University Press, 1989).

7. See, for example, E. Digby Baltzell, *Puritan Boston and Quaker Philadelphia: Two Protestant Ethics and the Spirit of Class of Class Authority and Leadership* (New York: Free Press, 1979), and Ronald Story, *The Forging of an Aristocracy: Harvard and the Boston Upper Class, 1800–1870* (Middletown, Conn.: Wesleyan University Press, 1980).

8. Paul E. Johnson, *A Shopkeeper's Millennium: Society and Revivals in Rochester, New York, 1815–1837* (New York: Hill & Wang, 1978); William J. Rorabaugh, *The Alcoholic Republic: An American Tradition* (New York: Oxford University Press, 1979); Neil Harris, *Humbug: The Art of P. T. Barnum* (Boston: Little, Brown, 1973); Joseph J. Ellis, *After the Revolution: Profiles of Early American Culture* (New York: Norton, 1979); Lawrence W. Levine, *Highbrow/Lowbrow: The Emergence of Cultural Hierarchy in America* (Cambridge, Mass.: Harvard University Press, 1988); Anne C. Rose, *Voices of the Marketplace: American Thought and Culture, 1830–1860* (New York: Twayne Publishers, 1995); Lewis Perry, *Boats against the Current: American Culture between Revolution and Modernity, 1820–1860* (New York: Oxford University Press, 1993).

9. Nathan O. Hatch, *The Democratization of American Christianity* (New Haven, Conn.: Yale University Press, 1989); Sellers, *The Market Revolution*, 30, 31; Richard E. Ellis, "A Transforming Revolution," in "A Symposium on Charles Sellers, *The Market Revolution: Jacksonian America, 1815–1846*," *Journal of the Early Republic* 12, no. 4 (1992): 449; Daniel Walker Howe, "The Market Revolution and the Shaping of Identity in Whig-Jacksonian America," in Stokes and Conway, *The Market Revolution in America*, 259–81; and Richard Carwardine, "'Antinomians' and 'Arminians': Methodists and the Market Revolution," in Stokes and Conway, *The Market Revolution in America*, 282–310.

10. Steven Mintz, *Moralists and Modernizers: America's Pre–Civil War Reformers* (Baltimore: Johns Hopkins University Press, 1995); Robert H. Abzug, *Cosmos Crumbling: American Reform*

and the Religious Imagination (New York: Oxford University Press, 1994); Stephen Longenecker, *Shenandoah Religion: Outsiders and the Mainstream, 1716–1865* (Waco, Tex.: Baylor University Press, 2002), esp. 79–112; Nathan Hatch, "The Second Great Awakening and the Market Revolution," in *Devising Liberty: Preserving and Creating Freedom in the New American Republic,* ed. David Thomas Konig (Stanford, Calif.: Stanford University Press, 1995), 249, 259. See also the recent collection of articles edited by Mark A. Noll, *God and Mammon: Protestants, Money and the Market, 1790–1860* (New York: Oxford University Press, 2002), pertinent to the market revolution from several perspectives, many of which are heavily influenced by Sellers's paradigm or reactions to it.

11. Mark S. Schantz, "Religious Tracts, Evangelical Reform, and the Market Revolution in Antebellum America," *Journal of the Early Republic* 17 (1997): 3, 428, 429, 465. See also David Paul Nord, "Religious Reading and Readers in Antebellum America," *Journal of the Early Republic* 15 (1995): 2, and "Systematic Benevolence: Religious Publishing and the Marketplace in Early Nineteenth-Century America," in *Communication and Change in American Religious History,* ed. Leonard I. Sweet (Grand Rapids, Mich.: Eerdmans, 1993), and R. Laurence Moore, *Selling God: American Religion in the Marketplace of Culture* (New York: Oxford University Press, 1994).

12. Dona Brown, *Inventing New England: Regional Tourism in the Nineteenth Century* (Washington, D.C.: Smithsonian Institution Press, 1995); Scott C. Martin, *Killing Time: Leisure and Culture in Southwestern Pennsylvania, 1800–1850* (Pittsburgh: University of Pittsburgh Press, 1995); Jon Sterngass, *First Resorts: Pursuing Pleasure at Saratoga Springs, Newport and Coney Island* (Baltimore: Johns Hopkins University Press, 2001); Charlene M. Boyer Lewis, *Ladies and Gentlemen on Display: Planter Society at the Virginia Springs, 1790–1860* (Charlottesville: University Press of Virginia, 2001); Thomas A. Chambers, *Drinking the Waters: Creating an American Leisure Class at Nineteenth-Century Mineral Springs* (Washington, D.C.: Smithsonian Institution Press, 2002); Cindy S. Aron, *Working at Play: A History of Vacations in the United States* (New York: Oxford University Press, 1999).

13. Eric Lott, *Love and Theft: Blackface Minstrelsy and the American Working Class* (New York: Oxford University Press, 1993); James W. Cook, *The Arts of Deception: Playing with Fraud in the Age of Barnum* (Cambridge, Mass.: Harvard University Press, 2001); Kevin G. Barnhurst and John Nerone, *The Form of News: A History* (New York: Guilford Press, 2001), 68–106; Christopher Morris, "What's So Funny: Southern Humorists and the Market Revolution," in *Southern Writers and Their World,* ed. Christopher Morris and Steven G. Reinhardt (College Station: Texas A& M University Press, 1996), 9–26; Brian Roberts, *American Alchemy: The California Gold Rush and Middle-Class Culture* (Chapel Hill: University of North Carolina Press, 2000); Mark M. Smith, *Listening to Nineteenth-Century America* (Chapel Hill: University of North Carolina Press, 2001).

14. Some attention has been paid to gender roles. See, for example, Samuel J. Watson, "Flexible Gender Roles during the Market Revolution: Family, Friendship, Marriage and Masculinity among U.S. Army Officers, 1815–1846," *Journal of Social History* 29, no. 1 (1995): 81–106.

2

The Market Revolution and Market Values in Antebellum Black Protest Thought

Patrick Rael

Considering the influence of the market revolution on African Americans conjoins two widely disparate themes: the economic changes at the forefront of American society and the people most left behind by the economic development of American society. While the market revolution brought untold novelty and progress to millions, few foundered in its wake more than American blacks. Still, the story of African Americans' relationship to the market revolution is not one of mere neglect or stasis—of a people left behind by progressive changes in the economy. The market revolution was a vital source of *change* for African Americans, and whether blacks benefited or lost by it, their story cannot be told without reference to those changes. By the same token, the story of the market revolution itself cannot be complete without assessing its impact on those it slighted.

Contradictorily, the economic revolution that birthed the industrial order affected African Americans most directly through the great boost it gave to the preindustrial system of southern agriculture. The manufacturing revolution in Britain and the northeastern United States fostered the vast expansion of cotton cultivation in the South. The spread of mechanized looms created a huge demand for the fiber, which was met only through the rapid development of southern agriculture and its "peculiar" labor system. Slavery, commonly thought to be doomed at the time of the American Revolution, found congenial company in the market revolution's growing demand for raw materials from the periphery. Contrary to much popular thinking, the civil war that was required to destroy slavery in the United States resulted not from economic competition between two incompatible forms of production but from the political and ideological struggles between the champions of these codependent forms, over which would yield the greatest influence over the political system.

While the market revolution most affected blacks through the growth of slavery that it spurred in the agricultural periphery, the sentiments that finally destroyed the institution developed as a result of the market revolution in the industrializing metropolitan cores. First, radical abolitionism appeared in the North, spearheaded by moral reformers such as William Lloyd Garrison. Considered "crack-brained fanatics" in their day, these radicals anchored a growing segment of public opinion that viewed slavery as sinful, antiquated, and antidemocratic. By weakening the radicals' message, political abolitionists such as Gerrit Smith and his Liberty Party offered antislavery fare more palatable to northern tastes. Still, success did not come until the original antislavery message had been compromised even further. Only in the 1850s, when the newly formed Republican Party hit on the dual formulation of "free labor" and "slave power conspiracy"—ideas that appealed as much to northerners' inherent racism as to their patriotism—did northern public opinion become sufficiently antislavery to challenge the slaveocracy for control of the union. Somehow, the market revolution had created an ideological atmosphere congenial to the destruction of slavery. Even so, complete abolition emerged only gradually on the Civil War agenda and as the result of military exigence rather than a revolution in racial sentiments. And in the wake of slavery's demise, the market revolution's much-vaunted cry of "free labor" went largely unheeded.

This tale neglects key players in the northern metropole. Along with the radical abolitionists—and, indeed, largely inspiring them—were important black voices urging incessantly for the end not simply of slavery but of racial prejudice. Free black leaders[1] from the antebellum North crafted a rich body of protest thought designed to sway an intransigent public to abolish slavery and promote the ideals of equality at the core of America's national founding myth. These free spokespersons, often culled from the elites of their communities, represent a crucial but little-understood group with important implications for assessments of the market revolution and its ideological consequences. They stood in curious relation to the powerful economic and social forces swirling around them. Not enslaved in the plantation South, neither were they truly free in the urbanizing North. Caught between slavery and freedom, between plantation and manufacturing capital, and between the social worlds that these forms of production created, their responses to their plight reveal much about the ideological consequences of the market revolution as well as its limitations in fulfilling the core promises of American democracy.

This chapter explores the ways black leaders in the antebellum North invoked the principles of the market revolution in understanding and fashioning responses to the troubles black people faced. It begins by surveying the significant context of the market revolution for the formation of African American protest thought. It goes on to explore black thinkers' analysis of "prejudice," the key concept that illustrates how black leaders understood their racial plight through market values and metaphors. The chapter then turns to African American responses to the problems of prejudice and racism, which were similarly directed by understandings of the market. Black leaders sought racial equality by embracing the bourgeois value of "respectability," which promised to both uplift individual African Americans and place white Americans in a position whereby they would be directed by their own market interests to relinquish prejudice. The chapter closes by discussing some of the ways this analysis of the market revolution in black leaders' thought challenges the most important interpretations of African American protest thought in the antebellum North.

Black leaders in the antebellum North formulated their protest rhetoric in the midst of the market revolution and the class formation it wrought. Their thought most clearly echoed the values of the emerging middle class, particularly middle-class reformers, a phenomenon requiring some explanation. Why would it be that black leaders' thought most clearly resembled the values of the white middle class rather than the white working class? For one, it is surely the case that some black leaders were themselves middle class and perhaps even more elite. Wealthy sailmaker James Forten, from Philadelphia, may be credited with converting William Lloyd Garrison to immediatism, while Detroit's George DeBaptiste, a frequent participant in the black convention movement, claimed $21,000 in property in 1860. Still, the case for black leaders' status as class elites must not be made too strongly. Many of the most prominent figures in black abolitionism were not wealthy but served out of a sense of community obligation or personal calling. Activism rarely paid well.

Black newspapers, for example, rarely lasted for more than a few issues, and editorial pleas for subscriptions frequently attested to their fiscal fragility. Even Garrison's *Liberator*—in relative terms a wildly successful enterprise—continually teetered on the brink of bankruptcy. It is thus not useful to describe antebellum black activists in general as middle class. Denied equal access to the antebellum economy and castigated in antebellum society, African Americans only rarely possessed the luxury of unqualified middle-class status. Rather, black leaders lived within a culture of activism that was related in important ways to emerging middle-class values.[2]

Black activism in the North shared roots with the middle-class reformism that later bred radical abolitionism. The earliest generation of free black activists were those such as Richard Allen, the freed slave from Philadelphia who became a minister and founded the first independent black church in 1794. These early leaders retained close ties to important white patrons. In the waning years of slavery in the North, Federalist-leaning whites had formed the core of Revolutionary-era antislavers. They founded societies dedicated to the gradual abolition of slavery, such as the Pennsylvania Abolition Society (1775), and aided slaves as they brought legal suits for their freedom. These white attorneys and philanthropists retained important roles in freedom, founding the first institutions designed for free blacks, such as the African Free School of New York City (1787). It was inevitable that their influence would outlive their immediate dealings with enslaved black northerners. Not content to merely free slaves, they took it on themselves to instruct their charges in what was expected of them in freedom.

The first generation of free black activists partook of this patronage, spouting the social philosophies of the benefactors back to them in appreciative tones. The earliest generation of free black activists in the North, then, came of age on the eve of mass politics and the Jacksonian expansion of the white electorate. Congenial to the patron-client model of social relations championed by their generally Federalist patrons, they drew sustenance from the ideological milieu of the social betters who assisted them. They founded institutions directly modeled on those of their elite patrons, such as literary societies designed "to aid the progress of those who . . . might behold the magnificent temple of the Ruler of the Muses."[3]

So closely associated were black elites with these Federalist patrons that white Jacksonians came to mock the Federalists' hold on black leaders' political loyalties in popular etchings and broadsides. For example, one of Edward Clay's "Life in Philadelphia" series satirizes blacks' alleged penchant for political unity and dependence on conservative whites (figure 2.1). In the image, an elderly and well-to-do African American man—likely the client and perhaps former slave of some wealthy white patron—grasps in one hand a switch, with which he intends to scold the black youth he clutches in the other. On his head, the child wears a hat made of a copy of *The Mercury*, a Democrat newspaper, and peddles copies of the *Democratic Press* at his feet. Referring to Democratic populist Andrew Jackson, the older man angrily chides him, "What de debil you hurrah for General Jackson for?—you black nigger!—I'll larn you better—I'm a 'ministration man!!"[4] The humor here, such as it is, depends on the older man's excessive desire to police black political solidarity, which is contrasted with his manifest failure to corral even the minimal challenge posed by a youthful renegade. The implication is not simply that African American leaders lacked the capacity to unite their people politically; it is also that the youth might actually prove wiser than his stodgy comrade, who has become nothing but the puppet of the conservative white power brokers who championed the capitalist class.

The era of patron-client politics was ending, however, just as the cartoon suggested. A new generation of American politics was brewing out of the social changes wrought by the market revolution. Cities grew, transportation and industry expanded, and immigrants entered the workforce in unheralded numbers. The political system responded with the birth of the first truly national mass parties, inaugurated by New York's Albany Regency and the Jacksonian Democrats it supported. In the 1820s and 1830s, most northern states rewrote their constitutions, expanding the suffrage to all white men regardless of their property holdings. But blacks bore the price of suffrage expansion, for most of the new constitutions traded the property requirement for racial exclusion.[5] Whiteness became the only property required to wield the rights of full citizenship. The word "white" entered the franchise stipulations, and blacks lost the vote.

In the new political order, blacks had few places to turn. Their old Federalist patrons were defunct, their elite style of politics out of favor. The white working classes, a potentially invaluable source of allies, offered little hope. The very egalitarianism breeding the Jacksonian expansion of the electorate

FIGURE 2.1

"I'm a 'ministration man!!" Black leaders' failure to enforce the political solidarity of their own constituents is lampooned in this cartoon, which also suggests the early-century political affinity between black social elites and their Federalist patrons. Lithograph by Edward Clary, *Life in Philadelphia*, plate 7 (Philadelphia: S. Hart, 1829), courtesy of The Library Company of Philadelphia.

led those in the forming white working class to predicate their identities as much on an embrace of their own whiteness as on their resistance to capitalist hegemony. As a spate of cheap new print media (penny newspapers, broadsides, comic almanacs, and offprint etchings) made clear, white workers tended to view blacks as double jeopardy. Working-class blacks were seen as labor competitors, while old associations with white elites rendered well-to-do blacks tools of a white capitalist class increasingly seen as oppressive.

A broadside from 1830s Philadelphia neatly illustrated the fears of an emerging white working class. Titled "The Results of Abolitionism," it graphically depicted the consequences of blacks' alliance with white capital (figure 2.2). In the poster, a well-dressed black man supervises the construction of a building by white and black laborers. The two white laborers at the base of the building are mixing mortar and carrying bricks to the black workers, who are laying the bricks at the top the building. The black supervisor admonishes a white worker, "White man hurry up them bricks." Meanwhile, the two black workers coarsely direct the white laborers: "Bring up the mortar you white rascals," says one, while the other remarks, "You bog-trotters, come along with them bricks." Emancipation would, the poster asserts, entail the inversion of racial and labor hierarchies to the detriment of the white worker.[6]

"The Results of Abolitionism" argued not simply against the consequences of black activism on the status of white labor; it also explored the mechanisms of class domination implicit in that degradation. In the image, the vehicle for the elevation of middle-class black managers over white laborers proves to be racially traitorous white capitalists who ally with blacks to undermine the interests of white labor. The addition of the figure of the white capitalist who manipulates the social aspirations of middle-class blacks for his own gain signals the besieged state of mind of white laborers, who easily conflated racial hatred with opposition to an increasingly repressive regime of industrial work. The broadside thus constituted a call for racial solidarity across class lines to defeat the larger menace of black competitors. It suggests that working-class whites proved poor prospects for a cross-race alliance with similarly oppressed African American workers. Instead, working-class white culture, at the very point of its formation, displaced its class antagonisms onto the bodies of black workers and the elites who claimed to represent them.

Into the vacuum of potential allies for African Americans stepped the radical abolitionists. Originally hailing from the ranks of old-money reforming

FIGURE 2.2

"The Results of Abolitionism!" This white labor broadside depicted the consequences of black freedom as a threatening elevation of blacks through the labor hierarchy, to the detriment of white labor. Wood engraving, artist unknown (Philadelphia, ca. 1835), courtesy of The Library Company of Philadelphia.

elites, a few important reformers, such as Arthur Tappan, began funding radical new efforts by alienated members of the middle class. William Lloyd Garrison, once editor of the reform-minded newspaper *Genius of Universal Emancipation*—which advocated the policy of "colonization," whereby slaves would be freed and "returned" to Africa to settle it—was the most important of these. In 1830, Garrison broke with the moderate colonization stand and became a radical abolitionist, demanding the immediate and uncompensated end to slavery on moral grounds. His conversion was fostered by his discussions with James Forten, a black leader in Philadelphia, who conveyed to him nonelite blacks' unequivocal rejection of the colonization scheme.[7] The largesse of those such as Tappan and the uncompromising rhetoric of those such as Garrison found union in the leaves of abolitionist newspapers such as *The Liberator*. This newspaper spread the message throughout the nation, polarizing popular feeling while publicizing the antislavery issue. Such an enterprise was made possible only by the market revolution's technological advances in printing and the revolution in inexpensive transportation, which made feasible the publication and wide transmission of so marginal a voice.[8]

In a few short years, white immediatists were championing middle-class alliances with blacks in which white abolitionists—relatively better off than their black compatriots—instituted a new kind of patron-client relationship. By the mid-1830s, a new generation of African American leaders had taken up the clarion call of reform, signaling their alliance with the radicals. Blacks helped found biracial reform societies, such as the American Moral Reform Society, which black Philadelphian William Whipper helped organize in 1837. Eventually, in the 1840s and 1850s, many black activists declared their independence from radical abolitionism, but the flavor of reform never left the movement, and even the most militant black activists of the 1850s never stopped calling for moral reformation. Black protest thought throughout the nineteenth century would remain heavily steeped in the ethos of middle-class reform from the antebellum North.

The market revolution had made all this possible. It provided the material basis for middle-class formation. In turn, middle-class formation bred a complex of ideas and values that deeply informed antebellum reform. And through reform, the market revolution influenced the radical ideological offshoots of black activism and white abolitionism. Yet this brief survey only begins to suggest the role of the market revolution in the development of black protest thought. The market revolution intruded into the content of black activist philosophies in myriad ways by supplying key metaphors and tropes. An examination of the great argument that black thinkers built to achieve equality reveals the depths to which black thinkers were indebted to the market for central ideological presuppositions.

At the core of black thinkers' critique of American society lay their understanding of prejudice. Their analysis of prejudice depended in turn on a broader idea, of "elevation," which served as the bedrock of much antebellum social ideology in the North. Elevation was the notion that people could "rise" along various "scales of being"—usually considered moral, mental, and physical. Antebellum sermons and advice literature consistently held out the possibility that individuals might develop their own natures to the fullest. Unitarian minister William Ellery Channing, for example, celebrated America's unique capacity to permit man "the unfolding and perfecting of his nature." He wrote, "In this country the mass of the people are distinguished by possessing means of improvement, of self-culture, possessed nowhere else."[9]

Blacks shared this interest in self-elevation, calling it a "primeval duty" owed to God and society.[10] In literally thousands of utterances, black leaders referred casually and incidentally to the concept. David Walker spoke of factors that kept blacks "from rising to the scale of reasonable and thinking beings," while Austin Steward urged African Americans to "never falter and grow weary, until we have reached the elevated station God designed us to occupy." Some began newspapers dedicated to "the general improvement of Society," while others wanted to restore blacks to the "former elevation in the scale of being" they had occupied in ancient Africa.[11]

In prejudice, however, blacks confronted a force dedicated to hindering their elevation. According to the *Colored American*, a black newspaper, prejudiced whites denied blacks "all the means of improvement, respectability and education."[12] According to this line of thinking, slavery imposed circumstances that hindered blacks from developing their natural moral and mental faculties. While slavery constituted the greatest obstacle to black elevation, prejudice against free blacks in the North also impeded the progress of the race. Black leaders said they faced hostile public opinion, which, according to Henry Highland Garnet, "in this country is stronger than law."[13] Prejudice, to northern blacks, was "the spirit of slavery." It was a "wrong exercise of the sentiments and sympathies"—a "disease of the will" that begat a "corrupt public sentiment," resulting in legal and social proscriptions against free blacks in the North.[14]

Understandings of the market were key to this analysis of elevation-inhibiting prejudice. Too much *of* the market order to ever challenge its fundamental legitimacy, black leaders never considered the market hopelessly corrupted. But their analysis suggested that their plight owed to certain features of the market—features that concerned a wide variety of Americans in the antebellum North and that were evident in black thought in three important ways.

First, black thinkers fused market metaphors with the popularized philosophy of those such as John Locke and David Hume to develop an epistemology uniquely suited for the age of the market revolution. Ideas, to black thinkers, were synonymous with the products offered in an increasingly anonymous marketplace of consumers who chose the ones that struck their fancy. Hosea Easton, a black clergyman from New Haven, imagined public sentiment as a "current" of mental influences on which the otherwise moribund mind is "borne along," until called on by changing events "to a new exercise of thought."[15] According to Frances Watkins, poet and author, these impressions worked for good or ill, depending on their content. "A thought is evolved and thrown out among the masses," she explained. "They receive it and it becomes interwoven with their mental and moral life—if the thought be good the receivers are benefitted, and helped onward to the truer life; if it is not, the reception of the idea is a detriment."[16] The problem was that consumers' fancies were at best amoral and at worst catered to the untutored passions of licentious masses. Those in the market consumed dangerous ideological products such as prejudice, with blacks the unfortunate victims.

Second, in black leaders' analysis, prejudice also led its consumers to negate the very principles of the free market by undermining the crucial market principle of meritocracy. Market values dictated that merit alone should foster social rising; those with habits and characters congenial to success would thereby prosper and the basic justice and rationality of the market order be affirmed. But racial prejudice introduced a nonmarket element into these calculations. It imposed obstacles to elevation on the mere basis of race—a biological accident, as far as blacks were concerned. Suffrage restrictions, the abrogation of civil rights and liberties, and popular malice all operated to deny blacks the level playing field demanded by liberal ideals. The result was a disruption of the market's system of incentives and rewards.

Charles L. Remond, a black Garrisonian from Boston, best captured the logic of this argument in an address to the Massachusetts House of Representatives in 1842. Speaking before a subcommittee formed to examine segregation in the state, Remond pointed out that segregation, by lumping together all people of African descent, obscured important and necessary distinctions in the moral characters of African Americans. Under a prejudicial system of segregation, "the most vicious is treated as well as the most respectable," he pointed out. In such a system, what incentives impelled men toward virtuous behavior? "If the colored man is vicious, it makes but little difference; if besotted, it matters not," Remond claimed, for both were treated with similar hostility. Such a system, wherein "virtue may not claim her divinely appointed rewards," seemed to Remond "well calculated to make every man disregardful of his conduct, and every woman unmindful of her reputation."[17] For Remond and his colleagues, a rational and race-neutral market order, in which virtue and merit alone determined success, was seen as the normative state of American life. Prejudice violated this order, introducing aberrations and irrationalities into American society to the detriment not only of blacks but of the market itself and the social and political order built on it.

Finally, and most important, black thinkers argued that immoral ideological products such as prejudice undermined the very notion of authenticity. The market revolution had created a huge variety of mechanisms for creating new ideas and putting them out before an idea-consuming public—ideas largely unregulated by anything but the market itself. Short of libel or obscenity, anyone could claim anything of anyone and face virtually no recrimination. How was one to know which ideas were true and which self-serving falsehoods? According to black leaders, prejudice served the needs of the slaveholders and white supremacists by setting forth false notions of African Americans as inherently and perpetually debased. Particularly irksome were the northern "penny press" newspapers, which gushed streams of antiblack calumny to antebellum readers. The *Colored American* lambasted these inexpensive dailies for corrupting the social and moral habits of their black readers, while other African Americans railed against the unprincipled man who edited such sheets: this "destroyer of virtuous character" operated "on a multitude of minds, and poisons the moral atmosphere around him," leaving his readers "*slaves* to a wicked public sentiment."[18] In short, those who propagated prejudice were frauds, falsely marketing slavery and discrimination to a gullible public.

Black leaders argued that an unregulated market of ideas imperiled not only their people but market society itself. According to J. Holland Townsend, who wrote for the *Anglo-African Magazine* in 1859, under the pressure of public opinion, consumers of ideas were "strongly tempted to forego their own convictions of what is right, and seek for a reputation among their fellow men as the greatest good." They adopted others' views of right, for they were goaded by the pressure to be publicly accepted "at any price" instead of waiting to acquire the knowledge of right and wrong "by diligence, patience and industry."[19] For white elites, the corruption of true sentiment by new and illegitimate media forces took the form of the disruption of traditional and local sources of political authority;[20] for black leaders, it took the form of racial prejudice. In their analysis, proslavery apologists, to further their own ends, exhorted the ignorant masses to hate blacks. Racial prejudice, which associated blackness with vice, entered the "public mind," festered, and influenced the behavior of white Americans, who responded by imposing obstacles to black elevation.

Of course, for black leaders, the most important consequence of the problem of prejudice in an expanding market society was its effect on racial politics. A "public mind" poisoned against blacks did not simply highlight the vices of individual African Americans; rather, it fused all people of African descent into a single group united by an ascription of their vicious characters. In this sense as well, racial prejudice violated the tenets of the rational marketplace. Purveyors of public opinion slandered all blacks on the basis of individual acts, thus effacing the successes of those who had overcome their liabilities to rise in competitive market society. Exasperated by this phenomenon, J. W. Lewis, a black racial theorist, proclaimed of African Americans, "Every indecorous act on their part is used as a weapon by the pro-slavery spirit of the age against the cause of freedom . . . to show that the colored people are not fit for freedom." Prejudice thus became an attack on the very principle of middle-class respectability. According to Lewis, "Popular prejudice will exaggerate the bad conduct of a colored man, while at the same time it closes all eyes to the claims of the colored man of moral worth."[21]

Black leaders believed that this problem of representation arose as a direct result of market forces in antebellum America. As fixing identity in an ever-expanding and increasingly anonymous public sphere became an ever more infeasible task, weak surrogate means arose. When black activist Lewis

Woodson wrote to Samuel Cornish that "nothing is more common in men, than to associate a cause, with him who advocates it,"[22] he may just as sagely have applied his formulation to ethnic and national groups. Nothing was more common in the antebellum North than to associate a people with the individuals who represented it. For this reason, black leaders incessantly warned their working-class brethren to consider the broad racial implications of their actions. In the 1840s, a southern black traveler noted this concern among Philadelphia's African American elite: "The sight of one man . . . whatever may be his apparent condition . . . is the sight of a community; and the errors and crimes of one, is adjudged as the criterion and character of the whole body."[23] In a world wherein it was impossible to know the character of the ones with whom the average urbanite interacted, ethnic, racial, and national signifiers—however faulty as determinants of character—seemed to offer desperately needed cues.

According to African American thinkers, the problem of representation lay at the roots of an even bigger one: it begat a self-reinforcing cycle of black degradation that proved nearly impossible to disrupt. Individual whites, moved by racial prejudice, supported legislation and customs that kept blacks enslaved or degraded, denied blacks admission into labor unions or public schools, and precipitated mob activity that targeted blacks and their abolitionist champions. Then, ludicrously enough, white commentators used the results of their prejudice—the resulting actuality of black degradation—as "facts" used to prove blacks' natural incapacity for freedom and full citizenship. The radical Henry Highland Garnet deftly summarized this sophistry of white supremacy: "It is one of the most malignant features of slavery, that it leads the oppressor to stigmatize his victim with inferiority of nature, after he himself has . . . brutalized him."[24]

Black leaders thus envisioned a vicious cycle of three mutually reinforcing elements: slavery and racially proscriptive practices, the degradation they caused among African Americans, and the attitudes they fostered in white minds. The obstacles to elevation that whites imposed had the effect of debilitating black progress. The resulting conditions of black life, which nearly all contemporary African American leaders admitted lagged behind whites, then suggested to whites not that they should remove the liabilities hampering black progress but that blacks were naturally and irredeemably inferior. As a consequence, whites felt the need to control blacks and restrain their participation in the life of the nation so as to protect the nation. And on and on the cycle went.

African American thinkers generally understood the challenge confronting them to be the interruption of this vicious cycle. Most black leaders viewed custom and law as the most visible manifestation of the problem but appreciated the great difficulties in attacking this component of the self-reinforcing cycle head on. African Americans performed tireless work in this realm: they employed the legal system to challenge segregated schools and public transportation, madly petitioned state and federal legislatures when their rights were threatened, and spoke eloquently and vociferously against the informal racial practices that seemed beyond all hope of legal remedy. But effecting this kind of change directly and immediately proved almost impossible; African Americans simply lacked the resources and influence to stem the tide of prejudice effectively. Other means seemed necessary—more indirect, perhaps, and far more commensurate with the limited agency blacks possessed. If blacks could not directly remove the obstacles confronting them, maybe they could undermine the other two components of the self-reinforcing cycle that created those obstacles: the degraded conditions of black life that resulted from iniquitous law and custom and the racist attitudes and beliefs that justified iniquitous law and custom. Such means, if practiced faithfully, promised fundamental transformations in black lives and American society.

In order to fully understand the changes black leaders sought to make, it is necessary to further explore African Americans' relationship to market society and, in particular, its key value, which black thinkers invoked to frame their responses to white supremacy: the notion of respectability. African American thinkers saw themselves as part and parcel of an antebellum northern mental world shared with a wide range of other Americans. Racial prejudice was clearly a bane to African Americans and one fostered by features of market society. Yet black thinkers understood that prejudice was but one example of the myriad ways the market could undermine authenticity, or "true sentiment." The black press, like the white, regularly debated the validity of novel medical treatments, frequently ran tales of rubes separated from their money and imposters unmasked, often informed readers of dangerous business deals unfolding, and universally declared religious movements such as Mormonism shams.[25] "The world is full of snares and temptations," a black woman activist lectured African American youth. In the current age, "vice will assume the

semblance of virtue, and falsehood by a thousand seducing arts deceive the in-
cautious heart to receive it as truth."[26] Prejudice was but a supreme instance
of this unfortunate phenomenon.

Such statements reflected concerns widespread in antebellum America.
Historians have suggested that the emergence of urban market society had
created a crisis in what may be termed social epistemology. Identity—one's
place in society—became unmoored from its traditional signifiers; it became
increasingly difficult to determine the social standing of anonymous strangers
merely from their appearance. Middle-class Americans and those aspiring to
middle-class status reacted to the resulting sense of dislocation by seeking
ways to "fix" or secure the public legitimacy of their class identities. The goal
was to communicate their inner sense of moral worth through a display of
"true sincerity," or the demonstration that one's inner qualities matched one's
external appearance. They did this through scrupulous attention to outward
indicators, such as dress, behavior, and home furnishings, which they hoped
might suggest to others the substantiality of their middle-class status.[27] Some
have begun to explore the issue of respectability among African Americans,[28]
but none of these concerns itself with the antebellum roots of the issue, which
remain largely unexplored.[29]

If one word encapsulated these efforts to secure one's worthiness in the
public estimation, it was "respectable." That term, uttered countless times in
the antebellum press with little regard for consistency, served as a master
value, encompassing a host of traits—not all of them compatible—that came
to define an ideal for human character in an expanding market society. In an
important sense, respectability buttressed the market order. As we have seen,
the market introduced new or exacerbated old moral inconsistencies in American life by undermining the principles of meritocracy and authenticity. The
discourse of respectability sought to reconcile the moral inconsistencies of the
market: it offered a set of rules that promised the rewards of success without
the need for falsity, the comforts of sincerity without the sacrifice of gain.

While its definition was vague, "respectability" connoted a set of values
closely linked with the qualities required for morally acceptable material success in the new America. Respectable individuals had, through dint of individual industry and perseverance, cultivated their inner characters sufficiently
to harvest the honest rewards of their efforts. Most important, according to
respectability's tenets, this potential was available to all those willing to un-

dertake the difficult art of self-government. The idea must have struck a chord in the hopeful ears of those seeking sure but moral routes to social rising.

African Americans stood in complex, curious relationship to this dogma. Of course, the benefits of the expanding market economy were not by and large enjoyed by black northerners. Yet such rewards were touted to them endlessly by philanthropists, abolitionists, and other liberal "friends" of blacks. In 1855, for example, the *New York Times* argued optimistically that "it matters little whether a man is black, white, or mingled. If he is respectable, he will be respected." Or consider what Republican Benjamin Wade told a convention of black Ohioans before the Civil War: "White people, while poor and ignorant, are no more respected than you are. I say again, color is nothing. When you have attained intelligence and independence, you will soon be admitted to your social and political rights."[30] Such, at least, was the lip service often paid to the race-neutral promises of the liberal marketplace. African American leaders seemed very often to have embraced it. Having critiqued the ideological shortcomings of the liberal marketplace, they chose not to regulate or limit it but rather to operate in it for their own betterment. A national convention of African American leaders asked merely for the restoration of a race-neutral liberal marketplace in which blacks hoped to compete on equal terms. "We do not solicit unusual favor, but will be content with rough-handed 'fair play,'" the convention addressed white America. It asked only "to be freed from all the unnatural burdens and impediments with which American customs and American legislation have hindered our progress and improvement."[31] The discourse of respectability offered all, not only African Americans, a way to critique the inconsistencies and injustices of the new market society without undermining the liberal values undergirding that society.

It was little surprise, then, that African American elites in the antebellum North, who saw themselves as very much a part of the liberal market order, invoked respectability in their responses to white supremacy. They did so through two arguments, each of which conjoined respectability to other lynchpins of antebellum liberalism. The first invoked respectability and the centrality of individual character in an effort to overcome the problem of blacks' limited agency and to change the conditions of black lives. Black thinkers reasoned that no matter how poor they were, rank-and-file African Americans could never be utterly destitute, for they could always control themselves. Agency over individual behavior offered a means of influencing

the racial balance to which all had access. To black leaders, a bourgeois concern with self-regulation offered the most potent means of breaking the cycle
of oppression and returning the nation to its race-neutral first principles. The
values of thrift, economy, and gratification delay—in short, everything encapsulated by the word "respectability"—resonated among black leaders precisely because they offered individual character as a space of uncontested
authority that could help change white minds. "We have to act an important
part, and fill an important place . . . in the work of emancipation," intoned
black editor Samuel Cornish. "On *our* conduct and exertions much, very
much depend."[32] Through their own actions, behavior, and comportment,
African Americans could rebut the racist claims that held them back. "I think,"
wrote Austin Steward, "that our conduct as colored men will have a great bearing on the question that now agitates this land. . . . Let it be shown that we as
a people are religious, industrious, sober, honest and intelligent, and my word
for it, the accursed system of Slavery will fall, as did Satan from Heaven."[33]

Relying on the same principle that premised their understanding of prejudice, that individual examples reflected on the whole, black leaders hoped to
use their very liabilities to reverse the self-reinforcing process whereby prejudice begat obstacles to black elevation and these obstacles begat the conditions
that rationalized prejudice. Instances of black elevation would offer material
refutations of the premises underlying racial prejudice. The black-led American Moral Reform Society of Philadelphia stated the philosophy baldly: "If
amidst all the difficulties with which we have been surrounded, and the pri-
vations which we have suffered, we presented an equal amount of intelligence
with that class of Americans that have been so peculiarly favored, a *very grave
and dangerous* question would present itself to the world, on the natural
equality of man, and the best rule of logic would place those who have oppressed us, in the scale of inferiority."[34]

While it surely had collective significance, this effort could be only an individual one. Black leaders constantly sought group elevation (through, for instance, agitation to rewin the franchise), but self-elevation could by its nature
be accomplished only through personal means. Indeed, its value lay precisely
in its applicability to every single African American regardless of status or
condition. "Each one for himself, must commence the improvement of his
condition," wrote Samuel Cornish. "It is not in mass, but in individual effort
and character, that we are to move onward to a higher elevation."[35]

In pursuit of the strategy of individual uplift, a veritable flood of advice issued from black leaders to the rank and file. Newspapers, speeches, and sermons listed virtues to cultivate and influences to shun, behaviors to avoid, and habits to embrace. Black northerners were advised to forsake black vernacular culture for the respectability of classical literature and music, to take up skilled rather than unskilled occupations, to construct domestic lives that modeled middle-class norms, to develop thrifty and economical habits, to move to the country where such virtues might best be cultivated, to dress decently but not foppishly, and to flee as they would the plague the tavern, gambling house, dance hall, theater, and brothel.[36]

The point of individual uplift ideology was not simply to benefit African Americans by making them better people. It would serve the overarching racial purpose of directly attacking the self-reinforcing cycle of white supremacy by undermining part of its underlying rationale. According to black thinkers, white supremacy operated by using the reality of debased black lives as evidence supporting its claims of innate and irrevocable black inferiority. If black lives could be lifted up from their admittedly sorry state, this crucial bit of evidence would be removed. Whites could no longer use the actuality of slave degradation or free-black impoverishment to claim that African Americans were naturally unfitted for equality. The self-reinforcing cycle—by which whites imposed barriers to black "elevation," which consequently diminished black life (as measured by the standards of the black elite and white critics), which in turn reinforced prejudicial attitudes, which justified further proscription—would be broken. By changing the individual behavior of everyday blacks, African American leaders might thus change the public mind on matters of race, impelling whites to dismantle the obstacles to black elevation that not only degraded black life but also perpetuated the conditions that fostered prejudice in the first place. The rational order of the race-neutral market would be restored, thus permitting anyone to rise based on merit and obviating the significance of race in the social order.

Complementing black leaders' strategy of individual uplift was a second component that relied on faith in the inherent rationality of the free marketplace. Using the moral uplift strategy, black leaders sought to place white Americans in a position wherein they would be compelled, by a calculation of their own rational self-interest, to relinquish their prejudice and change their practice. Black leaders' strategy turned on the notion that public standing and reputation constituted men's and women's greatest capital assets, which they would imperil only under the gravest circumstances. If, then, African Americans could shape public opinion so as to make slavery and racial prejudice disreputable—if they could make it so that white supremacy was punished rather than rewarded—they would gain a powerful lever with which they might remove the obstacles which impeded their self-elevation. As the black national convention of 1847 put it, the slaveholder "is reputable and must be made disreputable." He must be "outlawed" from "social respectability" and "execrated by the community" until he repented and freed his slaves.[37]

How was this enterprise of shaping the contours of respectability to be accomplished? It was no small task, for respectability entailed notions of autonomy and independence utterly at odds with dominant images of blacks. Antebellum political theory, mired deeply in the tenets of republicanism, treasured the independent man, who owed his livelihood to no one else and who shared a stake in society that ensured his civic virtue. In the early republic, the precious right of self-governance could be entrusted only to such men and never to the apprentice, servant, or wife—certainly not to the enslaved. As the market revolution transformed early national republicanism into the liberalism of the age of the common man and as the political system embodied this in the principle of universal white manhood suffrage, northern free blacks became "others"—vessels for the vice and licentiousness displaced from the formerly disenfranchised white working classes. But northern black leaders were too close to this process to fully comprehend how the social changes wrought by the market revolution had transformed racial ideology. Too much *of* the bourgeois order to critique it objectively, their very faith in the rationality of the market prevented them from understanding its perverse offshoots. They shared the belief that in a virtuous republic, rights were yielded only to equals, and they banked on whites' faith in those principles.

Respectability seemed to offer the key to uprooting prejudice because it appealed to the very standards middle-class northern whites used to publicly justify blacks' oppression. If blacks were excluded because they lacked respectability, surely the answer was to gain respectability. Black leaders focused on one particular manifestation of respectability: equal participation in the marketplace and its capacity to elevate African Americans to a level of equality with others. African American spokespersons were fond of aphorisms stressing this point: "True equality . . . can exist only among peers," wrote Boston doctor John S. Rock, while a national convention of African Americans declared that "it is only by placing men in the same position in society, that all cast[e]s are lost sight of."[38] In a competitive market economy ruled by the tenets of classical liberalism, respectability could accrue only to those who participated fully and equally in the race of life. Instead of being mere consumers, economically dependent on whites, who would therefore not respect them, black leaders hoped that African Americans would become producers as well. Wrote Henry Bibb, a former slave who sought to create an independent black community in Canada, "If we would be men and command respect among men, we must strike for something higher than sympathy and perpetual beggary. *We must produce what we consume.*"[39]

Black leaders thus strove not so much for economic independence from whites as for a greater degree of mutual dependence between whites and blacks. They stressed not so much the early republic's concern with economic (and hence political) independence as they did the Jacksonian era's gradual concession to the developing fact of economic (and hence social) interdependence among all. By becoming producers as well as consumers, African Americans hoped to equalize their market relationships with whites. If blacks could become producers as well as consumers, whites might become dependent on them. Black conventioneers in 1847 therefore resolved that "we must make white persons as dependent upon us, as we are upon them."[40]

Thus dependent, whites would yield the liberty and rights due to blacks *by whites' own self-interest.* As one black newspaper argued, "Towards an equal, every action becomes just, kind, and very often noble. Self-respect induces all equals to respect those who belong to their order, interest impels them to cultivate good understanding with those whose assistance may at any moment be necessary to preserve life or property."[41] This was the key: respectability implied leverage in the marketplace (of both ideas and products); those who commanded it commanded the attention and goodwill of the hungry consumers who grew dependent on the supply. "May we safely suppose," asked Lewis Woodson, "that a government which has shown such decided hostility towards us as individuals, would regard us with a more indulgent eye, when formed into communities, acquiring intelligence, wealth, and power?"[42] Others put it more optimistically, claiming that the strategy of respectability could even defeat whites' intractable prejudice: "Even this can be removed as circumstances shall show it to be their interest to do so."[43]

The interdependency black leaders called for was both abstract and literal. At one level, the market served as a potent simile through which black leaders sought to understand and resolve their problem. Prejudice was *like* an immoral ideological product, marketed to hungry white consumers who only increased its demand. It operated *in the abstract* to undermine values of authenticity and meritocracy. In seeking to shape public opinion, black thinkers sought to become producers *of ideas* that whites would slowly consume as alternatives to prejudice. In this trope of the market as metaphor for prejudice, we may note the degree to which the market had become a pervasive feature of life for African American spokespersons in the urbanizing North. But African American spokespersons viewed the market as far more than a powerful metaphor in their analysis. In myriad ways, they also argued forcefully for a literal application of their strategy of becoming producers. They sought to found manual training schools that would educate black youth in the skilled trades the antebellum economy demanded, and they urged their people to move to the country where they could become prosperous and independent yeomen farmers. In all instances, black leaders viewed deep integration into the most progressive parts of the liberal marketplace as the key to obtaining the respect of whites, changing the public mind, and hence compelling blacks' oppressors to change their practices.

From the crucible of market change in the antebellum North, black spokespersons thus forged a rich interpretation of the problems confronting their people and of the best way of addressing them. They sought to make African Americans key participants, as much as possible, in the most progressive parts of the national economy. Doing so would render African Americans producers as well as consumers—not only of material goods but of ideas as well. By producing goods, blacks would make whites as economically dependent on blacks as blacks were on whites. This would foster among whites a healthy respect for blacks, derived from a calculation of rational self-interest. It would also offer to consumers in the marketplace of ideas ideological fare that might counteract the effects of racial prejudice. These new ideological products would serve two purposes: to refute inaccurate stereotypes that fed the cycle of prejudice and proscription and to challenge ideological products that undermined important market values of authenticity and meritocracy.

Respectability, for African Americans, promised to break the self-reinforcing cycle of prejudice and racism. Blacks' efforts to elevate themselves would no longer be hampered by racist practices fed by prejudicial ideas. The normative state of market society—in which success accrued to those who had perfected the difficult art of self-government—would be sustained and the market order reinforced.

What, then, was the relationship between market change and black strategies for resistance? The most obvious observation is the close reliance of black thinkers' strategies on market ideas, metaphors, and principles. Relying on notions of respectability, African Americans formulated an appeal to whites' economic interests that they considered far more powerful than mere benevolence (which could never foster independence and respectability) or even faith in democratic ideals (which had offered no guarantee of universal liberty even in 1776). Their analysis of slavery and racism could not have been formulated in a nonmarket environment, for it relied on market understandings and market metaphors at every stage. Black leaders' ideological lineage lay in the middle-class reformers who became radical abolitionists. Black thinkers' concepts of prejudice were rooted in the vision of a rational and race-neutral marketplace of ideas, which prejudice was seen to violate and which blacks ultimately hoped to restore. And the notion of respectability so central to their thought was the direct product of middle-class formation, as were the moral admonitions they unceasingly fed to the black nonelite.

Of what significance was this close relationship between elite black protest and the market order? Some radical scholars have suggested that it constituted evidence of the deep assimilation of African-descended people into American culture. In contrast to those in the slave community, those African Americans from the antebellum North who forged the black public protest tradition often come across as deeply integrated into American life and thus hopelessly out of touch with the realities of African American vernacular culture. For example, according to V. P. Franklin, Frederick Douglass's status as elite spokesman separated him from the black rank and file such that he failed to understand and advocate the "mass cultural objectives" and "mass economic interests" of African Americans that "emerged directly out of the Afro-American slave experience."[44] It is but a short leap to conclude that black spokespersons' relatively well-to-do status rendered them particularly likely to fall prey to the hegemony of the expanding market and its values. As E. U. Essien-Udom claims of "articulate Negroes" in the nineteenth century, a "desire for acceptance by white Americans" amounted to a form of "cultural subordination" that deeply undercut the leadership's ties to the black nonelite.[45] Perhaps, as black radical scholars claimed of later generations of so-called black leaders, these men had even "sold out" their nonelite brethren for the promises of integration.[46]

It is certainly true that antebellum black leaders were deeply conversant with the discourses of the northern public sphere, just as it is true that black elites' incessant admonitions to the black nonelite seem to mirror the moral didacticism of middle-class white reformers. Yet it will not do to suggest that black leaders in the antebellum North were simply black versions of the middle-class whites who sought class hegemony at the expense of the less well off. Elite whites could afford to see the white working classes as solely antagonistic, and reforming middle-class whites had the luxury to consider the unwitting targets of their zeal mere objects, defined as working class precisely by their need for reformation. Black leaders had no such advantage. Whatever class preferment black elites enjoyed over the nonelite, it was not sufficient to sunder them from a deep and personal concern with the black masses. Lumped in the public mind with the nonelite by prejudice, black leaders could ill afford to consider nonelite African Americans distinct from themselves, as unelevatable objects of benevolent paternalism. As evidenced by black elites' apparent frustration with nonelite behavior, this forced association grated considerably, especially when it failed to acknowledge leaders' success at achieving the markers of middle-class status. There was surely some self-interest at work, then, in controlling the behavior of the nonelite: it promised to deliver the deserved class recognition that elites believed they had been denied.

Yet while black leaders' concern with nonelite behavior often seemed to mirror that of white reformers, it served far different ends. If scholars such as Clifford S. Griffin are right in suggesting that middle-class white reformers used reform to rationalize their class hegemony and distance themselves from their charges, their conclusions cannot simply be transferred to middle-class black leaders.[47] Indeed, elite blacks' regard for their working-class brethren reflected efforts to unite the community in a common purpose under a common identity. Black leaders first and foremost sought to use moral admonitions to the nonelite in the service of racial politics, to control black behavior so that hostile whites might be deprived of evidence to support their racist conclusions. After criticizing the African Americans in his audience for their ignorance, William Hamilton, a prominent community leader from New York, retreated: "I am sorry to say it," he conceded, "but I speak with the intention to quicken you."[48] Black leaders never considered the nonelite hopeless, if only because they could not afford to. Just as prejudice had to be eradicable, "degraded" nonelite blacks had to be elevatable. Otherwise, biological determinism would win the day, and blacks would all but admit the justice in keeping them oppressed.

The market revolution, far from luring black leaders away from their flocks with promises of incorporation into the middle class, indirectly provided them with the ideas and languages necessary to frame critiques of American society and to posit all people of African descent as a unified whole. In instance after instance, black leaders employed the language of the public sphere to unite all people of African descent under a common rubric and to argue for their liberation and elevation—to, in short, create a version of African American identity. Antebellum black protest drew its power from precisely the factors that rendered northern free blacks *less* culturally and ideologically autonomous of the white world than their enslaved brethren. It was in fact black thinkers' fluency in the language and ideas of the public sphere that made their words and deeds so powerful.

This fluency was not, in fact, evidence of "assimilation"—of some process whereby blacks internalized alien culture. Black spokespersons were cofabricators, albeit largely disenfranchised ones, of a bourgeois order to which they could lay undeniable claim. In the same way that their unpaid and unappreciated labor helped mold the nation's cities and farms, so too their words and ideas played critical roles in contesting the meanings of race, class, and gender in America. African Americans were present at the birth of the American public sphere and of the market revolution; American social classes formed amidst their presence, and blacks themselves took part in this process. Theirs were not makeshift arguments for freedom and equality, improvised from the ideological possibilities around them. They did not dress racial issues in the ill-fitting garb of bourgeois respectability; rather, they tailored respectability to their distinct racial plight. For black thinkers, racial uplift and complete human equality were the *meaning* of bourgeois values.

The history of race, then, suggests a considerably more complex narrative to the story of class formation than we have come to expect. Class formation—and the dialectical construction of class identities it entailed[49]—certainly owed to the market revolution. Yet so closely has class formation been tied to the market revolution that it has become nearly impossible to imagine the ideological consequences of the latter as anything other than bourgeois hegemony. The history of race suggests that the market revolution offered ideological possibilities not inevitably subordinated to the hegemony of an emerging middle class. The ideological world of the market revolution offered only possibilities, such as new moral values, that could be used in a variety of ways by a variety of social interests. It would be going too far to suggest an overly broad set of potentials for these ideas; surely their primary significance lay in securing the legitimacy of a new bourgeois order. It was, for example, highly unlikely that the market revolution would produce ideas that could have successfully destroyed the market order itself. As we have seen, even the radical challenge to the existing order posed by black activists had the unwitting consequence of buttressing key market values, such as meritocracy and authenticity. Yet it is also true that black activists did not see their work in the same terms that reforming whites did. They managed to steer emerging market values down a different path—one capable of subordinating class hegemony to the fulfillment of the nation's democratic promises. In the process, they demonstrated that they were not mere casualties in the market revolution but rather an advance force for a democratic revolution they never saw fulfilled.

The reinvigoration of black elites' agency along these lines is not without complications. First, it seems clear from the evidence offered throughout this chapter that African American leaders could not fathom a solution to their problems that involved alternatives to the liberalism of their age. Just as they served as bastions for the principles of democratic revolution, their efforts also buttressed the principles of the new market order.

Second, if African Americans were central crafters in the discourses of the antebellum public sphere, they must be held accountable for its ignoble legacies of classism, patriarchy, and even a degree of racialism. Additionally, black elites' strategy of influencing the public mind failed in important respects. To begin to break the self-reinforcing cycle of prejudice required exercising a degree of self-control and manifesting a level of success unparalleled by all but the young lads in Horatio Alger novels and McGuffy's readers. Abolitionist allies were especially fond of admonishing blacks that good behavior was all the more necessary from those assumed to be vicious by nature. Some seemed to take an almost perverse pleasure in speaking of the nearly uncrossable distance between white and black moral status in the public mind, lecturing blacks interminably on the hypermorality required to traverse the gulf. Gerrit Smith, the wealthy New York landowner who gave parcels of land to black freedpeople, told the objects of his benevolence that they were "under the necessity of being better than the whites, because prejudice of color . . . is for them, and against you. . . . They may be idlers, and yet be respected. But, if your industry relax, you are denounced as lazy. . . . They may be spendthrifts, without greatly, or at all, harming their reputation. But yours is ruined, unless you are rigid economists."[50]

Under the yoke of such pressures, many northern blacks chafed. Sarah Parker Remond, wife of black abolitionist Charles Remond, once wrote to a London newspaper, "We are expected to be not only equal to the dominant races, but to excel in all that goes toward forming a noble manhood or womanhood. We are expected to develop in the highest perfection a race which for eight generations in the United States has been laden with the curse of slavery. Even some of our friends seem to expect this, but our enemies demand it."[51] Only a few others, cynical but insightful, sensed that moral elevation did little to address the double standard underlying white images of blacks: when whites acted viciously, they were seen to have fallen from fulfillable ideals; when blacks did, they were seen to have merely manifested their inherently degraded natures.

More damaging than this, however, was a third qualification. The strategy of elevation contained a key, faulty premise: that black leaders' great faith in the values of the market revolution, and in particular the race-neutral liberal state, was shared by whites. Black elites imagined the public sphere as a realm of rational discourse, wherein it was assumed that words had power and arguments mattered. For them the public sphere was a democratic marketplace of ideas, ideally ruled by laws that rendered it mutable to anyone with access to it. The respectability strategy assumed that there were circumstances under which rational whites acting in their own self-interest would be willing to jettison their prejudice. As late as 1859, black editors could optimistically encant that "no kind of energy, however evil in its direction, can continue to go wrong in this glorious republic of ours." The "checks and balances of public opinion" would prevent it.[52] There were fewer more ardent apostles of what Jürgen Habermas would later describe as a rational, bourgeois public sphere than free African Americans in the antebellum North.[53]

Their faith ultimately proved groundless. It mattered little if blacks' arguments were sound, their logic spotless. Far too many white Americans were far
too willing to jettison principle (or even interest) when confronted with the
supplementary "wages" of their whiteness. Rather than convert hostile whites,
evidence of black elevation tended only to enrage them further.[54] Liberalism
and respectability proved to be only part of a Janus-faced America: one side
promised inclusion to all who comported themselves properly, while the other
issued a steady stream of exclusion and inequality.

Nonetheless, black leaders' reliance on the ideological vocabularies fostered
by the market revolution offered them the possibility of understanding features
of their plight they never could have otherwise. Their analysis of prejudice as a
force stemming from popular opinion and a corrupted "public mind" was not
far off, even if they erred in believing the public mind to be so easily altered.
They rightly understood the ideological component of their challenge. As the
black national convention of 1847 put it, "We struggle against opinions. Our
warfare lies in the field of thought."[55] Black thinkers' plan to change that public mind was far more radical than the alternatives offered by moderate colo-
nizationists (who could imagine the expatriation of blacks more easily than the
eradication of prejudice) and even by radical abolitionists (who never seemed
able to completely jettison their paternalism). Black thinkers' reliance on public sphere discourse offered the possibility of not only convincing whites that
slavery was immoral but also causing them to reappraise their entire understanding of race in American life. Through recourse to the ideological lingua
franca of their day—a language deeply tied to market society—African American spokespersons constructed an array of arguments far broader than can be
even mentioned here, drawing not only on individual uplift but also on popular values of nationalism, patriotism, and even racialism.

To a critical extent, they succeeded. They, even more than the radical abolitionists, spoke from the margins of American society. Yet gradually, from the
1830s on, the fierce and fiery rhetoric of mere handfuls of radical activists began to influence the center of American politics. Slowly and painfully, the
ideas of a scorned and rejected minority infiltrated public debate, polarizing
public opinion, and eventually precipitating the colossal ideological battles
that raged from 1848 to 1860. The antislavery ideology with which the Union
marched to war in April 1861 was a hopelessly co-opted descendent of its antebellum original, yet in the maelstrom of the Civil War it was sufficient to

spur the complete obliteration of the hated institution of slavery. Both that great conflict and the emancipation it demanded owed their origins to the efforts of black activists in the antebellum North.

NOTES

1. I use the term "leader" loosely, without pretense of any objective definition, to refer to the several thousand who left their imprint on the historical record through newspapers, convention proceedings, sermons, pamphlets, slave narratives, and other sources. It would be impossible and unproductive to draw strict correlations between the class status of particular African Americans (as measured by factors such as wealth, property, or profession) and their status on the black leadership pyramid. We would be wiser, perhaps, to think of leadership status as conferred from a variety of sources (from self-appointment to white patronage to community status). Still, in using "elite" as nearly synonymous with "leaders," I have sought to acknowledge that most of those sufficiently well resourced to have left their ideas in the historical record would have constituted better-off folk in their communities.

2. For more on the class identity of antebellum black leaders, see Patrick Rael, *Black Identity and Black Protest in the Antebellum North* (Chapel Hill: University of North Carolina Press, 2002), 14–44.

3. Prince Saunders, *An Address, Delivered at Bethel Church, Philadelphia; On the 30th of September, 1818, before the Pennsylvania Augustine Society for the Education of People of Colour* (Philadelphia, 1818).

4. Edward W. Clay, *Life in Philadelphia* (Philadelphia: W. Simpson, 1828), courtesy Prints Division, Library Company of Philadelphia.

5. James Oliver Horton and Lois E. Horton, *In Hope of Liberty: Culture, Community and Protest among Northern Free Blacks, 1700–1860* (New York: Oxford University Press, 1997), 168–69; Leon F. Litwack, *North of Slavery: The Negro in the Free States, 1790–1860* (Chicago: University of Chicago Press, 1961), chap. 3.

6. *The Results of Abolitionism!* (n.p., c. 1835), courtesy Prints Division, Library Company of Philadelphia.

7. William Lloyd Garrison, *Thoughts on African Colonization*, ed. William Loren Katz, (Boston, 1832; reprint, New York: Arno Press, 1969), i. See also Richard S. Newman, *The Transformation of American Abolitionism: Fighting Slavery in the Early Republic* (Chapel Hill: University of North Carolina Press, 2002), 113.

8. Ronald Zboray, "Antebellum Reading and the Ironies of the Technological Innovation," *American Quarterly* 40, no. 1 (March 1988): 65–82.

9. "Self Culture: An Address Introductory to the Franklin Lectures, Delivered at Boston, Sept. 1838," in *The Works of William E. Channing*, by William E. Channing (Boston: American Unitarian Association, 1882), 19.

10. *North Star*, January 21, 1848.

11. David Walker, "Address Delivered before the General Colored Association at Boston," *Freedom's Journal*, December 19, 1828; Austin Steward, *Twenty-Two Years a Slave, and Forty Years as a Free Man* (1857), 334; *The Rights of All*, May 29, 1829; *Colored American*, April 22, 1837.

12. *Colored American*, July 8, 1837.

13. *Weekly Anglo-African* 1, no. 9 (September 19, 1859), in *The Ideological Origins of Black Nationalism*, ed. Sterling Stuckey (Boston: Beacon Press, 1972), 167.

14. *Colored American*, March 13, 1841; speech of Theodore S. Wright, Utica, New York, October 20, 1836, *Friend of Man*, October 27, 1836, in *The Black Abolitionist Papers*, ed. C. Peter Ripley, Roy E. Finkenbine, Michael F. Hembree, and Donald Yacavone (Chapel Hill: University of North Carolina Press, 1985), vol. 3, 184 (hereinafter cited as *BAP*); M. H. Freeman, "The Educational Wants of the Free Colored People," *Anglo-African Magazine* 1, no. 4 (April 1859): 115.

15. Hosea Easton, *A Treatise on the Intellectual Character and Civil and Political Condition of the Colored People of the United States* (Boston, 1837), 7.

16. Frances Ellen Watkins, "Our Greatest Want," *Anglo-African Magazine* 1 (1859): 160.

17. Charles L. Remond, "Address to a Legislative Committee in the Massachusetts House of Representatives, 1842," in *Liberator*, February 25, 1842.

18. *Colored American*, August 8, 1840; *Freedom's Journal*, February 28, 1829; *Colored American*, March 18, 1837.

19. J. Holland Townsend, "Our Duty in the Conflict," *Anglo-African Magazine* 1, no. 9 (September 1859): 292.

20. Stephen Nissenbaum, *The Battle for Christmas: A Cultural History of America's Most Cherished Holiday* (New York: Vintage Books, 1996), chap. 2; Karen Halttunen, *Confidence Men and Painted Women: A Study of Middle-Class Culture in America, 1839–1870* (New Haven, Conn.: Yale University Press, 1982), 15–16; Leonard Richards, *"Gentlemen of Property and Standing": Anti-Abolition Mobs in Jacksonian America* (London: Oxford University Press, 1970), 52–62.

21. J. W. Lewis, "Essay on the Character and Condition of the African Race," in *Life, Labors, and Travels of Elder Charles Bowles, of the Free Will Baptist Denomination* (Watertown, Conn.: Ingalls, 1852), 252–53.

22. *Colored American*, July 22, 1837.

23. [Joseph Willson], *Sketches of the Higher Classes of Colored Society in Philadelphia* (Philadelphia, 1841), 13.

24. Sidney's reply to "William Whipper's Letters, No. 11," *Colored American*, March 6, 1841.

25. For medical treatments, see *North Star*, March 17, 1848, and June 8, 1849. For rubes and imposters, see *Freedom's Journal*, October 3, 1828; October 31, 1828; December 26, 1828; and January 16, 1829. For real estate deals, see *Colored American*, August 5, 1837. For Mormonism, see *Colored American*, September 29, 1838, and May 18, 1839.

26. Elizabeth Wicks, *Address Delivered before the African Female Benevolent Society of Troy, on Wednesday, February 12, 1834* (Troy, N.Y., 1834), 7.

27. My understanding of respectability and class formation and the discussion that follows are informed by Halttunen, *Confidence Men and Painted Women*; Stuart M. Blumin, "Explaining the New Metropolis: Perception, Depiction, and Analysis in Mid-Nineteenth-Century New York," *Journal of Urban History* 11, no. 1 (November 1984): 9–38; Steven Watts, "Masks, Morals, and the Market: American Literature and Early Capitalist Culture, 1790–1820," *Journal of the Early Republic* 6 (summer 1986): 127–49; John F. Kasson, *Rudeness and Civility: Manners in*

Nineteenth-Century Urban America (New York: Hill & Wang, 1990); Guy Szuberla, "Ladies, Gentlemen, Flirts, Mashers, Snoozers, and the Breaking of Etiquette's Code," *Prospects* 15 (1990): 169–96; Richard L. Bushman, *The Refinement of America: Persons, Houses, Cities* (New York: Knopf, 1992); David Scobey, "Anatomy of the Promenade: The Politics of Bourgeois Sociability in Nineteenth-Century New York," *Social History* 17, no. 2 (May 1992): 203–27; and Michael O'Malley, "Specie and Species: Race and the Money Question in Nineteenth-Century America," *American Historical Review* 99, no. 2 (April 1994): 369–95.

28. See Harry C. Silcox, "The Black 'Better Class' Political Dilemma: Philadelphia Prototype Isaiah C. Wears," *Pennsylvania Magazine of History and Biography* 113, no. 1 (January 1989): 45–66; Evelyn Brooks Higginbotham, *Righteous Discontent: The Women's Movement in the Black Baptist Church, 1880–1920* (Cambridge, Mass.: Harvard University Press, 1993); Willard B. Gatewood, *Aristocrats of Color: The Black Elite, 1880–1920* (Bloomington: Indiana University Press, 1990); Kevin K. Gaines, *Uplifting the Race: Black Leadership, Politics, and Culture in the Twentieth Century* (Chapel Hill: University of North Carolina Press, 1996); Paul Harvey, "'These Untutored Masses': The Campaign for Respectability among White and Black Evangelicals in the American South, 1870–1930," *Journal of Religious History* 21, no. 3 (1997): 302–17; and Victoria W. Wolcott, "The Culture of the Informal Economy: Numbers Runners in Inter-War Black Detroit," *Radical History Review* 69 (1997): 47–75.

29. An exception is James Brewer Stewart, "The Emergence of Racial Modernity and the Rise of the White North 1790–1840," *Journal of the Early Republic* 18, no. 2 (summer 1998): 181–217.

30. Both quoted in Eric Foner, *Free Soil, Free Labor, Free Men* (New York: Oxford University Press, 1969), 298.

31. "Address of the Colored National Convention, to the People of the United States," *Proceedings of the Colored National Convention, Held in Rochester, July 6th, 7th and 8th, 1853* (Rochester, N.Y.: North Star Office, 1853), 8.

32. *Colored American*, March 4, 1837.

33. *Colored American*, June 2, 1838.

34. *National Enquirer*, January 28, 1837, in *The Black Abolitionist Papers, 1830–1865*, ed. C. Peter Ripley, Roy E. Finkenbine, Michael F. Hembree, and Donald Yacavone (microform collection), reel 1, frames 921–22 (hereinafter cited as *BAPC*).

35. *Colored American*, April 22, 1837.

36. Rael, *Black Identity and Black Protest in the Antebellum North*, 188–98.

37. "Report of the Committee on Abolition," *Proceedings of the National Convention of Colored People, and Their Friends, Held in Troy, N.Y., on the 6th, 7th, 8th and 9th October, 1847* (Troy, N.Y.: J. C. Kneeland and Co., 1847), 32.

38. John S. Rock, March 5, 1858, in *Liberator*, March 12, 1858; *Minutes of the National Convention of Colored Citizens: Held at Buffalo, on the 15th, 16th, 17th, 18th and 19th of August, 1843* (New York: Piercy and Reed, 1843), 32.

39. *Voice of the Fugitive*, March 26, 1851.

40. "An Address to the Colored People of the United States," in *Report of the Proceedings of the Colored National Convention, Held at Cleveland, Ohio, on Wednesday, September 6, 1848* (Rochester, N.Y.: John Dick, 1848).

41. *Pacific Appeal*, July 12, 1862, in *BAPC*, 14:392.

42. Augustine (Lewis Woodson), in *Colored American*, February 7, 1837.

43. *Proceedings of the Colored National Convention, Held in Franklin Hall, Sixth Street, below Arch, Philadelphia, October 16th, 17th and 18th, 1855* (Salem, N.J.: National Standard Office, 1856), 17.

44. V. P. Franklin, *Black Self-Determination: A Cultural History of African-American Resistance*, 2nd ed. (New York: Lawrence Hill, 1992), 8.

45. E. U. Essien-Udom, *Black Nationalism: A Search for an Identity in America* (Chicago: University of Chicago Press, 1962), 20, 16.

46. This strain of thinking emerged in the late 1960s and 1970s, as Black Power began to influence scholarship on African American history. The antiassimilationist critique is clear in canonical works such as *The Autobiography of Malcolm X*, in which X speaks of "'integration'-mad so-called 'intellectuals,'" who were "fat, happy, and deaf, dumb, and blinded, with their crumbs from the white man's rich table." Malcolm X, *The Autobiography of Malcolm X*, ed. Alex Haley (1964; reprint, New York: Ballantine Books, 1991), 183. It is perhaps best exemplified in scholarship by Harold Cruse's scathing criticism of the contemporary "Negro intelligentsia," which he claimed had "sold out their own birthright for an illusion called Racial Integration." Harold Cruse, *The Crisis of the Negro Intellectual* (New York: William Morrow, 1967), 111. Scholars working in this vein tacitly or explicitly assumed that black intellectuals and "leaders" of the past must also have fallen prey to the temptations of class co-optation. For examples of black history inspired by this school of thought, see Nathan Hare, *The Black Anglo-Saxons* (New York: Marzani and Munsellm, 1965); Sterling Stuckey, ed., *The Ideological Origins of Black Nationalism* (Boston: Beacon Press, 1972), 1–29; Rodney P. Carlisle, *The Roots of Black Nationalism* (Port Washington, N.Y.: Kennikat, 1975); Alphonso Pinkney, *Red, Black, and Green: Black Nationalism in the United States* (Cambridge: Cambridge University Press, 1976); James E. Turner, "Historical Dialectics of Black Nationalist Movements in America," *Western Journal of Black Studies* 1, no. 3 (September 1977): 164–83; V. P. Franklin, *Black Self-Determination: A Cultural History of the Faith of the Fathers* (Westport, Conn.: L. Hill, 1984) (republished as *Black Self-Determination: A Cultural History of African-American Resistance* [New York: Lawrence Hill, 1992]); Sterling Stuckey, *Slave Culture: Nationalist Theory and the Foundations of Black America* (New York: Oxford University Press, 1987); Kwando Mbiassi Kinshasa, *Emigration vs. Assimilation: The Debate in the African American Press, 1827–1861* (Jefferson, N.C.: McFarland, 1988); Gayle T. Tate, "Black Nationalism: An Angle of Vision," *Western Journal of Black Studies* 12, no. 1 (1988): 40–48; Gayle T. Tate, "Black Nationalism and Spiritual Redemption," *Western Journal of Black Studies* 15, no. 4 (1991): 213–22; and John T. McCartney, *Black Power Ideologies: An Essay in African-American Political Thought* (Philadelphia: Temple University Press, 1992).

47. For the classic statement, see Clifford S. Griffin, "Religious Benevolence as Social Control, 1815–1860," *Mississippi Valley Historical Review* 44, no. 3 (December 1957): 423–44. For an overview, see Lawrence Frederick Kohl, "The Concept of Social Control and the History of Jacksonian America," *Journal of the Early Republic* 5 (1985): 21–34.

48. William Hamilton, *An Oration Delivered in the African Zion Church, on the Fourth of July, 1827, in Commemoration of the Abolition of Domestic Slavery in this State* (New York: Gray and

Bunce, 1827), in *Early Negro Writing, 1760–1837*, ed. Dorothy Porter (Baltimore: Black Classic Press, 1995), 103.

49. E. P. Thompson, *The Making of the English Working Class* (New York: Vintage, 1963); Sean Wilentz, *Chants Democratic: New York City and the Rise of the American Working Class, 1788–1850* (New York: Oxford University Press, 1984).

50. *North Star*, August 4, 1848.

51. Sarah P. Remond to Editor, *Daily News* (London), November 7, 1865, in *BAP*, vol. 1, 568–69.

52. "A Word to Our People," *Anglo-African Magazine* 1, no. 9 (September 1859): 297.

53. Jürgen Habermas, *The Structural Transformation of the Public Sphere: An Inquiry into a Category of Bourgeois Society*, trans. Thomas Burger (Cambridge, Mass.: MIT Press, 1989).

54. David R. Roediger, *The Wages of Whiteness: Race and the Making of the American Working Class* (London: Verso, 1991); Emma Jones Lapsansky, "'Since They Got Those Separate Churches': Afro-Americans and Racism in Jacksonian Philadelphia," *American Quarterly* 32, no. 1 (spring 1980): 54–78.

55. "Report of the Committee on Abolition," 18–19.

3

A Cultural Frontier: Ethnicity and the Marketplace in Charlotte, Vermont, 1845–1860

KEVIN THORNTON

THE NEW SETTLER

Like almost every other settler in Vermont, when Antoine Loraine acquired his homestead, his first task was to chop down trees. Loraine cleared a small area of land, then with an adz shaped the trees he had cut down into rough square timbers. Using the timbers, he built a small log house, carefully cutting the corners into half dovetails for a tight, square fit. By the end of his first year of ownership, Loraine had finished his house and begun farming his improved land.[1] Odds are that Loraine practiced the mixed-use, subsistence, or safety-first agriculture typical of small farmers on the frontier. His first priority would have been feeding a young and growing family, but we can surmise that he participated in the market economy enough to acquire some capital—he had to buy his land—probably by working as a farmhand for one of his neighbors.

It's a typical frontier story, but a frontier story with a twist. Because when Loraine, a French Canadian, settled in Charlotte, Vermont, sometime around 1845, Anglo-Americans had already been living in the area for sixty-odd years. A number of taverns and inns dotted an extensive road system that linked the town to Middlebury and Burlington. Substantial Federal and Greek Revival homes marked a long-settled landscape. A ferry service had been transporting travelers and livestock across Lake Champlain since 1795 on a regular, horse-powered run since the 1820s. In the same decade, a gristmill and a sawmill had been established on Lewis Creek. By 1830, Charlotte was a well-established, thriving rural community with a population of 1,702, most of whom lived on and worked their own farms. It had, moreover, benefited substantially from the Merino wool boom of 1815 to 1840. By the time Loraine arrived, the town had achieved an economic peak it would not attain again for over a century. He had hardly settled in a wilderness.[2]

Yet should we consider him a frontiersman nevertheless? The known details of Loraine's life reveal a man struggling with a "frontier" existence, an existence overlaid almost imperceptibly on a settled, market-orientated community. As we have seen, he built his own home, by hand, of logs, much in the manner of settlers sixty years earlier. He probably cleared his own land. For a French Canadian, he was living on the far edge of settlement. The chances are that his farm production was subsistence oriented. He was cash poor, one of the poorest home owners in Charlotte, with real estate worth $200 in 1850, and his homestead was not recorded in the agricultural census of that year. Loraine was apparently too small time, his production too devoted to subsistence, for his farm to matter in what was an accounting of marketable produce. To the marketplace he was nearly invisible.[3]

This is not to argue that Loraine lacked a "market mentality." On the contrary, if anything, he was struggling to establish himself in the market. He had saved enough to buy his land, probably by working for wages as a farmhand for one of his neighbors. Undoubtedly, he was a man with aspirations, a hardworking planner and saver. Within a few years of settlement, he had accumulated the means to both improve his home and expand his small holdings from six to nineteen and a half acres.[4]

Loraine's economic isolation, therefore, was far more likely the result of poverty than the absence on his part of a market orientation. Loraine participated in the market as much as he could and, judging by his behavior, saw wages as a means toward achieving the independence of a homestead. These were not contradictory aims for him. But he nevertheless came from a place in which most people did in fact practice something different from market-oriented agriculture. The *habitants* of Quebec were more peasants than yeomen. Subject to feudal obligations to church and seigneurs, organizing their farms "primarily around the principle of household self-sufficiency," resistant to agricultural improvements that put a premium on maximizing profits, Canadiens arrived in Vermont with a tradition and experience vastly

different from the intensive, market-driven, and specialized agriculture practiced in Vermont.[5]

But even conceding the question of orientation, I think, gives up rather little. The salient fact about Loraine was not necessarily his orientation but his
isolation. This isolation was only in part economic. More important, it was
broadly cultural. Loraine was invisible in the market only because he was
poor. But he was invisible socially and politically because he was French. Loraine, a noncitizen, would not have been able to vote in Charlotte. He was illiterate. His children did not attend a public school. Most probably, he could
attend church on only the rarest occasions—the nearest Catholic parish was
fifteen miles away, in Burlington, and even then he would not have been able
to hear preaching in French before 1850.[6] He had no role in Charlotte's life ex-
cept as an employee. While Lorraine certainly did not live in a wilderness,
while he lived in a place with a dense population, and while there certainly was
no struggle between ethnic groups for political control or social dominance in
Charlotte, Loraine was nevertheless on a sort of frontier—a French Canadian
one. Fully as much as Leatherstocking, Loraine lived apart from the voluntary
institutions that characterized Anglo-American society.[7]

If a frontier occurs on the peripheries of a culture, where its population is
spread thinnest and intersects with other cultural groups, then Loraine was on
a frontier. Charlotte may have not been sparsely populated, but when Loraine
arrived it was thinly settled in French Canadians. And the French Canadians
differed from other immigrants (in Charlotte's case, especially the Irish) in
that the center of their world abutted the United States. They *could* go home
again, and many of them did, across a remarkably porous border. Especially
after the construction of railroads, they could return for visits and important
occasions. They could go home seasonally, to get married, to return for good,
or for any number of reasons. Unlike the Irish, they had not irretrievably broken ties with home. They were not part of a diaspora but something more like
a dispersal, and this gave them a different mentality about settlement. For Vermont's rural French Canadians, isolation and poverty reinforced the sense of
cultural continuity rather than working to break it down. For them, the American frontier was a cultural one that did not necessarily coincide with the border. It was, rather, that permeable, tenuous point at which cultural attenuation
disperses into fragments. Loraine and those like him could see themselves as
in the hinterlands of the Canadiens rather than or at the same time as aliens

among the Americans. The difference from our expectation is this: the inter-
stices in Loraine's frontier were filled not by trackless forests but by the busy
commercial society of nineteenth-century Anglo-America.[8]

Loraine's experience on the Vermont cultural frontier, then, suggests how
the course and nature of nineteenth-century American market expansion
could interact with ethnicity, language, and especially culture. We will begin
examining this interaction by looking at a brief history of Charlotte and its
environs, focusing on the social and economic characteristics of the settlement. From there, we move to an examination of how "new" immigrants to
Vermont—the Irish and French Canadians—fared in the established, market-
oriented society they found there. A comparison of these groups demonstrates that ethnicity shaped the experiences of both but served to isolate
French Canadians such as Loraine from the market much more so than it did
the Irish. Finally, we will consider how viewing the upper Champlain valley as
a Canadien frontier sheds new light on the history of Vermont, French Canadians, and the market revolution.

A "NEW" NEW ENGLAND TOWN:
LAND AND STATUS IN A VERMONT SETTLEMENT

In one sense, Charlotte, chartered in 1763 but unsettled until 1784, had been
commercial from the start. Land speculation was one of the primary activities
everywhere in frontier Vermont, and Charlotte was no exception. To a man, the
town's original proprietors, the majority of whom lived in Duchess County,
New York, were speculators. Only one of the original grantees seems ever to
have lived in town, and with the exception of the surveying team that laid out
the original lots, none of the others even set foot in it. For the people who did
eventually settle, the fact that a substantial majority of the town's earliest
records concern land reveals the settlers' preoccupation with title and ownership. In an overwhelmingly agrarian economy, land remained the most important commodity, and in successfully exploiting land lay the key to success.[9]

Certainly land ownership was tied to status directly. Throughout the early
town records, a sprinkling of buyers and sellers refer to themselves as "Gentleman," "Esquire," "Yeoman," and (in one case that clearly points toward the
status anxieties of the twentieth century) "Physician." These titles were self-
awarded but made public, objective claims about the social status of the indi-

vidual in question. The most common yardstick with which to measure the validity of those claims was visible wealth, and in most cases that meant land. John McNeil, for example, was listed only by name on his original 1784 purchase of land in Charlotte (which made McNeil one of the first people buying into the town), but by 1793, when he was both an established, substantial landholder and a town officer, he was completely comfortable listing himself on another deed as "John McNeil, Esq." It did not matter that only a few years earlier he could not make such a claim. While still a resident of Bennington County in 1784, McNeil had bought three hundred acres of lakeside land from Ethan Allen, a notorious land speculator. Two years later he acquired thirty more adjoining acres from Ira Allen, which gave him all the land around what is still known as McNeil's Cove. In 1792, while serving as Town Clerk, he bought yet more acreage at a tax sale, including some of the land he had apparently purchased from Ethan Allen eight years before (Ethan Allen was not the most reliable name in real estate). By the time he was done, McNeil controlled over 450 acres. In less than a decade, he had acquired sufficient land and status to earn the title "Esquire."[10]

Yet in this very process, we can see the incipient end of a society based on deference. McNeil was an unusually enterprising man, but neither was his a terribly isolated case. Plenty of people were busy both acquiring more land than a single man could farm, either for long-term holdings or short-term speculative profit. A hundred and fifty years earlier, the best land and the largest lots in new Massachusetts towns had gone automatically to those proprietors with the highest status. In other words, status preceded and created wealth. In McNeil's case, however, and the cases of others like him, the acquisition of wealth preceded status. The ability to call oneself "Esquire" was a confirmation of success rather than a prerequisite of it. Claiming such a title for oneself was already becoming old-fashioned, if Charlotte's town records are any indication. Very few men did so. In the postrevolutionary society of frontier Chittenden County, where virtually all men were landholders and all were freemen and a title such as "Esquire" was open to any successful man able to claim it, a logic of democracy was already incipient at the time of settlement. Already in 1794, the Reverend Samuel Williams, in his *Natural and Civil History of Vermont*, found Vermonters in a state of "equality." Implicit in the legal exactness and close accounting of settlers' mortgages and deeds was the conviction that in ownership lay independence.[11]

In 1785, the "second division" of land in Charlotte (the reallocation of acreage unclaimed since the first division of town land in 1763) placed a "Town Lot" squarely in the center of the town grant. This Town Lot further was subdivided into small units, one for each proprietor, with others set aside for a church, the town's "first settled minister," and a school. All this appears squarely within the New England tradition. The centralized Town Lot, with its small individual units big enough for a house and garden, was designed to encourage the development of a village, and the land set aside for church, school, and minister was meant to create the center of a cohesive, homogeneous community.

It did not work out that way. The earliest New England villages had been settled by corporately preexisting communal bodies. In many cases, the community existed before the village did: people who knew each other moved collectively onto new land. At least that was the intention. But from the start, Charlotte, like the rest of northern Vermont, was chartered by outside proprietors and settled by whoever took the chance to pull up stakes and come. To all these people, the subdivided Town Lot was just more land to buy and sell. For over a century before the 1780s, New Englanders had been moving away from villages and onto their individual farms, a tendency that had only accelerated as scattered individual holdings became consolidated over time.[12] In Charlotte, land was consolidated into individual holdings from the beginning. Everyone who arrived intended from the start to live on his own land. In Charlotte, in other words, there was never an expectation of village life as a communal necessity, either by proprietors or by settlers. Consequently, not much of a village ever developed near the Town Lot. By the 1780s, it was (and had been for a while) a legal and cultural vestigial gesture and not a serious attempt at planning. Centrally located on a ridge between two hills and on the stage road, by 1800 the town center, such as it was, consisted of a store, a tavern and inn, and a handful of houses. It never grew much beyond that.[13]

Even the expectation of Protestant homogeneity is deceptive (the early settlers were nearly all Yankees). In Charlotte's case, despite the provision of lots for church and minister in the second division of land, no church was established until 1792, and even then it had no pastor between 1799 and 1807, during which time membership fell to a low of eleven families. In addition, as early as 1802, formal espousals of individuals' theological differences from the established church begin to appear in the town records. Whether these reflect genuine differences of conscience or not (there were at least one Baptist and

one Methodist in town by 1801), they served the additional purpose of allowing the attesting party to avoid supporting the church.[14] In any case, the apparent homogeneous Congregationalist uniformity of the town did little to
offset a real decline of ecclesiastical influence. This is not to say that all settlers
were impious, but it is to say that the church was not a tremendously influential institution in early town history.

All the apparent (and real) continuities of ethnicity and tradition disguised
the fact that emerging out of the rapidly disappearing wilderness was a new
kind of New England town. The fact that the town had been founded by in-
vestors and settled by eager wheelers and dealers, the small but confident beginnings of a commercial economy evident by 1800 and reflected in the ferry
service and the potash and lumber trades, the importance of land speculation,
the dispersed settlement pattern, the decline of status and incipient challenge
to status-based politics, the weakness of institutional religion—taken together, these point toward locating the town in an emerging nineteenth-
century world rather than in a continuing New England tradition. The mi-
grating Yankees who settled the town are readily identifiable as commercial
strivers, as individualists, and as democrats. That is, they were more like the
Americans Tocqueville would discover in the 1830s than they were the inher-
itors and conservators of a traditional past. At the same time, they continued
to be a homogeneous Yankee community. It was into this settled, commercial,
and thoroughly Yankee society that the next wave of settlers, typified by Antoine Loraine, would arrive in the 1840s.

THE NEW IMMIGRANTS

In the 1840s, significant numbers of French Canadian and Irish immigrants
began to arrive in town, their departures from their respective homes spurred
by the same forces—famine, land shortages, overpopulation, and political upheaval. The Irish were escaping the poverty, despair, and famine of home via
the St. Lawrence. The Canadiens were escaping similar agricultural disaster and
political upheaval. Since at least the beginning of the nineteenth century, rising
population and limited amounts of land had forced the subdivision of farms
down to marginal sizes. Primitive agricultural methods were also a problem. By
the late 1830s, these nagging issues had flared into rural crisis. Between 1827
and 1844, Quebec experienced a 75 percent drop in wheat production (as

much as 95 percent in some counties). The year 1836 yielded a particularly poor harvest, and after that, a spiral of debt, discouragement, and exorbitant prices made many farmers unable to reseed, which drove more and more of them into penury. At the same time, the Panic of 1837 froze business activity, and the American demand for specie crippled the money supply. Increasing numbers of families lived on potatoes, with no bread at all, in debt and becoming more indebted. The export economy to Britain fell off sharply. The political situation was no better. Abortive rebellions in 1837 and 1838 led by the *patriote* party added to this turmoil. Ineptly led, opposed by the church, and militarily disorganized, they were doomed to failure but nevertheless managed to create piecemeal chaos. The end of 1838 saw martial law established, scores of *patriote* rebels' farms and villages burned and looted in retribution, and at least several hundred *patriotes* dead and hundreds more imprisoned (of whom twelve would be hanged and fifty-eight deported to Australia). Nor was it clear that anything was settled: other rebels still plotted on the American side of the border, planning a long struggle. Crossing the border shortly after them were thousands of other refugees from poverty.[15]

As a result, the French Canadian population of Vermont is estimated to have risen from around four thousand in 1840 to over twelve thousand in 1850, with most settlement occurring on the northeastern border and along the Champlain valley. Charlotte was at about the halfway point of this expansion, about fifteen miles south of the largest concentration of French Canadians developing in Burlington, by then a burgeoning urban center. As these French settlers moved south, they mixed in with Irish refugees, continuing their movement south by water along Lake Champlain from Canada.[16]

While in 1840 Charlotte remained a thoroughly Yankee town,[17] by 1850 over a quarter (72 of 282) of the town's households were headed by immigrants, the overwhelming majority of whom were either French (at least forty-three households) or Irish (twenty-one households).[18] Of a total population of 1634, 126 (7 percent) were Irish, and at least 260 (16 percent) were French. Desperately poor, often illiterate, and, in the case of the French, sometimes unable to speak English, these refugees sought to find places for themselves in a society that was neither newly settled nor undergoing burgeoning industrialization. Unlike their counterparts in more urban places such as Burlington and Winooski, the new people in Charlotte could not get jobs in mills or on the waterfront, though a tiny number worked on the Rutland Railroad, which arrived in town in 1849.

For the most part, these rural people became employees, primarily servants and farmhands. Fully thirty-six of the forty-three French households in Charlotte (84 percent)[19] were headed by a "laborer" in 1850. For the Irish, the figure is twelve of twenty-one (57 percent), and this figure is probably skewed downward by the fact that four Irish households were headed by women, probably widows. Nor do the numbers tell the full story. For the first time in town history, these hired people included significant numbers of men who were heads of families. The fact that men with mouths to feed were doing what had been a young, single man's job hints at the economic situation they faced.

Moreover, almost none of the new immigrants had sufficient capital to purchase substantial property. Only three French and three Irish in Charlotte are listed as "farmers" in the 1850 census (Loraine was not among them, though he was one of the very few who owned property), and these men had an average net worth considerably below the average for Charlotte farmers. One of them was only worth $200, which put him at Loraine's level. In the overwhelmingly agricultural society of the rural Champlain valley, the inability to acquire land was crippling to a man's economic prospects. Artisanship apparently did not offer much of an alternative. A lone stonemason was the only artisan among the Irish. The French did somewhat better in this regard, with a blacksmith, shoemaker, carpenter, two tailors, and two joiners. But as with the Irish stonemason, none of these men owned enough property to be recorded on the grand list. Charlotte's working poor were overwhelmingly immigrants in the 1840s and 1850s.[20]

That immigrant status coincided with class is perhaps clearest when the French and Irish are contrasted with Yankee heads of households. Of Charlotte's 190 households headed by working native-born men, 128 (67 percent) are listed as "farmer" and only 20 (10.5 percent) as "laborer." The rest are artisans, professionals, merchants, and business owners, such as the town's two hotel keepers. Looking at these figures another way, forty-six of the sixty-six "laborers" listed on the census (69.6 percent) were immigrants, though immigrants made up only a quarter of the population. By comparison, French and Irish immigrants combined made up only 4 percent of the town's farmers (6 out of 135),[21] 24 percent of its artisans (8 out of 33), and none of its businessmen or professionals. These immigrants lacked the primary means of rural economic mobility, land (available to the first generation of settlers), and that alone placed them outside of accepted social norms. They also lacked much of a foothold among Charlotte's skilled tradesmen and had no access into the professions. In addition, of course, they were also foreign, Catholic, and from societies traditionally despised by the English. In the Charlotte of the 1850s, the immigrants constituted a new class—a class of the landless poor.[22]

THE IRISH: LIMITED MOBILIITY

By 1860, the overall population of Charlotte declined by 3 percent, to 1,589, in 274 households. The Irish population, however, had increased, in total numbers (198), number of households (30), and as a percentage of total population (12). Twenty-one people among that Irish population had been listed on the census of 1850, a retention rate of 17 percent.[23] One hundred and eighty-seven individuals made up the thirty Irish families. Seven of the thirty-five Irish households were living with families to whom they appeared to be unrelated by either birth or marriage—that is, a laborer's family counted as part of his employer's household.[24] There were also eleven Irish living as individuals with employers' families, the same total as in 1850—six women living as servants and five men as farm laborers.[25]

Most of these people experienced little change in status in the decade between 1850 and 1860. Two-thirds of the families in 1860 (twenty out of thirty) were headed by laborers, a higher percentage than the decade before. Over the same decade, however, the number of Irish farmers rose from three to eleven, and those listing other occupations quadrupled to four (a mason, the superintendent of the poor, a railroad section manager, and a clothier). According to the agricultural census and grand list, most among these two groups owned real property by 1860. Upward mobility, then, appeared to be beginning for *some* of the Irish.[26]

Even so, when this change is considered in real economic terms, it becomes apparent that this was only a limited beginning. The 1860 agricultural census, which listed 121 of the 141 Yankee households headed by farmers and 9 of the 11 Irish, reveals how limited. The Yankee farm values ranged from a low of $500 to a high of $40,000 with the mean value of $8,000 and an average of $11,500. Even if the lowest six evaluations ($2,000 or below) and the highest five valuations ($16,000 or above) of the Yankee-led farm households are not considered, the average value of a Yankee farmer remains high, at $10,500. Furthermore, of the forty-two Yankee households whose head either listed no occupation or engaged in other occupations or professions,[27] sixteen owned farms with an average value of $4,500. For the Irish, the values of farms ranged between $600 and $12,000, with an average value of $1,800—considerably below that of the Yankees.[28]

The rise in the number property-owning Irish is also reflected in the Charlotte grand list for 1860. The grand list accounted for all taxable real property in town, including houses and their lots, as well as farms. Its valuations are considerably lower than those of the agricultural census for those properties listed in both, but as an indicator of relative wealth, it tells the same story. In the grand list of 1860, fourteen Irish are designated as owning taxable appraised property. One hundred and eighty-nine Yankees are listed. Of the Irish, one owned property valued at less than $100, while nine Yankees owned property in the same range. Eleven Irish owned properties valued between $100 and $499 versus forty-one Yankees. One Irish farmer owned a farm appraised at between $500 and $1,999 versus sixty-nine Yankee families. Forty-nine Yankee families owned property appraised at between $2,000 and $4,999, but no Irish family did. The property of the richest landowner, John Quinlan, was appraised at $5,062. Twenty-one Yankees householders owned property appraised at $5,000 (although only ten owned property rated at a greater value than Quinlan's).[29] Taken in conjunction with the agricultural census, the grand list of 1860 fills in the picture of real, if uneven, progress in Irish upward mobility. Most Irish were still landless laborers. Most of the Irish landowners were at or near the bottom in terms of real property. But some had made substantial gains, and one could be counted as among the town's elite. In 1870, the *Burlington Free Press* paraphrased Quinlan on his pride in both his remarkable progress and his reception in Charlotte:

> Over thirty years ago, he landed in Burlington. . . . Since then he had resided in one of the best towns in Vermont, that of Charlotte. . . . In a community composed of a large majority of Americans and Protestants, and a strong Republican town, he had never denied that he was an Irishman and a Catholic and a Democrat; yet he had received all the kindness and encouragement he deserved, or that any man could ask for . . . and he could only wish that every Irishman in Ireland could be landed on the south dock [in Burlington] tomorrow.[30]

Quinlan, the proud owner of 1,200 acres of Charlotte's "finest farm land," achieved the remarkable feat of being elected Charlotte's representative to the legislature in 1884. The French had no one like him.[31]

THE FRENCH: THE BOTTOM RUNG

The French made up about 21 percent of Charlotte's 1860 population. Already they were beginning to lag behind the Irish. There were about forty-seven French households in Charlotte by 1860, containing around three hundred persons (these estimates are on the low end). Twenty-two individuals of that number had been listed on Charlotte's 1850 census, a retention rate of 8 percent. Three of the French households of 1860 appeared to live with their employers. An additional thirty-five or so people also lived in employers' households; of those for whom an occupation is listed, all the women were servants and all the men but one farm laborers (the last was an apprentice blacksmith). Of the independent households, thirty-seven out of the forty-seven (79 percent) were also headed by laborers (twenty-seven farm, nine day, 1 railroad). Four, possibly five (11 percent), were farmers. There were three artisans, a carpenter, a joiner, and a blacksmith (6 percent). One man was too elderly to list an occupation, and one's occupation is unknown.[32]

These numbers indicate that as a group the French had not made much if any economic progress. The percentage of households headed by laborers was down only incrementally (from 84 to 79 percent), while the number of French artisans had dropped over a decade from seven to four, even including the apprentice. There were still no French merchants or professionals. Moreover, a closer look at the farmers reinforces the impression that the French were lagging badly. Three of the four listed in the agricultural census owned fourteen or fewer acres; the fourth owned thirty. Their average net worth was $750. Even if we add the grand list's valuations for houses to the estimates of the agricultural census, the average net worth of the four French farmers is still only $912.50, about half the Irish farmers' average. The fifth and richest French property owner, Francis Ploof, held fifty-seven acres and was listed as being worth $1,053 in the 1860 grand list. But he may not have been farming any more. He was at least sixty years old in 1860 and does not appear in the agricultural census of that year. In 1850, his farm had been worth $1,500. The most upwardly mobile Frenchmen in Charlotte were Lapresse Cloffas, a laborer in 1850 who had become a carpenter/joiner worth $130 in 1860; Matthew St. Peter, a farmer who had raised his net worth from $200 to $950; and Francis Ash, a laborer in 1850 who in 1860 owned a thirty-acre farm worth $1,000.[33]

So much for the relatively well-to-do. The other French Canadians who owned any property at all in 1860 (ten are counted on the grand list) had an average net worth of $131 and owned an average of 2.4 acres, barely a toe-hold in the agricultural society of the rural Champlain valley.[34] Yet these, along with the farmers listed previously, were the most—indeed the only—propertied French Canadians in town. On the opposite end of the narrow scale of French wealth, twenty-four French male farm and day laborers and eleven female servants lived as members of their employers' households in 1860. In 1850, twenty-nine males and six females had been similarly situated. These numbers also mark a significant departure from the experience of the Irish; three times as many French were single servants or laborers living with their employers in both decades.[35] This did not, however, necessarily mark a significant departure from the experience of the French in Quebec. The day laborer, mainly but not solely agricultural, had become a substantial element in Quebec society by the 1830s as more and more young *habitants* failed to inherit land.[36] In any case, a decade in Charlotte had not changed the fact that the French were the poorest, most transitory, and least established peo-ple in town. If anything, their situation had declined relative to both the Yan-kees and the Irish.

The records of the new Catholic Church reinforce the impression of the poverty and isolation of Charlotte's French. In 1858, a group of Charlotte's Catholics determined to form a parish. The town's leading Catholic, John Quinlan, purchased a house for the parish, a portion of which was altered to provide an area where mass could be heard. Led by Quinlan, Charlotte's Catholics also bought a meetinghouse from the Quakers of adjoining Monk-ton. They moved the building to Charlotte over the course of the winter of 1858 to 1859, and in June 1859 Bishop Louis DeGoesbriand laid the corner-stone of a reconstructed church. Quinlan had advanced a total of $592.24 by 1861, when the bishop assumed his debt and formed the parish.[37]

Despite Quinlan's best efforts, the parish—a mission—got off the ground slowly. At the time of its formation, DeGoesbriand had only a dozen priests to serve the entire state, and until 1874 mass was said on weekdays far more of-ten than on Sundays. In 1862, the visiting priest did not know the number of families in the parish, and pew rent, the primary income, totaled $55. In 1863, it totaled $51. In 1866, the bishop visited the parish "and laid down to the con-gregation on what terms they would continue to have the services of a priest" at all. The basic problem was not a lack of piety but the overwhelming poverty of the French parishioners, which made it difficult for them to raise money or attend weekday masses. "This congregation would no doubt do a great deal better if a priest could say mass for them frequently on Sundays," the visiting priest, Father Cloarec, wrote in the parish report of 1872. "The French Canadians of the congregation suffer more than the Irish because they are hired out and have no opportunity to attend mass on week days." He restated the point about Sunday mass the next year as well, adding, "I find the greatest difficulty in teaching catechism to the children, especially the Canadian children as very few of their parents can read. I cannot attend to this parish as it should be attended to on account of my numerous duties in Burlington."

In 1874, the parish finally got its priest, Father Joseph Kerlidou: "Le pretre est venu definitement pour habiter Charlotte le 27 Sept," he wrote in the parish records. "Depuis le 9 Avril jusqu'a cette epoque la paroisse a ete dessirvir par les pretes de l'eglise Canadienne St. Joseph Burlington. Le presbytre etait habite par une famille Irlandaise." ["The priest finally came to live in Charlotte on September 27. From April 9 until that time the parish was served by the priests of the Canadian church, St. Joseph's, Burlington. The rectory was inhabited by an Irish family."]

Father Kerlidou would remain only until October 1877, at which time the parish reverted back to mission status, in which it remained until 1966. But by his departure and probably well before, its character was set as a thoroughly French-dominated parish. In 1879, the first-year parishioners were counted by ethnicity; parish records show that French parishioners outnumbered the Irish two to one, one hundred families to fifty. Beginning in 1889, the diocese began asking what language parishioners spoke. In Charlotte, a French-speaking majority of between two and three to one would last until 1912, rising to as high as five to one in 1900. Moreover, the church's reports would be written in French between 1884 and 1912. Then, the latter year, a roughly three-to-two French-speaking majority suddenly became a three-to-two English-speaking one. By 1918, the number of French-speaking families (or, more likely, the number of families wanting to claim status as French speakers during wartime) would dip to a low of thirty-five. The number of French-speaking families would never again make up much more than a quarter of the parish again. In 1938, the church dropped the language question from the parish survey.[38]

The church records therefore reinforce two impressions: first, that the rural French did not assimilate linguistically until well into the twentieth century, and, second, that they remained poor for a long time after arriving in

Vermont, longer than the Irish. If we can judge by the numbers of intermarriages, the French did not assimilate very much even with their fellow Catholics. In 1860, only four Irish women were married to French men; no French women were married to Irish men. French baptisms consistently outnumbered Irish ones by ratios at least as large as the language disparity, while "mixed" baptisms never made up more than a tiny handful of the total. Between 1858 and 1874, the French swamped the Irish with their fecundity, with Irish babies outnumbering French ones only once, in 1869. In 1870, the French outbirthed the Irish twenty-eight to ten; in 1871, French babies outnumbered Irish ones fourteen to three; and in 1874, an army of newborn French overwhelmed the supposedly fertile Irish forty-four to four. Just as significantly, in no year between 1858 and 1874 did "mixed" baptisms (one Irish and one French parent) exceed two. The separation between Irish and French may have well have been partially due to economics. In the 1870s, after all, Father Cloarec was not worrying about Irish poverty and illiteracy or an Irish inability to attend Sunday mass. But just as clearly, it was also due to culture and language. The French were set apart.[39]

THE CANADIEN FRONTIER

Rowland Robinson indicated just how set apart they were. Robinson, a Vermont local colorist famous for writing in painstaking phonetically accurate but near-impenetrable dialects, lived in Ferrisburgh, the next town south of Charlotte. The son of famously tolerant Quaker abolitionists and a man who made it his life's work to reproduce the myriad of speech patterns, accents, and social types he found in Vermont, Robinson could nevertheless sum up very little sympathy for French Canadians. In just one book in 1892, he variously managed to describe the French Canadians as "an inferior class," "professional beggars," "vagabonds," and "lazy." French women he considered "slatternly ... with litters of filthy brats, all as detestable as they were uninteresting."[40]

Nor was he was alone in these opinions. By the mid-nineteenth century, the decline of northern New England had already become a cultural trope, and immigrants were bearing a fair share of the blame. In at least one way, the decline of Yankee Vermont was very real. Vermont's population would actually have gone down in the 1850s had it not been for foreign immigrants (Charlotte's population declined even with the infusion of immigrants, and Charlotte was hardly hill town). Throughout the rest of the century, even though

Vermont's population held steady or grew, its Yankee population declined steadily. Nor did the perception of decline apply only to numbers. Perhaps more important, the cultural importance of the Yankee as the symbol of all that was good in America appeared to be eroding as well. For many people, the decline of the hill town foreshadowed the end of a social ideal. Yankees who stayed in the state, acutely conscious of these changes, increasingly articulated a self consciously and assertively Yankee cultural identity. Yankee superiority, for example, is a consistent theme in rhetoric devoted to dedicating Civil War monuments in the state. And the struggle over who represented the "real" Vermont would become the primary issue defining the politics of the second half of the nineteenth century. In this atmosphere, all immigrants were problematic. But the beggarly and lazy French Canadians, continuously swamping the border and breeding their endless new litters, were the special harbingers of social death in Vermont.[41]

As always seems to be the case, then, the French were despised both because they were inferior and because they were a threat. While the Irish (and other, later) immigrants could be problematic, the French, especially the rural French, were something else altogether: linguistically stubborn, culturally resistant to assimilation, and, most important (because it lay at the root of these other differences), at the edge of a contiguous culture. Moreover, they were on the frontier of a society and culture in which since at least 1763 identity was defined largely by resistance to English. The French arriving in Charlotte in the 1840s and 1850s had arrived near the far reaches of that cultural frontier. Set apart from the Yankees by class and from both the Yankees and the Irish by culture and scattered throughout a town that never developed a true center, lacking, for many years, even the opportunity to attend Sunday mass, French Canadian immigrants to Charlotte had to either cross the cultural frontier or remain permanent outsiders. Many—most—of them disappeared in plain sight, passing through the life of the town as migrants or a resident underclass, leaving very little trace. Others did not. They changed their names to Drinkwine or Ash or Strong, spoke English at home, and became, after a while, invisible in another way—invisibly French.

And what of Antoine Loraine? Was he a frontiersman? We began with him in a log cabin, isolated by poverty and cultural distance from his surroundings, presenting negligible agricultural production. But let us consider one more definition of the frontier. In 1981, Thomas Cochrane posited that the primary frontier for nineteenth-century Americans was the cultural divide between a precapitalist and a capitalist mentality. By that definition, Loraine was probably already across. Judging by his later life, he was no longer mentally a *habitant*. Instead, on his six acres in 1846, he was already, though a laborer for others, a classic Jacksonian man, making his first step toward autonomy—and to an embrace of the market. But Cochrane also argued that "continual migration accentuated the open class structure" of American society. "The new arrival in a community was judged by what he could do rather than who his parents were."[42] And in mid-nineteenth century Charlotte, I am not entirely sure that was the case. If Robinson is any indication (and he is), the French Canadians were certainly judged by who their parents were and the language they spoke. Men such as Loraine had to cross another cultural divide as well, one that was, well, cultural. As long as they remained, mentally and culturally, on the fringes of Quebec, they were less likely to succeed in America.

At some point in his life, Loraine appears to have crossed that second frontier. In 1854, he sold out and left Charlotte, just another transitory Frenchman who made little mark on the town. But he did not go far. He bought another farm one town away in Monkton, Vermont, and sold it two years later—at a profit.[43] About the same time, he invested again, this time in a much bigger farm, in New Haven, Vermont, one county away and about fifteen miles south of both Monkton and Charlotte. There he stayed the rest of his life. The 1870 census assessed his holdings at $7,000. He died in 1892; his youngest son, Henry, farmed in New Haven until the 1930s.[44] But it is his oldest son, Antoine Jr., who had been born in New York, who perhaps best shows the Americanization of the Loraines. In May 1861, as part of the first wave of volunteers, the twenty-one-year-old enlisted in the 2nd Vermont under the name Anthony Lawrence. By mid-September, he was dead of consumption, without ever leaving the state. When in 1873 a group of townspeople and schoolchildren gathered on Memorial Day "to decorate graves of local men who had died in the Civil War," the first on their list was "Anthony Loraine." That name, perhaps, fit best.[45]

Charlotte was and is a small town. Drawing inferences from the silences surrounding its poorest and most isolated inhabitants is a tentative business, especially when it can be difficult to determine who they were, and implying that the resulting conjured insights might be applicable to a large region bordering

Quebec is probably a foolish one. Nevertheless, fools rush in to fill an historiographic vacuum, so here I go: a look at Charlotte in the years from the mid-1840s to the Civil War suggests that it might be fruitful to think of a northern frontier along the same lines that historians have recently been looking at the West and especially the Southwest—that is an area in which contiguous culture groups are interacting. That perspective, I believe, will allow a fresh look at much of Vermont's history, and it will bring the rural French, overshadowed by their more urban brethren and obscured through inattention far too long, into the brighter light they deserve.

In 1937, the sociologist Elin Anderson published *We Americans*, a study of ethnicity in Burlington. Fifteen miles north, ninety years removed, and an economic universe away from the small log house of Antoine Loraine, she found that the French sense of the frontier still lingered. "The difference between the French Canadians and the other groups in Burlington," she wrote,

> cannot be understood without a recognition of the attitude with which the French Canadians regard the territory itself. They may not proclaim it from the housetops, but to them Burlington is a French city and they are its true citizens. . . .
>
> With this belief deep within them, their settling in New England has differed from that of other people. Their migration has been a "peaceful penetration" across an imaginary line. . . . When they [settled permanently] it was not so much like settling in a new land as extending the boundaries of the old.[46]

At some point, across time, space, and cultural distance, those boundaries become blurred. But one hundred years after the *patriote* rebellion, what she found was the remnant of the cultural frontier.

NOTES

1. Loraine's House was moved in 1953 to the Shelburne Museum in Shelburne, Vermont. A 1955 interview of an elderly Charlotte man suggests that Loraine may have worked as a woodcutter rather than a farmhand, but the report is unreliable. Shelburne Museum Archives, Building File, Settler's House (Sawyer's Cabin). For a view of what Loraine's progress as landowner and homeowner may have been like, see the A. F. Sayles 1860–1870 stereoviews, "Four Stages of the 'Green Mountain Boy,'" in *Vermont Landscape Images 1776–1976*, ed. William C. Lipke and Philip Grime (Burlington, Vt.: Robert Hull Fleming Museum, 1976).

2. On the settlement and early development of Charlotte, see Charlotte Historical Society, ed., *Around the Mountains: Historical Essays about Charlotte, Ferrisburgh and Monkton by William Wallace Higbee* (Charlotte, Vt.: Charlotte Historical Society, 1991); W. S. Rann, ed., *History of*

Chittenden County Vermont, with Illustrations (Syracuse, N.Y.: D. Mason, 1886); Hamilton Child, *Gazetteer and Business Directory of Chittenden County Vermont for 1882–1883* (Syracuse, N.Y.: printed at the Journal Office, 1882); Abby Maria Hemenway, *Vermont Historical Gazetteer, Chittenden County* (Burlington, Vt.: A. Hemenway, 1868); Zadock Thompson, *History of Vermont, Natural, Civil, and Statistical, in Three Parts, with an Appendix* (Burlington, Vt.: the author, 1853).

3. U.S. Department of Commerce, Bureau of the Census, *Seventh Census of the United States, 1850, Chittenden County, Vermont,* lists the net worth of each household. Because Loraine is not listed in the separate agricultural census of that year, it is impossible to know what use he was making of his land. However, the unusually detailed Charlotte grand list of 1873 gives a fairly thorough accounting of the property of the man to whom Loraine sold his homestead in 1854. On the same nineteen and a half acres in 1873, John C. Wilder owned one horse, two sheep, one cow, one heifer, and a dog, worth a total of $98 and real estate worth $641 (he had paid Loraine $400 for the property). Clearly, this was not a commercial property of any substance. Nor had it ever been, even if we assume the fall in land value was due to the neglect of Wilder.

4. Loraine purchased six acres of land from L. and W. R. Pease in 1845 for $180 ($20 mortgage). In 1846, his tax assessment was $60. (Tax assessments were generally lower than market value, as they are today.) In 1847, Loraine's assessment rose 20 percent (to $78), and for the first time the property was listed in the town grand list as containing a "house & lot" rather than mere acreage. This, along with architectural evidence, leads me to conclude that the house was constructed between the 1846 and 1847 assessments. In 1850, Loraine purchased thirteen and a half acres adjoining his original holdings from S. W. Stearns for $283. All records relating to Loraine's land and house ownership are in the *Charlotte, Vermont, Land Records,* vol. 12, 117, 118, 618; vol. 13, 234, and the *Charlotte, Vermont, Grand List, 1845–1854,* passim. Loraine is listed in the 1850 census as a "laborer," generally a designation given to the landless, rather than as a "farmer." This I take as a reflection of both his small holdings and his status as an employee.

5. Allan Greer, *The Patriots and the People: The Rebellion of 1837 in Lower Rural Canada* (Toronto: University of Toronto Press, 1993), chap. 2. The quotation is from p. 23.

6. The 1850 census lists Loraine as having been born in Canada. It also categorizes him as illiterate (this is confirmed by his inability to sign deeds) and notes that his son did not attend public school. U.S. Department of Commerce, Bureau of the Census, *Seventh Census of the United States, 1850, Chittenden County, Vermont,* entry 281. My assumption about Loraine's citizenship and level of political activity derives from his place of birth, his illiteracy, and his recent arrival in town. In 1840, he had been living in Chazy, New York, which put him on a common path for immigrants from Quebec to the Champlain valley (U.S. Department of Commerce, Bureau of the Census, *Sixth Census of the United States, Clinton County, New York, 1840.* On the immigration of French Canadians into Vermont, see Ralph Vicero, "French Canadian Settlement in Vermont prior to the Civil War," *The Professional Geographer* 23, no. 4 (October 1971): 290–94; Betsy Beattie, "Opportunity across the Border: The Burlington Area Economy and the French Canadian Worker in 1850," *Vermont History* 55, no. 3 (summer 1987): 133–52, and "Community-Building in Uncertain Times: The French Canadians of Burlington and Colchester, 1850–1860," *Vermont History* 57, no. 2 (spring 1989): 84–102; and Gerard Brault, *The French Canadian Heritage in Vermont* (Hanover, N.H.: University Press of New England,

1986). On the French Canadian church in Vermont, see Joseph Couture, "New England's First National Parish, or the History of St. Joseph's of Burlington, Vermont" (M.A. thesis, St. Michael's College, 1960); Jeremiah K. Durick, "The Catholic Church in Vermont: A Centenary History," in *One Hundred Years of Achievement by the Catholic Church in the Diocese of Burlington, Vermont* (Lowell, Mass.: Sullivan Brothers Printers, 1953); and David Rous, "The Soldier Monuments: Civil War Commemoration in Vermont, 1866–1924" (M.A. thesis, University of Vermont, 2000), app. D. Our Lady of Mt. Carmel, the Catholic parish in Charlotte, was established in 1858. On the Catholic Church in Charlotte, see Abby Maria Hemenway, *Vermont Historical Gazetteer, Chittenden County* (Burlington, Vt.: A. Hemenway, 1868), 744. Catholics in Charlotte were so isolated that there are only two recorded marriages by Catholic priests from 1860 to 1869 (*Charlotte Marriage Records*).

7. In his *American Frontiers: Cultural Encounters and Continental Conquests* (New York: Hill & Wang, 1997) Gregory Nobles defines "frontier" as "a region in which no culture, group, or government can claim effective control or hegemony over others" (xii). The Charlotte of 1850 certainly does not qualify as a French frontier by that definition. While social, political, and economic "control or hegemony" definitely changed at the border, it is my contention that the French, or at least many French, understood themselves to be part of a transnational culture.

8. In his discussion of Vermont's eighteenth-century settlement, Michael Bellesiles proposes a definition of "frontier" (2) that "implies confrontations born of diverse cultural contacts and structural developments" and adds that "it is now largely seen as an area where diverse cultures meet and interact and as a region not yet consolidated into a larger political unit." Oddly enough, the period Bellesiles describes is remarkably free of diverse cultures in Vermont, as eighteenth-century settlers were almost exclusively New England Yankees and the area almost devoid of Native Americans (Bellesiles acknowledges this on p. 52 and goes on to discuss diversity among Yankees). In mid-nineteenth-century Vermont, by contrast, though the question of the "political unit" had long been resolved, cultural interaction with Quebec was far more open. On early Vermont and the frontier issue, see, especially, Bellesiles, *Revolutionary Outlaws: Ethan Allen and the Struggle for Independence on the Early American Frontier* (Charlottesville: University Press of Virginia, 1993); Randolph Roth, *The Democratic Dilemma: Religion, Reform, and the Social Order in the Connecticut River Valley of Vermont, 1791–1850* (New York: Cambridge University Press, 1987); Chilton Williamson, *Vermont in Quandary, 1763–1825* (Montpelier, Vt.: Vermont Historical Society, 1949); and Paul Searls, "Yankee's Kingdom: The Imagined Community of Vermonters and the American Struggle with Modernity, 1896–1915" (Ph.D. diss., New York University, 2002). Searls's historiographic discussion of the literature of eighteenth- and nineteenth-century Vermont is particularly extensive. Good examples of the market-oriented school of thought that discuss rural New England generally are Christopher Clark, *The Roots of Rural Capitalism: Western Massachusetts, 1780-1860* (Ithaca, N.Y.: Cornell University Press, 1990), and Richard Bushman, *From Puritan to Yankee: Character and the Social Order in Connecticut, 1690–1765* (Cambridge, Mass.: Harvard University Press, 1967).

9. *Charlotte, Vermont, Proprietors' Records*, vol. A. The original charter is on p. 19. See also pp. 3 and 350.

10. MacNeil's transactions are recorded in the *Charlotte, Vermont, Land Records*, vol. 1, 28, 29, 30, 31, 48, 151, 354, and 405. On the latter two, he refers to himself as "esquire." The tax sale is 354. Town clerks through 1990 are listed in Charlotte Historical Society, *Around the Mountains*, 207.

11. On changes in northeastern land use patterns, see Kenneth Lockridge, *A New England Town: The First 100 Years* (New York: Norton, 1970); Alan Taylor, *William Cooper's Town: Power and Persuasion on the Frontier of the Early Republic* (New York: Alfred A. Knopf, 1995); and John Stilgoe, *Common Landscape of America, 1580–1845* (New Haven, Conn.: Yale University Press, 1982). When Stilgoe writes that by 1770 people in new communities "found it useless to think of discrete settlements focused about single centers" (83), he might as well have Charlotte in mind. Samuel Williams, *Natural and Civil History of Vermont* (1794); McNeil's transactions are in the *Charlotte, Vermont, Town Records*. Anyone interested in understanding how Democratic impulses were manifesting themselves in frontier Vermont would do well to follow the career of Matthew Lyon (1749–1822), the "Beast from Vermont."

12. Lockridge, *A New England Town*; *Charlotte, Vermont, Proprietors' Records*, 106 (map of second division).

13. There is a spring on the top of the hill, still the "town spring" (a small, rusty hand pump is hidden in some shrubbery). In 1850, a small town hall was constructed at the intersection, and a new Congregational church was built nearby a few years later. Beyond that, nothing much has ever developed.

14. Charlotte Historical Society, *Around the Mountains*, 51–53. *Charlotte, Vermont, Town Records*, vol. 2. The first disavowals of the Congregational Society begin on p. 53. See also pp. 120, 144, 145.

15. On the Quebec rebellions of 1837 and 1838, see Fernand Ouellet, *Lower Canada, 1791–1840: Social Change and Nationalism* (Toronto: McClelland and Stewart, 1980), chaps. 11 and 12, and Greer, *The Patriots and the People*.

16. Brault, *The French Canadian Heritage in Vermont*, 52; Vicero, "French Canadian Settlement in Vermont prior to the Civil War," passim.

17. There were twenty-three Charlotte residents with French last names in the 1840 census.

18. The difference this immigration made in the constitution of the town is quite striking and readily identifiable in census records. The 1840 census does not list birthplaces but in Charlotte lists only a handful—three or four—possible French names (such as "Tatro"). In the 1850 census, I counted as French Canadian only those households where a French surname coincided with a birthplace of Canada listed for the head of the house. In all, there were forty-six Canadian heads of household in Charlotte in 1850, some of whom undoubtedly had anglicized French names (for instance, a "Drinkwine" [Boivin]). Of these forty-six, I counted thirty-nine as French, which is conservative. The remaining non-Irish immigrants in Charlotte were born either in England (four) or Scotland (one). U.S. Department of Commerce, Bureau of the Census, *The Sixth Census of the United States, 1840, Chittenden County Vermont*, and *The Seventh Census of the United States, 1850, Chittenden County, Vermont*.

19. Counting the French is a difficult task for two reasons. First, many French names, particularly those of the illiterate, were badly transcribed, often in nearly indecipherable hands, by Yankee census takers and town clerks who either did phonetic guesswork or assigned an

English name that sounded something like what they thought they had heard. Second, some people, such as Henon Bishop, apparently translated French names into English sometime after arriving in America; determining who did that requires guesswork as well. In Charlotte, for example, William Drinkwine probably started life as a Boivin. As with Bishop, first names in the family shore up this assumption. But had Joseph Baker and Jeremiah Steady, both of whom were Canadian single men, been born as, respectively, a Boulanger and a Gibou dit Tranquille? Was John Miller, who had children named Lewis and Angeline, a French Canadian? It is not always easy to tell. Veronique Gassett offers somewhat of a path through this thicket with her extremely helpful pamphlet "French Canadian Names: Vermont Variants" (Montpelier, Vt.: Vermont Historical Society, 1994), but the way is easily lost nonetheless.

20. U.S. Department of Commerce, Bureau of the Census, *The Sixth Census of the United States, 1840, Chittenden County Vermont*, and *The Seventh Census of the United States, 1850, Chittenden County, Vermont.*

21. One of these farmers, Henon Bishop, had actually been born in Vermont. Since his wife had been born in Canada and the first names in his family indicate that "Bishop" probably was "Leveque" at some point, I count him as French. If we eliminate him, there were only five Catholic farmers in town in 1850.

22. U.S. Department of Commerce, Bureau of the Census, *The Seventh Census of the United States, 1850, Chittenden County, Vermont.*

23. Irish families positively identified in other town records were omitted from the 1860 census. Two families were "free colored," and almost all the remaining were native-born Protestant. Included in the Yankee listing are several British immigrants.

24. These seven families and fifteen individuals were listed as farm laborers or servants or had no listed occupation. For example, one of these individuals was listed as a "boarder."

25. U.S. Department of Commerce, Bureau of the Census, *The Eighth Census of the United States, 1860, Chittenden County, Vermont*, and *The Seventh Census of the United States, 1850, Chittenden County, Vermont.*

26. U.S. Department of Commerce, Bureau of the Census, *The Eighth Census of the United States, 1860, Chittenden County, Vermont*; *Vermont Agricultural Census, 1860*; *Charlotte Grand List, 1860.*

27. These forty-two Yankee householders included professionals (two clergymen and two physicians), other occupations (a merchant, a miller, and a clerk), and the usual skilled tradesmen and artisans (two masons, nine carpenters, two shoemakers, a wheelwright, a millwright, a carriage maker, a tailor, a saddler, a butcher, a broom maker, and a painter).

28. *Vermont Agricultural Census, 1860.* Two of the Irish who listed their occupation as laborer also owned farms, one valued at $600 and the other at $4,000, and one Irish head of household who occupation was included in the "other" grouping also owned a farm valued at $1,000.

29. *Charlotte Grand List, 1860.*

30. Article in the *Burlington Free Press*, March 18, 1870, in the Our Lady of Mt. Carmel parish papers, Roman Catholic Diocese of Vermont Archives.

31. John Quinlan obituary, *Burlington Free Press*, September 8, 1892, in the Our Lady of Mt. Carmel parish papers, Roman Catholic Diocese of Vermont Archives.

32. U.S. Department of Commerce, Bureau of the Census, *The Eighth Census of the United States, 1860, Chittenden County, Vermont.*

33. *Vermont Agricultural Census, 1860; Charlotte Grand List, 1860.* A decade later, Cloffas would be gone, and Ash would still own a thirty-acre farm worth $1,000. Of the three, only St. Peter had improved his economic position. His farm was listed as being worth $2,362.

34. *Charlotte Grand List, 1860.*

35. U.S. Department of Commerce, Bureau of the Census, *The Eighth Census of the United States, 1860, Chittenden County, Vermont,* and *The Seventh Census of the United States, 1850, Chittenden County, Vermont.*

36. Greer, *The Patriots and the People,* 30–31.

37. Our Lady of Mt. Carmel parish papers, Roman Catholic Diocese of Vermont Archives.

38. Our Lady of Mt. Carmel parish papers, Roman Catholic Diocese of Vermont Archives.

39. The rural poverty of the French relative to the Irish is interesting in part because in Vermont's (more) urban areas the French were more prosperous than the Irish and had higher-skilled jobs. On this, see Beattie, "Opportunity across the Border," 133–52, and "Community-Building in Uncertain Times." In Charlotte, after about 1880 the Irish become assimilated to the point that they become difficult to track.

40. Rowland E. Robinson, *Vermont: A Study in Independence* (Boston: Houghton Mifflin, 1892), quoted in Rous, "The Soldier Monuments," 66. See also T. D. Seymour Bassett, *The Growing Edge: Vermont Villages, 1840–1880* (Montpelier, Vt.: Vermont Historical Society, 1992), 175–97.

41. On population trends, see Vicero, "French Canadian Settlement in Vermont prior to the Civil War," 291; on population trends and the Yankee cultural response, see Hal S. Barron, *Those Who Stayed Behind: Rural Society in 19th Century New England* (New York: Cambridge University Press, 1984); on the rhetoric of Civil War dedications, see Rous, "The Soldier Monuments"; on mid- to late nineteenth-century politics, see Searls, "Yankee's Kingdom."

42. Thomas C. Cochrane, *Frontiers of Change: Early Industrialism in America* (New York: Oxford University Press, 1981), 12.

43. Loraine's various deeds and mortgages in Monkton are in the *Monkton, Vermont, Town Records,* vol. 13, 491–92, 560; vol. 14, 60–61. See also the *Monkton Grand List, 1855 and 1856.*

44. U.S. Department of Commerce, Bureau of the Census, *The Eighth Census of the United States, 1860, Addison County, Vermont,* and *The Ninth Census of the United States, 1870, Addison County, Vermont; New Haven, Vermont, Land Records,* vol. 14 (1852–1861), 533; *New Haven, Vermont, Vital Records,* book B, 19; *New Haven, Vermont, Grand List, 1857.*

45. Vermont General Assembly, *Revised Roster of Vermont Volunteers and Lists of Vermonters Who Served in the Army and Navy of the United States during the War of the Rebellion 1861–66* (Montpelier, Vt.: Watchman, 1892); Harold Farnsworth and Robert Rodgers, *New Haven in Vermont, 1761–1983* (New Haven, Vt.: Town of New Haven, 1984); *New Haven, Vermont, Vital Records,* book A, 111.

46. Elin L. Anderson, *We Americans: A Study of Cleavage in an American City* (New York, 1937), 26–27.

4

Native Americans, the Market Revolution, and Culture Change: The Choctaw Cattle Economy, 1690–1830

James Taylor Carson

The market revolution has emerged as an important interpretive paradigm for the study of cultural, economic, and social change among societies around the world. However, Charles Sellers, the preeminent historian of the American market revolution, excluded Native Americans from his study.[1] The early nineteenth-century cattle economy of the Choctaw Indians offers a striking example of how the Native Americans responded to the revolution. Generally speaking, students of the cattle economy of the Old Southwest have either overlooked the involvement of the Native Americans, or, as Richard White and Daniel Usner have done, considered it solely as an economic innovation without examining its cultural ramifications. Contrary to Sellers' argument that land was the most conservative force opposed to the American market revolution, culture proved to be an even more conservative force because it structures the Choctaws' adaptation to and participation within the market economy. Men adapted by incorporating cattle herding into their warfare and hunting traditions, and women exploited cattle and expanded their economic roles too without transgressing the cultural conventions that had patterned their lives well before the first cattle ambled into the Lower Mississippi Valley.[2]

Cattle and the cattle trade first became important in the Lower Mississippi Valley when the French settled the region at the end of the seventeenth century.

This chapter is reprinted from James Carson Tyler, "Native Americans, the Market Revolution, and Culture Change: The Choctaw Cattle Economy, 1690–1830," *Agricultural History* 71, no. 1 (1997): 1–18.

Tribes like the Houmas, Tunicas, Chitimachas, Pascagoulas, Natchez, Avoyelles, and Attakapas valued European trade goods, and they incorporated the French into what historian Daniel Usner has termed a frontier exchange economy. These tribes, the *petites nations*, traded, among other goods, cattle, which they had acquired as early as 1650 from tribes who traded with the Spanish in New Mexico, to the beef-starved French. In return these tribes received guns, ammunition, and other manufactured items. The commercial success of the *petites nations* was, however, short lived. By the mid-eighteenth century, disease, dependency, and European political and demographic expansion had reduced their remnants to economically and politically marginal groups. Moreover, by the 1740s French settlements at Opelousas and Natchitoches had begun to produce enough cattle to satisfy much of the Louisiana colony's needs.[3]

Only the Choctaws withstood colonial pressures and remained a forceful presence in the lower Mississippi Valley throughout the eighteenth and early nineteenth centuries. Among the region's tribes, the Choctaws were by far the most numerous and politically influential. They numbered around twenty thousand throughout the period, inhabited several towns in present-day east central Mississippi, and practiced a mixed economy of horticulture and hunting. Women directed domestic life and oversaw farming. They fabricated clothing and tools from animal skins and bones, manufactured earthen containers, prepared food, and sowed and harvested crops. Their expansive fields of corn, pumpkins, beans, and squash provided two-thirds of the Choctaws' diet and made the Choctaws what British surveyor Bernard Romans termed a "nation of farmers." Men, on the other hand, oversaw vitally important public ceremonies, but hunting, trading, and warfare were equally important occupations, and their social prestige depended on their success in these endeavors. Together men and women fashioned a surplus subsistence economy predicated on a sexual division of labor. Thus, when the frontier exchange economy made itself felt among the Choctaws in the eighteenth century, women traded foodstuffs, baskets, clothing, and firewood, and men offered deerskins and military service to the French in exchange for manufactured goods. Whether or not the Choctaws, like the *petites nations*, traded cattle in this economy is unclear, but linguistic evidence indicates they may have done so.[4]

Choctaws and other Indians of the Lower Mississippi Valley had conceived of the cattle as a trade good since their first contact with the animals in the late seventeenth century. Jesuit priest Pere Jacques Gravier visited them in 1701 and reported their use of the word *waka*, derived from the Spanish *vaca*, for cow. *Waka* is one of the few European loanwords Choctaws incorporated into their language. They typically named European goods with indigenous words that reflected their conception of their good's function or form. For example, Choctaws called horses *isuba*, deer-resembler, and guns were *tanampo*, from the verb *tanampi*, to fight. The use of the Spanish loanword was a regional phenomenon because the languages of many tribes that bordered the Lower Mississippi Valley and that had extensive contacts—belligerent and peaceful— with the Choctaws also included derivatives of *vaca*. The Mobilian trade dialect that served as a regional lingua franca employed *waka* as well. Linguistically, *waka* constructed cattle in such a manner that they became inseparable from the European colonial presence, and their use as a trade good conformed to Spanish expectations of regional trade and alliance. Moreover, the incidence and prevalence of the loanword suggests that the Choctaws and other tribes may not have integrated cattle into their daily lives like they had horses and guns.[5]

Frenchmen Regis du Roullet visited the Choctaws in 1732, and he recorded evidence that reveals the extent to which cattle were becoming an integral part of what historian James Merrell had called the "Indians' New World." While traveling westward from Mobile to the Choctaw nation, du Roullet crossed a small river about eight miles outside of Mobile, the Choctaw name of which translated to "bayou where cattle pasture." In contrast, the French name for the river, Mill River, reflected an altogether different conception of the river's utility. Perhaps this was the site where Choctaws raised cattle for trade with the French colonists. Regardless, by the 1730s cattle had become a feature of the postcontract landscape.[6]

Inferences drawn from toponyms are far from conclusive, but artifactual evidence substantiates the links between Choctaws and cattle in the early eighteenth century. Warriors and hunters used powder horns made of cattle horn; buffalo horn may also have been used. Native doctors used horns, open on both ends, to bleed their patients in a cupping fashion, and women fabricated winter cloaks from cowhides.

The impact of cattle on Choctaw place-names and material culture signaled an acceptance of the animals that allowed for more important and far-reaching innovative uses of cattle in community and individual life later in the century.[7]

By the last half of the eighteenth century Choctaws certainly had begun to raise cattle, and they altered their settlement patterns to accommodate their herds. In the early 1770s many Choctaws abandoned the towns and moved out to unsettled land that had been previously reserved for hunting and warfare. Here they dispersed along the Yazoo and Tombigbee Rivers to take advantage of the thick stands of cane and rich fields of grass that proliferated in the river bottomlands.[8]

The expansion of the Choctaws collided with the expansion of the United States. In other parts of the continent such conflict usually led to war, but the United States and the Choctaws signed the Treaty of Hopewell on 3 January 1786 to ensure peace on the frontier. The treaty, and the wane of imperial rivalries in the region, brought an end to the intertribal and imperial wars that had characterized the Lower Mississippi Valley throughout much of the eighteenth century. Consequently, the peace imperiled the social and political prestige of Choctaw warriors. The Hopewell treaty, however, reserved for the Choctaws the right to punish illegal American squatters "as they please," and "rouguish young men," coming of age in a society where the traditional forms of social advancement were no longer present, took to raiding the cattle of American squatters as a substitute for warfare. In 1803, eight warriors, for example, raided Daniel Grafton's farm outside of Natchez and killed one of his work steers and wounded the other. Other Americans who lived closer to Natchez complained to the territorial governor incessantly about Choctaw depredations against their herds. The young men so valued cattle raids that they incorporated *waka* into their war names. By the early nineteenth century several men named Wakatubbee, which means cow-killer, bore testimony to the juxtaposition of an innovative mode of warfare within the broader persistence of a more ancient tradition.[9]

The federal government had failed to foresee the "problems" that resulted from Choctaw enforcement of the punishment clause, and President Jefferson sought to end the cattle raids without resort to hostilities. In the early 1800s the trading firm of Panton, Leslie and Company, a company run by Englishmen that operated out of Spanish Mobile and Pensacola, began to demand from the Choctaws repayment of debts incurred by their purchase of bullets, guns, and powder on credit. By 1803 the debt exceeded $46,000, and the firm demanded a Choctaw land cession to retire it. Opposed to the cession of Indian land to private individuals, and wary of Spanish and British intrigues in the Lower Mississippi Valley, Jefferson intervened and federal commissioners held treaty talks with the Choctaws. The resulting 1805 Treaty of Mount Dexter ceded a substantial portion of southeastern Mississippi to the United Stated for $50,000, and the federal government extinguished the Choctaw debt owed to the company with most of the cash settlement. The federal government earmarked what cash remained after paying off Panton, Leslie and Company to compensate citizens who had suffered depredations committed "on stock, and other property by evil disposed persons of the said Choctaw nations." Holding the Choctaws corporately liable for the legal livestock raids and punishing them collectively for such actions brought an end to the raids.[10]

In addition to cattle's vital place in male warrior culture, the animals emerged as an important part of its counterpart, hunter culture. Although deerskins overwhelmingly dominated the Choctaw skin trade throughout its duration, cowhides and beef tallow became important exchange commodities by the early 1800s. In 1802 the federal government built a trading factory on the banks of the Tombigbee River in present-day western Alabama to facilitate trade with the Choctaws, and it flourished. (At a later date the factory was moved up-river closer to the Choctaws towns.) Though the quantities of cowhides brought to the factory were small in relation to the amounts of other skins, in terms of value they rivaled bear skins as the second most important skin traded. Unlike the deer, bear, fox, and wildcat skins and beaver pelts, cowhides were not destined for consumption in distant markets. Instead, American factors, that is, government traders and their slaves, cut the hides into strips and used them to tie up the bundles of deerskins and other furs for shipment. The factors also used cowhides to shield the decks and crews of the factory's two boats from balls and arrows shot by hostile Indians. Another important trade commodity was beef tallow, but it never overtook its rival, beeswax, which was used in the manufacture of candles and was worth twice as much per pound. Cowhides and tallow obtained an important but secondary position in the vast array of skins, peltries, and other products that the Choctaws traded at the United States factory, but this trade allowed hunters, like warriors, to establish a relationship with the animals that comported with cultural norms.[11]

By the 1810s the Choctaws had become entirely dependent on the deerskin trade. Never able to trade enough skins to pay off their debts, they had mortgaged their economic and political independence first to the French, then to the British, and then to the United States. This decline, as Richard White has written, further undermined their society and degraded their environment. When the United States trading factory closed its doors in 1822, the Choctaws lost perhaps the only source of credit available to them, as well as the guaranteed prices that had been set by the federal government. Left on their own to cope with an emerging market economy that set prices according to demand and had little need for deerskins, the Choctaws for the most part abandoned commercial hunting. As Unser and White have argued, cattle raising offered an alternative to the increasingly impracticable deerskin trade.[12]

After over a century of contact with cattle, Choctaw warriors and hunters laid down their rifles, saddled their horses, strapped on spurs, unfurled their rawhide whips, and began to herd livestock as their primary economic endeavor. How they managed their herds, beyond free-ranging them, is unclear because there is no evidence to indicate that they selectively bred animals or culled their herds, or that they used traditional land management techniques like burning to manage their cattle and the cattle range.

As Terry Jordan has urged, other features of the nineteenth-century Choctaw cattle complex bore a strong Anglo-American imprint. English traders and cattlemen from Georgia and the Carolina had settled in Mississippi in the late eighteenth and early nineteenth centuries, and they imparted much of their knowledge to the Choctaws. At round-up times, Choctaw herdsmen, *wak apistikelim*, summoned their cattle from the cane-brakes, pastures, and forests with loud cracks of the whip, herded the cattle on horseback, and enclosed them in cow pens. Once penned cattle could be driven down innumerable cow trails, *wak aiitanowa*, to markets in surrounding American communities. To distinguish between herds, they branded their animals, as was common practice among non-Indians of the region. Choctaw cowboys like Mushulatubbee, Puckshenubbee, Mastubbee, and Indian countrymen John Pitchlynn and Charles Juzan bartered deerskins and cowhides for, among other things, saddles, bridles, spurs, whips, cow bells, and salt. (Salt was essential for the cattle's nutrition, and they would never venture far from a secure source of it.) Although Choctaw men retained deeply rooted hunting and warfare values in their relationship to cattle, they nevertheless also had learned how to use the accoutrements and techniques of the Anglo-American cattle economy.[13]

Cattle raising was an innovative economic behavior that fit perfectly within the regional market economy. Choctaws could raise cattle with ease, and the demand for beef in the Old Southwest remained constant because the region's plantation and subsistence economies depended to a large extent on cattle. Indeed, federal Indian agent William Ward remarked that the Choctaws "generally supplied (in part) the neighboring whites with . . . beef." The average price for a cow in Mississippi in the 1820s was between eight and ten dollars, and the price of fresh beef was four cents a pound. In the late 1820s when the Choctaw herd numbered over 43,000 head, it had a maximum market value of almost four hundred thousand dollars on the hoof of a half million dollars when converted into fresh beef. In addition to its value, the Choctaw herd's size was comparable to that of non-Indian herds in the region.

In 1828 there were 2.07 cattle per capita in the Choctaw nation. In Spanish Natchez, for example, the same ration was obtained in 1784, and in 1840 the state of Mississippi had a much lover ration of 1.8 cattle per capita. The size of the Choctaw cattle economy meant that unlike their cotton economy it was not concentrated in the hands of a few entrepreneurs.[14]

Whether they owned herds of several hundred head or only a few animals, by all accounts most Choctaws participated in the cattle economy. Families would have had access to approximately 1,290,000 pounds of beef annually, or just under three ounces per capita per day, and incalculable quantities of milk and butter. Whereas formerly adults had taught boys to hunt and girls to farm, the Choctaws began impressing on the young the value and importance of stock raising, Sons and daughters received from their families, if possible, a cow and a calf, a sow and piglet, and a mare and colt. As the child grew older, his or her herd multiplied and provided the owner with a sound source of income and subsistence in adulthood. The recognition of cattle as the key for future generations' prosperity prompted Choctaw leaders to attempt to control strictly the trade of cattle with Americans.[15]

American cattle traders frequently ventured into the nation to buy and trade for Choctaw cattle. Mushulatubbee, one of the nation's principal leaders, often entertained buyers from Alabama at his home. With what such men bought Choctaw cattle is unknown, but the most noteworthy, and hence recorded, transactions between Choctaws and American buyers involved midnight swaps of cattle for alcohol. Indians took whisky from the traders and exchanged it with other Choctaws for their cattle, blankets, and guns and then traded these items back to Americans. Failing this, some tribesmen simply stole their fellow Choctaws' cattle for trade with the Americans, and this drew

the ire of reform-minded leaders such as Hwoolatahoomah, who banned livestock stealing and whisky trading in his district. Despite the trouble caused by
the whisky trade, most Choctaws seem to have adapted to the market economy by raising livestock.[16]

But not all uses of cattle reflected market concerns. Choctaws also incorporated them into rituals that affirmed kin and community relationships and
obligations. When a Choctaw died, kinfolk shot and killed the deceased persons' cattle, horses, and dogs for the funeral ritual. Choctaws reasoned that the
animals "would be equally useful and desirable in the state of being which
they enter at death." Of use to the deceased in the afterlife, the meat of the
slain animals served the kinfolk as well. Relatives feasted on the meat to honor
the passage of the deceased and to reaffirm symbolically the bonds of kinship
and community, and life and death.

Such a ritual use of cattle found further expression in another form of social behavior, reciprocity. At a council held in August 1819, Choctaw headmen
donated eighty-five cows and calves for the support of the Boston-based American Board missionaries, who had begun building the Elliot missionary station
and school in the western part of Choctaw nation. When the missionaries accepted this gift, they unwittingly committed themselves to the system of reciprocal social relations and obligations that characterized Choctaw society.[17]

Adam Hodgson, an Englishman who visited the Elliot mission in 1820, witnessed firsthand the juxtaposition of tradition and innovation among the
Choctaws, for he recorded both the use of cattle in traditional funerals and the
prosperity of the new cattle economy. During his journey through the Choctaw
nation, Hodgson stopped and visited two Choctaw brothers who raised cattle
for a living. The size of their herds, the lushness of their range, and the sturdy
prosperity of their farmsteads impressed him, and he decided to spend the
night at their home. As the sun set their cattle ambled in from the forest for
milking, and Hodgson's host shot one of the cows for supper just as, a half century earlier, he might have killed a deer or turkey. That evening the Englishmen
sat down with the family for a meal of fresh beefsteaks. What escaped Hodgson's normally observant eyes, however, were the women who had milked the
cows and who had cooked the steaks.[18]

The infrequent mention of Native American women in historical sources
makes any study of their lives difficult and any conclusions reached tenuous,
but linguistic evidence can open new lines of inquiry and illuminate what

otherwise would be overlooked or incomprehensible. Anthropologists Mary Haas and Amelia Rector Bell have shown that the Muskogee language family, to which the Choctaw language belongs, contains grammatical structures and vocabulary that differentiate in subtle ways the language that the men spoke from the language that the women spoke. By drawing on the Choctaw language and the few references to women and cattle in the documentary sources, a number of suggestions about Choctaw women and cattle may be offered.[19]

Gendered social structures historically have exerted a considerable influence on different societies' development of a cattle complex and their participation in a market economy. Among patrineal peoples such as the Marakwet and Nambi of Kenya, men controlled property like cattle and, consequently, entry into the market economy. Women could own cattle, but what animals they owned were added to the men's herds. More importantly, men had the final say in whether cattle owned by women would be sold, traded, or left in the men's herds. Women's participation in the market economy was thus limited to the marketing of vegetable produce and sex. In early nineteenth-century New England a similar process occurred whereby women were cordoned off into "separate spheres" and hindered by law and custom from participating in the male-dominated economy.[20]

Unlike the Marakwet and Nambi of Kenya and the Americans of New England, Choctaws were matrilineal. Descent was traced through the mother, and children belonged to the mother's family. Moreover, they were matrilocal. Families lived grouped in matrilieages that further enabled Choctaw women to have a considerable if not decisive say in the distribution and control of land, property, and labor. Matriliny, therefore, differentiates the Choctaws' experience from that of their Kenyan and American counterparts.[21]

Just as men's relationship to cattle was conditioned by their warrior and hunter traditions, so too was women's relationship with the animals structured by their link to the home and horticulture. Like male Choctaws, females incorporated *waka* into their names, and the names reveal much about the complex intersection and discrete segmentation of Choctaw gender structures. According to Amelia Rector Bell, the Creek language differentiates gender distinctions according to definitions of male behavior. Thus, the woman "food maker" can only be understood in secondary opposition to the primary male "warrior." One of the translatable female names that incorporated *waka*,

Wakaihoner, means "cow cooker." When contrasted to the male name *Wakatubbee,* which means "cow killer," the names bear a striking resemblance to the pattern described by Bell. For women, it seems cattle could define them in relation to men insofar as women performed a gendered function like food preparation that was predicated upon a male behavior like hunting. But cattle could also be defined in terms that were predicated upon distinctly feminine activities like farming.[22]

Another Choctaw term for cattle—*alhpoa*—means literally "fruit trees such as are cultivated" and suggests a uniquely feminine construction of the value and utility of livestock. The fruit trees that proliferated among the Choctaw towns offered a sensible linguistic construction of cattle for several reasons. Just as women tended plum or peach trees for their fruit, so too could they care for cattle and obtain milk. The association of women with the formidable power of fertility also may have created a special relationship between them and cattle because, like fruit trees, the annual reproduction of cattle was what made the animals particularly valuable. Above all, orchards were an integral part of the town landscape, and other cattle-related terms derived from *alhpoa* suggest this held true for cattle as well. For example, *alhpoa aiimpa* meant pasture, and *alhpoa imilhpak* meant fodder. Both terms imply the careful tending and close proximity to the towns that characterized women's farming as opposed to the neglect that characterized the free-range herding practiced by the men.[23]

The linguistic construction of cattle as fruit trees may have allowed women to adapt to changing Choctaw settlement patterns. When the Choctaws abandoned their towns in the 1770s, relocated in the borderlands that had once been reserved for hunting and fighting, and began to raise cattle, the women had to abandon the orchards that had been a part of their land holdings and subsistence cycle. Once settled in the borderlands, they would have been unable to reconstitute immediately their orchards because native fruit trees took at least three years before they started to bear fruit. But, in cognitive sense, women could have taken their cattle, as fruit trees, into the previously unsettled and uncultivated borderlands that had been reserved for male hunting and fighting and reconstitute immediately what had been an integral part of village life.[24]

The cognition and exploitation of cattle as fruit trees further facilitated women's entry into the market economy. Early in the contact period Choctaw

women had welcomed explorers, travelers, and traders with gifts of food and shelter, but newer market sensibilities pervaded this ethic and transformed it by the 1800s. Women obtained scarce hard cash from travelers who were beholden to their Choctaw hosts by selling them milk, beef, corn, fodder, peaches, and other foods. This hospitality economy allowed women both to participate in the wide range of opportunities made possible by the market economy and to obtain hard cash for further participation in it. What the women purchased with this money is impossible to discover, but cloth, sewing necessities, and agricultural implements constituted the bulk of purchases made by women at the United States trading factory. Although he hospitality economy grew out of an older ethic of reciprocity, its transformation reflected the extent to which custom had given way to innovation, and reciprocity and subsistence had given way to sale and profit.[25]

Whereas selling beef or milk had precedent in the hospitality economy, the selling of livestock as animals did not. Nevertheless, *alhpoa* constructed cattle so that women like men could trade or sell cattle. However, as a result of the *alhpoa* construct, women, like men, could trade or sell cattle. In July of 1820 a thirteen-year-old Choctaw girl tried to enter the Elliot missionary school, located in present-day west central Mississippi. The missionaries, however, denied her request for admission because the school was already overcrowded. Reluctant to crush the girl's hopes of going to the school, her friends told her that because she lacked a school uniform, she could not enter the school. Undaunted, the girl determined to sell her cow for cash to buy a uniform. Touched by her resolve, the missionaries agreed to take the girl in, and her uncle offered to pay any expenses to cover the cost of her schooling.[26]

What the missionaries mistook for youthful precocity, and what some might mistake for an everyday occurrence in the Old Southwest, in fact revealed the juxtaposition and interplay of Choctaw culture and newer market sensibilities. The girl's conception of the cow as a good that could be sold for cash suggests the prevalence of a distinctly market-oriented mindset. Furthermore, selling the entire cow rather than its milk or meat represented elaboration of the feminine hospitality economy that was nevertheless sanctioned by the language of the Choctaw's gendered economy and culture.

The Choctaws' transition from the early eighteenth-century frontier exchange economy to the nineteenth-century market economy failed to upset the gendered economic structures of their culture. By killing, hunting, raising, trading, and selling cattle, they adjusted to the new world wrought by European colonization and American settlement. Moreover, Choctaw women avoided the economic marginalization and social subjugation that had characterized women's experiences in New England and Kenya by drawing on their traditional roles and responsibilities to sanction innovative economic activities. Contrary to Charles Sellers, market revolutions are not contests of impersonal forces but struggles waged by individuals within a changing world economy, and language and culture are crucial elements in understanding how different peoples have managed the fight.

NOTES

1. Charles Grier Sellers, *The Market Revolution, Jacksonian America*, 1815–1846 (New York: Oxford University Press, 1991). The Indians in Sellers' study vanish from the scene before the market economy emerges. Among other studies of the market's impact, Nancy Cott's *The Bonds of Womanhood: "Women's Sphere" in New England*, 1780–1835 (New Haven, Conn.: Yale University Press, 1977) was the first to argue that women's "separate spheres" and a "cult of domesticity" emerged to segregate women from the market revolution in New England. In contrast to Cott, Catherine Clinton's *The Plantation Mistress: Women's World in the Old South* (New York: Pantheon Books, 1982) argues that southern women did not necessarily experience the same changes that had occurred in the North. Nancy Hewitt's *Women's Activism and Social Change: Rochester, New York, 1822–1872* (Ithaca, N.Y.: Cornell University Press, 1984) has broadened further the debate in American historiography on the market economy's impact on gender by examining women from different social classes and their responses to social and economic change.

Anthropologists Henrietta L. Moore, *Space Text, and Gender: An Anthropological Study of the Marakwet of Kenya* (Cambridge: Cambridge University Press, 1986); and Regina Smith Oboler, *Women, Power, and Economic Change: The Nandi of Kenya* (Stanford, Calif.: Stanford University Press, 1985) have argued that in Kenya the patriarchal structure of the Marakwet and Nandi peoples structured their responses to colonialism and the market revolution in ways that perpetuated men's dominance and weakened the position of women. Their work and that of Cott, Clinton, and Hewitt suggest that far from exerting a uniform influence, the market revolution caused disparate, culturally conditioned changes in economic production and gender segmentation.

2. Lewis Cecil Gray, *History of Agriculture in the Southeastern United States to 1860*, 2 vols. (Washington, D.C.: Carnegie Institution of Washington, 1933); Jack D. L. Holmes, "Joseph Peirnas and the Nascent Cattle Industry of Southwest Louisiana," *McNeese Review* 17 (1966): 13–26: Jack D. L. Holmes, "Livestock in Spanish Natches," *Journal of Mississippi History* 23 (October 1961): 15–37: John Hebron Moore, *Agriculture in Antebellum Mississippi* (New York: Octagon Books, 1971); John Hebron Moore, *The Emergence of the Cotton Kingdom in the Old Southwest: Mississippi 1770–1860* (Baton Rouge: Louisiana State University Press, 1988):

Kenneth D. Israel, "A Geographical Analysis of the Cattle Industry in Southeastern Mississippi from Its Beginnings to 1860" (Ph.D. diss., University of Southern Mississippi, 1970); John D. W. Guice, "Cattle Raisers of the Old Southwest: A Reinterpretation," *Western Historical Quarterly 8* (April 1977): 167–87; Terry Jordan, "The Origins of Anglo-American Cattle Ranching in Texas: A Documentation of Diffusion from the Lower South," *Economic Geography 45* (January 1969): 63–87; Terry Jordan, *North American Cattle-Ranching Frontiers: Origins, Diffusion, and Differentiation* (Albuquerque: University of New Mexico Press, 1993); Lauren C. Post, "The Old Cattle Industry of Southwest Louisiana," *McNeese Review 9* (1957): 43–55; Richard White, *The Roots of Dependency: Subsistence, Environment, and Social Change among the Choctaws, Pawnees, and Navajos* (Lincoln: University of Nebraska Press, 1983). See also Michael F. Doran, "Antebellum Cattle Herding in the Indian Territory," *Geographical Review 66* (January 1976): 48–58, for a discussion of cattle raising among the Choctaws in Indian territory, and Louise Spindler, *Culture Change and Modernization* (New York: Holt, Rinehart and Winston, 1977) for an overview of cultural change and adaptation.

    3. Charles W. Arnade, "Cattle Raising in Spanish Florida, 1513–1763," *Agricultural History* 35 (July 1961): 116–24; William Beer, ed., *Early Census Tables of Louisiana*, vol. 5 of *Publications of the Louisiana Historical Society* (New Orleans: Tulane University Press, 1911), 79–104; David I. Bushnell Jr., "Drawings by A. Debatz in Louisiana, 1733–35," *Smithsonian Miscellaneous Collections*, vol. 80, no. 5 (Washington, D.C.: Smithsonian Institution, 1927); Heloise H. Cruzat, trans., "Louisiana in 1724: Banet's Report to the Company of the Indies, Dated Paris, 20 December 1724," *Louisiana Historical History* 35 (July 1961): 125–30; M. de Remonville, "Memoir, addressed to Count de Pontchartrain, on the importance of Establishing a colony in Louisiana"; Andre Penicault, *Annals of Louisiana*, vol. 1 of *Historical Collections of Louisiana and Florida, Including Translations of Original Manuscripts Relating to Their Discovery and Settlement with Numerous Historical and Biographical Notes*, new series, ed. Benjamin French (New York: J. Sabin & Sons, 1869), 2–14, 62, 144; Gray, *History of Agriculture in the Southeastern United States to 1860*, vol. 1, 79; Pierre Margry, *Découvertes et Établissements des Francais dans l'Ouest et dans le Sud de l'Amerique Septentrionale* (1614–1754), vol. 6 (Paris: Imprimerie D. Jouaust, 1888), 245–46; Antoine Simon Le Page du Pratz, *The History of Louisiana Translated from the French of M. Le Page du Pratz*, ed. Joseph Tregle Jr. (Baton Rouge: Louisiana State University Press, 1975), 166; Lauren C. Post, "The Domestic Animals and Plants of French Louisiana as Mentioned in the Literature with References to Sources, Varieties, and Uses," *Louisiana Historical Quarterly* 16 (October 1933): 560–63; Lauren C. Post, "Some Notes on the Attakapas Indians of Southwest Louisiana," *Louisiana History* 3 (summer 1962): 233–34; Dunbar Rowlland and A. G. Sanders, eds. and trans., *Mississippi Provincial Archives, 1729–1740: French Dominion*, vol. 3 (Jackson: Press of Mississippi Department of Archives and History, 1932), 268; Nancy M. Surrey, *The Commerce of Louisiana during the French Regime, Jesuit Relations and Allied Documents*, vol. 57 (Cleveland: Burrows Brothers, 1900), 257; Danial H. Usner Jr., *Indians, Settlers, & Slaves in the Frontier Exchange Economy: The Lower Mississippi Valley before 1763* (Chapel Hill: University of North Carolina Press, 1992), see particularly chapters 1, 2, and 3.

    4. Bernard Romans, *A Concise Natural History of East and West Florida; a Facsimile Reproduction of the 1775 Ed.* (1775; reprint, Gainesville: University of Florida Press, 1962), 71,

76; White, *Roots of Dependency,* chap. 2, 4; Jean-Bernard Bossu, *Travels in Interior of North America, 1751–1762,* ed. and trans. Seymour Feiler (Norman: University of Oklahoma Press, 1962), 169–70; John Swanton, "An Early Account of the Choctaw Indians," in *Memoirs of the American Anthropological Association,* vol. 4, no 2 (Lancaster, Pa.: American Anthropological Society), 59, 67–68; Patricia K. Galloway, "Choctaw Factionalism and Civil War, 1746–1750," *Journal of Mississippi History* 44 (November 1982): 289–327.

    5. Marc de Villiers du Terrage, "Notes sur les Chactas d'aprés les journaux de voyage de Regis du Roullet (1729–1732)," *Journal de la Société des Américanistes de Paris 15* (1923): 234; Cyrus Byington, "A Dictionary of the Chotaw Language," Bureau of American Ethnology, *Bulletin 46* (Washington, D.C.: Government Printing Office, 1915).

    Besides the Choctaw language and the Mobilian trade language, the Wichitas, Biloxis, Cherokees, Creeks, and Chickasawa used some form of *vaca* for cattle. David S. Rood, *Wichita Grammar* (New York: Garland, 1976), 295; John Owen Dorsey and John R. Swanton, eds., *A Dictionary the Biloxi and Ofo Languages,* Bureau of American Ethology, *Bulletin 47* (Washington, D.C.: Government Printing Office, 1912), 301; Durbin Feeling, *Cherokee-English Dictionary* (Talequah.: Cherokee Nation of Oklanhoma, 1975), 187; Henry Frieland Buckner, *A Grammer of the Masjwke (Muskogee), or Creek Language: To Which Are Prefixed Lessons in Spelling, Reading, and Defining* (Marion, Ala.: Domestic and Indian Mission Board of the Southern Baptist Convention, 1869), 35; James M. Crawford, *The Mobilian Trade Language* (Knoxville: University of Tennessee Press, 1978), 4, 76, 83: Kenneth H. York, "Mobilian: The Indian *Lingua Franca* of Colonial Louisiana," in *La Salle and His Legacy: Frenchmen and Indians in the Lower Mississippi Valley,* ed. Patricia K. Galloway (Jackson: University of Mississippi Press, 1982), 139–45.

    See J. L. Dillard, "The Maritime (Perhaps Lingua Franca) Relations of a Special Variety of the Gulf Corridor," *Journal of Pidgin and Creole Languages* 2 (1987): 244–49, for a discussion of the diffusion of Spanish loanwords in the Gulf Coast region; Terry Crowley, *An Introduction to Historical Linguistics* (Oxford: Oxford University Press, 1992), 267, 308; Theodora Bynon, *Historical Linguistics* (Cambridge: Cambridge University Press, 1977), 256–61; M. Mosha, "Loanwords in Luganda: A Search for Guides in Adaption of African Languages to Modern Conditions," in *Language Use and Social Change,* ed. W. H. Whiteley (Oxford: Oxford University Press, 1971), 288–308; Florian Coulmas, ed., *Language Adaptation* (Cambridge: Cambridge University Press, 1989), for discussions on the development of pidgins and incorporation of loanwords.

    6. The river was named *bouk ouaka apouka* (*Bok wak hopohka*). Marc de Villiers du Terrage, "Notes sur les Chactas d'aprJs les journaux de voyage Rjgis du Roullet (1729–1732)," *Journal de la Société des Américanistes de Paris* 15 (1923): 234–35; James Merrell, *The Indians' New World Catawbas and Their Neighbors from European Contact through the Era of Removal* (Chapel Hill: University of North Carolina Press, 1989).

    7. Bushnell, "Drawings by A. Debatz in Louisiana, 1732–1735"; John R. Swanton, "An Early Account of the Choctaw Indians," *Memoirs of the American Anthropological Association,* vol. 4, no. 2 (1918): 71, describes a Choctaw medicine man using a horn in his treatments but does not specify whether it was a cow or a buffalo horn, but, like powder horns, Choctaws could have used both types.

    8. White, *Roots of Dependency,* 102–5; *Missionary Herald 25* (November 1829): 350; Horatio B Cushman, *A History of he Choctaw, Chickasaw, and Natchez Indians* (Greenville, Tex.:

Headlight, 1899), 389–91, 403; Francis Armstrong to Lewis Cass, 21 September 1831, Letters Received by the Office of Indian Affairs, 1824–1880, Choctaw Agency, 1824–1876, Reel 169, Microfilm Series M234, Bureau of Indian Affairs, Record Group 75, National Archives (hereafter RG 75); Adam Hodgson, *Letters from North America Written during a Tour in the United States and Canada*, vol. 1(London: Hurst, Robinson, 1824), 224.

9. John McKee to Choctaw Headmen, 11 December 1815, Letters Received by the Secretary of War Relating to Indian Affairs, 1800–1823, Reel 1, Microfilm Series M271, War Department, RG 75; Dunbar Rowland, ed., *Official Letter Books of William C. C. Clairborne, 1801–1816*, vol. 1 (Jackson, Miss., 1917), 13, 60; Dunbar Rowland, ed., *The Mississippi Territorial Archive, 1798–1803*, vol. 1 (Nashville, Tenn.: Brandon Printing, 1905), 32, 350, 393, 527–29; Lawrence Kinnaird, ed., "Spain in the Mississippi Valley, 1765–1794," *Annual Report of the American Historical Association*, vol. 4 (Washington, D.C.: Smithsonian Institution Press, 1949), 26; Roster of Choctaws claiming to have lost horses during removal, 8 October 1837, Letters Received by the Office of Indian Affairs, 1824–1880, Reel 184, Microfilm Series M234, Choctaw Agency West, 1825–1838, Bureau of Indian Affairs, RG 75; Treaty of Hopewell, 3 January 1786, Articles 4 and 5, Reel 2, Microfilm Series M 668, Ratified Indian treaties, 1722–1869, Bureau of Indian Affairs, RG 75.

10. William Simpson, Abstract of debts owed to Panton, Leslie and Company, 20 August 1803, Letters Received by the Secretary of War Relating to Indian Affairs, 1800–1823, reel 1, Microfilm Series M271, War Department, RG 75; Article 2, Treaty of Mount Dexter, 16 November 1805, Ratified Indian Treaties, 1722–1869, Reel 3, Microfilm Series M668, Bureau of Indian Affairs, RG 75.

11. Indent Books, 14 December 1805, 24 January 1809, 6 February 1809, and Miscellaneous Accounts, 3 April 1816, Reels 1, 2, 3, Microfilm Series T500, Records of the Choctaw Trading House, Under the Office of Indian Trade, 1803–1824, RG 75; Deborah A. Hay, "Fort St. Stephens and Fort Confederation: Two U.S. Factories for the Choctaw, 1802–1822" (master's thesis, Auburn University, 1979), 39–43, 88–93, 112.

12. White, *Roots of Dependency*, chap. 4, 5; Daniel H. Unser Jr., "American Indians on the Cotton Frontier: Changing Economic Relations with Citizens and Slaves in the Mississippi Territory," *Journal of American History* 72 (September 1985): 297–98; Michael F. Doran, "Antebellum Cattle Herding in the Indian Territory," *Geographical Review* 66 (January 1976): 102–4.

13. Jordan, *North American Cattle-Ranching Frontiers*, 182–83; *Missionary Herald* 18 (May 1822): 150; *Panoplist and Missionary Herald* 15 (October 1819): 460, 463; Hodgson, *Letters from North America*, 1: 23, 241, 253; Byington, *Dictionary of the Choctaw Language*, 74, 77, 361–62; Francis Baily, *Journal of a Tour in Unsettled Parts of North America in 1796 and 1797* (London: Baily Brothers, 1856), 373; Israel, "A Geographical Analysis of the Cattle Industry," 26, 65; Harry Toulmin, comp., *Digest of the Statutes of the Mississippi Territory* (Natchez, Miss.: Territorial Publisher, 1807), 403; Dunbar, "Colonial Cowpens," 125–30; Guice, "Cattle Raisers of the Old Southwest," 167–87; Forrest McDonald and Grady McWhiney, "The Antebellum Southern Herdsmen: A Reinterpretation," *Journal of Southern History* 41 (May 1975): 147–66; Daybook entries, 18 August 1808, 16 September 1808, 22 May 1809, 13 July 1809, 9 October 1809, 18 April 1810, 8 March 1811, and 19 February 1813, Daybooks, 1803–1824, Reel 4 Microfilm Series T500,

Records of the Choctaw Trading House, Under the Office of Indian Trade, RG 75; Henry Halbert, "Origins of Mashulaville," *Publications of the Mississippi Historical Society,* vol. 7 (Oxford: Mississippi Historical Society, 1903), 393; André Michaux, "Travels to the West of the Allegheny Mountains in the States of Ohio, Kentucky, and Tennessee," in *Early Western Travels,* 1748–1846, ed. Reuben Gold Thwaites (Cleveland: Arthur H. Clarke, 1904), 246.

14. *Niles' Weekly Register* 38 (3 July 1830): 345; Gray, *History in the Southeastern United States to 1860,* vol. 2, 812, 1042; United States Bureau of the Census, *The Statistical History of the United States from Colonial Times to the Present* (New York: Basic Books, 1976), 30. In 1828 the American Board missionaries took a census of the Choctaw cattle herd in the eastern district of the nation and counted 5,627 people and 11,661 cattle, yielding a ration of 2.07 cattle per capita. Using this ration I have reconstructed the Choctaw herd for a population of 21,000 Choctaws in 1828 to be over 43,000 animals. *Missionary Herald* 25 (February 1829): 61, 153; *Missionary Herald* 17 (April 1821): 110.

15. Senate, *Report on Indian Tribes,* 20th Cong., 2nd sess., 3 January 1829, vol. 1, S. Doc. 27, 6; Guice, "Cattle Raisers of the Old Southwest," 175–77; Israel, "A Geographical Analysis of the Cattle Industry," 5–7, 79; Thomas L. McKenney, *Memoirs, Official and Personal,* vol. 1 (New York: Paine and Burgess, 1846), 323.

In the absence of figures that might reveal how much of their herds Choctaws consumed annually, I have used Leonard Brinkman's estimates for cattle weight and Harold K. Schneider's figure of 10 percent of the herd annually as a maximum for consumption, coupled with his estimation that a cow yields half its body weight in meat. Choctaw cattle probably weighed about six hundred pounds. Harold K. Schneider, *Livestock and Equality in East Africa* (Bloomington: Indiana University Press, 1979), 62, 101; Leonard W. Brinkman Jr., "The Historical Geography of Improved Cattle in the United States to 1870" (Ph.D. diss., University of Wisconsin, 1964), 38.

16. William A. Love, "Moshulitubbee's Prairie Village," *Publications of the Mississippi Historical Society,* vol. 7 (Oxford: Mississippi Historical Society, 1903), 375; *Missionary Herald* 17 (March 1821): 74; *Missionary Herald* 19 (January 1823): 9–10; Samuel Brown, *The Western States and Territories* (Auburn, N.Y.: H. C. Southwick, 1817), 242.

17. *Panoplist and Missionary Herald* 15 (October 1819): 461; *Panoplist and Missionary Herald* 15 (December 1819): 535; Louis LeClerc de Milford, *Memoir or a Cursory Glance at My Different Travels & My Sojourn in the Creek Nation,* ed. John Francis McDermott, trans. Geraldine de Courcy (Chicago: R. R. Donnelly and Sons, 1956), 204; White, *Roots of Dependency,* 105.

For further discussion of Choctaw funeral rites, see Hodgson, *Letters from North America,* vol. 1, 216; Henry Frieland Buckner, "Burial among the Choctaws," *American Antiquarian and Oriental Journal* 2 (July–September 1879): 55–58

18. Hodgson, *Letters from North America,* 1: 224, 241, 253. Hodgson does not state that women milked cows and cooked the steaks. In the absence of documentary evidence, I have used the methodology of ethnohistory and my own interpretation of what we know about the Choctaws to infer that it was women who did this.

19. Mary Haas, "Men's and Women's Speech in Koasati," in *Language in Culture and Society,* ed. Dell Hymes (New York: Harper and Row, 1964), 228–33; Amelia Rector Bell, "Separate People: Speaking of Creek Men and Women," *American Anthropologist* 92 (June 1992): 332–45.

20. Moore, *Space Text, and Gender,* 66–67, 144; Oboler, *Women Power, and Economic Change,* 9–11, 25–28, 153–55, 191, 229, 243; Cott, *The Bonds of Womenhood.*

21. John R. Swanton, "Source Material for the Social and Ceremonial Life of the Choctaw Indians," Bureau of American Ethnology, *Bulletin 103* (Washington, D.C.: Government Printing Office, 1931), 139–40; Henry Clark Benson, *Life among the Choctaw Indians* (Cincinnati: L. Swormstedt & A. Poe, 1860), 31–32.

22. Amelia Rector Bell, "Separate People: Speaking of Creek Men and Women," *American Anthropologist* 92 (June 1990): 332–35. The Choctaw names come from a roster of Choctaws claiming to have lost possessions during removal, 8 October 1837, Letters Received by the Office of Indian Affairs, 1824–1880, Reel 184, Microfilm Series M234, Choctaw Agency West, 1825–1838, RG 75.

23. du Pratz, *History of Louisiana,* 234; Post, "The Domestic Animals and Plants of French Louisiana," 560; U. P. Hedrick, *The Peaches of New York* (Albany, N.Y.: J. B. Lynn, 1917), 44–45.

24. White, *Roots of Dependency,* 103–5, 130–37; *Missionary Herald* 25 (November 1829): 350; Hedrick, *The Peaches of New York,* 44–45.

25. Baily, *Tour in Unsettled Parts of North America,* 373; Eron Opha Rowland, "Peter Chester, Third Governor of the Province of West Florida under British Dominion, 1770–1781," in *Publications of the Mississippi Historical Society,* vol. 5, Centenary Series, Franklin L. Riley, ed. (Jackson: Mississippi Historical Society, 1925), 83–84; Lists of travel expenses, George Gaines, 31 March 1811 and 30 September 1811, Miscellaneous Accounts, 1811–1815, Reel 2, Microfilm Series T500, Records of the Choctaw Trading House, Under the Office of Indian Trade, 1803–1824, RG 75.

26. *Panoplist and Missionary Herald* 16 (July 1820): 320.

5

The "Sharper" Image: Yankee Peddlers, Southern Consumers, and the Market Revolution

JOSEPH T. RAINER

As the Industrial Revolution was gearing up in New England shops and factories in the early nineteenth century, the increased production by manufacturers of clocks, tinware, and other Yankee "notions" found a market outlet through thousands of young men who peddled these wares across the entire United States. Yankee peddlers were familiar figures on the American landscape in the first four decades of the nineteenth century. Timothy Dwight noted in 1821 how Yankee tin peddlers boxed the compass of the young republic:

> Every inhabited part of the United States is visited by these men. I have seen them on the peninsula of Cape Cod and in the neighborhood of Lake Erie, distant from each other more than six hundred miles. They make their way to Detroit, four hundred miles farther, to Canada, to Kentucky, and, if I mistake not, to New Orleans and St. Louis.

Yankee clock peddlers practiced their own "Manifest Destiny" to sell clocks on the very fringes of Anglo-American settlement. Shortly after hearing, in June 1836, the capture of Santa Anna at the battle of San Jacinto, clock peddler John Case wrote to his partner Hiram Barber that Texas would offer "a field for speculation." Indeed, clock peddlers worked any and all markets within their reach. Two Massachusetts peddlers, Washington Stevens and Elihu

This chapter is reprinted from Joseph T. Rainer, "The 'Sharper' Image: Yankee Peddlers, Southern Consumers, and the Market Revolution," *Business and Economic History* 26, no. 1 (fall 1997): 27–44.

White, carried Samuel Terry clocks to the island of Cuba in 1834 [Dwight, 1969, vol. 2, p. 33; S. Terry, 3/24/1834; Bates, 6/1/11836].

The Yankee peddling system was a manifestation of the "market revolution" that took place in the quarter century after the War of 1812. Yankee entrepreneurs adapted the timeworn practice of peddling to distribute the output of New England's nascent industries, overcoming the limitations of the early nineteenth-century transportation infrastructure and cumbersome banking facilities to distribute their products in virtually every market in the country. Young men in their early twenties who peddled for wages were the main source of labor in this long-distance distribution system. The exploitative nature of the contractual relationship between the young peddlers and their employers pushed these itinerant hawkers into "overreaching" their customers. Given the long lasting success of Yankee peddlers in the South, most Southerners probably accepted their presence in trade and social relations. Some southerners, however, did not appreciate the Yankee peddler or his "notions." Nullifiers saw the Yankee peddling system as an invasion of "Commercial Scythians" intent on prostrating the agricultural South under a yoke of Yankee manufactures. The relations between Yankee peddlers and their employers and southern consumers were both molded by market forces and shaped the market itself; Yankee peddlers were both agents and authors of the market revolution. Investigating the business and the reception of Yankee peddlers reveals how Americans behaved in the new world of market relations and how they reacted to the spread of national market networks into local exchange networks.

New England's tin peddling system dates back to the 1740s, when an Irish immigrant, William Pattison, set up a tin shop in Berlin, Connecticut. Pattison made more tinware than the households of Berlin demanded, so he hired peddlers to hawk his merchandise in neighboring towns. By the turn of the century, the tinware industry was reaching markets outside of New England. In the search for new markets, tinware manufacturers set up temporary tinsmith shops in towns and cities across the continent, where tin workers made wares to supply the peddlers hired to sell the stock. A tinsmith shop had been established in Charleston, South Carolina by 1810. New England manufacturers established tin depots in Baltimore, Columbia, New Bern, Norfolk, Petersburg, Philadelphia, Richmond, Savannah, and many other locations. These tin depots operated about nine months out of the year from fall to spring; when summer arrived, the proprietor, the peddlers, and the tinsmiths closed shop and returned to New England and usually to agricultural pursuits. Through its complement of twenty or thirty peddlers, a tin depot served a broad hinterland clientele with tin pots, pans, cups, patent ovens, candle sticks, lanterns, graters, and other utensils. Peddlers made numerous trips back to the tin depot to restock their outfits of tinware and other notions [Keir, 1913, p. 256; DeVoe, 1968, pp. 13, 24; Dwight, 1969, vol. 2, pp. 33–34; Filley; R. U. Peck; Alderman, 1992, p. 20; Peck Family].

Like antebellum alchemists, Yankee peddlers turned tin into silver. Epaphroditus Peck cleared one hundred dollars "all in Silver" on a peddling expedition around Columbia, South Carolina in 1810. A peddler by the name of Holmes left the Petersburg, Virginia tin depot of Richard and Benjamin Wilcox in 1819 with a load of tinware worth eighty dollars and returned with one hundred and ninety dollars, including eight-two dollars in "Spanish Mills." Yankee peddlers also transformed tin into silver in a less legitimate manner, fobbing off articles made of tin for silver. A popular story was of peddlers' selling "silver" sidesaddles that were actually trimmed with tin. William Andrus Alcott, who peddled tinware in Virginia in the early 1820s, met a woman in Suffolk Country, Virginia who paid a Yankee peddler twelve dollars for a silver toddy stick. If the tin toddy stick "ever had any silver about it," wrote Alcott, "the value of the whole could not have been twenty-five cents" [Peck Family, 12/5/1810; Wilcox, 4/17/1819; Greene, 1833, p. 26; Alcott, 1851, p. 111].

Within five years after Eli Terry developed the machinery to mass produce wooden works clocks in 1807, peddlers were selling the clocks in southern markets. Initially, the wooden clockworks were sold without cases; hung up they were known as a "wag on the wall." Clock manufacturers were not able to relocate their shops in southern cities as tinware makers did, because the machinery was bulky and required a power source. New England cabinet makers relocated to southern towns and cities to case the works and sell the clocks. Z. Bronson made cases in a shop at the courthouse in Mecklenburg, Virginia for clock works shipped to Virginia by Lamson, Sperry & Co., clockmakers of Waterbury, Connecticut. Bronson predicted "handsome profits" from clock peddling in 1812. Bronson claimed that "clocks afford a greater profit than any thing I can sell," and said that if he had "one good man to carry them about the country I make no doubt but a great many might be sold" [Lamson, 11/2/1812]. By 1812 Gideon Roberts of Bristol, Connecticut was shipping clock movements in bulk to Richmond, Virginia, where his sons assembled and sold tall case clocks in the surrounding countryside. This saved the expense of shipping completed, cased clocks [Buell and Barr, n.d., p. 6]. Chauncey and Noble Jerome established a clock "factory" in Richmond in 1835. The "factory" was actually an assembly plant where clock movements, cases, and faces manufactured in Bristol, Connecticut were made into complete clocks. The Jerome's motivation was not to lessen the expense of shipping completed clocks to Virginia, but to avoid Virginia's tax of one hundred dollars per county per year on peddlers of "foreign" clocks [Jerome, 1860, p. 54].

Middle to upper-class Yankee entrepreneurs started clock peddling companies on their own capital (or credit), or entered a contractual relationship with a clockmaker to sell clocks. Independent peddler-entrepreneurs bought lots of ten or twenty clocks to sell on their own, but most Yankee clocks were sold through the large firms [S. Terry, 11/23/1815]. In a given year, a clock manufacturer sold hundreds of clocks to a peddling business on six- to twelve-month credit. One of the partners in the peddling concern acted as agent, directing the clock manufacturer on the number and styles of clocks to ship and where to send them. Allen Case was the agent of Gunn, Mattoon, Gilbert & Company, a clock peddling firm based in early 1838 in Lexington, Virginia. Typically, a shipment of Eli Terry Jr. clocks began its trip from Terryville, Connecticut, to Lexington, Virginia, aboard a wagon which took them to a forwarding agent in New Haven. There the agent insured the clocks and sent them on to an agent in New York City. From New York the clocks were shipped to Charles M. Mitchell, probably a forwarding agent or merchant, of Richmond. The clocks finally ended up in the hands of Simon W. Gunn in Lexington, who distributed them to the company peddlers [E. Terry, 12/12/1837, 2/14/1838]. Seth Wheeler contracted with Chauncy and Lawson C. Ives to sell their clocks in Kentucky in the late 1830s and early 1840s. If the Ohio river was open to traffic, C. & L. C. Ives shipped their clocks from Bristol, Connecticut, to New York City, to Baltimore, to Wheeling, to Maysville, Kentucky. In winter the clocks went from New York, to New Orleans, to Louisville, Kentucky. From his headquarters in Paris, Kentucky, Wheeler kept track of receipts and expenses, paid peddlers and allocated clocks to them. In 1838, for instance, Wheeler disbursed about seventy-five to one hundred clocks to each of his six peddlers, four hundred and sixty-eight clocks in total [Wheeler, 11/5/1836, 12/3/1836, 1/13/1837, 3/4/1837, 1/8/1838]. Peddling clocks became an industry in itself. A farmer in Orangeburg, South Carolina, in 1825 described the multiple services which clock peddling gave rise to:

these clocks were introduced by pedlars from Connecticut, and in succeeding years they brought fresh supplies accompanied by cases, stating that the clocks would be injured by the dust and moisture of the atmosphere; another would pass along who "cleaned clocks," and get a job of every man who owned one; and, lastly, one would go the rounds bushing the pivot-holes with brass, after which the machine was thought to be complete [Schwaab, 1973, vol. 1, pp. 184–5].

By the 1810s clockmakers could manufacture a shelf clock for five dollars. Yankee peddlers sold these clocks in the South at enormous advances. A fictional clock peddler in a newspaper story paid two dollars and fifty cents for each of his clocks, "on which he expected to make a profit of what he called ten per cent, that is ten time as much as they cost." Chauncey Jerome heard that his Bronze Looking-Glass clock "sold in Mississippi and Louisiana as high as one hundred and one hundred and fifteen dollars, which was a good advance on the first cost." Southern consumers had no gauge as to the fair price of such commodities, and Yankee peddlers took advantage of their naïveté, as an interview with a South Carolina planter in 1843 attests:

"What do you think I gave for that?" asked an ignorant planter in Sumpter district, while pointing to a Connecticut wooden clock which stood upon a shelf in the corner of the room. "I don't know," was my answer; "twenty dollars, or very likely twenty-five!" "*Twenty-five dollars*, stranger!" replied the planter; "why, what do you mean? Come, guess fair and I'll tell you *true*!" I answered again that twenty-five dollars was a high price for such a clock, as I had often seen them sold for a quarter of that sum. The man was astonished "Stranger," said he, "I gave one hundred and forty-four dollars for that clock, and thought I got it cheap at that! Let me tell you how it was. We had always used sun-dials hereabout, till twelve or fourteen years ago, when a man came along with clocks to sell. I thought at first I wouldn't buy one, but after haggling about the price for a while, the agreed to take sixteen dollars less than what he asked, for his selling price was one hundred and sixty dollars; and as I had just sold my cotton at thirty-four cents, I concluded to strike a bargain. It's a powerful clock, but I reckon I gave a heap of money for it!" [Schwaab, 1973, vol. 2, p. 330].

In some regions at certain periods of time, competition among clock peddlers drove prices downward. David Bell sold clocks in Tennessee in 1824 for which he paid $3.25 apiece for as little as $8.00 per clock [Leavenworth, 2/7/1824]. Milo Holcomb noted that clock peddlers were "very thick" in southwestern Pennsylvania and western Virginia in 1831, but had confidence in overcoming the competition: "we have some champions in our company and we can do our part of the business" [Holcomb, 1/29/1831]. One of Holcomb's competitors, perhaps, was Frederick Kellogg. He also complained that western Pennsylvania was "over run with pedlars which are selling their clocks for whatever they can get" [Harrison, 11/11/1831]. By the mid-1830s many markets of the United States had been filled with wooden works clocks. A. L. Brown found the market saturated in Louisiana in 1834. Around this time Connecticut clock manufacturers began mass producing clocks with brass movements, which revitalized the clock peddling business. Brown discovered that brass clocks were "a very good article" in Louisiana and could be sold for from $40 to $70 each on a credit of nine to twelve months [Lewis, 5/12/1834]. Seth Wheeler and his peddlers sold hundreds of brass clocks in Kentucky from 1836 to 1841; in over half the transactions, customers traded in an old wooden shelf clock in partial payment for the brass clock. From sundials, to caseless "wags on the wall" to cased wooden works clocks to brass works clocks, Yankee peddlers might have initiated the consumer practice of the technological upgrade.

Peddling fever gripped the young men of New England in the 1810s. William Andrus Alcott, who participated in this rush for wealth, later compared the peddling rage to the California gold rush. Peddling was a manifestation of the broader cultural trend of "seeking the main chance" through the unbridled individualistic pursuit of success. The desire for speculative success infected Phineas T. Barnum, a contemporary of many of these young peddlers:

> My disposition was of that speculative character which refused to be satisfied unless I was engaged in some business where my profits might be enhanced, or, at least, made to depend upon my energy, perservance, attention to business, tact, and "calculation" [Barnum, 1930, p. 18].

It was common for "enterprising young men" in early nineteenth-century New England "to start off South, in the fall season, and spend the winter in some of the southern States, on trading expeditions, and return in the spring with the fruits of their industry and enterprise" [Douglas, 1856, p. 25]. A rising generation of speculators hoped they could mimic the success of the few peddlers who created "great estates" out of "the pencil box, and the orange basket," wrote William Andrus Alcott in 1834. Thousands of young men, most barely out of their teens, loaded up wagons with combs, clocks, tinware, and other Yankee notions, which they sold in the South and West "rapidly, at large prices and great profits," and "some of them appeared to be getting rich." (Alcott, 1834, pp. 136–37; Alcott, 1851, pp. 14–15]. Asa Upson noted that the half dozen peddlers who returned to Bristol, Connecticut in 1823 looked like they had "come as Clean as the Cat Come out of the Cream" [Upson, 4/6/1823]. William Sherman and his three peddling partners cleared three thousand dollars each in 1818 in the Mississippi Territory. Sherman boasted of his success to friends back home:

> This in Massachusetts would be called a pretty little fortune but we consider it here only as a tolerable good business for young men just embarking in business with a small capital & no credit and all strangers in the country & to the business we have been in [Sherman-Tabor, 11/21/1818].

Peddling fever spread as successful peddlers returned or wrote home from the South. Returns of 33 percent or more on a stock of goods were common. Bronson Alcott claimed that his "Articles afford escclusive of Expenses 1/3rd or 33 1/3 per cent profit" [Herrnstadt, 1969, pp. 1–2]. Samuel Peck estimated that peddling would earn his brother 25 to 30 percent profits, far greater than the returns from the more steady occupation of farming [R. U. Peck, 8/6/1826]. Thomas Douglas of Wallingsford, Connecticut, cleared $1,200 on $500 worth of goods that he carried through western Virginia during the War of 1812 [Douglas, 1856, p. 32]. Milton Bates was "wide awake to goin on to the south" after hearing of his brother Carlos's success peddling clocks in Virginia [Bates, 3/15/1831]. Truman Alderman urged his brother Manna to "pluck up courage & go to Georgia or some other place" where other Yankee peddlers were making "a Good Deal of money" [Alderman, 1992, p. 11]. The lure of wealth and social pressures to succeed compelled many young New England men "seek the main chance" at peddling.

Most of the New England men who took up peddling were in their early twenties. Until a young man reached the age of twenty-one, he could not enter contracts and obligations legally as an individual. "Infant" sons under the age of consent had to seek their parents' permission to engage in a peddling career. Employers were careful to have parents of underage sons or sons with

Table 5.1.   Ages of Peddlers in Georgia, 1825–1831

Age Range	Number (N=167)	Percentage
Under 21	9	5.4
21 to 25	84	50.3
26 to 30	42	25.1
31 to 35	22	13.2
Over 35	10	6.0

Note: Two hundred and two licenses were found. Individuals who appeared in more than one year are represented once at their youngest age. There were doubtless many more peddlers in Georgia in this period than the 167 who obtained licenses.

no assets give security for their son's debts. Truman Alderman counseled his brother Manna that Manna's former employer Elisha Dunham could not recover damages from Manna because he "was under age" when he peddled tin for Dunham, and Dunham "did not ful fil his agreement" [ibid., p. 7]. Burrage Yale, who hired about eight young men each year to peddle tin from his shop in South Reading, Massachusetts, specifically advertised for "young men of lawful age," twenty-one to thirty years old [New Hampshire Patriot State Gazette, 1/19/1829, 1/28/1833]. The youth of Yankee peddlers can be quantified from the published lists of peddlers licensed to trade in Georgia between 1826 and 1831 [Georgia Journal, 1/6/1826–12/21/1831]. Of the 167 peddlers listed in Georgia newspapers between 1826 and 1831, only nine were minors; fully half were between twenty one and twenty-six years of age; and four-fifths of them were thirty or younger (see table 5.1). The youngest licensed peddler was eighteen, the oldest was fifty-six. The median age for this group was approximately twenty-four, and the mean age was about twenty-six and a half.

These young peddlers were in need of guidance as well as capital. Peddling was an alternative to clerking in a store. Elijah Kellog offered a peddling contract to N. Collins provided Collins would "come at a low price" of $125 per year. There was not "sufficient encouragement" in Kellog's offer to attract Collins, who decided to take a position as a clerk instead. His friends, who did not "speak very flattering of" peddling affected Collins' decision as well [Harrison, 3/6/1822, 3/16/1822]. Phineas T. Barnum described his plight as a young, fatherless, yet ambitious teen in 1826 in his autobiography:

I was in that uneasy, transitory state between boyhood and manhood when I had unbounded confidence in my own abilities, and yet needed a discreet counselor, adviser and friend [Barnum, 1930, p. 18].

Yankee entrepreneurs tapped into this reserve of youthful energy and ambition. William Andrus Alcott claimed that "there is generally in the neighborhood some hawk-eyed money dealer, who knows that he cannot better invest his funds than in the hands of active young men" [Alcott, 1834, p. 90]. Bronson Alcott's view of such mercantile mentorships was jaded by his dealings with Joseph T. Allyn, a transplanted Yankee merchant who operated a store in Norfolk Virginia. Bronson felt himself the "gudgeon" to this "shrewd dealer in fancy goods." Having been cheated by Allyn, mused Alcott "Why should he hesitate, why need repent, To sell in turn at thirty-three percent?" Bronson Alcott was unsuccessful at peddling fancy goods and tinware in Virginia, and in 1822 had to relinquish is horse, wagon, and goods to Allyn for his outstanding debts to Allyn. Alcott's father had to pay off $270 of Bronson's debt to Allyn [Alcott, 1881, pp. 180–81, 22; Wagner, 1979, p. 252].

"Arithmetic," presumed Thomas Hamilton of the Yankees, came "by instinct among this guessing, reckoning, expecting, and calculating people" [Hamilton, 1833, p. 127]. Despite the Yankees' reputation for being "born to calculate shillings and pence," peddling did not come natural to young New England men [Murat, 1833, p. 6]. Selling almanacs in Norfolk, Virginia "required more confidence, at first," wrote Bronson Alcott, "than I could readily summon, to accost a person and offer my trifle. Habit, however, soon gave facility, even something of dignity, to my attitude, and won respect." Joseph T. Allyn provided Alcott with "Directions for selling certain Articles," suggesting prices for violin strings, beads, watch chains, pins and needles [Alcott, 1991, p. 180; Alcott, 1823, p. 107]. Such petty salesmanship was a school for scandal, wrote Timothy Dwight:

Men who begin life with bargaining for small wares will almost invariably become sharpers. The commanding aim of every such man will soon be to make a good bargain, and he will speedily consider every gainful bargain as a good one. The tricks of fraud will assume in his mind the same place which commercial skill and an honorable system of dealing hold in the mind of a merchant [Dwight, 1969, vol. 1, p. 223].

Tinware and clock manufacturers and entrepreneurs often had to train their new peddler in the arts and mystery of peddling. Hezekiah Griswold asked tinware manufacturer Oliver Filley to give his son "all the instructions and informations that you may think proper and necessary for him respecting the articles he may take and the manner in which he ought to proceed—He is young and unacquainted with business and needs instruction and I shall count it a great favor to have you take the liberty to talk with him" [Filley, 4/1/4/1824]. Chapin G. Deming was a "new hand" at clock peddling in 1839, who needed "instructions in relation to putting up clocks &c." C. & C. Ives suggested to Seth Wheeler that he take Deming under his wing

> in order that he might become a little acquainted how to manage business, would it not be better for you to go out with him awhile that he may start right, and if not consistent with you to go, let him go out at first with some other good hand [Wheeler, 2/12/1839].

"New hands" at peddling could also learn from relatives experienced at peddling. Unfortunately, perhaps, for Chatfield Alcott, his older brother Bronson saw it as his duty to show him the ropes at peddling [Herrnstadt, 1969, pp. 1–2]. Albert and Milton Bates queried their brother Carlos about the prospects for peddling clocks in the South in 1831:

> give me all the information you can about what kind of clocks and what they are worth there and what kind of watches and how much they will fetch. I wish you to give us the best information you can about what state will be the best and what part to land the property. I would wish you to inform me in what way to gone on in an open wagon or a covered one. And about what time in the season to go on and what capital would be necessary for us to start with. I would not confine you to anyone article but would have you inform me of those you think the best for profit [Bates, 3/15/1831].

The wages paid to tin peddlers ranged from $25 to $50 per month. Payment came at the expiration of the contracted period of six to nine months. Wages were in cash, or, as in the case of Chauncey Buck, two-thirds in cash and "the residue in Truck." As an added incentive to aggressive salesmanship, the peddler could keep half of what he was able to clear above his wages and the wholesale value of the tinware. Contracts often included harsh stipulations concerning the wages of inefficient or profligate salesmen. In his 1818 contract to peddle for Oliver Filley, Andrew Hays promised "not to sink s[ai]d Filley anything more than his wages." Hays's 1820 contract stipulated that Filley "shall not loose anything by me more than my wages and should there be any further loss I will make it up." Thomas Frazier contracted to sell tin for Filley for $50 a month for six months. Frazier's contract stated that if he failed to clear his wages in sales, he would have to make up half his salary—$150—to Filley. If Frazier cleared more than his salary in his sales, Frazier would receive half the profits [Filley; R. U. Peck; Alderman, 1992, p. 20; Keir, 1913, p. 256].

Clock peddlers were generally better paid than tinware peddlers. Seth Wheeler's employees earned from $50 to $75 per month peddling clocks in Kentucky. If a peddler could prove himself capable in making sales, Wheeler increased his salary. Deforest Wolcott's contract of 1836 promised him a salary of $55 per month. However, if Wolcott could perform as well as Ebenezer Plumb, another peddler in Wheeler's employ, Wolcott would receive a bonus of $5 per month. Wolcott had to conduct "a first rate business," making "as many sales and on as good terms as to prices and length of credits and as safe debts" as Plumb. Wolcott performed satisfactorily, and in the following year his contract promised him a salary of $62.50 per month. As they gained experience and skill at making a sale, clock peddlers could demand better wages. Timothy Colvin began peddling clocks for Wheeler in 1836 at $55 per month. The following year Wheeler increased Colvin's compensation to $60 per month, and in 1839 Colvin earned $67.50 per month [Wheeler].

Employers compensated their peddlers for concomitant, traveling expenses, such as board, lodging, and license fees, but usually not for medical expenses, clothing, or keeping their own wagon in repair. In Nathaniel Clark's contract to peddle tinware for Oliver Filley, Clarke's expenses were to be "borne out of the load he peddles from" [Filley]. Rather than compensate peddlers for their expenses, employers usually provided peddlers with an assortment of cheap "notions," the sale of which was meant to cover the peddler's expenses. A fictional account of the kinds of wares meant to cover expenses is probably faithful to reality:

> on the lid was placed a bag full of whip lashes, a few parcels of cigars, and a number of boxes containing all the variety of combs, from coarse horn louse traps to superfine ivory and high finished tortoise shell. . . . The box contained

an assortment on the profits of which he was to subsist himself and horse, and consisted of a great variety of "good-for-nothing" things which women are so fond of purchasing—such as beads, ear rings, breast pins, and all the little et ceteras of jewelry; besides a good store of essences, shaving soap, scissors, thread, needles, pins & stilettos [*Georgia Journal*, 4/5/1832].

Seth Wheeler provided his clock peddlers with dozens of combs to meet their traveling expenses. The peddlers kept accounts of selling the combs for about a dollar apiece, and often recorded swapping combs outright for a tavern bill. This was indeed economical, given that Wheeler paid about six and a quarter cents each for brass combs and less than fifteen cents for silver combs [Wheeler, 7/24/1837].

Burrage Yale of Reading, Massachusetts sought to hire peddlers through advertisements from 1823 to 1844. Yale wanted young men of "undoubted moral character," who were "capable," "honest," "trust-worthy," "industrious," and "well qualified to make good traders." As proof of such character, the potential peddlers had to produce "recommendations form the Selectmen of their town, and countersigned by a minister of the same place, that they possess the above qualifications" [*New Hampshire Patriot State Gazette*, 1823–1844]. Russell Upson Peck promised in his contract to peddle tinware "to be Prudent Faithful & Industrious" to his employer, James Brooks [R. U. Peck, 9/26/1826]. As a further protection against loss from dishonest peddlers, employers often required a parent or some other person to give security. Elijah Kellog's "caution of hiring peddlers is to have them give security that is provided I am not acquainted with them, and shall calculate the young man will procure such a recommend that will hold the security accountable for his performance" [Harrison, 3/6/1822]. On occasion, employers lost property to dishonest peddlers. Harvey Filley planned to take a trip in the spring of 1821 in western Virginia to find his "stray" and "runaway" peddlers, who had not returned to his Philadelphia tin depot. Filley figured these "doubtful debt[or]s" would not come to Philadelphia to pay him, so he resolved "to go after them" [Filley, 2/14/1821]. Richard Wilcox was cheated by a peddler, Mr. Bartlett, who peddled out of his Petersburg, Virginia tin depot. Wilcox discharged Bartlett in 1820, and in 1821 heard that he had "bit" his new employers "as well as he did us & I think he will bite any one that hires him" [Wilcox, 11/19/1821].

A peddler's bottom line was earning his wages in sales, or at least recouping the value of the load of tinware. Richard Wilcox kept his brother abreast of the profitability of their peddlers' performances, telling Benjamin Wilcox who cleared their wages and who came short. The Wilcoxes had a good Winter in 1822 when Richard Wilcox calculated that: "Our Peddlers I think will the most of them clear there wages this season." The performance of hired peddlers attracted the particular attention of manufacturers of tinware. The foreman of the Filley's Elizabethtown, New Jersey, tin shop reported to Oliver Filley in 1810 that "Joab has not done bad but very well for a new peddler." Initially L. Burr's performance at peddling worried Harvey Filley. On his first trip, Burr was out two months, and "did not fetch in anything." On a subsequent trip Burr regained the confidence of Filley by making $100 during a "middling good trip" of three weeks. Harvey Filley assured Oliver Filley that Burr "will gain the point after a while." Richard Wilcox criticized David Kelsey for not earning "money quite to the chalk." Though Wilcox supposed Kelsey was "good," he did not want to allow Kelsey's debts to run too far. Mr. Pardy, another Wilcox peddler, "did not pay up into fifty dollars for his loads." Thomas T. Hubbard was a bigger disappointment to Richard Wilcox. Not only did Hubbard bring in an inadequate amount of cash for a load of tinware, but some of the money was counterfeit. Richard Wilcox threatened: "if he does not come in better this time I shall Discharge him when he comes in again." Wilcox denied Mr. Whiting his wages entirely. Wilcox justified his actions on Whiting's performance as follows: "he did not quite clear his property, and as he quit peddling sooner than the time mentioned when we bargained with him, as he had a good opportunity of selling wagon & horse, I think it no more than justice not to pay him any wages at all" [R. U. Peck; Filley, 10/26/1818, 1/31/1819, 12/23/1810; Wilcox, 4/17/1819, 12/15/1819, 12/25/1819, 2/19/1822, 3/22/1822, 3/11/1823].

Many Southerners viewed Yankee peddlers as part of a larger problem of an imbalance of trade with the manufacturing and financial centers of the Northeast. Northern agents dominated the export trade of staple crops from Southern cities. Yankees and other "foreigners" composed the bulk of the mercantile class in southern cities, which were viewed as appendages of Northern seaports, "places where their agents and factors do business, and who, having but little local interest, withdraw from them after a few years residence, with all their gains, to swell the wealth of the place of their early affection and attachment" [Russell,

1923, pp. 19–20, 99–100; Sydnor, 1948; Potter, 1976]. Yankee peddlers added a personal dimension, a face on which Southerners could place the blame for their economic woes.

Peddlers were probably the only Yankees most Southerners ever met face to face. From accumulated encounters with Yankee peddlers in the first three decades of the nineteenth century many Southerners acquired a negative impression of all New Englanders. The editors of the *National Intelligencer* claimed to have heard Southerners use the expression "Damned Yankees . . . a thousand times" in 1829. "Damned Yankees" was popularized by "the mass of the people, who derive their notions of 'the Yankees' from tin-pedlars and wooden-nutmeg wenders" [*National Intelligencer*, 6/18/1829]. The *Camden Journal* of South Carolina also imputed the "disadvantageous impression of Northern character" upon "the petty cheating, the low lived imposition, and two penny trickery of the Connecticut peddlers." "By no very unnatural course of reasoning," the *Camden Journal* went on, "they have identified the Northern character with that of the Wallingford peddlers of Tin Ware and Wooden Wheeled Clocks" [reprinted in *Georgia Journal*, 3/30/1830]. The Yankee peddler, complained a northern critic, "is the most common object of the jeers and jokes of our Southern brethren, whose mythical and highly imaginative notions of the men of the North it seems quite impossible to correct" [*North American Review*, 1844, p. 211]. As a northern defender of New England character noted in 1837, since the Yankee peddler stereotype was "capable of producing a political effect," it bore "a charmed life" [*North American Review*, 1837, p. 241].

Tales of Yankee tricks and fraudulent bargains were current throughout the country, but were especially virulent in the South. These stories catalogued an enormous range of bogus goods that Yankee peddlers imposed upon southern consumers. Kentucky, noted Timothy Flint in 1826, was full of "fine stories about Yankee tricks, and Yankee finesse" [Flint, 1968, pp. 26, 52–53]. Peddlers of tinware and clocks figured prominently in these tales. William Gilmore Simms created a character named Jared Bunce, a Connecticut peddler, in his novel of frontier Georgia, *Guy Rivers*. Georgia Regulators seize Bunce and try him in the "court of Judge Lynch." Witness after witness accuses Bunce of frauds committed against them. Bunce had sold a Colonel Blundell "a coffeepot and two tin cups, all of which went to pieces—the solder melting off at the very sight of the hot water." Bunce claims that the tinware was built for a northern climate and posits that the Georgians boil their water "quite too hot" for his tinware. Bunce promises that his next lot of tinware "shall be calkilated on purpose to suit the climate." Bunce's wooden clocks are likewise deemed trash. Bunce sold a clock to a planter's wife and not two days had passed since Bunce left, "before the said clock began to go whiz, whiz, whiz, and commenced striking, whizzing all the while, and never stopped till it had struck clear thirty-one, and since that time it will neither whiz, nor strike, nor do anything" [Simms, n.d., pp. 77, 79].

Asa Green parodies the encounters between South Carolina planters and Yankee peddlers in his novel, *A Yankee among the Nullifiers*. A Yankee peddler sells a "St. Killigrew's clock" to a planter and warrants that the clock would never stop if he would set it running on that saint's day, and promised if the clock varied one minute over six months, he would refund the planter his $40. The planter looks in his almanac and can find no St. Killigrew, and to his further chagrin, the clock will not run at all. When the peddler returns a year later, the planter demands a refund. The crafty Yankee replies that if the clock "has stood *stock still* all the time, it sartinly could'nt a *varied* any," and refuses to refund the money. Another Yankee peddler sold this same planter's wife a counterfeit tortoise shell comb. Wearing the comb in her hair in a rainstorm, "she found the comb had all dissolved, and it took three weeks to clear her hair of the sticky mass of glue, sugar, and gum Arabic out of which it was composed" [Green, 1833, pp. 67–68, 70–71].

Southerners accused Yankee peddlers of passing a huge variety of bogus goods made out of wood: wooden nutmegs, wooden hams, wooden cheese, wooden garden seeds, and wooden candlesticks. The Yankees' counterfeit goods were made in other media as well: oakleaf cigars, horn gunflints, stonecoal indigo, and so on. In his 1832 novel, *Memoirs of a Nullifier*, Algernon Sydney Johnston also puts a Yankee on trial, not in a Regulators' court, but before the Judgment seat of Rhadamanthus. Rhadamanthus reads from a ledger "a terribly long account against" a Yankee peddler named Virgil Hoskins.

To selling, in the course of one peddling expedition, 497,368 wooden nutmegs, 281,532 Spanish cigars made of oak leaves, and 647 wooden clocks. . . . To stealing an old grindstone, smearing it over with butter, and then selling it as a cheese. . . . To making a counterfeit dollar of pewter, when you were six years old, and cheating your own father with it. . . . To taking a worn out pair of shoes, which you found in the road, and selling them to a pious old lady, as being actually the shoes of Saint Paul. . . . To taking an empty old watch case, putting a live cricket into it, and then selling it as a patent lever in full motion.

Rhadamanthus declares his exasperation with New England, which gives him "more trouble than all the rest of the world put together." He sentences Hoskins "to be thrown into a lake of boiling molasses, where nearly all your countrymen already are, with that same old grindstone tied to your neck, and to remain there forever" [Johnston, 1832, p. 40]. The *Georgia Journal* printed in humorous detail the composition of a fraudulent wooden candle as: "A piece of white oak wood turned in the shape of a candle, with a snug little wick in each end, cover'd with jut about tallow enough to grease the bill of a Longe Island misketer!" [*Georgia Journal*, 2/21/1833].

The wooden composition of these bogus goods is significant in that wood was a medium of the early mechanization of New England industry. Wooden clocks, gun stocks, bowls, shoe lasts, and other commodities were churned out of the newly patented machinery running New England's industry [Hindle, 1975, pp. 3–12]. Southerners and others hostile to the protectionism of New England manufacturers denigrated the flood of patents in the early nineteenth century as mechanical absurdities. Southerners were not Luddites, but they questioned the uses to which Yankees put their lathes and other machinery. Actual products evoked this ridicule, such as the foot stove advertised by Joseph B. Gilbert in the *Connecticut Courant* in 1812. Gilbert claimed that his tin box was "so constructed as to combine all the necessary properties of a foot-stove, tea boiler, chafing dish, plate warmer, and butter or liquor cooler, as the season may be" [*Connecticut Courant*, 11/30/1812]. A frequent target of these patents were their ludicrous, sesquipedalian names. Jacob Engelbrecht of Frederick, Maryland observed in 1825 "a Machine to prevent cows from Poking—It was an Iron Bow, Extending from the Extremity of one horn to the other in a Semi-circular form." Engelbrecht reckoned the contraption would be called "the patent Preventing Poker" [Quynn, 1976, 3/28/1825]. In the humor of the period, these Yankee devices promised a fabulous, yet worthless, mechanization of the mundane. The Virginia and North Carolina Almanack for 1834 described a fantastic contraption called the "New-England Sausage and Scrubbing Brush Machine. . . . Into the center of this machine . . . you drive a hog; set the screws a going, and it will produce *ready made sausages* from one end, and *patent scrubbing brushes* from the other" [Warrock, 1834]. The protagonist of Johnston's *Memoirs of a Nullifier* invests $20,000 of his inheritance into the factory of a Yankee inventor named Increase Hooker. The factory will product "Hooker's Patent Self animated Philanthropic Frying Pans." This was "a frying pan, upon a new and wonderful principle. The mechanism is such that the slices of bacon, when exactly half done, turn themselves over on the other side simultaneously." In a moment of fictional, wishful thinking, Johnston writes that the frying pan is a flop in the South Carolina market. The frying pans "were sold for next to nothing, amidst the ridicule of the assembly, who declared themselves resolved to stick to the real good old frying-pan of their forefathers" [Johnston, 1832, pp. 7, 8, 13].

State legislatures tried to regulate the peddlers out of business by raising license fees to prohibitive levels, up to $1,000 per year in some states. Clock peddlers had to pay high license fees of $100 per year per county in Virginia after 1832. The fees were meant in part to recirculate the large amount of cash that clock peddlers supposedly drained from the local economy. To evade restrictive licensing laws against selling clocks, Yankee peddlers, according to a long-lived, popular joke, switched to leasing clocks for ninety-nine years [*Georgia Journal*, 11/20/1833; *Lexington Gazette*, 8/5/1841]. Some Anti-Tariff Southerners suggested that the legal precedent for an extensive boycott of Western goods lie in anti-peddler legislation, and that "a very slight alteration" in these laws "would effectually control the horse, hog, mule, cattle, bagging, and bacon trade of the wet" [*Nile's Weekly Register*, 1828, p. 301].

For forty years Virginians complained to their state legislature that peddlers were draining specie from the commonwealth. In 1806 petitioners in Campbell, Cumberland, and Spotsylvania Counties estimated that peddlers removed $300,000 in "ready cash . . . not only out of the neighborhood, but out of the state." This depletion of hard currency adversely affected not only the internal circulation of money, but even the established banks were "constantly drained of their specie!" Frederick County petitioners in 1822 claimed that "at the lowest calculation," tin peddlers alone took away $75,000 annually from Virginia in cash as well as in other commodities, such as "Furs, Beeswax, Feathers, Old Copper, and Pewter, and indeed every valuable article of trade they can lay their hands on." A few years later petitioners from Brunswick, Fauquier, Prince William, and Shenandoah Counties complained that Yankee peddlers had "actually produced a balance of trade against the interior of the Commonwealth." As the Nullification crisis heated sectional tensions, Southerners began to point out how northern manufacturers benefitted at southern expense through the peddler trade. Hugh Henry Brackenridge opined in 1831 that: "The money of the southern farmer is at present collected and carried away, to reward the industry of the northern manufacturer; southern notes are taken, sold to the north at a discount, and sent back to cramp the operations of the southern banks" [Schwaab, 1973, vol. 1, pp. 244–45]. Petitioners from Fauquier County, Virginia added this sentiment to the traditional catalogue of complaints against Yankee peddlers:

> Amongst the evils arising from them may be enumerated with certainty; an extensive and unlawful traffick with the slaves, who are their principal dealers; the collection and transmission of the specia change in large quantities from the commonwealth; the introduction of the small note currency known as shinplasters and its circulation amongst ignorant persons; the interception of the business of the regular retail merchants; the imposition of counterfeit and insubstantial articles of wear and ornament upon purchasers; and finally, the removal of their gains to other states to whose wealth and advancement they contribute at our cost.

Southerners fought the inundation of Yankee manufactures in several ways: boycotts, restrictive legislation, and the encouragement of home manufactures. In Johnston's work of fiction, the people of South Carolina seem to naturally reject Increase Hooker's frying pans. But in reality such consumer boycotts were led by sectionalist southern leaders opposed to protectionist tariffs. However, there were certainly cases in which an aggrieved southern consumer might make such decisions on his or her own. James Dowdell made the kind of public notice expected by southern society of a man whose domestic domain had been violated. In a notice to peddlers published in the *Georgia Journal* on July 11, 1826, Dowdell protested that a "clan of designing, unprincipled mischief-makers" had "influence[d], misguide[d] and induce[d]" his fifteen-year-old wife to purchase a large quantity of merchandise without his "knowledge or approbation." Dowdell waited what he considered a sufficient amount of time for the peddlers "to reflect, repent and make amends" for their intrusion into his domain, but to no avail. The only satisfaction Dowdell could extract from these interlopers for taking advantage of his young wife was to boycott the purchase of any such commodities by his household for the space of eighteen months [*Georgia Journal*, 7/11/1826]. Southern planters led by example, dressing themselves in homespun or English imports. A Nullifier gentleman "would sooner go fifty miles and pay a hundred per cent more than a thing is worth if it by only imported, than have a similar article of American manufacture brought to [his] very door and sold at a fair price," claimed Asa Greene. A common joke of the Nullification era was of the Yankee peddler who pointed out all the New England made items in a Southern planter's supposedly Yankee-free vestments [Greene, 1833, pp. 39–41]. *Niles Register* joined in the attack on Anti-tariff boycotts by reporting that a Yankee inventor was earning "about 2,000 dollars a year by the manufacture of *shaving boxes* to assist the operation of *nullificating* the beards of southern gentleman" [*Nile's Register*, 1831, p. 149].

Home manufacturers were encouraged to staunch the flow of northern goods into the South, and southern wealth to the Northeast. Homespun garments might have made appearances at political rallies and other public events, but northern clothes still appeared on southern backs. The southern criticism of Yankee's bogus goods reached a paranoid pitch in 1828 when Georgia newspapers issued the following caution to southern consumers: "Sample Patterns of our Domestic cloth, have been sent on to the Northern manufactories, that they may be made there, and sent here to be impose on us as *Southern Homespun*. Therefore *beware of Counterfits* [sic]—they will soon be here." To fend off such impositions, the article advised consumers to purchase goods "only from the manufacturer, or such store keepers, whose veracity they can depend upon, when asked where their homespun was made." They certainly did not have Yankee peddlers in mind [*Georgia Journal*, 9/15/1828]. Petitioners from Frederick County, Virginia complained in 1842 that "even the poor Widdow who has earned an humble support for her orphan children by the industrious use of the needle is denied that privilege" by the flood of northern merchandize into southern homes [Va. Legislative Petitions].

The plight of southern mechanics against Yankee competition was reiterated time and again in the early nineteenth century. In 1821 the tinsmiths of Frederick County protested that the "vast monopoly" wrought by the tin peddling system rendered the livelihood of Virginia tinsmiths precarious. The petitioners complained that only the largest towns and cities of Virginia could support a native tinsmith, while in the absence of the tin peddlers and their depots, the towns, hamlets, and county courthouses of Virginia potentially could have supported thirty or forty additional, "regular" tinsmiths. Henry

Marie Brackenridge noted with concern in 1831 that small shops and stores filled with northern goods had taken the place of local mechanics in the South. Local artisans could not compete with the Yankee "hats, boots, shoes, ploughs, axes, hoes, buckets, tin-ware, ready made clothing, and a thousand articles of the first necessity," that stocked southern stores. The impact went beyond the cares of the local mechanic, and led to the decline of southern cities and towns [Schwaab, 1973, vol. 1, pp. 244–45]. In 1842 one hundred ninety-nine mechanics and others of Winchester, Virginia importuned the state legislature for an additional tax on peddlers and shopkeepers who sold northern manufactured goods. Judging by the enumerated list of goods, the sector of the artisan population that felt the competition of northern manufacturers had widened. The petitioners called for restrictions on the sale of boot, shoes, hats, caps, ready-made clothing, saddles, harnesses, saddletrees, chairs, "all description of cabinet furniture," and copper and tinware [Va. Legislative Petitions].

Yankee peddlers aggravated southern animosity over the imbalance of trade between North and South. William Gilmore Simms claimed in 1850 that "the southern people have long stood in nearly the same relation to the Northern States of this confederacy, that the whole of the colonies, in 1775, occupied to Great Britain." "Any nation that defers thus wholly to another," foreboded Simms, "is soon emasculated, and finally subdued" [Schwaab, 1973, vol. 2, p. 470]. The Yankee peddler, often a hired hand merely trying to make a start in life, was accused of acting as the agent of Northern colonization of the South. Agents of Northern Aggression, Abolitionist firebrands, slave stealers, counterfeiters, seducing rakes—Southerners attributed many anti-social behaviors to Yankee peddlers. Most of these young men were not born sharpers, but displaced New England farmboys who were initially as ignorant of market values and behaviors as their southern customers reputedly were. The many stories of tricks and fraudulent goods sold by Yankee peddlers had a kernel of social truth. They reveal the anxieties antebellum Americans, particularly Southerners, had as they warily embraced and were encompassed by National markets.

NOTE

I thank the American Antiquarian Society, the Virginia Historical Society, and the Massachusetts Historical Society for support.

REFERENCES

Alcott, A. B. "Autobiographical Collections," vol. 1–2 (1799–1823), Houghton Library, Harvard University.

———. *New Connecticut. An Autobiographical Poem* (Boston, 1881).

Alcott, W. A. *The Young Man's Guide* (Boston, 1834).

———. *Recollection of Rambles at the South* (New York, 1851).

Alderman, M. *Letters from a Burlington Peddler Who Traveled to North Carolina to Sell His Wares* (Burlington, 1992).

Barnum, P. T. *Struggles and Triumphs or, Forty Years' Recollections of P. T. Barnum* (New York, 1930).

Buell, C. W., and L. Barr. "Gideon Roberts: Clockmaker of Bristol, Connecticut," (n.d.) Manuscript in the American Clock and Watch Museum.

Carlos Bates Papers, Connecticut State Library.

[Hartford] *Connecticut Courant.*

DeVoe, S. S. *The Tinsmiths of Connecticut* (Middletown, 1968).

Douglas, T. *Autobiography of Thomas Douglas, Late Judge of the Supreme Court of Florida* (New York, 1856).

Dwight, T. *Travels in New England and New York,* ed. B. M. Solomon and P. M. King (reprint, Cambridge, 1969).

Filley Family Papers, Connecticut Historical Society.

Flint, T. *Recollections of the Last Ten Years in the Valley of the Mississippi* (Carbondale, Ill., 1968, reprint of Boston, 1826).

[Milledgeville] *Georgia Journal.*

Greene, A. *A Yankee among the Nullifiers: An Autobiography* (New York, 1833).

Hamilton, T. *Men and Manners in America* (Edinburgh, 1833).

Elihu Harrison Business Papers, Litchfield Historical Society.

Herrnstadt, R. I. ed. *The Letters of A. Bronson Alcott* (Ames, Iowa, 1969).

Hindle, B. ed. *America's Wooden Age: Aspects of its Early Technology* (Tarrytown, N.Y., 1975).

Holcomb Family Papers, Connecticut Historical Society.

Jerome, C. *History of the American Clock Business for the Past Sixty Years, and Life of Chauncey Jerome, Written by Himself* (New Haven, Conn., 1960).

Johnston, A. S. *Memoirs of a Nullifier; Written by Himself* (Columbia, 1832).

Keir, R. M. "The Tin Peddler," *Journal of Political Economy* 21 (1913): 255–58.

Lamson, Sperry, & Co. Papers, Mattatuck Historical Society.

Mark Leavenworth Clockmaking Accounts, Mattatuck Historical Society.

Legislative Petitions, Library of Virginia.

Milo Lewis Papers, Perkins Library, Duke University, Durham, N.C.

Lexington [VA] *Gazette.*

Murat, A. *A Moral and Political Sketch of the United States of North America* (London, 1833).

[Washington, D.C.] *National Intelligence.*

[Concord] *New Hampshire Patriot State Gazette.*

Nile's Weekly Register 34 (1828).

Nile's Register, 41 (1831).

The North American Review, 44 (1837).

The North American Review, 58 (1844).

Russell Upson Peck Papers, Connecticut Historical Society.

Peck Family Papers, Bristol [Conn.] Public Library.

Potter, D. M. *The Impending Crisis 1848–1861* (New York, 1976).

Quynn, W. R. ed. *The Diary of Jacob Engelbrecht 1818–1878* (Frederick, 1976).

Russell, R. R. "Economic Aspects of Southern Sectionalism, 1840–1861," *University of Illinois Studies in the Social Sciences* 11 (1923).

Schwaab, E. L. ed. *Travels in the Old South* (Louisville, Ky., 1973).

Sherman-Tabor Family Papers, Massachusetts Historical Society.

Simms, W. G. *Guy Rivers: A Tale of Georgia* (New York, n.d.).

Sydnor, C. S. *The Development of Southern Sectionalism 1819–1848* (Baton Rouge, La., 1948).

Eli Terry Jr., Letter Books, American Clock and Watch Museum.

Samuel Terry Collection, American Clock and Watch Museum.

George Rensseleaer Upson Papers, Connecticut State Library.

Seth Wheeler Papers, Connecticut State Library.

Wagner, F. "Eighty-Six Letters (1814–1882) of A. Bronson Alcott (Part One)," in *Studies in the American Renaissance*, ed. Joel Myerson (Boston, 1979), 239–308.

Warrock, J. "Virginia and North Carolina Almahack," (Richmond, Va., 1834).

Wilcox Papers, Berlin [Conn.] Historical Society.

6

"Well Bred Country People": Sociability, Social Networks, and the Creation of a Provincial Middle Class, 1820–1860

CATHERINE E. KELLY

While staying in Boston in 1804, George Bliss of Springfield, Massachusetts, was invited to dine at the Salem home of Mr. Prescott, a "brother lawyer." Bliss had heard that Prescott lived in luxury, but nothing he had heard or seen prepared him for the spectacle encountered. More than living well, Prescott lived in a "palace."[1] After Bliss rang the bell, a servant conducted him up a flight of stairs to a "large drawing Room," whose walls were "painted most elegantly with Landscapes & the mantle over the fireplace with fine figures." There Prescott sat, awaiting his guests. Bliss spent nearly an hour chatting with the Prescotts and their twenty-odd guests before the company adjourned to the dining room for a "superb & elegant feast." The dinner included soup, roast and boiled mutton, roast venison "alamode," beef, chickens, roast and boiled turkeys, pies, pastries, apples, raisins, nuts, wines, "besides many other dishes which [he] did not see or [did not] recollect." He was especially impressed with the venison, which was cooked at the table "by means of Dishes having under them a blaze made I think by burning spirits." More remarkable than the feast was Mrs. Prescott herself. He wrote his wife that "what I noticed was that Mrs. Prescott gave no order at the table." Nor had she left the drawing room to supervise the kitchen staff. Instead, she achieved the remarkable feat of "appear[ing] otherwise as a guest" at her own party. Charged with presiding over an enormous dinner, Mrs. Prescott managed

This chapter is reprinted from Catherine E. Kelly, "'Well Bred Country People': Sociability, Social Networks, and the Creation of a Provincial Middle Class, 1820–1860," *Journal of the Early Republic* 19, no. 3 (fall 1999): 451–80. Copyright © 1999, Society of Historians of the Early American Republic.

the evening with more ease than Bliss, who concluded "such a feast is a hard job—
I hope & trust I shall have no more of that work to perform before my return."

In the past ten years, historians have served up adventures like George
Bliss's to explain society and culture in the early republic. In particular, they
have looked to such anecdotes as part of a larger exploration of sociability, of
the myriad gatherings and networks that simultaneously pulled people together and set them apart. No longer the stuff of antiquarian catalogues and
antiques magazines, dinner parties, parlor socials, and neighborly visiting
now seem to reveal more than the broad outlines and the fine detail of bygone days. Instead, these occasions have assumed a new significance as part of
the informal, extrapolitical processes through which men and women delin-
eate distinctions of class, gender, and political affiliation. From this perspective, seemingly private patterns of sociability no longer stand in opposition to
the world of political parties, voluntary associations, and public rituals. Private and public no longer figure as opposite and oppositional worlds but as
points along a single continuum.[2]

More recently, sociability has captured the imaginations of rural historians.
Looking at neighborly visiting, work parties, and community organizations,
these scholars have been struck by patterns of sociability which they correctly
associate with the mutuality of the household economy and which persisted
well into the nineteenth century. The informal, inclusive style of rural sociability seems to confound the conventions of bourgeois culture, conventions
that placed the stamp of respectability on members of the urban middle class.
Holding the befuddled, mildly disapproving George Bliss up against the self-
confident elegance of Mr. And Mrs. Prescott, they have concluded that sociability served as a bulwark against the encroachments of bourgeois culture and
even against capitalist social relations.[3]

To be sure, provincial New Englanders never cast aside the sociability of their
parents and grandparents to ape cosmopolitan civility. But sociability hardly
served as the last bastion of the household economy. A closer examination of the
experience and cultural meaning of sociability in western Massachusetts, New
Hampshire, and Vermont reveals it as a far more contested, contradictory terrain.[4] Between 1800 and 1860, provincial women and men developed a hybrid
sociability, one that moved between the high fashion of the Prescotts and the
plain style of George Bliss. On the one hand, rural New Englanders increasingly
incorporated elements of cosmopolitan, genteel culture into their own patterns
of sociability. Many antebellum provincials appropriated the manners, customs,

and entertainments of the urban middle class, transforming and eclipsing the religious dimensions of women's self-presentation in the process. On the other hand, even the most casual nineteenth-century observers agreed that provincial sociability retained a special tenor, derived from translating community spirit into practice. Provincial gatherings were certainly less formal, less exclusive than their urban counterparts. And throughout the antebellum period, an etiquette of social proximity contributed to the sense of community.

At least as important as what women and men did was what sense they made of it. When provincial New Englanders considered sociability as a social process, rather than as an individual diversion, they generally overlooked the growing refinement of provincial culture. Instead, they emphasized the persistence of older forms of social interaction that derived from the household economy and from rural life more generally. In both published and private discourse, New Englanders exempted village sociability, and by extension, the social relations that obtained within towns and villages, from the wrenching social and cultural dislocation that accompanied the development of nineteenth-century capitalism. From their perspective, sociability placed New England's towns and villages not only beyond the boundaries of the city, but beyond the reach of bourgeois culture. Exaggerating the distinctiveness of their world, they constructed a vision of village sociability that obscured class differences and that articulated the ambitions of an emerging, rural middle class.

During the first half of the nineteenth century, growing numbers of northern, urban, middle-class women and men laid claim to something of the Prescotts' style, elaborating new and increasingly complex patterns of sociability. Mirroring the increasingly intricate and arcane rules governing commercial transactions, the manners described in countless etiquette books testified not simply to new kinds of entertainments but to new styles of interaction. Middle-class men and women worked hard to approximate the apparently effortless elegance of the Prescotts. In Boston, New York, and Philadelphia, ladies and gentlemen moved through parlors and promenades with grace and precision. Approaching each other with a studied sincerity, they fashioned new emblems of class and self.[5]

Provincial New Englanders tended to observe this transformation in much the same way as George Bliss. As a rule, they disapproved of such extravagant display. More often than not, they were slightly intimidated by the scale and splendor of urban sociability. Moses White of Lancaster, New Hampshire, worried that he would feel "rusty" and "out of fashion" when his daughter's wedding was hosted by Salem's prominent Peabody family. Notwithstanding his daughter's assurances that he was "made of a metal that does not contract rust" and that if White was "out of fashion the age must be more degenerate than even ours," he chose to remain at home. And White's fears were not unusual. While visiting the coast city of Newburyport, Elizabeth Phelps of Hadley, Massachusetts, faced a dinner party similar to the one attended by George Bliss. Phelps "dread[ed]" the thought of making conversation with twenty strange lawyers. After some fretting, she dodged the lawyers by taking tea with a friend.[6]

This is not to say that Phelps had no appetite for refinement. Shortly after her marriage to Dan Huntington took her from Hadley to Litchfield, Connecticut, she reported that she entertained Colonel Tallmadge and Mr. Gould, who were "both very fond of musick," by playing on her "guittar . . . while they sang"; together, the three "had quite a concert." A woman daunted by Newburyport's codes of genteel performance could nevertheless cut a fine figure in more intimate—and more provincial—settings. This sort of polite society, which Richard Bushman has termed "vernacular gentility," extended well beyond provincial centers like Litchfield.[7] As a resident of Guilford, Vermont, in the 1810s and 1820s, Mary Palmer Tyler and her family participated in endless rounds of informal visits with friends and neighbors. But the Tylers also enjoyed more formal entertainments, like a dinner party hosted by their dear friends the Denisons and a ball at "Mr. Blake's Hotel."[8]

Still, refinement is a relative quality, and the refinement exhibited in provincial sociability fell far short of the standard set by the Prescotts. Both the props and the style of provincial sociability set it apart from patterns elaborated by members of the urban middle class. If Tyler's friend "Madam Denison" threw a full-fledged dinner party, her menu centered on one lone turkey—slim pickings when compared to the mutton, venison, beef, chicken, and turkey that had graced the Prescott table some twenty years earlier. More telling, the Vermont party bore ample evidence of Madam Denison's labor in the household and the surrounding yards. While George Bliss marvelled that Mrs. Prescott could appear "as a guest" at her own party, Mary Tyler noted that her hostess "roasted her last Turkey (which she reared herself) for us." Indeed, women's labor pervaded the evening; after the fine meal, the hostess and her female guests settled in to quilt a comforter.[9]

The labor of women and men did more than decorate provincial sociability. Through the 1830s (and longer in some communities), sociability remained tied to the work rhythms of the agricultural calendar and more fundamentally to the reciprocity of the household economy. Theodore Huntington recalled that in the Hadley, Massachusetts of his youth, "winter was the time for making tea-parties on a large and generous scale." Only in farming's slack season could the Huntingtons hope to gather "not . . . less than ten or fifteen couples," the minimum required for an "old-fashioned teaparty . . . to go off well." Mary Palmer Tyler found that in Vermont, the agricultural calendar determined the guest lists: During the summer, male guests included only the host, the physician, the minister, and the lawyer.[10]

In many provincial communities, the grandest occasions—barn raisings, huskings, quilting parties—merged work and sociability. Ebenezer Fairbanks of Peterborough, New Hampshire, recalled that in the early nineteenth century, "wool breakins" were fashionable. After the wool was prepared for carding, "a general invitation [was] given to the ladies; who would collect from a distance of two or three miles bringing their cards with them, to card (or as it was called) to break the wool." In the evening, the "ladies" were joined by young men, who would "help complete the job, play button a while or some other amusement; and see that the ladies arrived safely home." For their part, Peterborough men "frequently had chopping parties to fall their trees, and log roolings [sic] to clear their land." Work-based sociability did not disappear in the antebellum era. Women continued to look to sewing circles to relieve the tedium of needlework. In 1856, Martha Rhoda Wilson of Keene, New Hampshire, attended a quilting parting similar to the "wool breakins" described by Ebenezer Fairbanks. After tea, the "married ladies" left the "*younger* part of the community," who were joined by "*most* of the gentlemen of the place" to play "Truth, cross question, Simon, ring, consequences, &c&c.[11]" And from the 1830s, provincial women regularly combined work, sociability, and benevolence, using sewing circles to further God's work on earth.[12]

Still, between 1820 and 1860, provincial women and men came to adopt some of the refinement that had set George Bliss agog during his visit to the Prescott home. This was by no means an even progress; styles that appeared in provincial centers like Springfield, Massachusetts or Concord, New Hampshire in the mid-1820s might only appear further into the countryside some fifteen years later. And in both provincial centers and more rustic villages, this transformation of sociability was both speeded by and part of the expansion of associational life. From the 1820s, provincial New Englanders increased their participation in a variety of religious and benevolent associations. But they also flocked to singing schools, dancing classes, and a wide variety of literary associations, groups that owed less to the "evangelical united front" than to the "Village Enlightenment."[13] Emphasizing self-improvement, or, more to the point, self-fashioning, these organizations encouraged provincial women and men to partake of some of the texts, props, and practices that had signaled gentility for earlier generations of New Englanders. Lessons learned in singing school or dancing class surely improved one's comportment in the parlor or at the ball; hours spent in polite conversation and graceful dancing encouraged an appetite for literary societies and singing schools.[14] Over the course of the antebellum period, private sociability and associational life worked together to increase the intricacy, the scale, and the pace of provincial sociability.

Impromptu, neighborly gatherings were overshadowed gradually by carefully planned "affairs" that compelled women to devote greater attention to setting, decoration, and entertainment. Elizabeth White Peabody, who had seen the best of Salem society before moving to Springfield, Massachusetts, gave high marks to a party at the Howard household. The family "received the company in one parlour, danced in the other, and had supper up stairs." More remarkable than the scope of the entertainment was the care that had gone into embellishing it. Peabody reported that one Margaret Emery, charged with arranging the supper table, had produced "astonishing decorations," carving roses out of "beets, carrots and turnips." Almost a decade later, the Cochran sisters of Northampton, Massachusetts, found themselves caught up in a whirl of "cotillion parties." Lizzie Cochran, the most musical of the three, borrowed "some Quadrilles from La Bayadere Masaniello & other operas with accompaniments for the flute & violin" and organized several local musicians to make "quite a *band* for dancing."[15]

By the end of the antebellum period, even residents of distinctly rural towns could enjoy a remarkably wide range of entertainments. Twenty-five years later Elizabeth White Peabody described Springfield's social season for Mary Jane White; sisters Agnes Gordon Higginson and Annie Storrow Higginson found comparable opportunities in Deerfield, a small farming community some forty miles up the Connecticut River. The two regularly availed themselves of the parties, dances, and book club meetings held in the homes of the town's better families. They also rode to Northampton to dance away the long winter nights at balls held in the town's hotel, and they rounded out their social life with frequent train rides to visit kin in Brattleboro, Vermont, where they enjoyed parties, cotillions, and parlor theatricals. In Derry, New Hampshire, residents organized "any quantity of levees" to while away the winter. According to one woman: "First there is Mrs. Morris. She has one once a fortnight then Caswell had had two or three," she wrote; if that was not enough, she added that "there is to be a *great Concert* at Chester Tuesday evening and another . . . Friday evening."[16]

Increasingly elaborate parties demanded increasingly elaborate—and abundant—provisions. In the summer of 1830, Springfield ladies and gentlemen enjoyed a "fruit party," featuring "strawberries, cherries, oranges, ice creams, and sponge cake" and "lemonade or wine" in place of coffee and tea. At an 1859 Deerfield wedding, guests were impressed by a "very magnificent supper" that covered "two long tables," each adorned with an "immense round flat loaf of wedding cake," which served more as ornament than food, for there was as much [cake] cut up beside as was necessary" to satisfy the guests. Even more ordinary teas and dinners boasted "fashionable dishes." Mary Ann Sanborn served "waffles, cold bread, sponge cake and Washington Cake" for tea in 1851, noting that "the waffles were very popular." Ten years later, an Oxford, Massachusetts, woman stuffed her dinner guests with "potted pigeons with paste cakes, & roast chicken with cauliflower, first course including of course all the minor vegetables." Those who saved room for dessert enjoyed apple slump pies and "splendid" grapes brought from Boston especially for the occasion.[17]

But despite its ornate decorations, elegant music, and dainty foods, provincial sociability never attained either the grandeur or the stilted formality that prevailed in the parlors of the urban middle class. Women accustomed to the rigid ritual of the city call quickly learned that provincial society defied many of their assumptions about the protocols of visiting. On a trip through Vermont in 1820, Julietta Penaimen was "not a little terrified" to arrive at her New Fane lodgings during tea. To her surprise, her hostess overlooked the gaffe, receiving the party with "smiles and many a welcome." Penaimen was more baffled still the next morning when her hostess indicated her displeasure when Penaimen's party failed to rise and dress until long after the other boarders had assembled for breakfast. For Penaimen, a world in which the protocols of tea might be disrupted while the morning meal remained sacrosanct was topsy turvy indeed. After Amelia White Peabody assumed the role of minister's wife in 1824, she expected to treat the Springfield congregation according to the etiquette that had prevailed in Salem, Massachusetts. Scheduling parish calls, she and her husband tactfully arranged afternoon visits for "such as are too humble to make morning calls." Unfortunately, the ladies of her husband's parish were unaware that even women without sufficient help to allow "morning calls" should be prepared to accept formal calls later in the day. To their horror, the couple surprised one woman who calmly "opened the door with a handkerchief over head & dressed in washing style, & a mop in her hand just in the act of cleaning the floor." The Peabodys beat a hasty retreat, promising to return later.[18]

The same women who paid each other the compliment of a "formal" call were just as likely to drop in at odd times. The diaries and letters of town women, especially, abound with makeshift tea parties honoring unexpected guests. Occasionally, provincial New Englanders dispensed with decorum altogether. One evening in 1859, twenty-seven-year-old Hattie Fuller, her twenty-one-year-old brother John, and a boarder named Matty decided to amuse family and friends with a "masquerade." With the two women "dressed up as young men" and John decked out in "a hooped skirt and bonnet," the spectacle was "too funny for anything." Not content to remain at home, the company took off on a series of surprise visits. Still in costume, they stopped at "Baxter Stebbin's & made a call, & afterwards went over to the Clary's."[19]

Even when provincial women and men set out to emulate the gracious sociability of an urban middle class, they often ended in failure. It was one thing to aspire to the rituals of cosmopolitan gentility, another to reproduce them. The realities of rural New England quickly deflated grand schemes. Royall Tyler, who never forgot his Boston beginnings and never lacked for social pretension, once insisted that his wife host an elegant soiree for his business associates and their "ladies." Ignoring their rustic "parlor" and primitive kitchen, oblivious to the untrained country "help" and the small children, he ordered up a dinner of "a roast and a boiled turkey, a fine ham, roast chickens, and a pair of very fine ducks, oyster sauce and cranberries" with nuts and apples for dessert. Mary Palmer Tyler struggled valiantly to fulfill her mission. She hired two extra women to help with the cooking, serving, and child care. She borrowed plates, dishes, knives, forks, glasses, and a cake for tea. At the last minute, she fussed with her appearance, for her husband "was naturally anxious that I should look and behave well on the occasion." Despite her best efforts, dinner was an hour late, the service was clumsy, and the baby shrieked throughout the meal. Insisting that they had had a marvelous time, the guests fled immediately after dinner, taking Royall Tyler with them. Years later, she recalled that

> this was the first and last time we attempted a dinner party, but contented our-
> selves with social tea parties with our intimate friends; there were but few in
> those days, and we could enjoy them without perplexity or more expense than
> we could afford, and in that way we avoided much unhappiness.[20]

Royall Tyler's pretensions had been crushed by the rustic conditions of early nineteenth-century Vermont. But even later in the century, circumstances could conspire to squelch social ambition. In 1858, a North Hadley family resolved to celebrate a wedding in grand style. Without considering that their house had been constructed for other purposes, they invited one hundred guests, a small orchestra, and a handful of singers to mark the occasion. As the orchestra and singers began the piece that preceded the vows, the floor collapsed and the entire party fell four feet. Rumpled and dirty but unhurt, the wedding party reconvened at the minister's house. There they successfully executed the ceremony if not the elegant affair.[21]

Grand entertainments like balls and theatricals may never have eradicated older forms of sociability or the habits of informality that accompanied them, but they did contribute much to the reshaping of provincial women's self-presentation. Until the 1840s, descriptions of sociability generally occupied a modest place in provincial women's diaries and letters. Certainly, these occasions offered women and girls a welcome respite from work and a chance to visit with neighbors and kin. But the social practices and material props of sociability rarely stood at the center of female self-presentations.[22] On the contrary, the rhythms of Christian practice marked the routines of women's lives; the struggle for faith stood at the core of self. Sociability appeared in women's diaries and letters both as a pro forma metaphor for the world and as a very real temptation that threatened to seduce the hapless from the path of Christ. By the 1840s and 1850s, the place of sociability in women's narratives changed dramatically. It no longer figured simply as one of many things that might occupy a woman's time, much less as a dangerous snare on the road to salvation. Instead, sociability eclipsed religion as the prism through which women measured themselves and each other. The myriad possibilities of polite society supplanted the struggle for salvation in women's narratives of self.

This sort of transformation is easier to describe than to explain; it resists both precise turning points and monocausal explanations. The shift from a Christian to a social self must have owed much to changes within antebellum Protestantism itself. As Richard Bushman has argued, over the first half of the nineteenth century, ministers and laity alike worked to soften the contrast between Christianity and gentility, between godliness and worldliness.[23] And the ever-increasing pace of sociability itself must also have contributed much to the transformation of women's self-presentations. As we have seen, by the 1840s and 1850s, provincial women devoted far more of their lives to social pursuits than had their grandmothers. And women bore the lion's share of the responsibility for generating and managing the rituals of this polite society. Men organized sleigh rides and the occasional excursion into the countryside. They also dominated the offices of local literary societies (although they were happy to share their duties—if not their titles—with female members). But it was women who assumed responsibility for the teas, dinners, parties, and balls that increasingly filled the diaries and memorandum books of provincial New Englanders. It is likely that the amount of time that women lavished on the rituals of sociability both evidenced and furthered the movement from a Christian self toward a social self. But whatever the causes, by the 1850s, refined leisure played a far more significant role in shaping the boundaries of the female self than it had earlier in the century.

In the journal she kept from the 1810s through the 1840s, Mary Tyler routinely noted the outlines of her social life. She recorded callers, tea parties, and dinner invitations in the same plain style she used to describe the number of candles made, pies baked, and shirts hemmed. She devoted considerably more attention to the triumphs of her adult sons on whose financial support the family depended; less frequently, she praised the selfless labor of her two daughters. But she reserved her most elaborate and graceful prose to mark the rare occasions when she contrived to travel the two miles from Brattleboro to Guilford to worship in the Episcopal church, where she could experience the "happiness of again listening to the effusions of true Piety breathed in language Simple yet Elegant." Inspired by the beauty and power of one especially "excellent" sermon, she described her hunger for grace, comparing herself to the fertile earth waiting for seed: "May the Infinite Being who saw and knows with what joy I receive this portion of the good seed, grant it may take root as in good ground well prepared, and spring up & bear fruit a hundredfold!" The solace she found in faith, as well as the pleasure she took in the liturgy, dominated her presentation of herself. Social activities had their place in the routines of everyday life, but opportunities to praise God in the church of her first choice constituted life's grand occasions.[24]

Elizabeth Phelps Huntington, a contemporary of Tyler's, kept several concurrent journals, which she used almost exclusively as a vehicle for secret prayer. Like Tyler, she described trips to church and moving sermons. She also made careful note of the many anniversaries that measured her years: the births and deaths of loved ones, her wedding day, the date she was admitted to Church, the dates on which her children experienced a saving grace—all warranted special prayers and dutiful fasting. In Huntington's journals, leisure hardly makes an appearance, and the everyday routines of family and household figure only as a heuristic device, providing inspiration for prayer. The same hierarchy of values dominate the scores of letters she wrote to her children in the 1830s and 1840s. If Huntington's letters contain a good measure of family news, including occasional descriptions of the social milieu beyond the family farm, they too are dominated by religious themes. Earthly activity, including sociability, always was yoked to a higher purpose. As she explained to her daughter in 1832, genteel behavior, "is indeed a secondary consideration; we must never forget that many things, 'which are highly esteemed among men are an abomination in the sight of God.'" Certainly, one should cultivate "true politeness," which was nothing more or less than the "unaffected graceful expression of real benevolence, kindness, or charity." Yet even these social graces were valued because they made a woman a more credible representative of Christ. "Do this not to make a display," she cautioned, "but that you may be enabled to recommend the Christian character."[25]

Still, it was one thing to define "true politeness," another to put it into practice. Huntington herself struggled to negotiate between the behavior required of a congenial guest and the behavior demanded of a pious Christian. The rigors of a large Northampton party in the late 1830s completely undermined her ability to gauge her self-presentation. She confessed that "it required some discretion, and much of the 'fear of the Lord, which is the beginning of wisdom,' to resist the temptation to levity on the one hand and to avoid the appearance of severity and moroseness on the other." Uncertain that she managed to strike the proper chord, she retreated to the moral high ground. At the very least, she wrote, such "occasions offer as good an opportunity as any to honour religion before the tho'tles." Far from reinforcing her sense of self, the demands of secular sociability compromised it.[26]

These tensions between the sacred and the secular could prove especially troubling for young women, who faced the temptations of society more frequently than their mothers. How was a young woman to demonstrate "that love which the Christian is required to feel towards the people of this world" when so many of those people conspired to draw her away from Christ? When nineteen-year-old Eliza Adams found herself caught in this dilemma, her friend Delia Willis reminded her of the Christian's final accounting. "Were one of our dear companions to be brought to a serious deathbed what would be her language in regard to parties and the manner in which professing Christians had treated them," Willis asked. "Would she not say it was time spent worse than in vain?" Nor were these abstract question. Willis pointed to "a lady of my acquaintance" who spent the past "25 years accustomed to the society of those who were fond of parties." Although the older women had been plagued by the same doubts that troubled Eliza, she admitted that simply by attending parties "she gave her sanction and when all was over she had done little different from them who went freely." But even Delia Willis was not immune to the lure of society. Several months later she confessed that she attended a "social visit" only to discover that "there was not in that whole group a heart which beat in unison" with hers. Returning home at the evening's end, Willis concluded that she "enjoyed more heartfull pleasure in one solitary half hour" of prayer than in "years of the 'happy confusion'" that characterized so much of society.[27]

It was one thing for a woman to encounter "happy confusion" among her neighbors and friends, another to confront it within her own home. When Adeline Young returned from a term at Mary Lyon's Ipswich school in 1833, she was mortified that her family received calls on the Sabbath. On the one hand, Young believed that "we ought not to separate ourselves from those that think different from what we do," especially when the heterodox included one's immediate family. On the other hand, "a person who intends to regard the Sabbath, does not wish to be disturbed." When family and friends ignored her gentle hints that "it was not a proper time to call," Young found that in "endeavoring to please the world" she had offended her "Maker." Turning to her older brother for guidance, she asked "*what shall I do?* any thing that I can see is duty, I will gladly do, though it may be *painful* . . . I . . . do not know what step to take."[28]

For a later generation of women, the commotion of society posed no problem at all. Far from figuring as moral dilemmas, social affairs commanded detailed descriptions, replacing accounts of inspiring sermons and spiritual struggles. These women lavished attention on the kinds of gatherings that Mary Tyler had only cursorily described and that Elizabeth Huntington, Eliza Adams, Delia Willis, and Adeline Young had found so bedeviling. For example, in the diary she kept during the 1850s, seventeen-year-old Agnes Gordon Higginson occasionally mentioned attending church, although she never listed the text of a sermon, commented on the quality of the preaching, or speculated on the state of her soul. But she kept a precise accounting of her social life. She took the time to list the titles of the "private theatricals" she had attended during a visit to Brattleboro: "Hour of a Lover," "Lend me five shillings," and "Boot at the Swan," all "Perfectly Splendid!!!!" productions. She had a "splendid time" on an excursion to Turner's Falls. And we can imagine that she also enjoyed the evening that she spent dancing with "the adorable Fred!"[29]

Agnes Cochran Higginson was not unusual. In the newsy letters she wrote to her daughter in the early 1860s, Mrs. Hodges of Oxford, Massachusetts, chose not to explore questions of faith, although she did describe a memorable Boston sermon in which the reverend upbraided his wealthy flock for napping in church. Instead, she turned to her own busy social life, recounting Boston vacations, family visits, and the menus of memorable dinner parties. Most especially, she described the constant shopping necessary to decorate her ambitious social calendar. For example, during a stay at Boston's Revere House, she wrote that she and her husband had invited "gentlemen" in to play "Euchre." The memory of that evening prompted her to add that "we have two new ornaments to our mantle here, the little clock which was sent here the other day and a beautiful little mug which Papa bought to shave in. It is dark blue with white figures on it of the muses." And although Mrs. Hodges sporadically reminded her daughter to pray, she was far more concerned with managing the intricacies of her daughter's social life and wardrobe. She sent gifts to family and friends on the girl's behalf and offered advice on budding romances. She instructed her daughter to have her dresses made "high in the neck as that is entirely the style" and to braid her hair, which would enable her to "wear ribbons or a net either & the changes would be pretty."[30]

By the standards of an Elizabeth Huntington or a Delia Willis, Mrs. Hodges and Agnes Higginson surely slighted matters of the soul. But other women mined the language of religious faith to create a vocabulary for sociability. In 1859, a young Deerfield woman named Rebecca complained to a friend in Boston that her own town was "not *gay*." A last dance proved "so disagreeable" that she had "determined not to attend another." Reversing the pieties of earlier generations, Rebecca urged her Boston friend to thank God that she was wintering among "better pleasures, more salutary influences." She wrote "'Rejoice & be exceedingly glad' for great is yr joy in Boston—You must have much to amuse and instruct your youthful mind."[31]

Yet other women extended the language and imagery of parlor sociability to events of religious importance, especially death. Receiving word in 1856 that her friend "Elwarder" had died, Agnes Higginson went to view the body. Recalling the incident in her diary, she drew on the same conventions she employed when describing the appearance of her living friends at parties and dances. Ignoring Elwarder's prospects for grace, she wrote only that her friend looked "*lovely beautiful*" with a funeral wreath round her head, the dead woman even looked "very natural." The year before, learning that "Sophie Harris of Brattleboro" had died, Higginson chose to memorialize her not as a Christian but as the kind of young woman who proved an asset at parties, "a lovely girl whom everybody liked." More striking still is Maria Clark's account of the death of a New Hampshire minister's wife. Clark wrote that the Reverend and Mrs. Willis had invited the "Sunday school scholars" over for a visit. "We had a very pleasant time," she wrote, because Mrs. Willis, "who was a very pretty woman" had "done all she could do to have us enjoy ourselves though her health was very poor." Unfortunately, the woman "over exerted herself," took sick, and died a week later. Describing the ill-fated affair, Clark chose to memorialize the woman's appearance and her hospitality rather than her faith or her prospect for salvation.[32]

By the end of the antebellum era, women and amusements which would once have been condemned as "tho'tless and gay" no longer threatened the standards of Christian piety, much less respectability. Gentility, made manifest in temperament, manners, and appearance, assumed an increasingly significant role in women's depictions of themselves and those closest to them. By the end of the antebellum period, provincial women were eyeing each other carefully, searching out evidence of refinement and polish. Indeed, their diaries and letters reveal a growing emphasis on looking, on spectatorship. For example, Martha Rhoda Wilson and her friends "noticed many things" on an 1850 sleigh ride that took them from Keene, New Hampshire, to Brattleboro, Vermont, and back again. But the "most prominent . . . was a gentleman, lady, & child." From "the Gent, the ladies received what was termed a complimentary remark;" not to be outdone, a man in Wilson's party "responded in good earnest." Women, especially, noticed each other and imagined others noticing them. Hattie Fuller of Deerfield was entirely pleased with the figure she cut at a "pleasant ball" to celebrate her twenty-third birthday. She boasted a new silk dress, a handsome escort, and concluded, "I 'expect' we were the best looking couple at the ball." Several years later, Annie Storrow Higginson cast her friends as the "*ornaments*" of another Deerfield party. Matty was "magnificent," she wrote, "Both Mr. Wells and Mr. Grennell admired her." Higginson's mother insisted that her own two daughters were the brightest ornaments in Deerfield society. "Aggy" was "the prettiest girl" while "Annie the most elegant and the best dancer." Looking—and looking good—had become central to the performance of gentility.[33]

Indeed, women's preoccupation with looking at each other became so pronounced that some men felt slighted. In an essay complaining about women's behavior at social gatherings, "Theophilus Thistle" described the painful realization that a lady was looking past her man to size up the women around her. "Sometimes we are doing our best to talk, when we catch your eye wandering about the room to see how your friends are dressed," he wrote. Surely, men who "worked hard all day, and tried to be agreeable all evening" deserved better than that.[34]

As we have seen, the diaries and letters of provincial New Englanders offer abundant evidence of a growing gentility. Those same sources suggest the ways in which that gentility reshaped not only patterns of provincial sociability, but provincial women's identities. But when men and women considered the broader significance of sociability, when they imagined it as something more than effect of individual preference, they paid scant attention to the growing formality of provincial parties, balls, and calls. On the contrary. After around 1840, the same diaries and letters that testify to the growing refinement of provincial life also insist upon the endurance of older patterns of sociability. Published accounts, in particular, gave short shrift to the growing formality of social life, emphasizing instead the survival, even the triumph, of older patterns of sociability. But if certain styles of sociability lasted through the antebellum period, those same styles took on new significance in the context of changing class and gender identities. In diaries and letters, memoirs and imaginative literature, provincial New Englanders elaborated new meanings for old practices. They conflated the style of provincial sociability with the structure of provincial social relations. They drew on the rhetoric of republicanism and the conventions of sentimental literature to clarify and magnify the significance of sociability. Playing off simplicity against fashion, authenticity against pretense, and country against city, they exaggerated the distinctiveness of provincial sociability.

Looking back at antebellum New England written from the close of the nineteenth century, memoirists took pains to describe the special tenor of provincial sociability. Villages and towns were distinguished by their informality and inclusiveness, qualities that set them apart from the stratification and pretense that characterized both the antebellum city and Gilded Age America more generally. In 1886, Susan I. Lesley recalled that "there were no very rich people in Northampton." "Envying no one," her neighbors lived happily on a "moderate competence." But make no mistake; these were no mere rustics. The men and women of antebellum Northampton exhibited "refined and aristocratic manners" and "practis[ed] a generous hospitality at all times." Theodore Bliss agreed. In Northampton "simple ideals of living made it unnecessary to assume an external gloss that did not belong to our everyday existence." This distinctive simplicity fostered an equally distinctive egalitarianism. Bliss insisted that social relations and social life were marked by "a certain tone of sincerity and self-respect" that enabled the "butcher, the baker, and candlestick maker" along with the "minister, teacher, and lawyer" to meet in a "large community of intelligent, thinking people" And although Francis H. Underwood was less enamored of provincial society than either Bliss or Lesley, he too argued that (relatively) widespread property ownership placed the "smith or the joiner who owned his house and shop . . . on equal terms with the farmer, his customer, and could hold up his head with the best." These "equal terms" defined the etiquette of everyday sociability. "It was the custom to salute on the highway or in public places," Underwood wrote. "To pass even a stranger without some recognition would have been considered rude." This congeniality was special to the countryside. Indeed, he explained, "one of the reasons city people were so disliked" was their refusal to bow, or "pass the time o'day."[35]

What are we to make of such comments? It is easy enough to dismiss them as self-serving nostalgia, as one more example of the ways in which fin-de-siècle New Englanders mythologized themselves. And nostalgia certainly permeates these constructions of "simple ideals of living" which obliterated class distinctions and "moderate competences" which yielded "aristocratic manners." Yet these accounts—like all good myths—contain an element of truth. Provincial sociability *was* distinctive. But its distinctiveness owed less to "simple ideals" than to the complex material realities that undergirded provincial social networks and to the ideological underpinnings of an emerging middle class.[36]

Population, occupational structure, and tensions within an emerging middle class all contributed to patterns of sociability. At the most basic level, community size reinforced the flexible social networks that Bliss and Underwood remembered. Because the relatively small populations limited the numbers of men and women who might be included within a local middle class, all but the most intimate gatherings necessarily encompassed a variety of people. Royall Tyler explained that when the residents of early nineteenth-century Guilford, Vermont, had "a social party the whole neighborhood are invited." The town's two merchants, two doctors and single lawyer socialized regularly with "well-bred country people" and with "well to do mechanics who aim to treat company equally well." This "truly primitive state of society," as Tyler termed it, prevailed most obviously in younger towns, like Guilford. But it also seems to have prevailed in towns that experienced either slight growth or population decline during the antebellum era. And, as we shall see, it even shaped patterns of sociability in well-established provincial centers like Northampton.[37]

But sociability was not simply a function of a town's age or size. The distinctive class structure of provincial communities played a more important role in shaping social networks. Numerous social and economic historians have traced a rise in economic inequality from the eighteenth century to the eve of the Civil War. Rural New England did not escape this sea change. In

Christopher Clark's succinct formulation, after 1840, provincials were increasingly divided by the "quantity of property that people held, the forms that it took, and the ways they could use it." This inequality early produced a recognizable rural working class. But it was far slower to produce a middle class that conformed to the occupational categories that historians have employed to trace middle class formation in cities like Boston, Philadelphia, Utica, and Rochester.[38] Middling, and middle-class, provincial townsmen defy straightforward distinctions between manual and nonmanual labor, between artisan and entrepreneur, between farmer and merchant. Seen in this context, the butcher and lawyer who enjoyed a relaxed, and intimate acquaintance in Theodore Bliss's memory may have been separated by far less than he imagined.[39]

Compared to its urban counterpart, the provincial middle class appears to have been far more varied. It may also have been more divided. Christopher Clark has demonstrated significant tensions among Connecticut River Valley wealth holders, whose access to the benefits of a national commercial and financial marketplace varied considerably. These same farmers, artisans, merchants and manufacturers were separated by more than economic opportunity: they were divided by the extent of their adherence to the ethos of the household economy, marked by either a commitment to "older patterns of family support and neighborhood assistance" or by the decision to heed the call of the market by relying on institutionalized finance and diversifying their property holdings. The provincial middle class was distinguished not simply by its permeability at the upper and lower margins but also by its internal contradictions.[40]

These hazy class distinctions and intra-class tensions combined with the intimacy of small town life to preserve the kind of familiar, face-to-face interactions that had all but disappeared from city streets by 1820. To be sure, social standards and social inclusiveness varied greatly among communities and within them, depending on the size and sophistication of the town as well as the resources available to particular families and the closeness of their connections to urban culture. Nor is this to deny the subtle, even petty, hierarchies of village life. But these divisions did not translate into a strict segregation of classes. Harriet Wood reported that she liked Concord, New Hampshire, "very much" precisely because "many different elements . . . mingle harmoniously in the most republican manner." Both the tone and the structure of provincial society allowed for considerable interaction between classes, linking an increasingly genteel middle class to uncultured farmers and even to the very respectable poor. Unlike the good citizens of Boston and Philadelphia, who grappled with the problems posed by rough-looking strangers, provincial men and women hammered out an etiquette of social proximity that allowed them to coexist with poorer neighbors whose names and histories they knew all too well.[41]

Theodore Bliss, who treasured Northampton's "certain tone of sincerity and self-respect" experienced this etiquette of social proximity firsthand, for he came from a family that had been destitute almost since his birth. After an ill-advised loan destroyed his father's finances and his reason, young Theodore was shuttled from one relative to another until he was finally apprenticed to a Northampton printer and bookseller. Such a young man could hardly be said to have travelled in the best circles. But when Mary Wright, whose family was prominent if not wealthy, began to attract his "respectful attention on the street," Bliss had no difficulty befriending her; he quickly became a regular visitor at the Sunday evening musicals hosted by Wright and her sister.[42]

Caroline Clapp Briggs, a contemporary of Bliss, found religion to be more important than wealth in drawing the boundaries of her social circle. During her youth, she recalled, "my acquaintances were mostly Unitarians. I had no intimate acquaintance with any family in the Orthodox church." Yet within her congregation, Briggs befriended members of Northampton's best families. In the 1840s, after her father lost his job as the town jailer, the young woman and her sister "did sewing, copying, or anything our hands could find to do, as well as taking in boarders" to help support the family. Scrambling to help support her family, Briggs was a regular visitor in the homes of her betters. She benefitted from the "large hospitality" of the wealthy Hunt family, whose house "was more tasteful than any other in the village, better furnished, with ornaments and pictures, and always decorated with tastefully arranged flowers"; she relaxed in silk manufacturer Samuel Whitmarsh's conservatory, with an "atmosphere so summerlike that one could easily forget all the frost and snow outside." She particularly enjoyed the Cochran women's company, taking great pleasure in Martha Cochran's keen wit.[43]

But there were clear limits to the liberality of Northampton's better families. While Theodore Bliss found Mary Wright easy to meet and easier still to love, marrying her proved far more difficult. His concerns about his future deterred him from proposing marriage until he had begun to make his fortune in Philadelphia. If Caroline Clapp Briggs often enjoyed afternoon teas, charitable sewing, and perhaps even cotillion parties at the homes of Northampton's elite, she was almost certainly not included among their intimates. Briggs idolized the rather formidable Martha Cochran, describing her as "one of the rarest women I ever met." But the young woman failed to make an equal impression on Cochran. Indeed, the Cochran women's newsy letters ignored the Clapp family altogether. Caroline Clapp Briggs remained at the edges of the Cochran's vision, one of the nameless women who regularly appeared in their parlor for meetings of the sewing society and the reading club.[44] Still, the intimacy of provincial society gave both Briggs and Bliss an entree that would have been denied them in a larger city. More important, it encouraged a mutual identification. By allowing Theodore Bliss, and Caroline Clapp Briggs a stake in the world of their betters, the familiarity of provincial sociability softened the harshest edges of class distinction. The growing awareness of class was muted by a shared sense of community.[45]

Provincial sociability did more than ease tensions between classes and shore up a sense of community. The same patterns of sociability that seemed to narrow the distance between members of an emerging middle class and their poorer farming and laboring neighbors, binding them together as a single community also served to emphasize and to exaggerate the cultural distance between country and city. Invoking the artlessness and inclusively of provincial life, middle-class women and men invoked the countryside. In their telling, their communities' virtues were inextricably bound up with the rural landscape. When Harriet Wood praised the "most republican" society of Concord in 1841, she also described it as a "village." Now Concord was certainly a far cry from Boston or New York, but it took a good deal of imagination to cast New Hampshire's state capital as a "village." Elaborating discourses of sociability, New Englanders paid scant attention to the ways in which the market revolution was refashioning the ties between city and country, just as they overlooked the increasing show and ceremony of their own sociability. Indeed, provincial sociability and the discourses surrounding it allowed men and women to construct a middle-class culture that owed less to urban, middle-class style than to its disavowal.[46]

Visits to the urban center regularly provided provincials with ample fodder for comparison. But even distant reports about city entertainments could prompt provincial women, especially, to comment on the distance between town and country. Marianne Cochran, for example, relished the society meetings and musicals which kept her away from her Northampton home three nights out of seven. But in her letters, these homely diversions stand in sharp contrast to the extravagant affairs of prosperous Bostonians with whom she had a passing acquaintance. With disapproval only slightly checked by envy, she contrasted the modest dimensions of her own social life with a "dinner & ball where a bouquet was placed at every plate & after meats &c all adjourned to another room & table for the dessert! . . . Much offense is given by these . . . *nobility*," she wrote.[47]

Distancing themselves from the elaborate conventions of bourgeois civility, Cochran and her contemporaries simultaneously constructed and took refuge in the respectability of New England's morality, a morality increasingly at odds with the show and display of bourgeois culture. When Sarah Olcott of Hanover, New Hampshire sent out invitations for an 8:00 P.M. wedding, all "nicely sealed with a white ribbon" and "with her card 'at home'" included, not all of her guests appreciated her attempt at gentility. "Such things I think are rather ridiculous in a small country village," concluded one woman. This lapse in taste and judgment was all the worse considering that bride was moving from a "small country village" to someplace even more rustic. "It is said Candia is to be her place of residence. What can she show off to there," the disapproving guest wondered.[48]

By the 1840s, some provincials self-consciously put on "rural style" in order to signal their virtue. Joseph Bartlett, a minister, planned his wedding to accord with the standards of provincial sociability and to represent rural virtues. He explained that "we have endeavored to make all things suitable for a country parson's bridal in regard to dress & c. There will be no wedding party—not even the indispensable cake." One woman recalled that even at Northampton's largest parties "everything . . . was managed after the most economical fashion." Disdaining "confectioners' commodities," guests contented themselves with simple fare—apples, walnuts, and a basket of oranges, or cake and wine. Reproaching a younger, more sophisticated generation, she boasted that "All the food was good, because it was home-made; and it was not the New England fashion to despise good, well cooked food." The homemade props of rural sociability kept it free from the taint of the urban market, just as social networks kept provincial New Englanders free from the corrupting divisions of bourgeois social relations.[49]

Such comments surely satisfy to the human propensity to censure others and to praise the good old days at the expense of the present. But they also reveal the ways in which provincial women and men participated in the construction of the New England village ideal, with its images of an organic social order based on widespread property ownership and maintained through neighborly society. Through the structure of social networks and the discourse surrounding sociability, middle-class women and men depicted New England's town and villages as standing outside of bourgeois class relations and transcending bourgeois culture. Their increasingly elaborate style of sociability revealed their deepening identification with genteel habits of the urban middle class. But to the extent that sociability recalled the corporate social relations of earlier generations, members of the emerging middle class could abstract their communities and themselves from social change and bourgeois social relations. Far from serving as a bulwark against the encroachments of bourgeois culture, social styles derived from the household economy could be turned to the needs of an emerging middle class. By contributing to the New England village ideal, the influence of this same sociability spread beyond provincial New England to shape Northern bourgeois culture. For the sentimentalized picture of village life that loomed large in nineteenth-century literary culture and political discourse sprang not simply from the imaginations of urban intellectuals and canonical writers, but from the experiences, strategies, and texts of provincial New Englanders themselves as they negotiated the transition from household economy to market society.

NOTES

I thank David Jaffee, Angela Woollacott, Carolyn Lawes, Michael A. Morrison, and especially Carol Lasser for their comments on various incarnations of this essay.

1. The Prescott party is described in George Bliss to Abigail Rowland Bliss, Jan. 31, 1804, Bliss-Morris Papers (Genealogy and Local History Library, Connecticut Valley Historical Museum, Springfield, Mass.).

2. These developments have accompanied historians' larger reconsideration of the origins and significance of the public sphere. See Jürgen Habermas, *The Structural Transformation of the Public Sphere: An Inquiry into a Category of Bourgeois Society*, trans. Thomas Burger (Cambridge, Mass.: MIT Press, 1989). For critical discussions of Habermas's concept of the public sphere, see, for example, the essays collected in Craig Calhoun, ed., *Habermas and the Public Sphere* (Cambridge, Mass.: MIT Press, 1992). For an overview of feminist critiques of Habermas, see Belinda Davis, "Reconsidering Habermas, Gender, and the Public Sphere: The Case of

Wilhelmine Germany," in *Society, Culture, and the State in Germany, 1870–1930*, ed. Geoff Eley (Ann Arbor: University of Michigan Press, 1996), 397–426. For Americanists' attention to and interventions in these debates, see David Waldstreicher, review of Craig Calhoun, ed., *Habermas and the Public Sphere*, in *William and Mary Quarterly*, 52 (Jan. 1995): 175–77; David S. Shields, *Civil Tongues and Polite Letters in British America* (Chapel Hill: University of North Carolina Press, 1997); Kathleen M. Brown, *Good Wives, Nasty Wenches, and Anxious Patriarchs: Gender, Race, and Power in Colonial Virginia* (Chapel Hill: University of North Carolina Press, 1996); David Scobey, "Anatomy of the Promenade: The Politics of Bourgeois Sociability in Nineteenth-Century New York," *Social History* (May 1992): 203–27.

3. On rural sociability see esp. Karen V. Hansen, *A Very Social Time: Crafting Community in Antebellum New England* (Berkeley: University of California Press, 1994). Other useful studies include Mitchell Snay, "How the Country Folk Frolic: Sociability in late Eighteenth-Century Rural New England," paper presented at the Sixteenth Annual Conference of the Society for Historians of the Early American Republic, July 1994, Boston; Jane Marie Pederson, *Between Memory and Reality: Family and Community in Rural Wisconsin, 1870–1970* (Madison: University of Wisconsin Press, 1992); Nancy Grey Osterud, *Bonds of Community: The Lives of Farm Women in Nineteenth-Century New York* (Ithaca, N.Y.: Cornell University Press, 1991); Barbara Karsky, "Sociability in Rural New England," in *Time and Work in Pre-Industrial America*, ed. Barbara Karsky and Elise Marienstros (Nancy, France: Presses universitaires de Nancy, 1991). While all of these historians suggest that sociability served as a check against bourgeois culture, Osterud (*Bonds of Community*, 280) extends this argument furthest, suggesting that the kin-based mutuality and the heterosociability of Nanticoke Valley served as a "bulwark" against capitalist social relations.

4. I describe the region under consideration (western Massachusetts and the southern halves of Vermont and New Hampshire) as provincial rather than rural. Although the regional economy remained dominated by agriculture throughout the antebellum period, the region also included a number of good-sized towns and an increasingly diversified economy, as historians of rural New England readily concede. "Rural" seems an awkward term for an area like the one under consideration. But the word "provincial" does more than skirt questions about the fine distinctions between villages, towns, and cities. More important, for my purposes, is the way that the term locates the farms, villages, and towns within a regional economic and cultural system that was increasingly dominated by metropolitan centers. Writing about the nineteenth-century Midwest, Timothy R. Mahoney similarly describes the provincial town as a "place that contributes to the center, interacts with it but . . . is not a center," noting that by the 1850s, the rise of the "great metropolitan centers" transformed "hundreds of towns, once the centers of small local worlds, into 'provincial' places." Mahoney, *River Towns in the Great West: The Structure of Provincial Urbanization in the American Midwest, 1820–1870* (New York: Cambridge University Press, 1990), 24.

5. See Richard Bushman, *The Refinement of America: Persons, Houses, Cities* (New York: Knopf, 1992); Scobey, "Anatomy of the Promenade"; John F. Kasson, *Rudeness and Civility: Manners in Nineteenth-Century Urban America* (New York: Hill and Wang, 1990); Karen Halttunen, *Confidence Men and Painted Women: A Study of Middle-Class Culture in America,*

1830–1870 (New Haven, Conn.: Yale University Press, 1982). Stuart Blumin argues that although the parlor etiquette described by Halttunen was aimed at "the wealthiest and most socially ambitious middle-class families," the rank and file of the urban middle class also "found that the parlor made demands on their deportment." See Blumin, *The Emergence of the Middle Class: Social Experience in the American City, 1760–1900* (New York: Cambridge University Press, 1989), 184–85, 179–91.

6. Elizabeth White to Moses White, July 5, 1824, Everett-Peabody Family Papers (Massachusetts Historical Society, Boston, Mass.); Elizabeth Phelps to Elizabeth Porter Phelps, Oct. 4, 179, Porter-Phelps-Huntington Family Papers, (Amherst College Archives and Special Collections, Amherst, Mass.). For discussions of refinement of the countryside and the relation between this process and the shifting cultural dynamics between city and hinterland, see Catherine E. Kelly, *In the New England Fashion: Reshaping Women's Lives in the Nineteenth Century* (Ithaca, N.Y.: Cornell University Press, 1999); and Bushman, *Refinement of America*, 270–80.

7. Elizabeth Phelps Huntington to Elizabeth Porter Phelps, Jan. 11, 1801, Porter-Phelps-Huntington Family Papers. Following her marriage to Dan Huntington, Elizabeth Phelps lived for several years in Litchfield, Connecticut; it was in Litchfield that she entertained Tallmadge and Gould with her guitar. For other accounts of women's musical accomplishment and genteel sociability in provincial New England, see Eliza Adams to Harriet Adams Aiken, Mar. 18, 1829, Adams Family Papers (Dartmouth College Library, Hanover, N.H.); Theodore G. Huntington, "sketches by Theodore G. Huntington of the Family and Life in Hadley written letters to H. F. Quincy," typescript, Porter-Phelps-Huntington Family Papers. On "vernacular gentility," see Bushman, *Refinement of America*, 208–9, 382. On women's musical talents and the cultivation of gentility in the eighteenth century, see Shields, *Civil Tongues and Polite Letters*, 154–55.

8. See Mary Palmer Tyler Diary, 1821–1842, Mar. 20, 1822, Jan. 31, 1822, Jan. 2, 1822; Royall Tyler Daybook, 1817–21, Nov. 16, 1817 in Royall Tyler Collection, Gift of Helen Tyler Brown, (Vermont Historical Society, Montpelier, Vt.). Prosaic visits are so frequent in the diaries and letters of antebellum men, and women, especially, that they have often escaped historians' analysis if not their notice; for one attempt to make sense of the social meaning of visiting, see Hansen, *A Very Social Time*. The social meaning of more elaborate gatherings beyond the urban center has received even less attention. On the role of hotels as centers for village gentility in general and dancing in particular, see Bushman, *Refinement of America*, 376. For manuscript collections especially rich in their references to an descriptions of provincial sociability in the early nineteenth century, see in addition to the Porter-Phelps-Huntington Family Papers and the Royall Tyler Collection, the Fuller-Higginson Papers, and Mary Hoyt Wilson Diary (both at the Pocumtuck Valley Memorial Association, Deerfield, Mass.) and the Adams Family Papers.

9. Mary Palmer Tyler Diary, 1821–1843, Mar. 20, 1822, Royall Tyler Collection. See also Royall Tyler Daybook, 1817–1821, Dec. 16, 1819, Dec. 16–17, 1817, June 11, 1818, Royall Tyler Collection.

10. Theodore G. Huntington, "Sketches," 45, Porter-Phelps-Huntington Family Papers. Huntington added that if winter afforded the leisure for tea parties, winter weather might spoil them. Living two miles outside Hadley, the Huntingtons knew that "if a storm should intervene

there would be great danger of failure." Mary Palmer Tyler, *Grandmother Tyler's Book: The Recollections of Mary Palmer Tyler (Mrs. Royall Tyler), 1775–1866*, ed. Frederick Tupper and Helen Tyler Brown (New York: G. P. Putnam, 1925), 270. Because the observations of both Huntington and Tyler were recorded in memoirs as general descriptions of social life and customs, it is difficult to affix a precise date to the periods they are describing. But calculating from Huntington's birthday (1813) and the dates of Tyler's residences in Guilford and Brattleboro, it seems likely that in both cases, the memories describe social life in the 1820s and early 1830s.

11. "A Historical Sketch of Some of the Customs and Fashions of Fifty Years Ago," attributed to Ebenezer Fairbanks (b. 1794) and written ca. 1847–1876, papers of Mrs. Ephriam Holt (New Hampshire Historical Society, Concord, N.H.); Diary of Martha Rhoda Wilson, Mar. 6, 1856, Cheshire County Diaries, (Historical society of Cheshire County, Keene, N.H.). On the intersection of work, sociability, and community, see Daniel Vickers, "Competency and Competition: Economic Culture in Early America," *William and Mary Quarterly*, 47 (Jan. 1990): 3–29; Laurel Thatcher Ulrich, "Martha Ballard and Her Girls: Women's Work in Eighteenth-Century Main," in *Work and Labor in Early America*, ed. Stephen Innes (Chapel Hill: University of North Carolina Press, 1988); Jack Larkin, *The Reshaping of Everyday Life, 1790–1840*, (New York: Harper & Row, 1988), 266–71; Karsky, "Sociability in Rural New England; Hansen, *A Very Social Time*; and Osterud, *Bonds of Community*.

12. For archival accounts of women's benevolent work in provincial New England, see, among many, Elizabeth Phelps Huntington to Catherine Carey Huntington, Feb. 18, 1829, Porter-Phelps-Huntington Family Papers; Angelina Bodman to Joseph Bodman, may 19, 1846, Angelina Bodman to Oliver B. Bodman, Jan. 10, 1845, Philena Hawkes Bodman to Luther Bodman Jr., June 1, 1845, all in Bodman Family Papers (Sophia Smith Collection, Smith College, Northampton, Mass.); Elizabeth Parsons Hidden to Emily Parsons Tenney, June 20, 1847, Emily Parsons Tenney to Elizabeth Parsons Hidden, Mar. 29, 1847, Parsons Family Papers (Schlesinger Library, Radcliffe College, Cambridge, Mass.); Sophronia Grout Diary, [n.d.] Sept. 1825, [n.d.] Nov. [c. 1830] and scattered references 1828–1829 (Pocumtuck Valley Memorial Association); Sophronia Grout to parents, June 23, 1828, Sophronia Grout Papers (Pocumtuck Valley Memorial Association); Julia Dutton to Lucretia Wilson Dutton, Dec. 19, 1845, Dec. 18, 1947, Lucretia Wilson Dutton Papers, (Special Collections, University of Vermont Library, Burlington, Vt.); Nancy Avery White Diary, vol. 6, Mar. 3, 1836, Dec. 13, 1837, Apr. 9, 1940, White-Forbes Papers (American Antiquarian Society, Worcester, Mass.); Records of the Northampton Martha Washington Temperance Society (Forbes Library, Northampton, Mass.); Records of the Northampton Anti-Slavery Society, (Forbes Library, Northampton, Mass.); Records of the First Congregational Church ladies' Benevolent Society (Jones Library, Inc., Amherst, Mass.). The historiography of women's benevolent activities is too large to cite here in any detail, but see esp. Mary P. Ryan, *Cradle of the Middle Class: The Family in Oneida County, New York, 1760–1865* (Cambridge: Cambridge University Press, 1981); Nancy A. Hewitt, *Women's Activism and Social Change: Rochester, New York, 1822–1872* (Ithaca, N.Y.: Cornell University Press, 1984); and Lori D. Ginzberg, *Women and the Work of Benevolence: Morality, Politics, and Class in the Nineteenth-Century United States* (New Haven, Conn.: Yale University Press, 1990).

13. I do not mean to suggest here that associations devoted to religion were antithetical to those devoted to refinement. Surely there was a good deal of overlap between the two. But just as surely there were also differences, and tensions, between, say, an association aimed at eradicating sin and one devoted to teaching dance. For a thoughtful account of the connections and tensions between nineteenth century religion and refinement, see Bushman, *Refinement of America*, 313–52. The term "evangelical united front" originated with Charles I. Foster, *An Errand of Mercy: The Evangelical United Front, 1790–1837* (Chapel Hill: University of North Carolina Press, 1960); quoted in Blumin, *Emergence of the Middle Class*, 193. David Jaffee, "The Village Enlightenment in New England, 1760–1820," *William and Mary Quarterly*, 47 (July 1990): 327–46, coined the term "Village Enlightenment" to describe the interconnection of commerce and culture that transformed rural New England in the hundred years before the Civil War; he has done more than any other historian to explore this process of cultural change.

14. Archival sources offer rich testimony to the growing importance of these associations in the lives of women and men. On singing schools, see Diary of Mary Hoyt Wilson, Nov. 26, 1826; Harriet Holkins to Eliza Minot Adams, May 14, 1824, Sarah Hazen to Eliza Adams, Mar. 20, 1830, Adams Family Papers; Emmeline Flint to Mary Ann Tarble Flint, Feb. 25, 1839, Haile Papers, (Vermont Historical Society); Julia Dutton to Lucretia Wilson Dutton, Sept. 26, 1847, Dec. 18, 1847, Lucretia Wilson Dutton Papers; Diary of Marion Hopkins, Feb. 22, 1851, (New Hampshire Historical Society); Martha Rhoda Wilson Diary, Jan. 13, 1851, Cheshire County Diaries; and Theodore G. Huntington, "Sketches" Porter-Phelps-Huntington Family Papers. Good descriptions of dancing schools appear in the Marion Hopkins Diary, scattered entries between Feb. and Mar., 1850; Milton Reed to Missouri Reed, Nov. 26, 1857, Milton Reed to Missouri Reed, Dec. 18, 1857, Feb. 11, 1858, and Jackson Reed to Missouri Reed, Jan. 10, 1858, all in Reed Family Papers (Historical Society of Cheshire County, Keene, N.H.). On literary societies and reading clubs, see, among many, Thomas Tenney to Bezaliel Smith, Nov. 3, 1825, 825603 (Dartmouth College Library); Mary Hoty Wilson Diary, Aug. 30, 1826, Sept. 28, 1826; Sarah Hazen to Eliza Minot Adams, Nov. 16, 1829, Adams Family Papers; Henry Willard to the Hon. John Willard, Feb. 17, 1849, 849167 (Dartmouth College Library, Hanover N.H.); Agnes Cochran Higginson to Stephen Higginson II, Feb. 21, 1856, Fuller-Higginson Papers. Cultural associations, especially those outside metropolitan areas, have received far less attention from historians than they merit. But see Kelly, *In the New England Fashion*; Larkin, *Reshaping of Everyday Life*, 239–44, 252–56.

15. Elizabeth White Peabody to Mary Jane White, Jan. 16, 1830, Everett-Peabody Family Papers (Massachusetts Historical Society); Marianne Cochran to Agnes Cochran Higginson, Jan. 6, Feb. 10, 1839, Fuller-Higginson Papers. Mrs. Howard was not the only woman in Peabody's Springfield circle to entertain elaborately; in the same letter she described one Bessey Howard, who planned to use her "north parlour for a supper table, the other for her company to sit in, her kitchen for dancing, and bedroom for refreshments" at an upcoming party and another friend who hoped to impress *her* guests with the "great simplicity but real richness" of her furnishings. For further descriptions of Springfield sociability in this period, see Mary Jane White to Charlotte White, July 4, 1830, Everett-Peabody Family Papers. Jack Larkin pointed to the increasing formality of antebellum provincial communities in "The View from New

England: Notes of Everyday Life in Rural America to 1850," *American Quarterly* 34 (Bibliography Supplement 1982): 258.

16. This description of the social lives of Agnes Gordon Higginson and Annie Storrow Higginson is based upon Agnes Cochran Higginson to Stephen Higginson II, Apr. 20, 1854, Dec. 8, 1855, Dec. 28, 1855, Feb. 21, 1856; Agnes Gordon Higginson [Fuller] Diary, 1855–1856; Annie Storrow Higginson to Agnes Gordon Higginson Dec. 9, 1859, all in Fuller-Higginson Papers; Sarah Upton to George Upton, Feb. 9, 1862, Upton Family Papers (New Hampshire Historical Society). See also Georgiana Drake Carpenter to Frank Drake [n.d., c. 1860s], Drake Family Papers (Dartmouth College Library); Henry Hills to Adelaide Spencer, Jan. 12, 1855, Hills Family Papers (Amherst College Archives and Special Collections); Hattie Fuller to Elijah Fuller Mar. 1, 1855, Fuller-Higginson Papers. By the 1850s, the expectation of an active social life was so deeply entrenched in the minds of provincials that a slow season was cause for comment. In 1857, Milton Reed reported because of "hard times," "there does not seem to be a great stock of 'Balls' on hand for Thanksgiving. I have heard of only one or two;" Milton Reed to Missouri Reed, Nov. 26, 1857, Reed Family Papers. See also Harriet Cossit to Lucy Clarke, Nov. 3, 1851, Morris-Clarke Papers (New Hampshire Historical Society); and Hattie Fuller to George Fuller, Jan. 30, 1853, Fuller-Higginson Papers. The impulse to organize more elaborate forms of sociability, especially dances, extended beyond the middle class. For an account a leap-year ball organized by women working in the Lowell textile mills, in which the "ladies . . . asked for the pardners, and paid al[l] the bills, and got up a sleigh ride," see Caroline Wallace to Hannah Dearborn, Mar. 1, 1848, Deerfield Family Papers (New Hampshire Historical Society).

17. Annie Storrow Higginson to Agnes Gordon Higginson, Dec. 9, 1859, Fuller-Higginson Papers. Mary Jane White to Charlotte White, July 4, 1830, Everett-Peabody Family Papers. See also Amelia White Peabody to Mary Jane White, Aug. 1, 1829, Everett-Peabody Family Papers; S. E. Hodges to Katherine Craddoc Hodges, Oct. 22, 1861, Hodges Family Papers; and Mary Ann Webster Sanborn to Achsah Webster, Feb. 25, 1851, Sanborn Family Papers, (Dartmouth College Library). Elizabeth Phelps Huntington referred to the "fashionable dishes" served at a casual Northampton dinner party in 1840. Elizabeth Phelps Huntington to Frederic Dan Huntington, Mar. 18, 1840, Porter-Phelps-Huntington Family Papers.

18. Julietta Penaimen to Jonathan Dorr Bradley, Feb. 18, 1820, Bradley Family Papers (Schlesinger Library), E. Goddard, a young woman travelling through New Hampshire with her father in the early nineteenth century, was less charitable than Penaimen in her assessment of provincial hospitality. E. Goddard Diary, [n.d], 1976–58 (New Hampshire Historical Society). See also Hattie Fuller to Elijah Fuller, Apr. 30, 1854, Fuller-Higginson Papers, for an account of one young Deerfield woman who, in the course of visiting, burst unannounced into the wrong house, where she encountered a scene that "wasn't perfectly proper"; for the young woman and her friends, this was less a faux pas than a source of humor. For historians who describe the growing formality of middle-class sociability, see note 5.

19. Annie Storrow Higginson to Agnes Gordon Higginson, Dec. 9, 1859, Fuller-Higginson Papers.

20. The dinner party is described in Tupper and Brown, eds., *Grandmother Tyler's Book*, 284–91 (quotations at 288, 287, 290).

21. *Hampshire Gazette* (Northampton, Mass.), Apr. 27, 1858, Tasteful weddings could also be compromised by local customs. Following their 1847 wedding, one Claremont, Massachusetts, couple was "serenaded . . . by a band with their guns and ten trumpets until after midnight." The band continued to carouse through the next day, when they made "considerable trouble" at a local store "by blowing out the lights, throwing things about making a noise with their feet & holloring & etc. etc." Philena Hawkes Bodman to Luther Bodman Jr., May 17, 1845, Bodman Family Papers.

22. Not surprisingly, such women were discomfited when others suggested that the pleasures of society occupied too much of their time or played too large a role in their identities. When ten-year-old Lavinia Bailey Kelly devoted too much of her journal to descriptions of her mother's socializing, the older women intervened. "Ma thinks it improper that I should keep a journal of her tea takings," Kelly wrote in 1828, "so all I can say about it is that Mrs. Mead took dinner with Ma and the account was cleverly balanced before sunset." Lavinia Bailey Kelly Journal, Aug. 18, 1828 (New Hampshire Historical Society). Similarly, Marianne Cochran fretted that on an outing of Northampton's walking club in 1838, the aptly named Miss Church seemed to disapprove of her own "free to easy manners . . . I thought she might have joined rather more in our gayety without materially lessening her dignity." Marianne Cochran to Agnes Cochran Higginson, Sept. 16, 1838, Fuller-Higginson Papers.

23. Bushman, *Refinement of America*, 313–31. Karen Halttunen, *Confidence Men and Painted Women*, 98–99, has also pointed to the intersection of politeness and piety in antebellum etiquette manuals.

24. Royall Tyler Daybook, 1817–21, July 15, 1821, Royall Tyler Collection. Mary Palmer Tyler Diary, 1821–1843, Aug. 18, 1822, *ibid.*

25. Elizabeth Phelps Huntington to Mary Dwight Huntington, June 1, 1832, Porter-Phelps-Huntington Family Papers.

26. Elizabeth Phelps Huntington to Frederic Dan Huntington, n.d. [c. 1838], Diary of Elizabeth Whiting Phelps Huntington, *ibid.*

27. Delia Augusta Willis to Eliza Minot Adams, Oct. 11, 1829, Adams Family Papers. For similar accounts of the temptations of society, see Bertha Throop Huntington Common Place Book, May 24, 1839, Porter-Phelps-Huntington Family Papers; Ester Grout Diary May 30, 1830, June 6, 1830, (Pocumtuck Valley Memorial Association); and Louisa Stone to Eliza Wheeler, Oct. 8, 1837, Stone Family Papers (Dartmouth College Library).

28. Adeline Young to Ira Young, Jan. 12, 1833, Adams Family Papers.

29. Diary of Agnes Gordon Higginson [Fuller], 1855–1858, Fuller-Higginson Papers.

30. The sermon and descriptions of the mug and fashion instructions are described in Mrs. Hodges to Katherine Craddoc Hodges, Dec. 17, Mar. 11, 1860, Hodges Family Papers.

31. "Rebecca" to Agnes Gordon Higginson [Fuller], Jan. 11, 1859, Fuller-Higginson Papers. By the mid-nineteenth century, women and men extended the language of Christian faith to describe a variety of earthly connections. On the use of religious language to describe romantic love, see Karen Lystra, *Searching the Heart: Women, Men, and Romantic Love in Nineteenth-Century America* (New York: Oxford University Press, 1989), 237–57; and Kelly, *In the New England Fashion.*

32. Diary of Agnes Higginson [Fuller], Mar. 7–8, 1855, Fuller-Higginson Papers. Maria Clark to Mr. And Mrs. Morris Clark, Aug. 12, 1846, Morris Clark Papers (New Hampshire Historical Society). Compare this to Eliza Minot Adams's 1829 account of a visit with a minister's wife who "appeared tired & woebegone. Surely, minister's wives have trials peculiar to themselves, trials which demand the constant exercise of grace and strength from above." Eliza Minot Adams to Harriet Adams Aiken, June 26, 1829, Adams Family Papers. On the intersection of Christianity and gentility, see Bushman, *Refinement of America*, 313–52. For analysis of the sentimentalization of death in nineteenth-century middle-class culture, see Halttunen, *Confidence Men and Painted Women*, 124–52; David E. Stannard, *The Puritan Way of Death: A Study in Religion, Culture, and Social Change* (New York, 1977), 173–88; and Gary Laderman, *The Sacred Remains: American Attitudes Toward Death, 1799–1883* (New Haven, Conn.: Yale University Press, 1996), 54–62.

33. Diary of Martha Rhoda Wilson, Jan. 4, 1850; Hattie Fuller to Elijah Fuller Mar. 1, 1855. Annie Storrow Higginson to Agnes Gordon Higginson, Dec. 9, 1859; Agnes Cochran Higginson to Stephen Higginson II, Feb. 21, 1856, all three in Fuller-Higginson Papers.

34. Theophilus Thistle, "A Last Word to the Girls," *Hampshire Gazette*, Apr. 20, 1858.

35. Arthur Ames Bliss, ed., *Theodore Bliss; Publisher and Bookseller. A Study of Character and Life in the Middle Period of the XIX Century*, (Northampton, Mass.: Northhampton Historical Society 1911), 37–38; Susan I. Lesley, *Recollections of My Mother* (Boston, 1886), 84; Francis H. Underwood, *Quabbin: The Story of a Small Town with Outlooks upon Puritan Life* (Boston: Press of G. H. Ellis, 1893), 73–74, 99.

36. The creation of the New England myth is particularly well described in Steven Nissenbaum, "New England as Region and Nation," in *All Over the Map: Rethinking American Regions*, ed. Edward L. Ayers et. al. (Baltimore: Johns Hopkins University Press, 1996), 38–61; and Joseph S. Wood, with a contribution by Michael P. Steinetz, *The New England Village* (Baltimore: Johns Hopkins University Press, 1997). My thinking on social networks is influenced by Stuart Blumin, *Emergence of the Middle Class*, 264–65, who defined social networks as "the arrays of interactions characteristically experienced by the members of specific groups of people in their daily rounds—within the home, at work . . . and in whatever other public and private spaces people confront and interact with one another."

37. Tyler's description of Guilford's social scene is quoted in V. S. Hemenway, *Vermont Historical Magazine*, 96. For discussions of the connections between population, economic development, and social structure in New England, see esp. Hal S. Barron, *Those Who Stayed Behind: Rural Society in Nineteenth-Century New England* (New York: Cambridge University Press, 1984); and Robert W. Doherty, *Society and Power: Five New England Towns, 1800–1860* (Amherst: University of Massachusetts Press, 1977).

38. Christopher Clark, *The Roots of Rural Capitalism: Western Massachusetts, 1780–1860* (Ithaca, N.Y.: Cornell University Press, 1990), 264. For other studies that reveal and analyze growing levels of economic inequality in New England's hinterland, see Randolph A. Roth, *The Democratic Dilemma: Religion, Reform, and the Social Order in the Connecticut River Valley of Vermont, 1791–1850* (New York: Cambridge University Press, 1987); Jonathan Prude, *The Coming of the Industrial Order: Town and Factory Life in Rural Massachusetts, 1810–1860* (New York: Cambridge University Press, 1983); and Doherty, *Society and Power*.

39. My description of the occupational structure of the provincial middle class is drawn from Clark, *Roots of Rural Capitalism*; and Prude, *Coming of the Industrial Order*. Significantly, although Clark and, especially Prude, describe the emergence of a rural "working class," they never use the terms "middle class" or "bourgeoisie" when referring to the elites of their communities; instead, they refer to coalitions of merchants, manufacturers, artisans, farmers, and the odd professional. Classic studies of urban middle class formation include Paul E. Johnson, *A Shopkeeper's Millennium: Society and Revivals in Rochester, New York, 1815–1837* (New York: Hill and Wang, 1978); Ryan, *Cradle of the Middle Class*; and Blumin, *Emergence of the Middle Class*.

40. Clark, *Roots of Rural Capitalism*, 264.

41. Harriet F. Wood to Eliza Adams Young, May 24, 1841, Adams Family Papers. For an especially biting description of provincial hierarchies, emphasizing rural folk's pettiness and narrow-mindedness, see Frances Underwood's *Quabbin*. Stuart Blumin, *Emergence of the Middle Class*, 231, argues persuasively that the shift from the "personalized, face-to-face hierarchies of the eighteenth century . . . to the more distant, categorical hierarchies of the nineteenth century" was central to the experience of class in the nineteenth-century city. On the threatening presence of strangers in Northern cities, see Halttunen, *Confidence Men and Painted Women*; and Kasson, *Rudeness and Civility*.

42. Bliss, ed., *Theodore Bliss*, 45.

43. George S. Merriam, ed., *Reminiscences and Letters of Caroline C.* [Clapp] *Briggs* (Boston: Houghton Mifflin, 1897), 60, 58–59, 77, 65.

44. Briggs, *Reminiscences*, 58; Bliss's courtship is described in *Theodore Bliss*, 45–47. It is useful here to compare the Briggs's perceptions of Unitarian fellowship with those of Elizabeth White Peabody, whose husband presided over Springfield's Unitarian congregation. In 1842, the Peabodys hosted a series of parties to "establish a more intimate" relationship with the poorer members of their congregation. In planning the parties, Peabody invited groups of the working men and women who were "in the same circle among themselves, & then add half a dozen or so of our own circle, of such as are disposed to make themselves agreeable to [the working-class congregants]." Peabody's claim that "we never had pleasanter parties" notwithstanding, the degree of division is obvious. In general, the smaller the town, the more democratic and flexible the sociability. Elizabeth White Peabody to Mary Jane White, Mar. 22, 1842, Everett-Peabody Family Papers.

45. This conclusion is congruent with Michael H. Frisch's description of political culture and associational life in antebellum Springfield, Massachusetts, which he characterizes as possessing an "informal community of association, at once structured and deferential and yet fluid, open, and inclusive." Michael H. Frisch, *Town into City: Springfield, Massachusetts, and the Meaning of Community, 1840–1880* (Cambridge, Mass.: Harvard University Press, 1972), 32–49 (quotation at 47–48).

46. Harriet F. Wood to Eliza Adams Young, May 24, 1841, Adams Family Papers.

47. Marianne Cochran to Agnes Cochran Higginson, Feb. 10, 1839, Fuller-Higginson Papers.

48. M. C. Hale to Rev. Bingham Hale, June 24, 1834 (Dartmouth College Library).

49. Joseph Bartlett to Samuel C. Bartlett and Mary Bartlett, Oct. 11, 1847, Bartlett Family Papers (Dartmouth College Library); Merriam, ed., *Reminiscences and Letters of Caroline C. [Clapp] Briggs*, 66. Hard times could make hospitality simpler still. During the 1857 depression, the "gentlemen" of the Brattleboro's Lawrence Water Cure Establishment recast their Wednesday night socials. As Mary Tyler reported, "they are not to have any refreshments—and the Ladies are to agree to have no new dress—but wear such as they have and it is called the 'Hard times club.'" Mary Tyler to Thomas Pickman Tyler, Dec. 1, 1857, Royall Tyler Collection. Nineteenth-century, middle-class provincials were not alone in their enthusiasm for simplicity; city residents idealized simplicity without yoking it to a rural landscape. See David E. Shi, *The Simple Life: Plain Living and High Thinking in American Culture* (New York: Oxford University Press, 1985), 100–24; and Halttunen, *Confidence Men and Painted Women*, 56–91.

7

"In the Sweat of Thy Brow": Education, Manual Labor, and the Market Revolution

Jeffrey A. Mullins

This is emphatically the age of mechanics. Look at the increased power of man as obtained from the development and combination of the powers of mechanism. And yet how many of our mechanics, worthy and good citizens as they are, are mere machines, and know nothing of the principles which they are every day putting into practice. There is much to be done in making our practical mechanics scientific ones also.[1]

At their request, Col. James Madison Porter addressed a crowd of nearly five hundred artisans following their July 4 parade in 1835 through the streets of Easton, Pennsylvania. In his speech to the assembled mechanics, Porter encapsulated many of the concerns that tradespeople had about the network of changes we now label the "market revolution": that manufacturing would shift from a skilled trade to wage slavery, that workers would have to do more work for less pay, and that an unbridgeable chasm would open up between those who worked in industry and commerce and those for whom they worked. In his speech, too, Porter summarized many of the typical responses on the part of nonmanual laborers to such concerns. If they were industrious, artisans would find that "one hour alone, out of the twenty-four, bestowed on the acquisition of scientific knowledge," would bring forth an "astonishing" amount of information and learning. And if they were frugal, saving the "daily expense, which almost every one incurs, of a six-pence," for amusements or drink, then the assembled mechanics could raise over $10,000 a year, enough to construct a Mechanic's Institute, complete with a library and an annual series of edifying lectures "on the various subjects connected with the sciences of Natural Philosophy and the Mechanic Arts." Industrialism, mechanization, displacement of workers, dependence on wage labor, and the other arrangements that came with the market revolution need not be a fear of the resourceful artisan.

As a lawyer, an entrepreneur, and later a judge, James Madison Porter gave advice that was of a piece with the innumerable early nineteenth-century assurances and exhortations to those in economic jeopardy on the part of those who were financially secure. One thing, however, set Porter apart from the majority of those who articulated such advice to the working classes: he put his words into action. As chairman of the board of trustees of Lafayette College, Porter played the leading role in bringing Lafayette College and its manual labor education system to Easton when it opened there in 1832. Porter and the other founders of Lafayette saw it as an antidote to the potential ills of the economic and social changes of the era. Like the other manual labor schools that came into existence across America in the 1820s and 1830s, Lafayette College gave access to education to those who might otherwise be excluded by allowing them to work three hours a day doing agriculture or woodworking, applying their wages toward tuition and living expenses. According to exponents such as Theodore Dwight Weld, the chief agent of the Society for Promoting Manual Labor in Literary Institutions, the manual labor system of education had the additional advantages of promoting cross-class understanding, using physical exercise to avoid the debilitating diseases thought to often accompany a learned lifestyle, fostering independence and self-reliance by having students support themselves and learn a reliable trade in an uncertain economy, and instilling the virtues of masculinity among its students. Despite the promise of personal mobility and social progress offered by the market revolution, contemporaries had grave concerns about its potential to corrupt individuals and to harden social divisions into rigid classes. Manual labor schools, it would seem, were the ideal response to difficulties attending the market revolution.

The story was not so simple, however. The collection of social and economic changes commonly denoted the "market revolution" was bound up with significant changes to the concepts of labor and class and to the cultural practices that constituted these categories.[2] Even as institutions such as

Lafayette College attempted to bolster conventional social norms in the face of economic innovations, the new means they devised to implement their goals often did as much to give shape to emerging concepts of labor, class, and other social norms as they did to preserve those already in play. In particular, four of Lafayette's principal goals stood in a complex relationship to the forces at work in the market revolution: the college's founders and instructors hoped to make education more widely available beyond the sphere of the elite, to give students a "manly" independence that would allow them to weather all economic shifts in the wind, to maintain their health in the face of dissipating effects of a "learned" lifestyle, and to ensure that by earning their keep "in the sweat of thy brow," students would not become estranged from the laboring population that made up the bulk of the country. Along with dozens of other manual labor academies and colleges taking shape across the nation, Lafayette's pursuit of these goals was part of an ambiguous relationship to the sweeping changes afoot in America's economic and social structure, especially the fluctuating understandings of labor and class.

In order to make sense of these changes, we need to expand the political, social, and economic examinations of the market revolution to include the perspective of cultural history. Joyce Appleby has recently called for just such an addition, encouraging historians to engage in a "recovery of meaning" through "cultural analysis" whereby they can delve into the motives and actions that made up Americans' responses to the "crisis of meaning" brought on by the influence of market capitalism. Doing this, in turn, requires several substantial reorientations of our historiographic assumptions. This is not the place for a lengthy methodological disquisition, but the observations of three leading students of culture and history will serve us well in the effort to understand the collection of developments commonly assembled under the heading of the "market revolution." Overarching all these points is a methodological touchstone explicitly identified by two of these scholars on culture—Roger Chartier and Pierre Bourdieu—that "all cultural analysis must take into account [the] irreducibility of experience to discourse." That is, cultural history ought not to treat the world solely as text. Instead, the "fundamental object of a history" lies in "the tension between the inventive capacities of individuals or communities and the constraints, norms, and conventions that limit . . . what is possible for them to think, to express, to do." Applied more specifically to the market revolution, Joyce Appleby has sounded the related theme that "the key issue in the transformation from a traditional to a modern economy lies with the social *response* to innovation" and that historians will best find a common agenda in this field when they look not only at "machinations of power" but also at "vehicles of meaning."[3]

These observations about the irreducibility of experience and the importance of human motivations help shed light on that vein of scholarship that has been concerned with *when* the market revolution—or, in associated literature, "capitalism"—came about. The arrival, existence, and character of a market revolution is to be discovered not only in the material arrangements of society but also in the dynamic between such arrangements and the thoughts and actions of all those people encountering them. In thus exploring the dynamics of the market revolution, we should bear in mind Mary Poovey's observations that ideology (defined as a "system of ideas and institutions") develops "unevenly." Even if one confines one's examination to a particular group (farmers, dock workers, merchants), setting (urban, rural), or region (New England, South), the social and cultural ramifications of the market revolution were "articulated differently by the different institutions, discourses, and practices that it both constituted and was constituted by." There is thus no definitive moment at which one can say that market capitalism prevailed in America at large. Certainly, historians can discern trends and patterns across a given category of experience, for example, planters in the Chesapeake or booksellers in the backcountry. No imperative for a methodology of radical particularity is being suggested here. Historians will, however, need to acknowledge that there are more categories of experience than we have tended to recognize in practice and that only by looking at the particular conditions of constraints and possibility for innovation can we make sense of activity in a given category. As Appleby has suggested, such a history will turn our attention to the "reasons" and "motives" inspiring action in framing historical change, in place of invoking sweeping "causes" to explain change.[4]

The search for motives very quickly raises the question of agency, and this brings us to those methodological observations regarding the debates about whether the spread of a market economy (and its social corollaries) was embraced or resisted by most Americans. Roger Chartier has demonstrated that historians need to understand the wide range of possible "appropriations" of ideas, texts, and practices by individuals and groups who may use them in ways sharply at variance with the intentions of their creators. No single concept or practice, therefore, has a fixed function or significance (although neither is it completely plastic at any given time). In contrast to Charles Sellers's vision of an all-powerful commercial ethos, then, we need to bear in mind that reactions to the market revolution are particular, that they will not follow a uniform development, and that they help constitute the phenomenon itself (and are not simply variations on an overall theme).[5]

Finally, as we search for meaning in the market revolution, we need to be clear about which groups we are investigating, what constraints and imperatives shaped their perceptions, and how their responses to the market revolution realigned the lineaments of their cultural world. In this case, we will be examining what appears to be a liminal zone wherein manual labor schools are employed to create a new kind of professional man. By very explicitly taking cultural norms from both "head" and "hand" workers, manual labor educators such as those at Lafayette College hoped to fashion a new class of men who would partake of the best qualities of each. As Pierre Bourdieu has demonstrated, there is often a strong clustering effect among various social and cultural practices, producing what he has dubbed the *habitus* of a class or group. Thus, if one likes classical music and fine wine, it is likely that one will be drawn to certain other values and practices as well. This gravitational pull among different elements of culture to make up a *habitus* Bourdieu calls "elective affinity," whereby certain people and things appear naturally more attractive than others as a result of a sense of taste that has actually been constituted by one's cultural background.[6]

In the case of Lafayette College and manual labor education movement, its leaders attempted to transform the prevailing understanding of social rank by altering the accepted definition of labor. To do so they appropriated some familiar concepts: the biblical injunction for humankind to "earn thy bread in the sweat of they brow," the educational maxim that only those who had "liberal" or "scientific" knowledge could truly understand the world, the cultural imperatives to be "masculine" and "independent," and a version of the republican goals of civic virtue and cross-class cooperation. As they would discover, however, not all these goals were mutually compatible in the context of early nineteenth-century America. Drawn from different *habitus*, they did not all have an elective affinity for one another. Manual labor educators were well aware of this: they were explicitly trying to reform society in order to permit these disparate values to cohere in a new *habitus*, one that would provide an acceptable response to the problems they perceived as accompanying the market revolution.

Ultimately, the manual labor program at Lafayette College failed within a decade of its initiation, just as it did at nearly every other institution across the nation. What remains, however, are three questions. First, why could the manual labor education movement not sustain itself? Second, in addition to their stated motives, what ideological work on the issue of class did a commitment to manual labor education do for the movement's leaders? Finally, what is the broader significance of this ambivalent response to the concerns attending the market revolution? Following a brief account of the origins and circumstances at Lafayette College, we shall scrutinize the degree and type of success Lafayette had in meeting four of its principal goals. By doing so we can witness how both middling Americans and those whom they were helping achieve such a status grappled with their various—sometimes conflicting—concepts of class and labor. The four goals were expanding access to education and opportunity for advancement, cultivating "useful" citizens, fostering masculine independence, and promoting cross-class understanding. As one of the most systematic and integrated responses to the challenges posed by the market revolution, the manual labor education movement allows us a window into the cultural dynamics surrounding a process that is normally considered for its economic, social, and political aspects. Lafayette College, embodying so many of the central values of this movement, is illustrative of the ways in which cultural values seemingly distinct from the market revolution were ultimately pivotal in determining how many Americans appropriated those aspects of the era's socioeconomic transformation with which they came into contact in their everyday lives.

ENTERING THE MARKETPLACE:
ACADEMIC ACCLAIM AND FINANCIAL STRUGGLE

Throughout its first several decades of existence, Lafayette College continually struggled to reconcile its educational and cultural goals with the imperatives of the market. As we shall see, this struggle was not necessarily one of direct opposites, of pure ideals contending with harsh fiscal realism. Rather, the leaders of the manual education movement sought a catalyst that could transform seemingly fixed and incompatible social elements into components of a stable synthesis. The philosopher's stone of Lafayette's founders was an institution that could make opportunity, utility, masculinity, and social harmony compatible with market forces that tended to promote exclusion, selfishness, effeminacy, and social division. As the alchemists found, however, such a goal could prove elusive, requiring compromise and legerdemain in order to give even the appearance of success. From its founding, we can see some of these tensions already at work in the mission of Lafayette College. Among the elements that made up this unstable compound were Lafayette's location, facilities, student body, curriculum, and relationship to the larger manual labor education movement.

The founders of Lafayette College believed that Easton was an ideal place for their institution. Well aware of the economic changes and "internal improvements" taking place across the nation, those who launched the project were especially sensitive to the need to make this a financially viable endeavor. At the confluence of two navigable rivers (the Delaware and the Lehigh), with daily transportation to both New York and Philadelphia, and a hub of regional stagecoach routes, Easton appeared well situated to attract students from across the region. Furthermore, as a starting point for wagon travel to the expanding West, with up to a thousand wagons departing annually, Easton symbolized the boundary between the settled and the developing parts of the nation. Alternatively, its modest size (3,700 people, in roughly five hundred dwellings, in 1832) and rustic location were potential selling points in a culture that believed that the fashioning of character—be it through education or reform—was best done at a remove from the physical and social dangers inherent in cities. If Lafayette College was designed to respond the concerns about class and labor that were generated by the market revolution, then Easton's role as an inland market hub placed it squarely in the path of such developments.[7]

Lafayette's history, however, did not begin in 1832. Indeed, the college arose from the confluence of two very different educational missions. On the one hand, Eastonians gathered together in 1824 to found a college when the Easton Union Academy closed after thirty years of operation. Inspired by the Marquis de Lafayette's visit to the United States in that year, the town leaders who gathered in White's Hotel on December 24, 1824, resolved to establish a college that would combine a "literary institution" with a military academy and that would bear the name of the Revolutionary War hero. Led by James Madison Porter, this group managed to obtain a charter from the Pennsylvania legislature in 1826, but they had insufficient funds to provide anything more than land and lodging for the college. Any educators who might wish to actually launch the college would have to live off the tuition proceeds and bear the full financial responsibility and risk of regular operations. Not surprisingly, given the marginal profitability of academies and colleges, it was some years before Porter and his comrades found anyone who would accept these terms.

In 1832, Porter learned that Reverend George Junkin might be interested in relocating the Manual Labor Academy of Pennsylvania from its current location in Germantown, just north of Philadelphia. The Manual Labor Academy had been founded by the Presbyterian Church in 1829 as a means of providing healthful and affordable education to young men of modest means intent on joining the ministry. By 1832, however, Junkin's commitment to "Old School" Presbyterian theology ran afoul of the largely "New School" board of trustees. Thus, when the opportunity arose to start a manual labor program at Easton, Junkin readily took it, agreeing to drop any specifically Presbyterian focus, as sectarianism was prohibited by the original college charter. For their part, Porter and company agreed to abandon their hopes of military instruction, allowing the exercise involved in manual labor to substitute as a means of preserving the health and virtue of the students.

Throughout Junkin's attempts to soften the effects of the market revolution on young Americans, he found his educational endeavors themselves plagued by the economic vagaries of the market. When Junkin moved his school from Germantown to Easton, he left behind what would be considered a medium-size school for its day. In the fall of 1830, the Manual Labor Academy had twenty-three students and expected another ten at the beginning of the new term. It occupied a large farmhouse in Germantown, expanded to accommodate thirty-seven students, and added a new shop to house manufacturing operations. By all accounts, the academy was a pedagogical success. As a financial venture, however, the academy suffered from its proximity to Philadelphia. The school was close enough to the metropolitan center that Junkin had to pay city prices for his carpentry supplies, but the school's peripheral location entailed the added cost of transporting first the raw materials and then the finished product to and from the urban market. Combined with the religious sectarian strife, these market circumstances provided ample incentive for Junkin to accept Porter's offer.[8]

The mixture of academic success and fiscal marginality continued at the institution's new location. When Junkin moved his school to Easton, the student body continued to grow: forty-three students from Germantown accompanied him, thirteen more came into the college during the first term, and eleven more were day students, making a total of sixty-seven when Lafayette College opened on May 9, 1832. Whereas the Manual Labor Academy of Pennsylvania had been staffed by Junkin as principal, an assistant teacher, and a farmer, the newly established Lafayette College had three faculty members, including Junkin as president, as well as one person each to supervise the farming and the construction and woodworking labor. What it lacked, however, was a suitable place in which to conduct classes. After beginning its first term in a rented farmhouse on sixty acres of land on the Lehigh River, in 1833 the trustees eventually raised enough money to buy nine acres on a bluff overlooking the town. By the outset of 1834, Lafayette had one building and its grounds but was also $8,000 in debt. As with so many endeavors of the era, social vision came with substantial financial risk.

In terms of curriculum and pedagogy, Lafayette was thoroughly in keeping with the educational norms of its day. The education offered at Easton was designed to reinforce, not challenge, the cultural conventions of the social elite (although this was identified as an active, worthy elite, not a dissipated, useless hierarchy). As we shall see in the next section, to the extent that the three and a half hours a day of manual labor was deployed as a means of changing society, it was to bring it back onto its original course. In keeping with this strain of cultural conservatism, students at Lafayette received a classical education centered on Greek, Latin, mathematics, theology, mental philosophy, and moral philosophy. Junkin took on the usual teaching duties of a college president, serving as professor of mental and moral philosophy. He also taught the courses in logic, rhetoric, and evidences of Christianity. Although Lafayette was nonsectarian, it still had a strong spiritual core, and the day began at 5:00 A.M. with morning prayers. It included as well three and a half hours for study and three hours of recitation.[9]

Where Lafayette branched off from the mainstream of American collegiate education was in its adoption of the manual labor program. As with other manual labor schools across the nation, Lafayette College's reform aspirations were principally social, not curricular, in nature. Among these shared values were those of opportunity, utility, masculinity, and social harmony already mentioned. These and other values of the manual labor education movement gained further prominence shortly before the opening of

Lafayette College through the newly formed Society for Promoting Manual Labor in Literary Institutions. The society was formed in July 1831, when a number of the nation's most prominent educators and reformers gathered "under the conviction that a reform in our seminaries of learning was greatly needed, both for the preservation of health and for giving energy to the character by habits of vigorous and useful exercise."[10] Among its founders were Yale President Jeremiah Day, education reformers William Woodbridge and Thomas Gallaudet, and abolitionists Joshua Leavitt and Lewis Tappan.[11] Its most visible representative was Theodore Dwight Weld, who traveled around the country giving lectures and visiting manual labor institutions to report on their progress and methods. While we shall examine both the values of the movement and Lafayette's relation to the larger movement in the next section, the important point here is that the educational project at Easton was part of a larger national trend, one that appealed to students, faculty, and trustees because of its synthesis of cultural goals and fiscal innovation.

Easton was by no means the only representative of this trend in the region. As it did in New England and the expanding West, the manual labor education movement caught hold in Pennsylvania. Indeed, with Philadelphia as a site of radical labor activity that often included demands for greater educational opportunities, the plan of having students work in artisanal shops or on farms in order to offset their expenses was especially popular, and Pennsylvania became one of the leading states in the development of the manual labor movement.[12] After the Manual Labor Academy opened at Germantown in 1829, both Bristol College and Jefferson College opened in 1830, and a number of other institutions followed suit.[13] Indeed, the state legislature heard arguments for the benefits of the manual labor system in 1832, and the following year Representative Benjamin Matthias proposed a state-sponsored manual labor program.[14] Though Matthias's bill was narrowly defeated, the 1834 Pennsylvania common school law allowed for manual labor along with intellectual and moral instruction.[15] This movement had some longevity in Pennsylvania, and as late as 1847 the Farmer's High School was established on a manual labor basis.[16] Lafayette College, then, was in tune with many of the same larger social trends that helped spawn the manual labor education movement and helped launch this movement in the mid-Atlantic region.

A NEW KIND OF STUDENT: LAFAYETTE, CLASS VALUES, AND LABOR IDEOLOGY

Having reviewed Lafayette's early circumstances, we need to ask how successful Junkin, Porter, and others were in bringing to life their vision of an appropriate response to the market revolution. In many ways, the early years of Lafayette College—and its prior Manual Labor Academy incarnation—seemed to fulfill the stated goals of its leaders. By at least four measures, there was reason to believe that the rhetoric and reality of Lafayette had converged. First, Lafayette was in fact attracting the kind of students its founders had stated were their main audience. Second, students were indeed engaged in "useful" labor, first building the college edifice and then engaging in farming and carpentry. Third, both the physical exertion and the accompanying trade skills worked toward bringing Lafayette students into line with the ideal of masculinity that so concerned contemporaries. Finally, there were promising signs that the manual labor curriculum, in which students learned to "earn thy bread in the sweat of thy brow," would help diminish the gap between the educated elite and the rank-and-file laboring population. Taken together, Lafayette's exertions in these four areas indicate a deep concern with educating a new type of "learned" professionals, one that would encompass not merely "head" workers but "hand" workers as well. Educators believed that such a new category of workers was necessitated by the market revolution. For Junkin, Porter, and the other leaders of the new college, the goal was not merely to expand the number of places available to Americans for higher learning but to do so in a way that furthered a particular vision of American society.

In understanding this vision, we need to understand something about varied components of the nascent middle-class culture of the period. On the one hand, a number of historians have argued some version of Charles Sellers's position that the "so-called middle class was constituted not by mode and relations of production but by ideology." Though generally not employing as stark a picture of ideological warfare as does Sellers, scholars such as Stuart Blumin, Richard Bushman, Kenneth Cmiel, Karen Haltunnen, and Mary Ryan have noted the importance of cultural attainments and presentation in the crystallization of a middle class in antebellum America.[17] On the other hand, the existence and fervency of the manual labor education movement demonstrates some Americans' great unease with the apparent spread of educational and professional opportunity, particularly with the growth of "head" work occupations. Even as they hoped to make education more relevant to—and more attainable for—a different class of students, the instructors, trustees, and supporters of manual labor institutions wished for their charges to shun many aspects of elite life, such as effeminacy and dissipation.[18]

What set the manual labor education movement apart from these other forces of cohesion for a nascent "middle class" is the fact that rather than emphasizing the difference or distinction between the genteel and the prosaic, manual labor educators underscored common interests among the learned and the laborers. Most antebellum writers and speakers stressed the reasons why farmers, artisans, the poor, and others ought to adopt practices quickly becoming associated with the middle class, often using the rhetoric of "science" as an explanation of the "universal" value of such practices. Manual labor educators reversed this equation—at least in part—by having aspirants to gentility plow, hoe, saw, hammer, and generally sweat their way through the enculturating process of a "liberal" education.

Although we shall return to the question of just how universal (in terms of both accessibility and adherence) were the values propagated by institutions such as Lafayette, a note about the methodology of studying class, social reform, and the market revolution will be helpful here. It would be easy to underscore the ways in which the manual labor education movement fell far short of a thoroughgoing reconfiguration of society and its inequalities, such as was attempted by communitarian movements such as Owenism or Fourierism. Likewise, it is possible to argue that many middling reformers did as much to solidify their own class position as they did to erase class divisions. We must acknowledge both of these points, but we must also not rest with such critiques. To do so would be to fail to answer the call for a history of "motives." Before we can truly understand the meaning of any social movement or cultural trend, we must understand the reasons why people participated in it. To fail to do this, to let social structural explanations entirely displace an understanding of what people believed they were doing, would be to substitute our own worldview in place of that which we are trying to evaluate. With this in mind, we must first reconstruct the aims of the manual labor education movement before we can assess either the success or the significance of these goals. That said, we can now turn to an analysis of the four goals already outlined.

In order to give form to their vision of a new hybrid professional, Lafayette's leaders first had to attract students to their institution, preferably students who came from socioeconomic backgrounds that would not generally allow for a collegiate education. Much of the evidence indicates that they were in fact attracting the kind of students they claimed to wish to serve. These students, having already started their careers and generally paying their own way, are what present-day educators often refer to as "nontraditional" students. The kinds of students whom the founders of Lafayette College wished to attract were a function of the larger goals of the manual labor education movement. A larger portion of the population would need to be educated if the republican experiment was to succeed. Although schools and colleges were proliferating in the 1820s and 1830s as a result of the work of education reformers across the nation, manual labor school reformers believed that these new institutions still excluded the vast majority of the population. The cost of tuition, room, board, and fees at most colleges and academies was too much for any but the most elite to afford, costing between $100 and $200 exclusive of expenses for travel to, clothing for, and leisure at such institutions. Roughly 1 percent of American families could afford to give their children such an experience.

The social consequences of America's exclusive system of higher education were made clear in 1833 by Theodore Dwight Weld, the spokesperson for the Society for Promoting Manual Labor in Literary Institutions. In the first annual report of the society, Weld was emphatic on the point that under the present education system, "nineteen twentieths of our population are shut out from the advantages of education in the higher branches," and since this excluded many from social advancement, "society is divided into *castes*." This inequity had grave consequences for the future of the nation:

> The laboring classes become hewers of wood and drawers of water for the educated. The two parties stand wide asunder, no bond of companionship uniting them, no mutual sympathies incorporating them into one mass, no equality of privileges striking a common level for both. The chasm between them, even in this republican government, already yawns deep and broad; and if it be not speedily bridged, by bringing education within the reach of the poor, it will widen into an impassable gulf, and our free institutions, our national character, our bright visions of the future, our glory and our joy, will go down with it.[19]

Even as it allowed for certain expanded opportunities for some individuals to exchange their labor or goods for cash, the market revolution created a system wherein for most people such limited opportunities were dwarfed by the overall structural division between those with ample resources and those without. For Weld, education was an ideal point at which to heal this rift.

The trustees at Lafayette harbored similar sentiments. Shortly before the release of Weld's report, they argued that theirs was "the only plan whereby classical and scientific attainments can be brought to the door of the poor as well as the rich." By keeping their total expenses for tuition, room, and board for the two terms (forty-six weeks) between $86 and $109 (depending on board arrangements) and by allowing students to work to pay for up to $46 of this, Lafayette opened up collegiate education to an audience that could not otherwise afford it. At this time, the most expensive colleges had total annual expenses near double those of Lafayette, and even the institutions with rates closer to Lafayette's did not provide any means for offsetting the cost.[20]

Lafayette's leaders saw their mission to expand access to higher education not simply as an end in itself but as an explicit means of adapting to the changes associated with the market revolution. Indeed, they believed that the boom in education and opportunity that accompanied the notable economic and political changes of the 1820s and 1830s could be as harmful as it might be helpful if not properly directed. During this period, there was an explosion in the number of academies and colleges dotting the nation. A young man's lifetime of education was likely to be wasted, however, if there were not changes made to the manner of education. Reverend Junkin announced what was at stake in his 1834 inaugural speech at the opening of the new campus on the heights above Easton:

> Should the love of gain, for example, become strong and demand frequent indulgence, it will carry off the mind ever and anon into speculations of money, calculations of profit, until it degenerates into mere avarice; one of the foulest passions that degrade the human character. Thus the man sets up his gods of gold. He sees nothing, he hears nothing, he thinks of nothing but percentage and bonds and mortgages. With him the sum and perfection of education is the art of getting money.[21]

The obsession with the possibilities for substantial improvement in one's economic status that attended the speculation and entrepreneurship of the market revolution, on this account, created a fundamentally different type of student than that which prevailed in earlier generations. Junkin and other manual education leaders worried that young men just gaining access to such entrepreneurial possibilities would be particularly susceptible to set financial gain above all else. In order to secure and maintain a healthy, virtuous, and productive republic, education did not simply need to expand; it needed to be changed to address this new student emerging from a new socioeconomic milieu. Lafayette proposed to offer just such changes.[22]

That there was a need and a desire for such changes is evidenced by the wide draw Lafayette enjoyed: students found the college's offer quite appealing. Lafayette was often in the position of having to turn students away for lack of dormitory space, as students came not only from Pennsylvania but also from Georgia, Maryland, New Jersey, Tennessee, and New Hampshire. Furthermore, the composition of the student body in the early years of Lafayette suggest that it lived up to the first ideal of manual labor education, that of giving producers a chance at higher education. The best evidence for this are the student records kept by the Manual Labor Academy, which supplied the first cohort of students to Lafayette. These records indicate that students came from "hand" work backgrounds and that they had typically already begun their working lives prior to coming to the Academy. In 1830, for example, the students at the Academy ranged in age from fifteen to twenty-eight, with the average age being nearly twenty. This was far above the typical age of students at nonmanual labor institutions, which commonly had youths of fourteen and fifteen and often would not accept anyone beyond their early twenties.[23] The student records also indicate that over two-thirds had been farmers or artisans before arriving at the Academy.[24] Many of the students who first arrived at Lafayette, then, were not of the same sort as would be found in the nation's more established colleges.

The records of the backgrounds of the following group of students (who started their higher education at Easton) are not quite as thorough, but even after the initial cohort passed through Lafayette, there is both statistical and anecdotal evidence to indicate the modest origins of the college's charges. Furthermore, they underscore the faculty and trustees' observations that most students paid for their own education rather than having it paid for by their parents (as was typically the case at other colleges). In his memoirs, David Coulter recalled, "I had never been from home more than thirty miles before—had never been out of my own native State of Delaware." Coulter arrived at Lafayette in 1833 at the end of the winter term, and Junkin gave him work in the garden during the vacation. Two years into his studies, Coulter's finances required him to leave Lafayette to teach school, but he later returned to finish up his education. Even so, it was necessary for Junkin to recommend him to the Presbyterian Church's Board of Education to receive $75 a year of "assistance." Coulter noted, "I also received some assistance in clothes and money from the ladies of the Presbyterian church of Lewistown and Cool Spring." Even so, in 1838 Coulter realized that in "my final settlement of expenses at the College I found that I was a little in arrears," and he had to borrow money temporarily to make up the difference. All told, it took him five full years to work his way through college. Already launched into the working world and coming from modest backgrounds, students in the early years of Lafayette often did not have the kind of family network from which they could draw financial backing.

Lafayette's second goal—to make students "useful citizens" of the republic—was a response to a widespread concern over who was a "useful" or "productive" citizen. Such a concern had been a part of literate discourse on the part of intellectuals and political leaders for some time. As Martin Burke has demonstrated, however, by the beginning of the 1830s "the question of who constituted the productive and unproductive classes had moved from the technical discourse of college professors to the wider arena of political debate." For the workingmen's parties that blossomed during the 1820s, the term "producing class" was limited to those who literally made something tangible. Merchants, manufacturing entrepreneurs, lawyers, bankers, and related occupations did not count. On this view, America was defined in part by class antagonism—not everyone shared the same socioeconomic interests. Given their perception of this divide, workingmen's parties believed that more producers should be involved in political affairs. This is what gave rise to the mechanic's institutes that Porter mentioned that would help artisans understand the broader context of their world.[25]

The social model of class antagonism found its counterpart in the belief in an underlying harmony of social and economic interests among all citizens no matter what their occupation or level of wealth. Proponents of this latter view noted that "producer" ought to be given a wider meaning so as to include anyone who added value to society. This perspective would broaden the definition to include a variety of professionals and potentially everyone working in any endeavor. Such a view emphasized the fundamental shared interests of all members of society. On this view, social harmony was of paramount value. As James Madison Porter's July 4 speech indicates, class harmony was a value held by many of Lafayette's leaders. As Martin Burke has argued, it was during this period that members of the professions created "a durable convention in public discourse that represented the United States as a society formed by classes but freed from class conflict."[26] One way in which they did this was to replace the language of productivity with that of utility, and the manual labor education movement's focus on "useful labor" supported this shift.

Lafayette's president had long experience in making students useful. Even before he took over the leadership of the Manual Labor Academy of Pennsylvania, Reverend Junkin had trained students for the ministry in his own home, where he took them under his roof in exchange for several hours of daily labor. This practice carried over to the Academy, where in 1830 the trustees reported that while the "studies of these pupils are the same as those in other academies or seminaries . . . the hours of recreation are not hours of waste and idleness." Rather, at their institution these hours were "employed in useful bodily labour by every student."[27] When they made the journey from Germantown to Easton with Junkin in the spring of 1832, Lafayette's first students were quickly put to work constructing buildings to supplement those on the rented farm. When the college acquired its own plot the next year, the students were likewise employed in constructed the three-story main edifice and the outlying buildings. Once this was complete, students labored in the woodworking shop and in the college's agricultural plots.

The third core value that Lafayette's directors promised to promote was a "masculine independence." The rhetoric of masculinity was common in both the eighteenth and the nineteenth century, and descriptors such as "manly" sprinkle both the correspondence and the printed works of the period. The notion of what constituted manly virtue, however, was neither fixed over time nor agreed on at any given time by all spheres of society. As at other academies and colleges, the young men at Lafayette fostered male sociability through literary and debating clubs—the Franklin and the Washington Societies—each of which had its own meeting space and libraries. Without banishing this more elite form of masculinity, however, manual labor education leaders called for a more visceral form of male identity, one typically associated with laboring ranks. As we shall see, the desire to promote a sweaty masculinity in a starched-collar milieu stemmed from another response to the market revolution, the crystallization of free-labor ideology.

Some of the rationales for a more corporeal masculinity are evident in the advocacy of the region's promoters of the manual labor education system. Episcopalian minister Stephen Tyng, for example, was a supporter of the original Manual Labor Academy in Germantown, on the board of managers of the Society for Promoting Manual Labor in Literary Institutions, and a member of the Episcopal Education Society of Pennsylvania. In 1830, Tyng outlined to a Philadelphia audience "a plan for a self-supporting, or manual labour institution," noting that the cycle of financial dependency directly undermined masculine independence. Tyng observed that poor and middling students attending standard institutions often had to take out loans, later forcing them to earn money far beyond their actual expenses in order to pay back these debts. Tyng charged that this plan, "by educating the poor in the sedentary and luxurious habits of the rich, entails all the destructive habits of life upon them which wealth is supposed to generate." In addition to leading men into immoral lives, "it enervates them and makes them incompetent for active exertion," thereby preventing them from fulfilling their duties even if they should pursue the correct path. Alternatively, Tyng argued that manual labor education allowed the "youth [to] leave the institution with an independent mind," one of the keys to self-government, and thus he "can eat his bread with gladness and singleness of heart, because no consuming tithe is urging its demands, for those who have paid for his education, and who think as they look upon him, that they have made him what he is."[28] The critique of social elites as physically debilitated—a debility leading to moral ennervation and effeminacy—was a staple of the manual labor movement. Indeed, as I have argued elsewhere, it is a central component of many strains of antebellum social reform.[29]

The halls of Lafayette College likewise resonated with the critique of effeminate professionals and the promotion of a new kind of professional, one prepared to meet the challenges of the new world created by the market revolution. In this view, self-possession was composed partly of independence of mind and partly of independence of wallet. Theodore Porter, Lafayette's chairman of the board of trustees, told students, "The knowledge of how to earn your own bread, under any vicissitudes of life, is calculated to bear a man up under its ills, and give him a feeling of independence, which the mere learned book worm, or citizen, can never attain."[30] Thus, gaining "useful knowledge" in school and engaging in a physical trade as a means of masculine identity and physical exercise while there were central goals of the manual labor system.

In fashioning the emphasis on these goals, manual labor advocates were influenced by free-labor ideology, which quickly became one strong influence on the discourse of masculinity in America in the 1820s and 1830s. The ideology of free labor was inspired by changing work relations that narrowed previously standard opportunities for social and economic advancement and by a growing concern about the economic and moral implications of slavery. This ideology idealized the white man who either owned and operated his own means of production or else worked in a shop or factory until he gained the skill and resources to be an independent producer. A key theme was production—production of tangible goods through physical labor. Such qualities were set against the "indolence" of moneyed elites and the "intellectual labor" of the traditional professions since both groups relied on the producing classes for their basic needs yet failed to grant those involved in physical toil either the social respect or the economic benefits due to them. Free-labor ideology entailed a commitment to the legal independence of the worker and to the need for the worker to be economically independent so he could be a free moral agent.[31] This latter concept, this stress on the need for individuals to be "self-governed" or "self-possessed" so that they might be individual moral agents and competent citizens of the republic, was a vitally important one for the ideology of free labor.[32]

The manual labor education movement was not alone in the 1820s and 1830s in stressing that a central component of masculinity was physical health and vigor. Academies and colleges across the country, wealthy and modest, were adopting some combination of physical exercise and dietary reform. Indeed, consciousness of the need for such measures extended well beyond educational institutions and into public discussions of the state of the nation. On his arrival at Lafayette, for example, David Coulter told Reverend Junkin, "I had hoped for the ministry but did not know if my health would be impaired by the close study it required." Neither the Manual Labor Academy nor Lafayette College was an exception to the nationwide push for physical health and vitality, and both institutions often noted the health status of each student over the course of the academic year. In their annual reports, the trustees made a point of the importance of preserving health since for that student for whom "death should not prove to be the seal of his diploma, he draws out a miserable existence," continually ill. Rather, "*regular, daily, systematic* exercise secures health of body, and by necessity health of mind."[33]

In their participation in the widespread concern about physical culture, however, manual labor schools took a unique path, combining the goal of masculinity with their aim to promote cross-class understanding. Whereas other schools typically adopted gymnastics as the route to student health and vigor, manual labor advocates viewed such exercises as both effeminate and selfish, the very embodiment of some of the perceived problems entailed by the market revolution, and the antithesis of the necessary solution to these problems. When he was the director of the Pennsylvania Manual Labor Academy, John Monteith shared the bias against gymnastics and other "contrived" activities usually adopted by more elite schools and called for labor that would be useful and fit a man for real work.[34] Likewise, in his *Report of the Society for Promoting Manual Labor*, Theodore Dwight Weld criticized gymnastics on four counts: "It is dangerous"; "It is unnatural"; "It is unphilosophical"; and "Gymnastic exercises excite aversion and contempt in the public mind." On this last count, Weld brought home the point of needing to support a producer identity, observing that the "laboring classes, who make up nine tenths of the community, are disgusted and repelled by the grotesque and ludicrous antics of the gymnasium." The reason for this is that "the exercise benefits *only the student*; [it] makes no contribution to the resources of his country, and no addition to the means of human subsistence."[35] Gymnastics was selfish, lacking in utility, effeminate, and unpatriotic.

At Lafayette College, President Junkin echoed the critique of gymnastics on the grounds of its inutility and solipsism: "We propose to direct the exertions of bodily power, which must be made in order to [preserve] health, to *profitable use.* Instead of putting a youth to the ignoble service of beating the air, we put a hammer into his hand."[36] Like Weld, who commented that "the time spent in [gymnastics] affords *no pecuniary advantage*," Junkin wished to link education and physical health with a form of financial prosperity that would further the welfare of the nation.

Porter, Junkin, and other manual labor advocates argued that such pecuniary advantage could best be reached by an education that also served to foster cross-class understanding. Specifically, they made the case that America needed a greater merger between the abstract or "scientific" understanding of the world generally found among the educated elite and the practical know-how generally found among artisans. As proponents of "useful labor"—in school and out—Lafayette's leaders underscored the *practical* need for some theoretical knowledge so that workers could better direct their practical efforts at production. In his promotional pamphlet, Junkin asked the rhetorical question, "Is the practical artizan [*sic*], for the most part, ignorant of the science whose principles he applies; and the scientific man equally ignorant of the habits of detail in its application?" Such differences in education were at the root of pernicious social divisions:

> It is notorious that learned men are looked upon by the multitude, as ignorant and to a great degree useless. And this feeling is not productive of those intercourses which would cement society but the reverse. Now the system we advocate takes away this feeling, for it makes a practical artizan [*sic*] of the scientific man, and brings him upon common ground with some class among the men of detail. Its influence in cementing the bonds of society, is not without practical benefit.[37]

Social harmony thus required a conjoining of mental and intellectual labor, one best brought about by the manual labor system of education. In Porter's July 4 speech to Easton's artisans, he stressed the need for them to learn the "science" behind their practice, suggesting the specific means of establishing a mechanic's institute. Conversely, schools such as Lafayette were meant to create a new kind of professional who would have a facility with the practical skills associated with manual labor. By doing so, Lafayette and its kindred institutions promoted work that was both practical and profitable, and they helped heal some of the rifts that were developing as a result of the commercialization of American society.

In light of the opening observations about the uses of cultural history, we can reach some important conclusions from the efforts of the manual labor movement leaders to promote their four goals of expanding educational opportunity, engaging students in useful labor, promoting masculine independence, and building cross-class understanding. Like some of figures identified by Charles Sellers and other historians, they wished to preserve some of the values that had prevailed prior to the market revolution; but they did not do so in any of the ways typically mentioned by proponents of the capitalism-as-forced-change model of historical explanation. Whether real or imagined, the image of earlier generations earning their own keep through physical exertion, thereby embodying republic principles of both masculinity and independence, was indeed a strong motivation for the manual labor education movement. They did not hope, however, to preserve these values by a simple-minded conservatism, a stubborn resistance to all change. The meaning that educators such as Junkin gave to the market revolution is quite different from either a clear celebration of expanded opportunity or a Cassandra cry against these innovations. This is so because, to borrow Mary Poovey's phrasing, "what may look coherent and complete in retrospect was actually fissured by competing emphases and interests."[38] One's perception of and reaction to the changes brought under the heading of the market revolution would vary widely, depending on one's connection to different institutions, groups, and discussions. Furthermore, even allowing for the normal range of variation within any historical category, these different reactions cannot be comprehended under the dual rubric of pro- or antimarket revolution. Understanding Americans' encounter with the market revolution requires understanding their responses to perceived changes, and the shape of these responses was substantially dependent on types of cultural resources—institutions, beliefs, practices—that individuals and groups chose to appropriate. In the remainder of this chapter, we shall further examine what manual labor education leaders chose to appropriate, what motivated them to do so, and why their efforts to bridge the gap between what they saw as two distinct social worlds failed.

EDUCATING FOR CLASS: FAILURES OF THE MOVEMENT

In 1839, after seven years in Easton and three years before that in Germantown, Lafayette's manual labor program shut down, leaving the institution to carry on as a conventional college. President Junkin wrote to the board of trustees that after "nine years of experience in conducting Manual Labor operations, in connexion with study" he had arrived at the conclusion that the system was not economically feasible, at least not at a large institution. In the years since the trustees had placed the financial responsibility for the regular operations of Lafayette on Junkin's shoulders, he had paid out $10,020.52 in wages to students while at the college, of which "one third was in excess above the actual value of labor." Junkin explained that he found himself in this situation as a result of keeping the overgenerous pay scale that he found in place when he took over running the Manual Labor Academy from its previous leader. Ultimately, this burden became too much to bear, and the trustees concurred with Junkin's decision to drop the manual labor part of Lafayette's curriculum. By the early 1840s, a similar sequence of events had played itself out at manual labor schools across the country.[39]

The financial failure of the manual labor education system, however, still leaves unanswered the question of the efficacy of the pedagogy itself. If we can identify some successes on the part of manual labor movement leaders, we also have to acknowledge that in some deep sense the movement failed. The attempt by manual labor leaders to appropriate elements from the *habitus* of both manual and nonmanual labor culture in order to reshape American society seems to have entailed too many tensions. The participating schools did indeed expand educational opportunity. This was within limits, however, and as we shall see, the results of this expansion were ironic. The drive to promote useful labor was less successful since the utility of the labor while in school was questionable, and the near universal flight from labor following school was unquestionable. As a corollary, the attempt to fashion a hybrid masculinity— one with independence and exertion yet allowing for professional endeavor— failed. If nascent middle-class professionals were criticized for their emulation of nonmanual labor of the effeminate elite, the evidence is overwhelming that this critique was not strong enough to keep many people from pursuing the expanding sphere of "head" work. Finally, the attempt at cross-class understanding enjoyed little success either on the part of Lafayette students or among those manual laborers who were acquainted with them. On closer examination, it appears that the manual labor education died out because the foundational ideological goals of the movement were compromised by competing ideological commitments. Even as educators were urging their charges to adopt the practices and attitudes of manual laborers, they were also instilling in their students core values that would lead them to shun both manual labor and those who performed it.

We can best assess Lafayette's success in attaining its first two goals of expanding access to education and engaging students in useful labor by looking at them in conjunction. As part of this, in order to discover what forces might be at work in the paradoxical outcome of students' education at Lafayette, we would do well to begin by looking at what kinds of transformations happened to the student body of the college. When students entered both the Manual Labor Academy and Lafayette College in the early 1830s, they tended to come from modest backgrounds. In 1830, there were twenty-three students at the Manual Labor Academy. Of the nineteen students whose occupations were identified, nine (47 percent) were artisans prior to coming to the school, and four (21 percent) had been farmers. Two (10 percent) had been in entrepreneurial endeavors, one (5 percent) was a clerk, and three (15 percent) were the sons of merchants. Their average age was nineteen and a half, and most had already begun their working lives before coming to the school.[40] While there was some shift away from the manual trades, later cohorts of entering students were still largely from such backgrounds, and most of these students went on to Easton when the school became Lafayette College.[41]

In 1836, four men graduated from Lafayette, and forty-three nongraduating students and thirty-six preparatory students finished their time there. Looking at this cohort sheds some light on the role Lafayette College played in forming their ideas about class and the appropriate occupations for those trained by the manual labor system. All four of the full graduates went on to distinguished careers. George Washington Kidd became a sugar dealer in the South, eventually becoming secretary of the Board of Trade and Cotton Exchange in Houston. David Moore soon became deputy superintendent of public schools of Pennsylvania for half a decade and then taught at a number of schools, including one that he founded. James Beverlin Ramsey was ordained at the Princeton Theological Seminary, then undertook a stint of missionary service among the Choctaw Indians before settling down in Virginia as principal of the Lynchburg Female Seminary and an author of religious texts. Finally, Nathaniel Barret Smithers pursued a career in law, then in politics, first becoming clerk of the Delaware House of Representatives, then secretary of state for Delaware, before representing that state in Congress and finishing his career as a bank president.[42]

Even among those young men who did not complete the full course of study at Lafayette, there is a marked propensity to enter into occupations that were not at all connected to physical labor. Of the forty-three nongraduating students, thirty (70 percent) went into the traditional professions (sixteen ordained ministers, nine lawyers, four physicians, and one who was both a physician and a minister). Among this number was a member of Congress and two members of state legislatures. Three others (7 percent) became merchants. None went on into farming, and only one (2 percent) entered the artisanal trades (becoming a printer). The fate of six is unknown. After they left

Lafayette, twenty-four (55 percent) went on to other colleges, most receiving degrees.[43]

Finally, for those thirty-six students finishing in 1836 who were not pursuing collegiate studies but were rather in the "preparatory department" (loosely analogous to present-day high school), there was a similar occupational trend. Not as much is known about these preparatory students, but of the nineteen for whom information survives, six (31 percent) went into the traditional professions (three ministers, two physicians, and one lawyer) and five (26 percent) pursued entrepreneurial endeavors. Two (10 percent) became artisans (a saddler and a confectioner), one (5 percent) became a farmer, and five (26 percent) went into assorted other occupations (most of which might be called "new middle class," such as bank clerk and railroad conductor).[44]

In light of this information about the fate of Lafayette College graduates, we need to reconsider the claims of the institution's leaders. Doing so, it is not at all clear that they were in fact creating a new kind of professional, one who came from a nonelite background and who would engage in endeavors that were "useful" in some sense more limited than the all-inclusive meaning ascribed to this term by elite apologists for class divisions. From the evidence, then, it appears that despite their manual labor backgrounds, on the whole these students were clearly not destined for manual labor futures.

The fact that Lafayette helped convert students into precisely the kind of professionals that leaders of the manual labor education movement often attacked was not an accident. Rather, this conversion was the result of conceptual tensions that were inherent in the manual labor mission. On the one hand, we have to conclude that Junkin, Porter, and other manual labor education leaders were genuinely interested in furthering the goals of the movement. While many socially prominent figures of the period merely gave lip service to such goals, people such as Junkin devoted most of their waking hours and a good bit of their own money to achieving these aims. It is highly improbable that anyone would go to such extremes without a firm commitment to the ideology of manual labor education. On the other hand, it is quite likely that people such as Junkin and Porter had multiple ideological commitments. While they may indeed have wished for genuine cross-class understanding and for a new kind of professional who would have a physical foundation for virtue, they were also members of a learned elite culture in which membership was at least as dependent on one's gentility of mind and manners as it was on one's occupation and financial standing. Unless they chose to simply turn their back on this world, educators such as Reverend Junkin had to reconcile the radical antielite implications of their movement with the fundamental assumptions about what constituted a complete education. Conceptually, manual labor school leaders understood that to merely inculcate their students with the gentility requisite for business or the professions would be to replicate the existing class divisions, and so they strove to tutor their charges in all the values already discussed. In practice, however, these educators had to find a lingua franca among the various social ranks, and in their efforts to do so they nearly always fell back onto what they knew best. Thus, even as it attempted to heal the rift between classes associated with the market revolution, the manual education movement furthered the process of class differentiation.[45]

Seen in the light of conflicting ideological commitments, we can better understand the failure to meet the first two goals—expanding educational access and promoting "useful" labor—by examining Lafayette's efforts to achieve the third and fourth aims—fostering masculine independence and cross-class understanding. When we turn to these latter goals, we find that the messages that Junkin delivered directly to his students were rather different than the messages conveyed in venues such as the trustees' annual reports or Weld's *Report*. In the material that follows, we can witness both the struggle in the mid-1830s to reconcile the conflicting cultural imperatives of the manual labor education movement and the eventual triumph by the 1840s of an increasingly hypostatized notion of class over the understanding of useful labor as entailing physical exertion.

We can witness this dynamic by returning to the cohort of students who finished their education at Lafayette in 1836. On their graduation, President Junkin sent them off into the world with the advice that they and others should not disparage literary men. He counseled that while literature, as a "monopoly," had the potential of "degenerating into an aristocracy" if not secured by "its appropriate checks and balances,"

> the cure for the evil does not lie in ignorance. He who opposes liberal education under the apprehension that he thereby diminishes class, has forgotten the first lesson of republicanism, viz. that virtue and intelligence constitute its basis. On the contrary the multiplication of literary men—especially if they have

formed other habits of friendly alliance with the labouring population—proportionally diminishes this dangerous tendency. . . . Hence for your country's welfare, we would that the habits you have formed, of viewing manual labour as honourable, should go with you through life; thus you become so many cords binding the extremes of society together. Let your conduct tell your fellow-citizens everywhere, that you esteem literary pursuits more honourable than manual labor, only because they enable you to contribute more efficiently to the public good.[46]

This passage is replete with evidence of the conceptual tensions that plagued the manual labor education movement. Most obviously, even as Junkin urged a respect for the laboring classes, he implicitly degraded them by his remark that Lafayette's graduates would be able to *better* serve the republic in their literary pursuits than was possible through physical endeavors. Here Junkin believed that if his students projected this message to physical laborers, it would be well received, understood as an overture of goodwill and cooperation.

Such a message was not well received, however. Part of the reason for this is that the entire message was based on a highly contentious assumption, one that seemed to undermine many of the stated goals of the manual labor education movement. In choosing the cords that would bind "the extremes of society together," leaders of the movement typically assumed that the most appropriate lineaments of this new composite would be those of the educated gentility. Even as they critiqued many elites for their unhealthful physical habits and moral dissipation, educators such as Junkin also unquestioningly adopted the norms of a "liberal" or "scientific" education. This was the education that was suitable for everyone, and if it happened to look surprisingly like the standard collegiate education already in place, then it was the laborer and tradesman—not the genteel professional—who would have to change in order to accommodate themselves to this solution to the nation's ills.

The goal of the manual labor education movement was to synthesize two very different types of education—and two very different types of people—in order to address the social and economic ills that attended the market revolution. In the early republic, "liberal" and "scientific" were often used synonymously in an educational context. Both terms referred to knowledge of the natural and moral laws that structured and organized the world, standing in opposition to mere "practical" knowledge of how to do very specific tasks without knowing the underlying principles at work. Junkin attempted to bridge the divide between useful knowledge and theoretical understanding by casting the latter as a part of the former—a knowledge of abstract principles was itself a tool. Linking liberal education to national destiny, he argued that "the union of art and science in a course of liberal education, must lead to a still more rapid and extensive development of the physical resources of the state and country." Just as did Porter in his July 4 address to the assembly of Easton artisans, Junkin explained that, "the application of science to art is a labor saving machine."[47] A liberal education was thus justified on the grounds of its utility to the mechanic in overcoming physical conundrums.

The idea that a liberal or scientific education would promote cross-class understanding did not always work out in practice, however, as demonstrated by the attitude of some Lafayette students towards their laboring countrymen. In his 1834 letters to a friend, Alexander Ramsey referred to the "mobocracy of Easton" and delivered a stinging commentary on some of the laborers whom he encountered in his travels around the region. Describing his trip up the recently built Lehigh canal, Ramsey wrote, "Sometimes you will meet a huge 'Goliath of Cath' [sic] sort of a monster, bareheaded and bear-footed, mounted on a 'wee' bit of a mule, his face, legs and apology for a shirt as black as the deepest shaft in Mauch Chunk coal mine, towing one of these boats, alternately whistling and singing." Whatever they might have heard in Lafayette's lecture halls, pulpits, and workshops, it would seem that students at the college on the hill looked down on the majority of townspeople below.[48]

The hard feelings were returned in kind. One did not need to read between the lines to discern the "hostile" attitude toward Lafayette College among Easton's artisans, farmers, and day laborers. The hostilities occasionally escalated into physical violence. The *Northampton Whig* noted one such example, reporting that on a Tuesday evening in October 1837, "as several students from Lafayette College were on their way home from the town between nine and ten o'clock, they were attacked on the Buskill bridge by a party in masks, who treated them in a shameful manner. One of the students had his face covered with tar and Spanish brown, and others came off not much better."[49]

Such instances of violence toward Lafayette students were a manifestation of widely felt resentment of the institution itself. In 1839, Easton's voters held meetings to protest the proposed appropriation of state funds to Lafayette College. The group passed several resolutions to which those present signed their names. The signatories did not wish to give to Lafayette College "the hard earnings of the farmers and mechanics, to be raised at some future time in the shape of State Tax, to keep up a private manufacturing establishment and its officers, which is an out rage [*sic*] upon the peoples [*sic*] rights." Among their other determinations were the conclusions that "we did not vote for J. M. Porter to be Governor of the East[ern part of the state], nor to be at Harrisburg to legislate," and "Resolved, that we have a poor opinion of Dr. Junkin."[50]

Eventually, Junkin and the board of trustees had to acknowledge this mutual animosity between Lafayette and Easton. In his letter to the trustees explaining why the manual labor program ought to be shut down, Junkin expounded on this point: "Another consideration which forces me, however reluctant, upon the determination of abandoning Labor as an essential part of the system, is the verdict of the laboring public. I am constrained to believe, that all classes of men who live by manual labor are hostile to its introduction into a College. It operates, even with them, to make the Institution unpopular."[51] In addition to financial burdens, then, Lafayette faced opposition from those "hand" workers who resented having key elements of their *habitus* appropriated by the genteel for purposes that had no apparent benefit—and obviously costs—for the manual laborers from whom they were borrowed.

THE PERSISTENCE OF IDEOLOGY

As it stands, the story of the rise and fall of the manual labor education movement and of Lafayette College in particular leaves us with a number of questions. Chief among these is the problem of how one is to explain the continued assertions in the 1840s that Lafayette could fulfill many of the founding goals of the college, even after the manual labor program—once held up as pivotal in achieving these aims—had been abandoned. If financial strain and a hostile reception conspired to bring Lafayette's manual labor operations to a close, what allowed the college's directors to carry on with their claims for class harmony and the power of their mission to redeem society from the ills of the market revolution? The answer to these questions lies in the reformulation of the concepts of labor and class in order to endorse an extremely broad definition of "useful" and to expound an understanding of a middle class comprising universally applicable (and accessible) values. The means of attaining these values and thus respectable standing was to pursue just the sort of liberal or scientific education offered by institutions such as Lafayette College.

In the 1820s and early 1830s, Junkin and others did not find it acceptable to simply embrace market capitalism, not so much because it had a negative impact on the truly poor but because it transgressed certain key values of the genteel and nascent middle-class culture. According to educators, having an abstract understanding of the world was one such value, as one can see in the comments of educational spokespersons throughout the early republic and reaffirmed in the 1828 "Yale Report."[52] Many of them hoped that the chaos and chance that seemed to define the marketplace might be brought under control by those who knew the underlying principles of the world; some of them were committed enough to this ideal to found entire institutions meant to bring it to life.

As it did for so many social reform movements, the end of the 1830s brought disappointment to the effort to establish manual labor education as a widely available option for young Americans. As with other reform movements, financial strain (especially after the Panic of 1837) combined with modest results and an increasingly ethnic cast to class debates to cause most manual labor schools to either shut their doors or change their pedagogy. By the 1840s, manual labor educators such as Junkin came to embrace openly not only the reality that they were training the next cohort for the professions but also the perspective that the "scientific" or "liberal" knowledge that defined the professional would relieve them of any moral imperative to physically exert themselves. Thus, by 1845 we find Junkin explicitly reversing his earlier praise of manual labor: "Is it not clear as day, that EDUCATION is working out man's redemption from the bondage of physical labour?—that SCIENCE, the parent of the arts, is rapidly freeing man from whatever is painful in the curse—'in the sweat of thy brow shalt thou eat bread.'" What a decade before had been a biblical injunction to physical exertion was now an empty phrase, an unfortunate burden to be borne only by those who could not manage to avoid it. Education became a means of escaping from that labor. Science, the knowledge of organizing principles, was the key to the escape from physical exertion. A liberal education resulting in professionalism eventually displaced actual craft practice in manual labor schools as the means to virtue.[53]

Indeed, by the mid-1840s, Junkin cast his defense of professionals as an explanation of the very progress of civilization. He told his audience that "centuries ago," the world decided—after long, laborious and painful experimenting on poor humanity—decided, once and forever decided, that the learned professions are an indispensable element in social organization. If you dispense with them, you dispense with civilization itself. . . . It cannot be done, my friends. You would thus revert speedily to barbarism.[54]

The professions, not the producing classes, were the essential element of society. Thus, the mission of manual labor schools to keep open the professional ranks to all classes was of national importance. According to Junkin, manual labor schools were the means to achieve social harmony and fulfill the republican vision and were constitutive of both the social order and its relation to individual character.

Like a number of other reformers in the era, Junkin ultimately appropriated what he needed from working-class conceptions of labor, masculinity, and independence without validating working-class culture more generally. Thus, he touted the notions of useful labor, physical masculinity, and self-reliance but diluted each of these to the point where they might be aptly applied to persons who would have been excluded from the original formulation of the concept. Thus, professionals received the accolades of these qualities without having to undergo the rigors (physical labor, sparse diet, and minimal creature comforts) that they required. Instead of finding a middle ground, a synthesis of "head" and "hand" values, on which to found a new class, in the end Junkin and others returned to the notion that the new class of professionals should be defined by its abstract knowledge of the workings of the world, its liberal or scientific education. Posed as a universally accessible quality—anyone might conceivably attain such knowledge—in reality it ended up excluding precisely the majority of "hand" workers, most of whom would never be able to afford the years of training required. Posed as a universal class, based on universal principles, in practice Junkin's professionals stood on the opposite side from manual laborers across the "chasm" his movement hoped to bridge. The elective affinities holding together the nonmanual labor *habitus*, from which Junkin and most other reformers emerged, combined with the various practical obstacles to reform, would require a greater force to realign them than the manual labor education movement had at hand.

Ultimately, we need to recognize the dual character of the manual labor education movement as a response to the perils of the market revolution and use it as a window into the cultural dynamics that helped give shape to concepts of class and labor in the period. On the one hand, even as they tried to mitigate the impact of the market revolution on American culture, manual labor education movement leaders actually exacerbated the problem. As members of the professions found their cultural influence waning in market-oriented society, some of them appropriated notions of labor and utility in order to distinguish themselves from the "idle" rich and from concerns with financial gain in general. Even as committed reformers such as Junkin were willing to critique the dissipation of the wealthy, however, they were not willing to erase the distinctions separating themselves from those below them on the social ladder. Like other middling reformers, leaders at Lafayette College and similar institutions invoked the language of science and liberal education in order to promote a cultural outlook that they argued was universally applicable and accessible but that required a level of education and resources available to only a fraction of the population. Seen in this light, then, the manual labor education movement was ultimately more concerned with solidifying the position of a nascent middle class than it was with engaging with other socioeconomic groups or transforming the social dynamics that structured such engagements.

On the other hand, seen in the light of a history of "motives," we must also acknowledge that the movement was neither a simple play for power nor a disingenuous attempt to propagate a value system in order to attain "social control." Like people working in higher education or social outreach today, antebellum reformers such as Junkin had the education, cultivation, and contacts to allow them far easier routes to financial gain and class interest than those paths they in fact followed. Given this, any explanation of their behavior based chiefly on self-interest (understood either as individuals or as a class) oversimplifies what was a complex cultural dynamic.

Furthermore, while both readings just presented of this movement might apply equally well to a number of antebellum social reform movements, the manual labor education movement has some distinctive traits when placed in the context of the market revolution. We need to recognize the movement as one of the few attempts to implement a concrete solution to the economic, social, and moral problems voiced by so many in response to the changes going on around them. Many of those who were striving to make the market revolution safe for the republic—to reconcile increased social division and opportunity with egalitarian and communal ideals—made overtures similar to those of Porter in his July 4 speech to Easton's artisans: they exhorted the less well-off to adopt a certain set of cultural values and practices, and sometimes they even provided some form of aid to help them achieve this transformation. Yet almost no one put forward a plan, much less designed an operational system, for inculcating into the expanding professional classes any of the values of the "hand" workers who made up the vast majority of the American population. If for no other reason, this sets Lafayette College and its fellow manual labor institutions apart from nearly every other response to market revolution. It is hoped that this study of one set of motives and responses to social and economic changes, rather than being a final conclusion, will help to further yet deeper and more diverse inquiry into the cultural meanings of the market revolution.

NOTES

I would like to thank Richard Bushman, Toby Ditz, Scott Martin, Cathy Matson, Andrew Rieser, and Dorothy Ross for their helpful observations on earlier versions of this chapter.

1. James Madison Porter, *An Address to the Mechanics of Easton Pennsylvania, Delivered at Their Request, by James Madison Porter, on the Fourth of July, 1835* (Easton, Pa.: J. P. Hetrich, 1835), 15.

2. A methodological aside is necessary here. This chapter engages with three concepts and their attendant discourses, one of which antebellum Americans would have clearly recognized and two of which would have been recognizable but not in quite the reified form that present-day historians invoke them. The discussion of labor ideology was very explicit, and historians have conducted their analysis in much the same terms as did contemporaries. The invocation of a "middle class," however, was not something that would be generally recognizable in the 1820s and 1830s. Social hierarchy was certainly present, acknowledged, and extensively commented on, but contemporaries generally did not discuss it in terms of being an amalgam of family practices, residential patterns, work practices, reform ideology, consumption patterns, and so forth. The same kind of disjuncture holds for the social and economic changes that we denote the "market revolution." Antebellum Americans were well aware of both the push for "internal improvements" (roughly equivalent to the "transportation revolution") and the drive for financial advancement that seemed to be in conflict with other core values. For them, however, this was less a "revolution" that served as a watershed by which to explain the later advent of widespread industrialism than it was a sense of a new world yet to be charted and a challenge to the republican, Christian, and agrarian values on which the country had so recently been founded. This said, I am somewhat suspicious of simply assuming the discreet existence of the "market revolution" and even more suspicious of doing so for a "middle class." I am working on

a further piece that explores the ways in which their multiple valences might bring us to reconsider the fundamental ways in which we discuss these phenomena. For this chapter, however, while I have tried to keep the amorphous status of these two concepts in mind, I do not have the space to fully flesh out these larger methodological issues.

3. Joyce Oldham Appleby, "The Vexed Story of Capitalism Told by American Historians," *Journal of the Early Republic* 21, no. 1 (spring 2001): 16–17 (emphasis added); Roger Chartier, *Forms and Meanings: Texts, Performances, and Audience from Codex to Computer* (Philadelphia: University of Pennsylvania Press, 1995), 1–5, 83–97.

4. Mary Poovey, *Uneven Developments: The Ideological Work of Gender in Mid-Victorian England* (Chicago: University of Chicago Press, 1988), 2–4. On the extensive debate regarding the fear of fragmentation and possibility of synthesis in historical explanation, see Thomas Bender, "Wholes and Parts: The Need for Synthesis in American History," *Journal of American History* 73 (1986):120–36; and Peter Novick, *The Noble Dream: The "Objectivity Question" and the American Historical Profession* (Cambridge: Cambridge University Press, 1988), 415–629; and Joyce Appleby, Lynn Hunt, and Margaret Jacob, *Telling the Truth about History* (New York: Norton, 1994).

5. Chartier, *Forms and Meanings*, 96.

6. Pierre Bourdieu, *Distinction: A Social Critique of the Judgement of Taste*, trans. Richard Nice (Cambridge, Mass.: Harvard University Press, 1984; original French edition, 1979), passim.

7. David Bishop Skillman, *Biography of a College: Being the History of the First Century of the Life of Lafayette College* (Easton, Pa.: Lafayette College, printed by The Scribner Press, 1932). On the yearning in early republican and antebellum America for an imagined bucolic past, see Paul Boyer, *Urban Masses and Moral Order in America, 1820–1920* (Cambridge, Mass.: Harvard University Press, 1978).

8. *Second Annual Report of the Board of Trustees of the Manual Labour Academy of Pennsylvania, November 9, 1830* (Philadelphia: W. F. Geddes, 1830), 5.

9. For details of the physical arrangements of the college and of the various technical problems encountered in the early years at Easton, see David Bishop Skillman, *The Biography of a College: Being the History of the First Century of the Life of Lafayette College* (Easton, Pa.: Lafayette College, printed by The Scribner Press, 1932), 56–75. On antebellum collegiate education, see David F. Allmendinger Jr., *Paupers and Scholars: The Transformation of Student Life in Nineteenth-Century New England* (New York: St. Martin's Press, 1975); Howard Miller, *The Revolutionary College: American Presbyterian Higher Education, 1707–1837* (New York: New York University Press, 1976); Mark Noll, *Princeton and the Republic, 1768–1822* (Princeton, N.J.: Princeton University Press, 1989); Douglas Sloan, *The Scottish Enlightenment and the American College Ideal* (New York: Teachers College Press, 1971); W. Charles Lahey, *The Potsdam Experience: A History and a Challenge* (New York: Appleton-Century-Crofts, 1966); and Richard Hofstadter and Wilson Smith, eds., *American Higher Education: A Documentary History* (Chicago: University of Chicago Press, 1961).

10. S. V. S. Wilder and Joshua Leavitt, "Introductory Statement," in *First Annual Report of the Society for Promoting Manual Labor in Literary Institutions, Including the Report of Their General Agent, Theodore D. Weld. January 28, 1833* (New York: S. W. Benedict & Co., 1833).

11. The slim existing historiography on the manual labor movement focuses on the imperative to solidify the identity of the independent producer—of the autonomous physical laborer who worked in the shop or the field or perhaps occasionally in the factory. Brief but interesting treatments of the manual labor movement can be found in Robert H. Abzug, *Cosmos Crumbling: American Reform and the Religious Imagination* (New York: Oxford University Press, 1994), 116–24; Jonathan A. Glickstein, *Concepts of Free Labor in Antebellum America* (New Haven, Conn.: Yale University Press, 1991), 78–81; Joseph F. Kett, *The Pursuit of Knowledge under Difficulties: From Self-Improvement to Adult Education in America, 1750–1990* (Stanford, Calif.: Stanford University Press, 1994), 129–32; and Paul Goodman, "The Manual Labor Movement and the Origins of Abolitionism," *Journal of the Early Republic* 13 (fall 1993), 355–88. Older narrative-style accounts of the movement include L. F. Anderson, "The Manual Labor School Movement," *Educational Review* 46 (1913), 369–86, and Charles Alpheus Bennett, *History of Manual and Industrial Education Up to 1870* (Peoria, Ill.: Manual Arts Press, 1926), 182–92.

12. In Pennsylvania, though, the lyceum movement was associated largely with the promotion of public schools, and lending libraries and reading rooms seemed to have greater longevity after the initial goals of public education were met. Carl Bode, *The American Lyceum: Town Meeting of the Mind* (New York: Oxford University Press, 1956), 68–69, 146–48.

13. *Outline of the Plan of Education to Be Pursued in the Bristol College* (Bristol, Pa.: John Taylor, 1830); *Catalogue of the Officers and Students of Jefferson College, Canonsburg. July, 1832* (Pittsburgh, Pa.: D. & M. Maclean, 1832); Joseph Smith, *History of Jefferson College* (Pittsburgh, Pa.: J. T. Shryock, 1857), 127–29; *A Prospectus of the Woodside Institute for Physical Education, and Agriculture; Including Some of the Prominent Points of Fellenberg's Institution in Switzerland. Under the Superintendence of John M. Keagy, M.D.* (Harrisburg, Pa.: John S. Wiestling, 1828); *Classical, English, and Agricultural Institute, at Bolton Farm, Bucks County, PA* (circular, 1830).

14. Mr. [Benjamin] Matthias. *Report of the Committee on Education, on the Subject of Manual Labor Academies, in Pursuance of a Resolution Passed by the House of Representatives, Dec. 14, 1832. Read in the House of Representatives, February 21, 1833.* (Harrisburg, Pa.: Henry Welsh, 1833). Appended to this report is "An Act for the Establishment of a State Manual Labor Academy, for the Education of Teachers." Like most calls for manual labor, this report was conscious of working within a tradition of European-inspired educational reform and specifically cited Emmanuel Fellenberg's school at Hofwyl, Switzerland. It also mentioned Lafayette College and the Oneida Institute as examples to be emulated.

15. J. P. Wickersham, *A History of Education in Pennsylvania* (1886; reprint, New York: Arno Press and New York Times, 1969), 430.

16. Wickersham, *A History of Education in Pennsylvania*, 432; Jim Weeks, "A New Race of Farmers: The Labor Rule, the Farmers' High School, and the Origins of the Pennsylvania State University," *Pennsylvania History* 62 (1995): 5–30.

17. Charles Sellers, *The Market Revolution: Jacksonian America, 1815–1846* (New York: Oxford University Press, 1991), 237; Stuart Blumin, *The Emergence of the Middle Class: Social Experience in the American City, 1760–1900* (New York: Cambridge University Press, 1989); Richard Busman, *Refinement in America: Persons, Places, Houses* (New York: Vintage Books, 1992); Kenneth Cmiel, *Democratic Eloquence: The Fight over Popular Speech in Nineteenth-*

Century America (Berkeley: University of California Press, 1990); Mary Ryan, *Cradle of the Middle Class: The Family in Oneida County, New York, 1790–1865* (New York: Cambridge University Press, 1981).

18. Note that this is a fundamentally different type of concern than that displayed by the well-to-do, who were concerned to establish distinctions between themselves and the lower orders. On this latter kind of social class "gatekeeping," see John F. Kasson, *Rudeness and Civility: Manners in Nineteenth-Century Urban America* (New York: Hill & Wang, 1990); Lawrence W. Levine, *Highbrow/Lowbrow: The Emergence of Cultural Hierarchy in America* (Cambridge, Mass.: Harvard University Press, 1988); Cmiel, *Democratic Eloquence;* Norbert Elias, *The History of Manners: The Civilizing Process, Volume I,* trans. Edmund Jephcott (1939; reprint, New York: Pantheon Books, 1978).

19. Weld, *First Annual Report of the Society for Promoting Manual Labor,* 40–41.

20. Weld, *First Annual Report;* Kett, *The Pursuit of Knowledge under Difficulties;* Colin B. Burke, *American Collegiate Populations: A Test of the Traditional View* (New York: New York University Press, 1982).

21. *Inaugural Charge by J. M. Porter, Esq., President of the Board of Trustees, and Inaugural Address of the Rev. George Junkin, D.D. President of Lafayette College. Delivered at the Installation of the Faculty, in the New College Edifice at Easton, Pa., May 1, 1834* (Easton, Pa.: J. P. Hetrich, 1834).

22. In this regard, Lafayette is representative of the manual labor school movement. Compare Junkin's statement, for example, to an 1834 address by Bristol College President Chauncey Colton defending the manual labor system in which Colton cautioned that educators had "to guard . . . against that mercenary version of utility in education, which would turn every thing into dollars and cents." Reverend Chauncey Colton, *An Address Delivered at the Inauguration of the Faculty of Bristol College, Bucks County, Pennsylvania, April 2, 1834. Second Edition, with an Appendix, Embracing the First Annual Catalogue of Bristol College* (Philadelphia: Key & Biddle, 1834), 16–17.

23. On the age of college students in the period, see David F. Allmendinger Jr., *Paupers and Scholars: The Transformation of Student Life in Nineteenth-Century New England* (New York: St. Martin's Press, 1975).

24. *Second Annual Report of the Manual Labor Academy,* 7–8.

25. Martin Burke, *The Conundrum of Class: Public Discourse on the Social Order in America* (Chicago: University of Chicago Press, 1995), 65. See also Paul Conkin, *Prophets of Prosperity: America's First Political Economists* (Bloomington: Indiana University Press, 1980).

26. Burke, *The Conundrum of Class,* 54.

27. *Second Annual Report of the Board of Trustees of the Manual Labor Academy, of Pennsylvania. November 9, 1830* "Health preserving labour of the hands defrays the expenses of education" (title page quotation) (Philadelphia: W. F. Geddes, 1830), 7.

28. Stephen H. Tyng, *The Importance of Uniting Manual Labor with Intellectual Attainments, in a Preparation for the Ministry. A Discourse, Preached at the Request of the Episcopal Education Society of Pennsylvania, and Printed by Their Direction* (Philadelphia: William Stavely, 1830), 8, 14, 18; Charles Rockland Tyng, comp., *Record of the Life and Work of the Rev. Stephen Higginson*

Tyng, and the History of St. George's Church, New York, to the Close of his Rectorship (New York: E. P. Dutton & Co., 1890), 117.

29. Jeffrey A. Mullins, "Duties to Science, Duties to God: Medical Theory, Physiology, and the Discourse on Morality in Nineteenth-Century America," *Transactions and Studies of the College of Physicians of Philadelphia* 17 (1995): 45–60. See also Thomas A. Horrocks, "'The Poor Man's Riches, The Rich Man's Bliss': Regimen, Reform, and the *Journal of Health, 1829–1833*," *Proceedings of the American Philosophical Society* 139 (1995): 115–34; Charles Rosenberg, "Medical Text and Social Context: Explaining William Buchan's *Domestic Medicine*," *Bulletin of the History of Medicine* 57 (1983): 22–42; and Kathryn Kish Sklar, *Catharine Beecher: A Study in American Domesticity* (New Haven, Conn.: Yale University Press, 1973).

30. James Madison Porter, *An Address Delivered before the Literary Societies of La Fayette College, at Easton, PA. July 4, 1832* (Easton, Pa.: J. P. Hetrich, 1832), 14. At Amherst College, Professor Edward Hitchcock—well known as both a health reformer and an activist in educational matters—likewise counseled students on the wisdom of having an independent means of livelihood in an uncertain world. Edward Hitchcock, *The Physical Culture Adapted to the Times: An Address Delivered before the Mechanical Association in Andover Theological Seminary, Sept. 21, 1830*, (Amherst, Mass.: J. S. and C. Adams, 1831).

31. Classic studies of the transformation to a capitalist economy and society include Paul G. Faler, *Mechanics and Manufacturers in the Early Industrial Revolution: Lynn, Massachusetts, 1780–1860* (Albany: State University of New York Press, 1981), and Paul E. Johnson, *A Shopkeeper's Millenium: Society and Revivals in Rochester, New York, 1815–1837* (New York: Hill & Wang, 1978). Eric Foner, *Free Soil, Free Labor, Free Men: The Ideology of the Republican Party before the Civil War* (New York: Oxford University Press, 1970), is still the standard work on the relation of concepts of free labor to slavery and its western expansion.

32. This vision of the independent producer was also set against the idea of slavery, either actual or wage. See Jonathan Glickstein, *Concepts of Free Labor in Antebellum America* (New Haven, Conn.: Yale University Press, 1991).

33. *The Second Annual Report of the Board of Trustees of Lafayette College* (Easton, Pa.: J. P. Hetrich, 1833).

34. [John Monteith] *A Report on the Subject of Connecting Manual Labor with Study. Presented to the Trustees of the Philadelphia Manual Labour Academy. At a Meeting Held Dec. 11, 1828.* (Philadelphia: W. F. Geddes, 1828), 6.

35. Weld, *First Annual Report of the Society for Promoting Manual Labor*, 55.

36. George Junkin, *Fellenberg, or An Appeal to the Friends of Education on Behalf of Lafayette College* (Easton, Pa.: J. P. Hetrich, 1835), 9.

37. Junkin, *Fellenberg*, 12.

38. Poovey, *Uneven Developments*, 3.

39. Letter reproduced in *The Seventh Annual Report of Lafayette College* (Easton, Pa.: J. P. Hetrich, 1839), 5–6. Junkin maintained the wage rates he inherited at Germantown because he believed that to start his service by giving students a pay cut would be "a very unpopular beginning." Now, however, the cost of keeping up this system was bankrupting Junkin, and he was asking for some reimbursement from the trustees for past wages paid to students, even as he

canceled the manual labor program. For their part, the trustees were still paying off the mortgage on the college property and relying in part on a quarterly stipend from the Pennsylvania Commonwealth to keep Lafayette afloat and so were not inclined to pay Junkin what he termed a "debt of honor."

40. *Second Annual Report of the Board of Trustees of the Manual Labor Academy, of Pennsylvania. November 9, 1830* (Philadelphia: W. F. Geddes, 1830), 8.

41. In 1831, for example, there were fifty-one students at the Manual Labor Academy. Of the thirty-two whose occupations are known, ten (31 percent) were artisans, eight (25 percent) were farmers, six (19 percent) were involved in entrepreneurial endeavors, three (9 percent) were planters, and three (9 percent) were engaged in assorted other activities. All but three of the artisans were twenty or younger (these three were sixteen, eighteen, and nineteen); the same trend held among the farmers. *Third Annual Report of the Board of Trustees of the Manual Labor Academy of Pennsylvania. November 8, 1831* (Philadelphia: W. F. Geddes, 1832), 14.

42. John Franklin Stonecipher, ed., *Biographical Catalog of Lafayette College, 1832–1912* (Easton, Pa.: Chemical Publishing Company, 1913), 29.

43. Stonecipher, *Biographical Catalog of Lafayette College*, 29–34.

44. Stonecipher, *Biographical Catalog of Lafayette College*, 34–36.

45. For an insightful analysis on the reasons why certain cultural practices (such as occupation, education, diet, fashion, and family structure) will seem "natural" to certain social classes, see Pierre Bourdieu, *Distinction: A Social Critique of the Judgement of Taste,* trans. Richard Nice (Cambridge, Mass.: Harvard University Press, 1984; original French edition, 1979).

46. George Junkin, *Baccalaureate Address, Delivered at the First Commencement of Lafayette College, September 22, 1836* (Easton, Pa.: J. P. Hetrich, 1836), 7.

47. Junkin, *Fellenberg,* 18.

48. Alexander Ramsey to Rudolph Kelker, October 12, 1834, and September 28, 1834, Alexander Ramsey Collection, Minnesota State Historical Society.

49. *Northampton Whig,* October 4, 1837.

50. *Northampton Whig,* March 13, 1839.

51. *The Seventh Annual Report of Lafayette College,* 6.

52. "Original Papers in Relation to a Course of Liberal Education," *American Journal of Science and Arts* 15 (1829): 297–351.

53. George Junkin, *A Plea for North-Eastern Pennsylvania. The Tenth Baccalaureate in Lafayette College* (Easton, Pa.: J. P. Hetrich, 1845), 14.

54. Junkin, *A Plea for North-Eastern Pennsylvania,* 14.

8

"I Have Brought My Pig to a Fine Market": Animals, Their Exhibitors, and Market Culture in the Early Republic

Brett Mizelle

In 1805, a writer for the *Boston Magazine* surveyed the early republic's cultural scene. He did not particularly like what he saw. Complaining, "the rage for novelty will never cease," "the Huer" directed his ire at forms of commercial leisure—balloon ascensions, puppet and magic shows, and animal exhibitions—that were "attract[ing] almost universal admiration." These entertainments, he argued, put "the whole town in a bustle" and created a situation in which "business, friends, [and] study" were "all pushed aside." Lamenting the popularity of those "'Little Things' that make our *elegant* Ladies laugh" and that "induce our '*well-bred* Gentlemen' to forego the most sublime and greatest," this writer was particularly hostile to those cultural entrepreneurs who "make fortunes out of our Credulity and Vulgar Tastes, while objects of highest moment and most refined gratification, are patronized with a miserly hand."[1]

One exhibitor, William Frederick Pinchbeck, quickly responded to what he saw as an "*insufferable critique* touching the *taste, judgment, manners* and liberality" of the citizens of Boston. Pinchbeck was known for his exhibitions of mechanical ingenuity and philosophical experiments but was most famous for his performances in the late 1790s with his Learned Pig, which could read, spell, tell time, and perform magic tricks with cards. In responding to "The Huer" in his 1805 book *Witchcraft, or the Art of Fortune Telling Unveiled*, Pinchbeck defended novelty as "the sovereign stimulus, and original spring of conception" behind all the world's "conveniences, privileges, acquisitions, and amusements." Arguing that attractions such as the "singular exhibition of the "*Knowing Pig*"

> impart pleasure and gratification, *to those who are not too wise to be amused*— and also, they have no little claim in cultivating and improving the mind, by solid confirmation to the superstitious eye, that ingenuity, patience, and perseverance, are all the *mighty magick* in the wonder they behold.[2]

Pinchbeck's defense of the propriety of animal shows and "novelties" created by exhibitors who provided "instructive amusement" to their audiences demonstrates the intensity of the contestation over amusement and leisure in the early American republic. This debate was itself part of Americans' efforts to come to terms with their rapidly changing postrevolutionary society. While there were many avenues through which Americans sought to understand their society, themselves, and others, public culture was one terrain "in which classes, sexes, and ethnic groups fought their relations out."[3] Commercial leisure activities in general and animal exhibitions in particular were a "contested cultural space" in which Americans articulated and developed ideas about ethnicity, class, gender, and community and created identities and defined values in a society being transformed by political revolution and market expansion.[4]

Struggles over what constituted acceptable leisure, of course, were not only provoked by animal exhibitions. Leisure activity was hotly contested in the early American republic, partly because public culture had been tied to concerns about national virtue and the character of the American people during the Revolution. Debate over "the boundaries of morally acceptable nonwork activity" continued in the early republic, heightened by the resumption and indeed expansion of commercial amusements that were "divorced from both work and communal regulation." Commercial leisure came under fire from both religious and secular critics who saw "trifling" amusements as a "waste [of] precious time and property." Morality was also an issue because, in the words of one pamphlet, purveyors of commercial leisure, whether animal exhibitors or "play-actors, puppet-show masters, winners in horseraces, and in gambling, live in idleness, and often in pride and luxury."[5]

Concerns about the morality of participation in commercial leisure, animal exhibitions included, were frequently expressed in terms of respectability. Respectability was increasingly an issue in the composition of audiences in the early nineteenth century, one accompanied by distinctions between proper and improper spectatorship. Related to both were concerns about artifice. While Americans were generally optimistic about individual and social progress, they were, as Karen Halttunen has argued, increasingly fearful of being taken in by confidence schemes and confidence men.[6] With increasing urban anonymity, the decline of face-to-face transactions, and the development of financial instruments such as credit and paper money that "involved an exchange of precarious and potentially competing claims to authority," America entered what has recently been called the "Age of Confidence."[7] While concerns about leisure and artifice would crystallize around the (much-studied) career of P. T. Barnum, who first came to broad public notice with his exhibition of Joice Heth beginning in 1835, in the early American republic animal exhibitions and their proprietors prefigured many of these developments by serving as "sites" and "sights" for conflicts centered, both explicitly and implicitly, on Americans' changing relationships to their increasingly market-driven society.

As part of an expanding world of commercial leisure, animal exhibitions had much in common with the theater, museums, and other, less institutionalized, public entertainments. Animal exhibitions, however, performed different cultural work precisely because of their animal content. Early nineteenth-century America was a society of people and their animals in which the former were beholden to the latter "for their sustenance, comfort, and most aspects of their everyday companionship and culture."[8] While many Americans had affective relationships with their livestock and other domestic animals, these animals were also valuable commodities in both household economies and the larger world of market exchange. Americans were used to being around animals, watching them, working with them, and buying and selling them as commodities as part of an economy crucially connected to animal husbandry.

Americans were also increasingly used to paying to see exotic animals from remote locations (such as the lion and elephant or, for many Americans, the bison and moose) or animals that had special physical or behavioral attributes (such as a six-legged cow or performing dogs, pigs, and monkeys). Exhibitions of these types of animals began in the 1720s, when a "Lyon, being the King of Beasts" could be seen in Boston.[9] Other exotic imports, such as lions, leopards, camels, and polar bears, and native curiosities, such as moose and catamount, were sporadically exhibited in colonial British North America until the 1770s, when growing tensions with Great Britain served to check the importation of animal curiosities and led to the prohibition of leisure activities, such as the theater, cockfights, and horse races, that tended to waste money and encourage dissipation.[10] After the interruption of the revolution, Americans witnessed an explosion of cultural activities in the form of new museums, theaters, and public exhibitions of all kinds, many devoted to the creation and articulation of a distinctive American culture. Animal exhibitions, in particular, began to flourish in the 1790s. In this critical decade, audiences saw many "firsts" in terms of form and content, including the "Menage of Living Animals," the elephant, and spectacular animal acts featuring performing pigs, dogs, and monkeys.

Animal exhibitions in the early republic were embedded in many of the social and cultural developments in this postrevolutionary society. The creatures seen by audiences at exhibitions generated ideas about animals and animality that helped Americans make sense of their world. Exhibitions of "American productions" from the trans-Mississippi West, for example, helped display the expanding nation to itself. Similarly, animals were used symbolically and practically in the new nation's partisan politics, most effectively by elites who drew on ideas about animals and animality to bestialize the "people" and their representatives and to lament the loss of an old political world of deference. While Federalists used a living elephant to draw crowds away from a Republican political festival in Litchfield, Connecticut, in 1806, most of the political uses of animals in the early republic were rhetorical. For example, satirists for the *Port Folio* used the popularity of the learned pig to lampoon Jefferson's cabinet and his supporters as enemies of proper "restraint." Hugh Henry Brackenridge's *Modern Chivalry* similarly satirized democracy by positing its ultimate extension, noting "from the right of suffrage, to the right of delegation, the transition was easy; and hence the idea of admitting beasts to a vote in elections, naturally led to that of beasts being voted for, and elected to a representative body."[11] Animal exhibitions also served as a locus for the (re)conceptualization of ideas about race, gender, and hierarchy, particularly when shows of performing animals or of monkeys and apes problematized the boundaries between human and animal.[12]

In short, animals were, to borrow Lévi-Strauss's famous formulation, "good to think with."[13] As recent scholarship in the emerging field of animal studies has demonstrated, animals have always proven central to the human understanding of the self. As Erica Fudge has noted, "The innate qualities that are often claimed to define the human—thought, speech, the right to possess private property . . . are actually only conceivable through animals; that is, they rely on animals for their meaning." Historical studies of both the material and the rhetorical uses of animals can not only tell us about human social identities and cultural environments but can also help us recognize that the very category of "human" is not intrinsically stable and that humans are "embedded within and reliant upon the natural order."[14]

This chapter suggests that there are connections between how Americans in the early republic thought about animals and how they thought about themselves and their culture. While exhibitions of exotic and performing animals were useful "sites" and "sights" for thinking about shifting and uncertain identities, the animal exhibition business itself was shaped by and extended developments in market and consumer culture. The first section of this chapter situates animal exhibitions within this milieu and shows how they helped make market culture thinkable, although often prompting resistance in the process. The second section looks at the marketing of and venues for animal exhibitions, showing how these processes involved the definition and segmentation of American audiences. Finally, I return to William Frederick Pinchbeck, examining how his use of a novel strategy—exposure—to deal with the vexing questions of leisure and artifice makes him a crucial transitional figure in the history of American popular culture.

ANIMAL EXHIBITIONS AND MARKET CULTURE

The circus and the zoo are so well established in modern American culture that it is hard to imagine a time prior to these cultural institutions. In postrevolutionary America, however, there were few institutions that exhibited animals. While live exotic animals could occasionally be seen in the early republic's museums, most of the exotic animals brought to the United States were seen in small, itinerant exhibitions. From the 1790s until the Panic of 1837, there was a gradual pattern of consolidation in the animal exhibition business, one that resulted in the formation of the short-lived Zoological Institute (a menagerie holding company) in 1835. For the most part, however, animal exhibitions were the work of individuals, most of whom have disappeared from the historical record, rarely leaving even a surname to be linked with their advertisements for their animal curiosities.

Individuals who hoped to make a living through the exhibition of animals faced many of the same challenges as the thousands of other men seeking economic independence in the new nation. In their "widespread willingness to be uprooted, to embark on an uncharted course of action, to take risks with one's resources," these men participated in "the creation of a popular, entrepreneurial culture that permeated all aspects of American society."[15] Although not working in more traditional channels such as manufactures, commercial agriculture, banking, and trade, those who chose animal exhibitions as their economic undertaking undoubtedly shared what Hezekiah Niles called Americans' "almost universal ambition to get forward."[16] In facing the additional difficulties related to acquiring, handling, and displaying their cultural product in a way that proved acceptable to a wide range of American audiences, these men took advantage of and helped promote the developments in transportation and consumerism that defined the market revolution.[17]

It appears that few men devoted the majority of their working lives to exhibiting animals. In fact, most of these cultural entrepreneurs pursued a number of diverse economic opportunities throughout their lifetimes, as did Secondo Bosio, who at various times opened an ice cream house, ran a tavern, and owned an ostrich. Sometime around 1800, Bosio began to exhibit an ostrich recently imported from Africa. At his death in 1826, this "Ostrich Burd" was still alive and proved the most valuable item in his estate, valued at $300. As one of many economic pursuits, this ostrich provided Bosio with a nice supplemental income; his estate included $219 in assets received from exhibition of this bird.[18] For a few, however, animal exhibitions were their entire livelihood. Samuel Dean, a disabled military veteran, brought a bison back with him from "the Miame Indian Village" in 1795 that was his sole means of support for several years.[19]

Other men, particularly ships' captains and sailors who were already transporting commodities throughout the world, speculated in exotic animals. The most spectacular animal import and perhaps one of the most successful speculations in the early republic resulted from the efforts of Captain Jacob Crowninshield of Newburyport, who purchased "a fine young elephant two years old, at $450," that he hoped would "bring at least $5000" in America. On the arrival of his ship *America* in April 1796, a New York paper noted that "this animal is sold for $10,000, being supposed to be the greatest price ever given for an animal in Europe or America."[20] Crowninshield had hoped to gain fame from bringing this exotic animal to America but instead made a tremendous profit from his risky venture by shifting the risk to the elephant's purchaser. While Crowninshield directly profited, the elephant's new owner had to feed, transport, promote, and exhibit his new acquisition, one that was not guaranteed to survive in its new American environment. Fortunately, the elephant that historians have come to call the Crowninshield elephant for lack of any knowledge of its actual owner, thrived (see figure 8.1). Thousands of Americans saw this elephant and the others that followed her during the early republic, making the phrase "to see the elephant" part of the American vernacular, used by individuals in the nineteenth century as they "encounter[ed] the unbelievable."[21]

Ships' captains such as Crowninshield and Benjamin Russell (who brought "two Royal Tigers, male and female" to Salem from Surat in 1806), were, in essence, early dealers in exotic animals.[22] Eventually, individuals who purchased multiple animals exhibited them in menageries rather than individually and began to actively trade them. The unnamed proprietor of the self-described "Greatest and Most Curious Natural Collection which has ever been exhibited in this country"—the earliest American menagerie—was a dealer of animals as well, noting in one of his 1789 advertisements in the *Massachusetts Centinel* that "he has to sell, besides his collection, one live Tygeress."[23] As the market revolution swept the Northeast, animal exhibitors increasingly drew on developments in the emerging capitalist economy to pool their resources and control risks by consolidating holdings and trading shares of animals. The area around Somers, New York, became the center of the traveling menagerie and circus business in America, as local men, such as Hachaliah Baily, Isaac Purdy, and Benjamin Lent, imported, traded, and exhibited all sorts of exotic animals while establishing the business networks and tools that helped stabilize the industry.[24]

Before this consolidation was completed in the Zoological Institute, early national museum keepers, who were constantly on the lookout for new curiosities for their collections, were frequent buyers of exotic animals. Cultural entrepreneurs such as Charles Willson Peale and Edward Savage, for example, were always seeking new animal specimens, both living and preserved, for their museums. Although Savage purchased the second elephant brought to America for his New York museum "at a great price," Peale generally preferred to have his specimens donated instead of paying for them and tended to exhibit mounted animals instead of live specimens.[25]

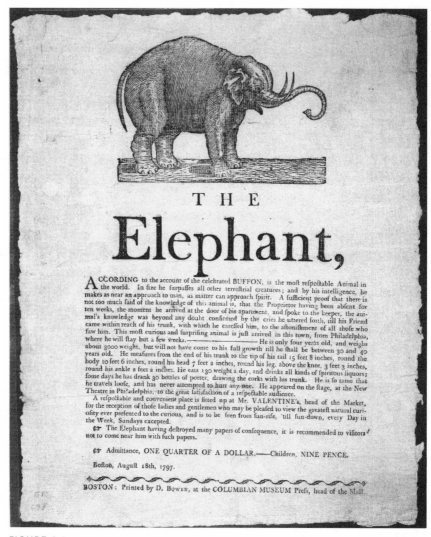

FIGURE 8.1

"The Elephant, According to the Account of the Celebrated Buffon, is the Most Respectable Animal in the World." Broadside (Newburyport: Printed by William Barrett, 19 September 1797), American Antiquarian Society, courtesy Peabody Essex Museum.

Purchasing and exhibiting a living exotic animal, especially one as large and as expensive as an elephant, required a willingness to accept the challenge of a novel economic venture. Many of these risk takers, particularly those who performed with animals, came to America from Europe, seeking new markets and opportunities for their talent in training and marketing animal acts. In contrast to American elites' efforts to create a national culture distinct from that of Europe,[26] the careers of these men highlight the transatlantic nature and foreign origins of American popular culture. Cultural entrepreneurs and animals alike circulated throughout the Atlantic world. John Bill Ricketts brought the first equestrian "circus" to Philadelphia and New York from London, performing from 1793 until his death at sea in 1800. Gabriel Salenka arrived in New York "from Europe" with his "sagacious dog"; this odd couple traveled throughout the Northeast in 1796 promising, among other feats, that the dog could "beat any person at playing at cards." William Frederick Pinchbeck exhibited various philosophical experiments, including his "pig of knowledge," after his arrival from England, while the Frenchman known as "Citizen Cressin" also performed in the 1790s with his monkeys "Gibonne" and "Coco," which delighted audiences with their mimicry of human behaviors.[27]

None of these men left behind any indication of why they came to America with their animal acts, although in doing so they established a new form of American popular culture, for shows of performing animals were virtually unknown prior to the Revolution. It is likely, however, that they saw the United States as a new world of opportunity for men of their abilities. Because they made their living with animals, however, they faced several challenges unique to their profession. It was undoubtedly difficult to handle, transport, and share their lives with animals, perhaps even more so for those men who dealt with wild exotic creatures. While it was likely an easy switch for many men from working with animals on the farm to working with animals in the field of commercial leisure, there was quite a difference between domestic and wild animal husbandry. James Capen Adams found this out the hard way in his youth, when he was nearly killed attempting to break an unruly tiger. The resulting disability temporarily ended his career as an animal wrangler, as he returned to shoemaking for the next twenty years. After losing his fortune in a speculation that was destroyed in a warehouse fire, he headed to California to start over, eventually to return east in his earlier profession as the famous "Grizzly" Adams.[28]

Adams died in 1860 from the lingering effects of a head injury caused by his supposedly tame grizzly named General Fremont. For most exhibitors, however, the bigger struggle was to keep the animals and their popular appeal alive. Since exotic animals frequently had difficulty acclimatizing to their new environments, the museum and menagerie proprietor Gardiner Baker noted that "those who wish to gratify themselves with a sight of those remarkable productions of nature" he had received from South America "had better make early application, for it is not uncommon for those that are foreign to live but a short time."[29] The lack of knowledge of exotic animal health and nutrition certainly contributed to what must have been short life spans for some proprietors' investments.

Public interest could be even shorter lived. After being exhibited extensively in the surrounding area, saturating the market, a "beautiful Creature, called a Leopard" was "expos'd to Sale to the highest bidder" in Isle of Wight County, Virginia. Although this animal could have been purchased on twelve months' credit, any buyer would have had to take this animal somewhere where it could again prove a novelty.[30] This overexposure highlights the importance of itinerancy, for although some entrepreneurs could make a consistent living in some of the larger cities, especially if they (like the museum owners) provided diverse entertainments, most of them had to take their creatures on the often suspect roads of the early republic to reach new audiences once the novelty of their exhibition had worn off. In doing so, they drew on developing transportation networks and furthered the spread of commercial leisure.

Improvements that were part of the transportation revolution made it easier for proprietors to make their often-long journeys. While the Crowninshield elephant walked yearly from northern New England to Savannah, Georgia, animals that required cages were transported on wagons.[31] Their owners were undoubtedly big supporters of internal improvements that facilitated the spread of their exhibitions into the American interior. A floating menagerie known as "Noah's Ark," for example, plied the recently completed Erie Canal in 1825. By the 1840s, menageries and other attractions were common in remote areas of western Pennsylvania. Wagons and riverboats gradually gave way to steamboats and railroads in the transportation of circuses and menageries, a development that culminated in 1852 with the "Floating Palace" of Spalding and Rogers' Circus.[32]

While many Americans undoubtedly relished the opportunity to see these exotic and performing animals firsthand, resistance occasionally accompanied the penetration of commercial leisure into the American interior. Benjamin Brown, a young man just starting his career in the circus business, recalled how exhibitors traveled at night "so that folks wouldn't see the animals" for free. Despite this precaution, they were still occasionally confronted by angry crowds that "collected in the road some times and tried to stop us."[33] Animal handler Hugh Lindsay recalled getting involved in fights with rowdies who came "to break up the show and lick the showmen." In his memoirs, Lindsay generally failed to mention what accounted for this opposition, although he described how in Christian Bridge, Delaware, a riot broke out after a man attempted "to pass the door keeper without paying, got pushed back and fell over a box." This man "raised a crowd of his friends and come back with axes, pitch forks and clubs. They tore down the canvass, and we to save ourselves rushed to a room, and locked ourselves up." A fight then broke out between these men and others from the town who had already paid to enter the menagerie until the sheriff arrived. To make matters worse, "a rich niggardly scoundrel of the place" arrived and claimed that the animals were actually his, leading to an impromptu trial through which this claim was easily dismissed. Given the tensions raised, however, the sheriff and the proprietor's "brothers of the Masonic order" helped escort the show to safety.[34]

The most significant conflict over itinerant animal exhibitions, however, occurred in 1816, when an elephant was killed by an irate farmer in Alfred, Maine. Apparently upset with the way this traveling exhibition was taking money out of the community, this "diabolical miscreant" outraged the American public by "murdering" this "noble, generous, high-minded, intelligent animal."[35] Hezekiah Niles, America's foremost business journalist in the early nineteenth century, noted that this event "much excited the public sensibility." A year later, he recorded the importation of another elephant, this time noting the amount ($5,000) for which this animal was insured.[36]

While the expansion of commercial leisure could provoke resistance, it could also provide individuals with metaphors for thinking about the political, economic, and social ramifications of market expansion. While imaginative conceptions of animals were, of course, not the only way that Americans sought to come to terms with their changing society, it is striking how frequently these animal metaphors appear in describing the political economy of the early republic. Many opponents of the Bank of the United States likened it to the mythical "many-headed hydra," while in New York, at least, counterfeit currency was called "the rhino."[37] Animal metaphors seemed to crystallize around the political turmoil of the Jackson administration. Nicholas Biddle, the director of the Bank of the United States, described Jackson's bank recharter veto message as having "all the fury of a chained panther biting the bars of his cage." Jackson was also frequently satirized and lampooned as an animal, both in texts and in political prints, such as the lithograph "Exhibition of Cabinet Pictures," which depicted him as an ape.[38]

Some of these metaphoric uses of ideas about animals were quite complex. In the spring of 1819, as poorly managed state banks that had issued notes without adequate reserves of specie were collapsing amidst a credit crisis sparked by a drop in world agricultural prices, Niles included a curious essay titled "How to Tame an Elephant" in his *Register*. Drawing an analogy from accounts of how elephants were captured and tamed in India (an account that may have accompanied the animal's exhibition), Niles described how the people (who "may be considered as the elephant") had been seduced by the paper system and speculators, only to be beaten into accepting an "unconditional submission" by the Bank of the United States. Niles hoped that eventually "the deceived elephant will cast off his pretended friends" and regain a lost "peace, liberty, and safety."[39]

Niles's analogy, however strained, points to the thinkability of animals, here directed toward the market. While it seems clear that animal exhibitions provided useful metaphors and analogies for thinking about market relations, it is more difficult to find accounts of how specific audience members at a given exhibition reacted. We have already seen how many individuals tried to see animal curiosities for free, believing, apparently, that such things, while interesting, were not worth spending hard-earned money on. In another instance, however, individuals proved more than willing to spend money on an apparently spurious exhibition. In 1838, some of the men of Dedham, Massachusetts, gladly paid to see a "striped pig" at a militia muster, for they received a free glass of whiskey as they contemplated this painted animal. This exhibition circumvented a state temperance law that prevented the sale of alcohol in quantities of less than fifteen gallons. The "striped pig" soon became a popular symbol of resistance to elite reformers that could be found in songs, in prints, and even in the name of a short-lived political party.[40]

In another suggestive case, an animal exhibition brought California Indians an understanding of Anglo-Americans' willingness to pay to observe the novel and exotic. Miwok Indians in the southern mines of California saw their first traveling circus in 1854; they were apparently most intrigued by the elephant, which they called the "animal with a tail at each end." Leonard Noyes, a New Englander who later recorded his recollections of California life, remembered that the Indians subsequently built a structure in which people danced and gambled, adding, "Young Indians taking the que from what they had seen at the circus concluded to make something out of the show so they stationed themselves at the opening demanding 2 bits each admittance, saying white man all same as Indian 2 [bits]." As Susan Lee Johnson has observed, this creative adaptation enabled Miwoks to use "market-based relations with outsiders to their own advantage without at the same time substantially altering ceremonial and social practices for themselves."[41]

It is not known how many others may have learned about forms of market behavior from traveling animal exhibitions. Individuals undoubtedly (although perhaps unconsciously) thought about market relations when they gave their money to a stranger from out of town who was promising them the novel exhibition of an exotic or performing animal. In this sense, audiences themselves took substantial risks in a new world of commercial leisure, hoping to get their money's worth from an exhibition that may or may not have lived up to the expectations aroused by its advertising. It is to that advertising and to the venues that proprietors chose to showcase their animals that we now turn.

ANIMAL EXHIBITIONS AND THEIR AUDIENCES

While itinerancy spread market culture, it worked for proprietors only if they could successfully attract audiences to their animal exhibitions. By looking at the ways animals were marketed and exhibited, we can chart the ways proprietors drew on and shaped developments in commercial leisure and begin to trace the taming of the audience, a process that favored the middle-class, respectable audience. Although scholars continue to disagree over the periodization for and mechanisms of this segmentation of what Lawrence Levine famously called a "shared public culture,"[42] this division was evident in the early republic in proprietors' efforts to construct their audience, those audiences' concerns about venues, and a related societal interest in defining proper spectatorship. The creation, disciplining, and segmentation of audiences for animal exhibitions, then, reveals much about the cultural impact of market expansion.

Newspapers, handbills, and broadsides advertising exotic and performing animal exhibitions reveal the reciprocal relationship between proprietors and audiences. While audiences obviously could choose whether to attend a given exhibition, their power can also be seen by looking at proprietors' advertisements for their shows, which reveal how audiences could more subtly structure the choices made by exhibitors. Sometimes audiences' interests could be seen in the very choice of format used to exhibit animal exhibitions. Acclimating themselves to the new market environment, exhibitors learned that the kinds of advertising they used helped determine the audience drawn to their exhibitions. While appearing in New York in 1795, for example, Cressin noted that "unruly boys" attracted by his handbills and broadsides were keeping a "genteel company" away. As a result, Cressin promised to run notices only in newspapers such as the *Daily Advertiser* for the remainder of his stay in town.[43]

While cultural entrepreneurs took advantage of the explosion in the number of newspapers in early nineteenth-century America, they also helped support this development with their paid advertising.[44] In addition to newspaper advertisements, they also promoted their enterprises through illustrated broadsides and handbills. As the number and quality of engravers in America improved, these advertisements depicted animals in an increasingly lifelike way. Other technological developments in the printing industry, such as the steam-powered press, enabled the production of both larger and more elaborate posters and a multitude of smaller handbills and cards, all at a decreasing cost. The diversity of this advertising material and its widespread circulation, particularly in urban settings, "underscored the jarring contiguities and transitions of an urban culture rife with new possibilities for individual self-presentation and mass action."[45] Yet while signifying the ways individuals dealt with their commercial culture in American cities, these advertisements could also bring modern marketing—with its excitement and, occasionally, a related need for skepticism—to rural areas as well. One Scottish traveler believed that the gigantic, wall-size posters he saw while traveling along the Erie Canal in 1834 tended to exaggerate the content of animal exhibitions. David Wilkie remarked on an "excellent specimen of Yankee puffing" he encountered in a tavern. The "huge bill" displayed "portraits of every ill-shaped brute which the caravan contained," along with "wonder-working" descriptions (see

FIGURE 8.2

"Exhibition of Natural Curiosities, To be Seen on [Blank] at the House of [Blank] in [Blank] for [Blank] Day Only." Broadside (Batavia, 1826), courtesy American Antiquarian Society.

figure 8.2). "No nation in the world," Wilkie mused, "understands the science of puffing more profoundly than the American."

Wilkie's complaint about puffed-up advertising is reminiscent of the debates about P. T. Barnum's famous "humbugs"—debates, of course, that further enticed the public to attend his exhibitions.[46] Yet in the postrevolutionary cultural marketplace, audiences were not yet as willing to accept either facetious or spurious public entertainments. As David Brigham has noted, a cultural emphasis on "useful knowledge" and "instructive amusement" structured debates over the meaning and propriety of public culture, functioning "as a kind of shorthand" that contained important "assumptions about economic priorities, social distinctions, and moral beliefs that were central to life in the early republic."[47] Given the pervasiveness of this language, many animal exhibitors understandably sought to promote their exhibitions in similar terms, often prefacing their advertisements with an invitation "To the Curious."

This strategy worked best for exhibitions of exotic animals, which were marketed as providing knowledge of the natural world. This use of enlightenment natural history to contextualize these exhibitions both made intuitive sense and enabled proprietors to couch their offerings in terms of a broader public good. Yet, as James Cook has noted, "each early American showman reacted to the expanding market economy in his/her own distinctive ways." Some, such as Charles Willson Peale, went overboard in efforts to "dispel any public uncertainty about the contents of his popular museum."[48] Others, however, particularly those hoping to make a living with animal acts, often attracted viewers by blurring the boundaries between viewers' expectations and the animal object. Cressin, for example, frequently described his performing monkeys Gibonne and Coco as miniature people without reference to the tails that would immediately establish them as nonhuman. His illustrated broadsides and live performances alike served to dramatize the "continuities and discontinuities between man and animal," raising questions about the uniqueness of human abilities that attracted audiences interested in thinking about race, gender, and hierarchy in postrevolutionary America.[49]

Because of the boundary blurring that was produced by the feats these animals performed, animal acts, rather than exotic animal exhibitions, best reveal audiences' fascination with these questions. William Frederick Pinchbeck, proprietor of the most successful exhibition that challenged conceptions about the boundaries between the human and the animal, perhaps faced this problem most acutely. Pinchbeck's Learned Pig

> reads print or writing, spells, tells the time of Day, both the hours and minutes, by any person's watch in the company, the date of the year, the day of the month, distinguishes colours, how many persons there are present, ladies or gentlemen, and to the astonishment of every spectator, will answer any question in the four first rules of Arithmetic. To conclude, any lady or gentleman may draw a card from a pack, and keep it concealed, and the PIG without hesitation will discover the card when drawn.[50]

Given the presence of pigs as nuisances in the streets of American cities at the time,[51] the fact that Pinchbeck had elevated such a lowly animal added to the appeal of his exhibition and to the wonder of his audiences. This inversion of the categories of "high" and "low" consistently appealed to audiences, helping to account for the popularity of both "learned" animals and those monkeys and apes that mimicked human behaviors.[52] While audiences enjoyed these inversions in other cultural forms as well, when confronted by direct or overt fraud, they felt empowered to take action. In July 1806, for example, an unnamed cultural entrepreneur in Boston promised the exhibition of a "nondescript biped from the East Indies." When this "nondescript" turned out to be a shaved black bear, the "mobility" assaulted the proprietor and freed the animal. As the poor animal "attempted to make his escape on all fours," the crowd chased it through the streets.[53]

As this incident illustrates, animal exhibitors confronted the problem of attracting audiences and regulating their behavior as they entered the new market for commercial leisure. Like other cultural entrepreneurs, they wished to draw large crowds but realized the liabilities associated with audiences dominated by uncouth and unruly lower-class spectators. Advertisements for animal exhibitions invited a wide range of potential observers but also reflected larger cultural concerns over the social acceptability of leisure in the early republic, as Pinchbeck implicitly excluded the "lower sort." This rhetorical appeal to a broad public, albeit one accompanied by subtle distinctions of social rank, was a common (and necessary) strategy used by most cultural entrepreneurs. While museum keepers and proprietors of itinerant entertainments depended on public support, they seldom directly excluded particular segments of the population despite privately betraying anxieties about the deleterious effects of "the lower sort" on both their audiences and the exhibitions themselves. Peale, for example, complained to his son about how "the Rude and uncultivated" failed to behave properly in his museum, often standing on benches for better views and, even worse, defacing defaced exhibition cases. Accordingly, Peale increasingly began regulating visitors' habits. While new signs and verbal admonitions could help ensure a proper audience inside the museum, the rhetoric of Peale's newspaper advertisements, which "presented the collections as a storehouse of utility and a source of moral education," also gave audiences reasons to self-select along class and status lines.[54] In this sense, animal exhibitions paralleled the larger marketplace, which itself "offered a highly visible model for an inclusive public," albeit one equally stratified by both income and aspiration.[55]

The rhetoric of proprietors' advertisements was not the only way that social distinctions were drawn, however, as the venues for exhibitions ("sites") and their content ("sights") also served to define and segment early national audiences. Prior to the development of the tented circus and menagerie and to a limited extent afterward, entrepreneurs proved willing to exhibit exotic and performing animals almost anywhere they thought they could make a profit. Given its role as the center of community life in both cities and the countryside, it is not surprising that many animals were exhibited at taverns. Because exhibitions at or near taverns, however, might not appeal to the broadest possible audience, some proprietors tried to exhibit in more formal settings. Pinchbeck, for example, generally exhibited his Learned Pig and other philosophical experiments in public halls. When he was forced to use a building adjacent to a Boston pub, he noted "the place now for Exhibition is entirely fitted up for that purpose" and would "have no communication with the Tavern."[56] Pinchbeck was trying to make sure that potential attendees in Boston—including women and children—were not deterred by his exhibition's physical proximity with what was likely perceived of as a disreputable tavern culture.

While taverns were the most common exhibition venue, exotic and performing animals could be seen virtually anywhere that people would gather. Proprietors took their animals to towns where circuit courts were meeting in order to take advantage of the temporary increase in the local population. College commencements and militia musters served the same purpose; as a result, graduates of Harvard saw a cassowary in 1800 and a menagerie of animals, including a stuffed lion, in 1804.[57] Street corners and barns or stables that were easily accessible also served as exhibition venues, as did other public institutions of amusement and edification, such as museums and theaters. Charles Willson Peale, for example, occasionally kept a menagerie of living animals outside his museum in Independence Hall in Philadelphia. When these animals grew too large or too unruly to be exhibited to the public, Peale killed, mounted, and displayed them inside the museum.[58] Exotic animals were also lent out for use in theatrical productions, most spectacularly when an elephant appeared on stage in a performance of *Forty Thieves* in New York in 1812. Other animals appeared closer to home: Peter Daspre of Providence exhibited monkeys in his front room, while Portsmouth hairdresser M'Reding kept an ostrich in his shop.[59]

Proprietors exhibiting in public spaces often had to obtain permission for the opportunity to reach a larger audience. In April 1794, Gardiner Baker, owner of the American Museum in New York, was granted his request "for the use of the small Corner Lot at the end of Pearl Street." Baker quickly set up this lot for his "Menage" (which for the unfamiliar he described as "a place for living Animals and Birds"), announcing his "Natural Curiosities" in a broadside.[60] In the spring of 1796, however, residents complained that Baker's menagerie was a "nuisance" and petitioned the New York City Council for its removal. Baker, initially ordered to "remove those Animals and deliver up the said Lot in clean & good order" by July 15, successfully petitioned for a reprieve that allowed him to keep his animals on Pearl Street until May 1798, when he moved his collection to what he bitterly described as "an out of the way dirty part of the City."[61]

Baker's conflict with his neighbors and the authorities paralleled other conflicts between new industries' use of space and more traditional definitions of land use.[62] It also illustrates how proprietors and exhibitors had to deal with local authorities who prohibited certain kinds of public entertainments or required licensing fees for others. Regulation and taxes, however, do not seem to have been significant impediments to proprietors in the early republic.[63] Of much greater concern was the fear that particular venues, especially those that might attract a rowdy crowd, would scare the better sort away. Proactively addressing this concern in Providence, for example, Cressin announced that "A civil Officer will attend, to keep good Order," while in Newburyport he moved his exhibition from a tavern near the unruly wharves to the center of town after several residents suggested "that if he had a more convenient place for his exhibitions, they would visit him with their families."[64]

These efforts to assuage potential audience members' anxieties reached their apex in proprietors' offer of private showings for select parties who, in Pinchbeck's notices, "cannot make it convenient to attend in the evening." Although this was a strategy used by Cressin as well to reach those unable (or unwilling) to attend these public performances, these private showings ultimately betrayed legitimate public concerns about the safety, morality, and respectability of these entertainments.[65] Given that groups of men and boys were "known to have pulled boards off [early circus] arenas, reviled passersby and to hound people leaving the hall," proprietors had to work hard to guarantee potential audiences' safety and comfort, promoting in the process a class-based segmentation of American audiences into the rowdy and respectable.[66]

It should come as no surprise that this effort to cultivate a respectable audience was also heavily gendered, given the larger renegotiations of the roles of men and women in postrevolutionary America. Cressin, for example, further justified his shift of location in Newburyport by noting that had he stayed in the tavern, this would have been "the first town where Mr. Cressin has not been honored with the presence of the Ladies." Pinchbeck similarly noted in his Boston advertisements that "strict attention will be paid always, to keep the place fit for the reception of Ladies—and nothing immodest or immoral will ever be introduced during the performance."[67] This effort to appeal to women, while primarily an effort to maximize gate receipts by opening up the show to the other half of the population, also prefigured the later process through which "theater was redefined as a feminine, rather than a masculine or family, entertainment." As Richard Butsch has noted in his study of the nineteenth-century theater, a female audience served as a crucial index of the respectability that some better-off cultural entrepreneurs sought to cultivate.[68]

One woman's comments about her attendance at an animal exhibition begin to illustrate this process. After Elizabeth Drinker went to see the Crowninshield elephant in 1796, she wrote in her diary that she "could not help pitying the poor Creature, whom they keep in constant agitation, and often give it rum or brandy to drink." She concluded, "I think they [the crowds] will finish it 'eer long."[69] Drinker's concern about the intensive audience participation at this exhibition was shared by the Reverend William Bentley of

Salem. As an educated observer, Bentley expressed a preference to see animals in the "style of nature," without "pranks," so that they could be compared to written natural histories. Not surprisingly, Bentley was also disturbed by the way working-class audiences interacted with exhibition animals, as their behavior led him to complain that he "could make no enquiries" about an animal.[70] After observing the Crowninshield elephant on its visit to Salem in 1797, the Bentley expressed his frustrations with "the crowd of spectators [which] forbad me any but a general & superficial view of him," although he was able to see enough to know that this elephant, advertised as male, was really "a female," as "teats appeared just behind the fore-legs." In his description of this exhibition, Bentley provided a glimpse of a chaotic scene:

> He [the elephant] was six feet four inches high. Of large Volume, his skin black, as tho' lately oiled. . . . The Keeper repeatedly mounted him but he persisted in shaking him off. Bread & Hay were given him and he took bread out of the pockets of the Spectators. He also drank porter & drew the cork, conveying the liquor from his trunk into his throat. His Tusks were just to be seen beyond the flesh, & it was said had been broken.[71]

Despite the proprietor's claim that he would provide a "respectable and convenient place" of exhibition, much of the audience, perhaps one used to more direct interactions with animals, again seemed more interested in getting the elephant drunk.

Bentley's and Drinker's concerns reflect an emerging distinction between legitimate and problematic displays of animals, one that was most frequently drawn between exhibitions of exotic creatures that provided "instructive amusement" and those animal acts that did not. Shows of performing animals were further suspect given the assumption that cruel and inhumane methods were used in the process of training them. The English writer Priscilla Wakefield most clearly articulated this critique when she attacked proprietors of performing animals for the "cruel discipline" used to produce these "ridiculous accomplishments." She also scolded potential audience members for even contemplating attending exhibitions that she considered a waste of time and money; such entertainment could appeal only to "unthinking spectators."[72]

Concerns about the humane treatment of animals, combined with the larger moral and economic opposition to commercial leisure activities, never seriously threatened the livelihood of animal exhibitors in the early nineteenth century. However, such critiques do reveal how belief in rational, detached viewing and a sentimental attraction to the animal under observation were becoming increasingly important to the middle class in both Europe and America in the late eighteenth and early nineteenth centuries. While these developments would culminate in the moralistic "menagerie good, circus bad" literature of the 1830s and 1840s,[73] the emergence of a distinction between both types of audiences and types of viewing in the 1790s may require a reassessment of arguments concerning the segmentation of the early nineteenth-century audience. Although recent scholarship has generally posited the class and gender segmentation of American audiences as a process that began in the Jacksonian era, that account may need to be revised when looking outside the theater at more ephemeral and itinerant animal exhibitions, where disdain for the participatory actions of what Drinker called the "tag. rag &c." and sympathy for the animal body empowered a distinction between the serious and the spurious.[74] Evidence from animal exhibitions suggests that early in the century, before the "sacralization" of culture by American elites noted by Lawrence Levine had begun, market forces were already operating to segment and discipline American audiences.

ANXIETIES ABOUT LEISURE AND THE MARKET

William Frederick Pinchbeck's career as an animal exhibitor and cultural entrepreneur illustrates many of the issues raised by the expanding market for commercial leisure. Pinchbeck's Learned Pig became as popular in America as it had been in Europe, where the illustration accompanying the music for a song singing the praises of "the Wonderful Pig" exhibiting in London featured a member of the audience thinking, "I should like it for a Tithe Pig." Meanwhile, the proprietor smugly acknowledges, "I have brought my Pig to a fine Market."[75] With success, however, came competition from other entertainers who attempted to capitalize on its popularity. While Pinchbeck benefited from references to his pig that heightened public awareness of his exhibition (such as the song "The Learned Pig," which was sung after a performance of *Isabella, or The Fatal Marriage* at the John Street Theater in New York), the popularity of this animal act also led competitors to exhibit their own pigs that were not always up to standard.[76] In Providence, Pinchbeck was forced to advertise "The Original and Real Pig of Knowledge," having "been informed the Public were lately much imposed upon by a Mr. Brigshaw, who attempted to show Something for the Learned Pig, that was not by any Means competent to what was advertised." To reassure those who "were much disappointed" with this imposture, Pinchbeck sought to establish the exhibition pedigree of his pig of knowledge by noting that

> this Animal is the same that merited the golden Collar in Europe, and exhibited before President ADAMS and Family, with great Applause, and was also shewn at the Museum in Boston, at Half a Dollar each Person; and then at Major King's Tavern, Market-Square, where he remained six months, at a Quarter of a Dollar.[77]

Invoking European awards, presidential praise, and long-standing public appeal in both museum and tavern settings, Pinchbeck's text validated his exhibition without resorting to sheer hype, for, as Pinchbeck noted, "this exhibition needs no vain puffing, allusive advertisement."[78]

Because his claims about the remarkable feats performed by such a lowly animal seemed too good to be true, Pinchbeck billed his pig as "a curiosity without deception" and took great pains to reassure the public that his pig of knowledge was "an actual living animal." This disclaimer reflected public knowledge of exhibitions of mechanical ingenuity and automata, the best of which (such as Jacques de Vaucanson's *le canard artificiel*) could imitate the physical movements and actions of living beings. Pinchbeck himself came from a well-known English family of automaton builders and exhibited many such philosophical amusements himself in the 1790s, perhaps leading him to conclude his advertisements for his "grunting professor" by promising that "in case of its not proving a real PIG, and equal to the description," audience members "shall have the money returned, [or] to be at liberty to pay after they have convinced themselves by seeing him perform."[79] Although it is not known whether any audience members asked for their money back after a performance, Pinchbeck was, at least, exhibiting a real pig

The public, as well as Pinchbeck, seems to have been concerned about misleading advertising but for different reasons. Pinchbeck feared that deceptive advertisements, or "puffs," would undermine the public's support of commercial leisure in general and his animal act in particular. This public anxiety, however, was not entirely misplaced at a time when deception seemed increasingly common in American life. Pinchbeck attempted to allay public fears by supplementing paid advertisements with letters "From a Correspondent" that were sent to a newspaper's editor. These letters, almost surely crafted by Pinchbeck himself, enumerated the benefits of patronage while identifying Pinchbeck's preferred or ideal audience:

> We are happy to learn that the Pig of Knowledge, which has been so long a subject of admiration and wonder, is actually arriving at Union Hall, and has been shown two successive evenings to a crowded and respectable audience. As this exhibition tends to instruct the youth, raise ambition in the tender mind and heart—where the philosopher may speculate, the serious admire, and the gay be elevated—We shall indeed be still more happy to find the Proprietor meets with that encouragement due him on this occasion, more especially as this phenomenon proves to demonstration that what is too often thought impossible wants only the dint of perseverance and assiduity to surmount every difficulty.[80]

Noting the exhibit's popularity ("crowded") and clientele ("respectable"), this correspondent provided a pedagogical rationale—to demonstrate the triumph of patience and applied rationality over the supposedly "impossible"—for this entertainment. Connecting education and amusement, this announcement in Newburyport urged the attendance of "all those persons who have not yet had the opportunity of viewing this great phenomenon in nature—*the friends and promoters of invention, the lovers of novelty and philosophy, such as are not too wise to be amused.*"[81]

Pinchbeck, then, was acutely aware of the distinction between serious and spurious entertainments, at the level of both the "site" (the venues for performances) and the "sight" (the legitimacy of the show itself). One way of addressing public concerns about commercial leisure might have been to encourage audiences to judge for themselves the legitimacy and reality of the Learned Pig, making epistemological uncertainty the subject of his advertising and the key to his success, as Barnum did later.[82] But until the early years of the nineteenth century, market conditions would not permit this, for any suggestion of deception undermined his efforts to attract an audience. I would like to end this chapter by exploring in more depth how he hoped to resolve these interrelated concerns about leisure and artifice, as these themes were also central to the emerging market revolution. As we have seen, leisure activities served as a contested site where Americans dealt with the social and economic transformations produced by market expansion, especially as they were discussed in terms of the virtue and restraint traditionally associated with republicanism. Artifice was also of increasing interest to Americans, especially those seeking their main chance in rapidly expanding cities or coping with the proliferation of representative currencies. The exploration of the cultural manifestations of these developments has traditionally focused on antebellum figures, such as P. T. Barnum or the confidence man. I would like to suggest, however, that Pinchbeck's two 1805 publications, *The Expositor, or Many Mysteries Unraveled* and *Witchcraft, or The Art of Fortune Telling Unveiled*, presage many later developments. These self-published texts, the first two original works on conjuring published in America, were intended to expose the secrets behind many of the animal acts, magic shows, philosophical amusements, and other performances available to the early national public. In leaving what he hoped to be a lasting legacy to the world, however, Pinchbeck not only richly described this popular culture but also demonstrated why Americans experiencing social and economic transformations were not yet ready to be amused by deception.

The Expositor (see figure 8.3) begins with Pinchbeck's explanation of the mystery behind the Learned Pig's education. In a series of letters to his anonymous but initialed correspondent "A. B.," Pinchbeck reveals how to train a young pig with behavioral reinforcement, not cruelty, until it can pick up the correct cards imprinted with letters or numbers. The key to this process is the signal between the human and the animal when the pig reaches the correct card; Pinchbeck suggests that "snuffing the nose" at the proper moment works best. Eventually, he notes, one can remove the signal, for "the animal is so sagacious that he will appear to read your thoughts. The position you stand in . . . [that] will naturally arise from your anxiety, will determine the card to your pupil."[83]

By describing a method that could elevate this lowly animal to a point where it seems to "read . . . thoughts," Pinchbeck virtually guaranteed that a properly trained pig would excite the admiration of its audience. In fact, after diligently applying Pinchbeck's techniques, A. B. wrote,

the Pig is completed. I have already exhibited him to a number of persons, men of ingenuity and talents, in whose judgment I can confide: They are astonished beyond description. None can account for the knowledge he apparently possesses,

The PIG of KNOWLEDGE ! !

T *be* *wife,* *obferve ;* *for* *obfervation* *is* *the* *fource*
of *wifdom.*

FIGURE 8.3
"The Pig of Knowledge!!," frontispiece of William Frederick Pinchbeck, *The Expositor; or Many Mysteries Unravelled* (Boston: Printed for the Author, 1805), courtesy
American Antiquarian Society.

or discover the secret communication betwixt myself and the Pig. In fact, amongst
the learned, I am thought a man of talents, whilst others less informed accuse me
of the Black Art, and condemn me as a wizard.

While this passage articulates a desire for respect from "men of ingenuity and
talents" that Pinchbeck himself perhaps shared but could not express, it simultaneously highlights the segmentation of the audience, as the writer
wishes to be seen not as a mere magician but as an inventor, experimenter, and

philosopher.[84] To that end, A. B. suddenly writes in his next letter "the Pig no longer excites admiration," as "there is a certain Philosophical Machine lately arrived from France, which engrosses universal attention." It appears that the public had tired of learned pigs, for they all but vanish for the next twenty years until Toby the Sapient Pig and his contemporaries became a sensation in London in 1817.[85]

The Expositor thus embeds revelations about learned pigs in a larger discussion of the principles and mechanisms behind a wide variety of exhibitions (such as the Penetrating Spy-Glass) and conjuring tricks (such as how to make a stack of coins move through a table and how to stop a gentleman's watch). These "mysteries" did not problematize the boundary between "man" and "beast" but, like the pig of knowledge, did create controversy about the respectability and value of spurious entertainments. Not surprisingly, then, Pinchbeck devoted parts of *The Expositor* and his second book, *Witchcraft*, to a passionate defense of novelty and amusement. This emphasis resonated with his times, a period in which Americans "demonstrated a heightened awareness of 'firstness'" and witnessed a host of inventions and innovations that depended on human ingenuity.[86] Because "novelty, [and] newfangledness, must be matters of excitement for an aggressive commercial and capitalist world," Pinchbeck's exhibitions and his published defenses of novelty helped promote the acceptance of cultural consumerism and modernity.[87] Yet his insistence that public culture can be good for the nation, providing "pleasure and gratification" while "cultivating and improving the mind," also had practical ramifications. After all, Pinchbeck was trying to attract many of the same individuals who were being urged by writers such as "The Huer" *not* to attend such shows.

But why, given Pinchbeck's need to make a living as an entertainer, did he reveal the secrets of his Learned Pig and dozens of other exhibitions and conjuring tricks by publishing *The Expositor* and *Witchcraft*? Certainly Pinchbeck used his books to demonstrate and promote his skills in animal training, magic, and mechanism; after all, he was "the inventor" of some of the tricks covered in his books and had "ocular demonstrations of the other feats."[88] Certainly, the books demonstrated his self-made abilities "as a mechanic and a philosopher."[89] More important, however, Pinchbeck's texts can be seen as guidebooks for readers who themselves may be trying to make their way in the world. Even if they were not trying to become magicians or exhibitors of mechanical experiments, they could take comfort in Pinch-beck's repeated declarations that anything (including making a pig spell) was possible with the right amount of patience and effort.

Pinchbeck's books can thus be considered as part of the larger canon of lit-erature about self-making in the early republic. While Pinchbeck mentions that he has been strongly discouraged by his colleagues in the entertainment world from publishing these secrets, he ultimately chooses the public good over private commercial interest, emphasizing that he has produced both *The Expositor* and *Witchcraft* in order "to combat superstition in all its forms; [and] to prove the folly and impropriety of attributing that we do not imme-diately comprehend, to the influence of diabolical agency."[90] Reflecting the en-lightenment call for "pushing back the boundaries of darkness and barbarism and spreading light and knowledge" so that America could emerge from what William Livingston described as "the rude unpolished Condition of an Infant country," Pinchbeck intended his books

> not only to amuse and instruct, but also to convince superstition of her many rediculous errors,—to shew the disadvantages arising to society from a vague as well as irrational belief of man's intimacy with familiar spirits . . . and lastly, [to demonstrate] how dangerous such a belief is to society, how destructive to the improvement of the human capacity, and how totally ruinous to the common interests of mankind.[91]

This obsession with the harmful effects of superstition and his revelations to "undeceive the ignorant, and gratify the inquisitive" was part of a larger transatlantic shift toward "rational entertainments."[92] Nonetheless, it served Pinchbeck well in the contested terrain of early national commercial culture, enabling him to offer instructive amusements for an emerging middle-class audience, one that increasingly demanded edifying public amusements. This strategy also allowed Pinchbeck to sidestep questions of artifice by showing what was precisely artificial or "magical" about these performances and exhi-bitions. In doing so, he made attendance at these shows respectable; the in-formed audience, after all, can attend these shows comfortable in their superiority to unenlightened audience members while feeling a sense of par-ity with the performer.

Pinchbeck's texts also aligned him with republican conceptions of virtue and self-sacrifice that had not yet fully transformed into the more chaotic, democratic, each-man-for-himself environment that would mark the period after the War of 1812, when the market revolution began to fully take off. His books attempted to distinguish his serious and useful entertainments from the spurious and degrading while exposing secrets that "would procure him a more than ample livelihood" for the public good. Yet ironically, these revelations for the public good themselves took the form of individualistic, self-interested display. Like the novelist Charles Brockden Brown, Pinchbeck was trapped "between a dying republican culture and a maturing liberal one" while being implicated within these larger transformations in public and print culture.[93] Pinchbeck, however, was additionally situated between Enlightenment ideas about exhibition and those that would emerge in the age of confidence. In short, William Frederick Pinchbeck, like those Americans who were concerned with public culture from the consumer's perspective, was caught amidst a number of conflicting social forces in the early republic. His revelation of secrets for the public good and his attempts to distinguish his serious and useful entertainments from the spurious and degrading align him (at least in his publicly addressed texts) with traditional conceptions of virtue and self-sacrifice while demonstrating his desire to be taken seriously as an inventor and entrepreneur. Yet his extremely competitive industry, full of opportunists seeking their "main chance" who pirated his shows (for example, by exhibiting learned pigs that were "not by any means competent to what was advertised") and took advantage of his good name, was deeply implicated in the larger move toward a modern, liberal, and self-interested America that would be marked later in the nineteenth century by the ascendancy of showmen such as P. T. Barnum.

NOTES

1. The Huer, "Novelty," *The Boston Magazine*, September 9, 1805, 10–11, reprinted in William Frederick Pinchbeck, *Witchcraft, or The Art of Fortune-Telling Unveiled: From the Low Ambition of the Celebrated Mary Pitcher, To the More Elevated, but Equally Vague Pretensions of The Injudicious Astrologer. Delineated in a Series of Letters, between a Friend and his Correspondent. Comprizing Arguments to Prove the Non-existence of Spirits . . . Philosophy of the Air and Fire Balloons . . . Method of Preparing the Gas, or Inflammable Air . . . Phantasmagora, or Magick Well . . . Italian Shades . . . Puppets . . . Reluminating Automaton . . . Opinions on Ancient Oracles . . . A few Philosophical Experiments . . . Art of Balancing . . . Remarks on Prejudice. Together With Poetic Compositions On Different Subjects* (Boston: Printed for the author, 1805), 98–100.

2. "The Fly" [William Frederick Pinchbeck], "A Critique on a Critique, with some candid remarks on the Theatre, its Auditors and Actors," in *Witchcraft*, 100–108. Although Pinchbeck likely sent this material to Belcher and Armstrong, it never appeared in print in *The Boston Magazine*.

3. David Waldstreicher, *In the Midst of Perpetual Fetes: The Making of American Nationalism, 1776–1820* (Chapel Hill: Published for the Omohundro Institute of Early American History and Culture by the University of North Carolina Press, 1997), 10.

4. Scott C. Martin, *Killing Time: Leisure and Culture in Southwestern Pennsylvania, 1800–1850* (Pittsburgh, Pa.: University of Pittsburgh Press, 1995).

5. *The Richmond Alarm; A Plain and Familiar Discourse: Written in the Form of a Dialogue between a Father and His Son* (Pittsburgh, Pa.: Robert Ferguson and Company, 1815), cited in Martin, *Killing Time,* 6.

6. Karen Halttunen, *Confidence Men and Painted Women: A Study of Middle Class Culture in America, 1830–1870* (New Haven, Conn.: Yale University Press, 1982).

7. David M. Henkin, *City Reading: Written Words and Public Spaces in Antebellum New York* (New York: Columbia University Press, 1998), 139; Terence Whalen, "Introduction," *The Life of P. T. Barnum, Written by Himself* (Urbana: University of Illinois Press, 2000), xi.

8. Peter Benes and Jane Montague Benes, "Introduction," in *New England's Creatures, 1400–1900,* ed. Peter Benes (Boston: Boston University Scholarly Publications, 1995), 5.

9. *Boston Gazette,* September 19, 1720.

10. See, for example *Boston Gazette,* September 25, 1721 ("Just arrived from Africa, a very large Camel"); *Boston Weekly Rehearsal,* December 3, 1733 ("A Fine large white Bear, brought from Greenland"); *Pennsylvania Gazette,* October 18, 1744 ("A Beautiful Creature, but surprizingly fierce, called LEOPARD"); *Boston Weekly News-Letter,* May 5, 1737 (moose); *Boston Gazette,* April 6, 1741 ("a Wild Creature . . . called a Catamount"); and Ann Fairfax Withington, *Toward a More Perfect Union: Virtue and the Formation of American Republics* (New York: Oxford University Press, 1991).

11. *Litchfield Monitor,* August 16, 1806; *The Port Folio* 2, no. 2 (January 21, 1802), and 3, no. 12 (March 19, 1803); Hugh Henry Brackenridge, *Modern Chivalry* (1792–1815; reprint, New York: American Book Company, 1937), pt. 2, 4:661.

12. David Brett Mizelle, "'To the Curious': The Cultural Work of Exhibitions of Exotic and Performing Animals in the Early American Republic" (Ph.D. diss., University of Minnesota, 2000), and "'Man Cannot Behold It without Contemplating Himself': Monkeys, Apes, and Human Identity in the Early American Republic," *Explorations in Early American Culture: A Special Issue of Pennsylvania History* 66 (1999): 144–73.

13. Claude Lévi-Strauss, *Totemism,* trans. Rodney Needham (Boston: Penguin, 1963), 89.

14. Erica Fudge, "A Left-Handed Blow: Writing the History of Animals," in *Representing Animals,* ed. Nigel Rothfels (Bloomington: Indiana University Press, 2002), 10, 15. Another important work on the thinkability of animals is Steve Baker, *Picturing the Beast: Animals, Identity, Representation* (Manchester: Manchester University Press, 1993).

15. Joyce Appleby, *Inheriting the Revolution: The First Generation of Americans* (Cambridge, Mass.: Harvard University Press, 2000), 88–89.

16. Harry L. Watson, *Liberty and Power: The Politics of Jacksonian America* (New York: Hill & Wang, 1990), quotation on p. 29.

17. Charles Sellers, *The Market Revolution: Jacksonian America, 1815–1846* (New York: Oxford University Press, 1991); Melvyn Stokes and Stephen Conway, eds., *The Market Revolution in America: Social, Political, and Religious Expressions, 1800–1880* (Charlottesville: University Press of Virginia,

1996); Daniel Feller, "The Market Revolution Ate My Homework," *Reviews in American History* 25, no. 3 (1997): 408–15. While most scholarship on the market revolution posits its beginning after the War of 1812, many of its major elements, including developments in transportation, the expansion of print culture, and the rise of consumerism, were well under way in the 1790s.

18. Richard N. Juliani, *Building Little Italy: Philadelphia's Italians before Mass Migration* (University Park: Pennsylvania State University Press, 1998), 68–69. The ostrich died just two weeks after its owner; its carcass was sold for $45.

19. *Providence Gazette*, June 20, 1795. When Dean exhibited his Bison in Salem, William Bentley noted that "such persons gave as pleased to compensate the man for his Trouble" (*The Diary of William Bentley, D.D., Pastor of the East Church, Salem, Massachusetts*, 4 vols. [Salem, Mass.: The Essex Institute, 1907], 2:156 [April 1, 1795]).

20. Robert McClung and Gale McClung, "Captain Crowninshield Brings Home an Elephant," *The American Neptune* 18, no. 2 (April 1958): 137–41; *New York Argus*, April 18, 1796.

21. John Phillip Reid, *Law for the Elephant: Property and Social Behavior on the Overland Trail* (San Marino, Calif.: Huntington Library, 1980), ix, x; Drew Gilpin Faust, *Mothers of Invention: Women of the Slaveholding South in the American Civil War* (New York: Vintage Books, 1996), 120. Thanks to David Hacker for calling these references to my attention.

22. These tigers were described as "so harmless that a boy may play with them without danger, and so tame as to lie down to sleep with the people on board ship," *United States Gazette* (Philadelphia), June 13, 1806. The auction was also advertised in the *Columbian Centinel* in Boston, the *New York Gazette*, and the *Salem Gazette*. It is not known who bought these tigers or for how much.

23. See advertisements in the *Massachusetts Centinel*, November 4, 7, 18, and 25, 1789. Records of sale prices and names of purchasers have proven extremely difficult to find.

24. See Richard W. Flint, "American Showmen and European Dealers: Commerce in Wild Animals in Nineteenth-Century America," in *New Worlds, New Animals: From Menagerie to Zoological Park in the Nineteenth Century*, ed. R. J. Hoage and William A. Deiss (Baltimore: Johns Hopkins University Press, 1996), 97–108.

25. Donors expressed their personal and professional interests by presenting them to Peale, who used these objects to create a sense of community ownership in his museum. See David R. Brigham, *Public Culture in the Early Republic: Peale's Museum and Its Audience* (Washington, D.C.: Smithsonian Institution Press, 1995), 107–44; *Boston Independent Chronicle*, May 24 and June 11, 1804. This elephant was "attended by a keeper, a native of Bengal, who will be of great service to a purchaser." Interestingly, several of the handlers mentioned in advertisements were described as "black" or as natives of the same regions as they animals they took care of. When the Crowninshield elephant appeared in Providence in 1797, newspaper announcements warned, "The Public are hereby cautioned against trusting William, the black Man attending the Elephant, as the Proprietor will not pay any Debt of his contracting" *United States Chronicle* (Providence), June 29, 1797; *Providence Gazette*, July 1, 1797.

26. See, for example, Joseph Ellis, *After the Revolution: Profiles of Early American Culture* (New York: W. W. Norton, 1979), and Eve Kornfeld, *Creating an American Culture: A Brief History with Documents* (Boston: Bedford/St. Martin's Press, 2001).

27. James S. Moy, "Entertainments at John B. Rickett's Circus, 1793–1800," *Educational Theatre Journal* 30, no. 2 (May 1978): 186–202; *American Minerva; an Evening Advertiser,* February 17, 1796; *Philadelphia General Advertiser,* July 31, 1794. The fates of Salenka and Cressin are unknown. Neither can be found performing in the United States after 1796 and 1797, respectively.

28. Theodore H. Hittell, *The Adventures of James Capen Adams, Mountaineer and Grizzly Bear Hunter of California* (Boston: Crosby, Nichols, Lee, and Co., 1860); Richard Dillon, *The Legend of Grizzly Adams: California's Greatest Mountain Man* (New York: Coward-McCann, 1966).

29. *New York Minerva and Mercantile Evening Advertiser,* May 4, 1797.

30. *Virginia Gazette,* February 20, 1792.

31. Traveling in Pennsylvania in 1804, for example, Joseph Gibbons encountered "3 men who had a large Box fixed on a waggon Carriage, drawn by 3 horses—containing they said a *Lion* weighing 600 lb. Wt. which they were taking about for a Shew" (Joseph E. Walker, "The Travel Notes of Joseph Gibbons, 1804," *Ohio History* 92 [spring 1983]: 142). Although the size of the cage depended on the animal inside, it seems that the leopard seen by William Bentley "confined in a wooden cage with rounds about 6 feet by 3 feet" had typical accommodations (Bentley, *Diary,* 3:408 [January 11, 1809]).

32. Paul Johnson and Sean Wilentz, *The Kingdom of Matthias: A Story of Sex and Salvation in 19th-Century America* (New York: Oxford University Press, 1995), 67; Martin, *Killing Time,* 53; Penelope M. Leavitt and James S. Moy, "Spalding and Rogers' Floating Palace, 1852–1859," *Theatre Survey* 25, no. 1 (May 1984): 15–27.

33. "The Oldest of Showmen: Aged Benjamin Brown's Recollections of Pioneer Circus Life" (undated clipping from the *Croton Falls News,* attributed to Horace Greeley, 1879, Somers Historical Society photocopy).

34. Hugh Lindsay, *History of the Life, Travels and Incidents of Col. Hugh Lindsay, the Celebrated Comedian, for a Period of Thirty-Seven Years. Written by Himself* (Philadelphia: n.p., 1859), 50, 34–35.

35. *Murder of the Elephant. An Accurate Account of the Death of that Noble Animal, the Elephant, Furnished by a Gentleman of Alfred, York County, July 6, 1816* (Boston: Printed by Nathaniel Coverly, 1816), 3. This pamphlet contrasted the "shameless villain" who disgraced his community with the noble elephant and his black handler, who collapsed in "grief and despair . . . when he saw the majestic animal in the struggle of death, and heard him breathe out the last moan of expiration" (3–4).

36. *Niles' Weekly Register,* August 10, 1816; *Niles' Register,* November 29, 1817.

37. I thank Scott Martin and Paul Erickson for calling those references to my attention.

38. Louis P. Masur, *1831: Year of Eclipse* (New York: Hill & Wang, 2001), 144, 112.

39. *Niles' Weekly Register,* April 24, 1819. Thanks to Wayne Knutson for calling this reference to my attention.

40. See, for example, *A History of the "Striped Pig"* (Boston: Whipple and Damrell, 1838), and the lithograph "Death on the Striped Pig, or, an Illustration of the Present Attitude of That Noted Animal as He Appears to New England" (Boston: Thomas Moore's Lithography, 1839).

41. Susan Lee Johnson, *Roaring Camp: The Social World of the California Gold Rush* (New York: W. W. Norton, 2000), 310.

42. Lawrence W. Levine first called scholars' attention to the existence of an underanalyzed shared public culture in his essay "William Shakespeare and the American People: A Study in Cultural Transformation," *American Historical Review* 89, no. 1 (February 1984): 46.

43. *New York Daily Advertiser,* April 16, 1795.

44. Appleby, *Inheriting the Revolution,* 99–100.

45. Henkin, *City Reading,* 72.

46. See Bluford Adams, *E Pluribus Barnum: The Great Showman and the Making of U.S. Popular Culture* (Minneapolis: University of Minnesota Press, 1997), and Neil Harris, *Humbug: The Art of P. T. Barnum* (Boston: Little, Brown, 1973).

47. Brigham, *Public Culture in the Early Republic,* 17.

48. James W. Cook, *The Arts of Deception: Playing with Fraud in the Age of Barnum* (Cambridge, Mass.: Harvard University Press, 2001), 90, 91.

49. Jennifer Ham, "Taming the Beast: Animality in Wedekind and Nietzsche," in *Animal Acts: Configuring the Human in Western History,* ed. Jennifer Ham and Matthew Senior (London: Routledge, 1997), 146; Mizelle, "'Man Cannot Behold It without Contemplating Himself'" (passim).

50. *Massachusetts Mercury,* January 9, 1798.

51. This is the theme of an illustrated children's book, *Some very gentle touches to some very gentle-men by a humble country cousin of Peter Pindar, Esq.* (New York: n.p., 1806).

52. On the pleasures of this inversion of high and low, see Peter Stallybrass and Allon White, *The Poetics and Politics of Transgression* (Ithaca, N.Y.: Cornell University Press, 1986).

53. *Boston Gazette,* July 7, 1806.

54. Brigham, *Public Culture in the Early Republic,* 28–29, 34.

55. Henkin, *City Reading,* 11. Henkin suggests, "While extending the logic of an expanding market culture, the public sphere of urban letters also reinforced the formation of a new subjectivity congenial to market relations" (12), a process that animal exhibitions furthered through their promotion of novelty.

56. *Massachusetts Mercury,* February 9, 1798.

57. Hugh Lindsay noted the practice of following the circuit courts in his *History,* 28, 46. *Massachusetts Mercury,* July 18, 1800: "It [the cassowary] will stay in town until Commencement, and those who may wish to see it before that time, are requested to call and view this singular Bird"; William Bentley "saw the Ostriches, Genet, Ichneumon, stuffed Lyon, &c. which were exhibited" at the commencement at Cambridge in 1804 (Bentley, *Diary,* 3:107–8 [August 29, 1804]). Broadsides for the Crowninshield elephant also mentioned that the creature would be headed to Cambridge for commencement.

58. President Thomas Jefferson gave Peale two grizzly bear cubs captured by Zebulon Pike in 1807. Eventually, Peale noted, these animals "thirsted for blood and any animals coming within their reach were sure to suffer." After dismembering a monkey and escaping to terrify his family, Peale killed the bears and displayed them inside his museum. See Charles Coleman Sellers, *Mr.*

Peale's Museum: Charles Willson Peale and the First Popular Museum of Natural Science and Art (New York: W. W. Norton, 1980), 206–7.

59. *New York Evening Post,* June 8, 1812 ("in Act I the procession of the caravan with the living elephant"); *Providence Gazette and Country Journal,* November 27, 1792; *New Hampshire Gazette,* December 26, 1809.

60. "Living Curiosities," broadside (New York: Printed by John Harrison, 1794), Massachusetts Historical Society; "Museum & Wax-Work, at the Exchange, New-York," broadside (New York, November 25, 1793), New York Historical Society.

61. David Maydol Matteson, ed., *Minutes of the Common Council of the City of New York, 1784–1831* (New York: City of New York, 1930), 2:70, 248, 250, 401; Robert I. Goler, "'Here the Book of Nature Is Unfolded': The American Museum and the Diffusion of Scientific Knowledge in the Early Republic," *Museum Studies Journal* 2, no. 2 (spring 1986): 18.

62. See accounts of such conflicts in Carol Sheriff, *The Artificial River: The Erie Canal and the Paradox of Progress, 1817–1862* (New York: Hill & Wang, 1996), 79–109.

63. In Vermont, heavy taxes kept the larger traveling circuses and menageries from exhibiting there through the mid-1820s. At the same time, the Connecticut legislature held several debates over the merits of the circus despite having previously banned "feats of agility of the body for money" in 1798. Cultural entrepreneurs simply avoided these areas to perform elsewhere. See Stuart Thayer, "Legislating the Shows: Vermont, 1824–1933," *Bandwagon* 25 (July–August 1981): 20–22, and "The Anti-Circus Laws in Connecticut, 1773–1840," *Bandwagon* 20 (January–February 1976): 18–20.

64. "Exhibitions, comic and experimental," broadside (Providence, 1796); "Innocent amusement," broadside (Newburyport, 1796), New York Public Library. The larger space afforded by the move may also have been necessary for Cressin to make the most of his simian performers, as his advertising depicted Coco riding a dog and performing on the tightrope.

65. *Newburyport Herald and Country Gazette,* May 29, 1798. Cressin also offered the option of showing his "Exhibitions Comic and Experimental" featuring Gibonne and Coco "to private parties" at "any hour most agreeable." Cressin's awareness of the concerns about the morality and respectability of entertainments is also evidenced in the differing titles he gave his shows, for what were "Exhibitions Comic and Experimental" in Providence and Salem became "Innocent Amusement" in the more conservative town of Newburyport.

66. Stuart Thayer, *Annals of the American Circus, 1793–1829* (Manchester, Mich.: Rymeck Publishing, 1976), 14.

67. "Innocent amusement," broadside (Newburyport, 1796), New York Public Library; *Massachusetts Mercury,* February 9, 1798.

68. Richard Butsch, "Bowery B'hoys and Matinee Ladies: The Re-Gendering of Nineteenth-Century American Theater Audiences," *American Quarterly* 46, no. 3 (September 1994): 374–405, and *The Making of American Audiences: From Stage to Television, 1750–1990* (Cambridge: Cambridge University Press, 2000), 6.

69. *The Diary of Elizabeth Drinker,* ed. Elaine Forman Crane (Boston: Northeastern University Press, 1991), 2:860 (November 12, 1796).

70. Bentley, *Diary,* 4:398 (July 12, 1816); 2:34 (July 15, 1793).

71. Bentley was most interested in determining for himself whether this elephant could bend at the joints, as this was a major controversy in natural histories of the elephant. He added that despite the fact that this elephant was female, "We say *his* because the common language" (2:235 [August 30, 1797]).

72. Priscilla Wakefield, *Mental Improvement; or the Beauties and Wonders of Nature and Art, in a Series of Instructive Conversations* (New Bedford, Mass.: Abraham Shearman Jr. for Caleb Greene & Son, 1799), 191.

73. See, for example, the editorial in the *Massachusetts Spy*, May 16, 1832.

74. See Butsch and Lawrence W. Levine, *Highbrow/Lowbrow: The Emergence of Cultural Hierarchy in America* (Cambridge, Mass.: Harvard University Press, 1988).

75. "The Wonderful Pig," reproduced in Ricky Jay, *Learned Pigs and Fireproof Women* (New York: Villard Books, 1987), 8.

76. *New York Minerva and Mercantile Evening Advertiser*, August 29, 1797.

77. *Providence Gazette*, September 8, 1798.

78. *New Hampshire Gazette*, June 5, 1798.

79. See *New York Minerva and Mercantile Evening Advertiser*, August 24, 1797. Pinchbeck held an "Automaton Exhibition" in Philadelphia in 1796 that was advertised in the *Aurora General Advertiser* on December 9. A typical "money-back guarantee" can be found in the *Salem Gazette*, May 4, 1798, and the *Massachusetts Mercury*, January 28, 1798.

80. *Newburyport Herald and Country Gazette*, May 25, 1798. Another "correspondent" writing in Boston's *Columbian Centinel* for February 24 observed that the Pig of Knowledge was "the topic of every conversation, in every polite circle.—In fact, not to have seen this extraordinary animal is to become unfashionable; tho' we are not in the habit of passing eulogiums on exhibition in general, yet we must allow, that great merit is due the teacher of this stubborn animal; as it proves to demonstration, how far assiduity and perseverance will surmount every difficulty." Note the similarity of the concluding sentences in both of these letters.

81. *Newburyport Herald and Country Gazette*, June 1, 1798. This notice appeared as "A CARD" above a reprinting of Pinchbeck's original Newburyport notice.

82. Cook, *The Arts of Deception*, 73–118.

83. William Frederick Pinchbeck, *The Expositor; or, Many Mysteries Unravelled. Delineated in a Series of Letters, between a Friend and his Correspondent. Comprising the Learned Pig,—Invisible Lady and Acoustic Temple,—Philosophical Swan,—Penetrating Spy Glasses, Optical and Magnetic, and Various other Curiosities on Similar Principles: Also, a Few of the most Wonderful Feats as Performed by the Art of Legerdemain. With some Reflections on Ventriloquism* (Boston: Printed for the author, 1805), 26–27.

84. *The Expositor*, 25. At the conclusion of his second book, Pinchbeck claims, "For my own part, as a shew-man, I seek not to impose, but to amuse; and the chief talent I have, is the love of variety and enterprize" (*Witchcraft*, 107–8).

85. Ricky Jay has argued, "This eagerness to embrace every new amusement (often at expense of the old)" likely accounts for the disappearance of learned pigs from the scene. *Learned Pigs and Fireproof Women* chronicles this "second wave" in substantial detail (19–23). Learned pigs

appear every twenty to thirty years during the nineteenth century to be seen by a new generation of audiences.

86. Appleby, *Inheriting the Revolution*, 23, 63–64.

87. J. H. Plumb, "The Acceptance of Modernity," in *The Birth of a Consumer Society: The Commercialization of Eighteenth-Century England*, ed. Neil McKendrick, John Brewer, and J. H. Plumb (Bloomington: Indiana University Press, 1982), 316. "The middle and lower classes, not only in England but increasingly too in Western Europe, particularly the Netherlands, had been taught to buy, to expect novelty, to relish change. Not all were happy about it, many feared that it would create greed and excess. Hence the constant iteration in the sale of any amusement that it would be instructive either in knowledge or in moral improvement" (332).

88. *The Expositor*, 6.

89. *The Expositor*, 30. Many men in the early republic entered into the rapidly expanding world of print to profit directly from the sale of books. Pinchbeck also hoped to profit indirectly from their publicity value. On print entrepreneurs, see Rosalind Remer, *Printers and Men of Capital: Philadelphia Book Publishers in the New Republic* (Philadelphia: University of Pennsylvania Press, 1996).

90. *Witchcraft*, 2. Both Pinchbeck and A. B. referred to audiences who assumed that the performance of the learned pig was the result of the "Black Art" (*The Expositor*, 10–11).

91. Cited in Gordon S. Wood, *The Radicalism of the American Revolution* (New York: Vintage Books, 1991), 191, 195; *The Expositor*, 5.

92. Pinchbeck's books sought to demonstrate how, in the words of Barbara Stafford, "what is marvelous, extravagant, or extraordinary is very often the result of astonishing manual skill, disturbingly capable of creating both genuine and ungenuine effects" (Barbara Maria Stafford, *Artful Science: Enlightenment Entertainment and the Eclipse of Visual Education* [Cambridge, Mass.: MIT Press, 1994], xxv–xxvi).

93. Steven Watts, *The Romance of Real Life: Charles Brockden Brown and the Origins of American Culture* (Baltimore: Johns Hopkins University Press, 1994); *The Republic Reborn: War and the Making of Liberal America, 1790–1820* (Baltimore: Johns Hopkins University Press, 1987), esp. 3–62.

9

Temperance Nostalgia, Market Anxiety, and the Reintegration of Community in T. S. Arthur's *Ten Nights in a Bar-Room*

GRAHAM WARDER

In the wake of the market revolution, temperance activities became a common feature in the American cultural landscape. With its roots among artisans, the populist Washingtonian fervor of the early 1840s explosively expanded the social base of the temperance reform. It also freed representations of drinking and drunkards from the control of the formal temperance movement and its evangelical ministers. Temperance entertainments purveyed by reformed drunkards and cultural entrepreneurs achieved a commercial legitimacy far beyond the desires of the staid reformers of the American Temperance Society. Experience speakers and dramatists exploited the popularity of temperance imagery and its potential for strong emotional responses. Writers and publishers similarly capitalized on the popularity of temperance by legitimizing the consumption of novels. The relationship between temperance and publishing was symbiotic. Ultimately, temperance promoted the consumption of books as much as books promoted the practice of temperance. Timothy Shay Arthur, one of the most popular writers of the 1840s and 1850s, exploited this confluence of interests to make himself a victor in a competitive literary marketplace.

In novels and short stories, American readers and writers worked their way through the disturbing cultural upheavals of the market revolution. The publishing boom of the 1840s and 1850s was both a product of and a reaction to the commercialization of everyday American experience in the nineteenth century. As Charles Sellers writes, the mass of print revealed "the cultural schizophrenia of capitalist transformation." In Sellers's view, writers extolled the virtues of a romanticized nature for a people who had decimated wilderness. The rational egotism of market relationships was buried beneath an avalanche of emotional sentimentalism. As simultaneously a force for change and a voice ruing the very changes it brought, antebellum commercial culture suggests what Renato Resaldo calls "imperialist nostalgia." New cultural productions accelerated the very changes they mourned. In particular, an older notion of community was remembered with fondness by the people most responsible for its death. Temperance writing was both a product of commercialism and a reaction against the instabilities introduced by the market revolution. It was forward looking in its support for such capitalist virtues as hard work and self-control but looked back nostalgically at the communal supports of traditional society, wistfully ignoring the central role of drinking in the lives of premarket folk.[1]

Temperance fiction also dealt with the nature of evil in a time of seemingly boundless theological and economic optimism. Writers such as Arthur took on the role of preacher as the authority on perfectionist goals. By wresting evil from the Calvinist confines of human nature and installing it in that voluminous repository for all things bad, Demon Rum, temperance writers popularized perfectionist aspirations and increasingly centered them on the home. To do this, they focused explicitly the gaze of the domestic reader on the social and moral degradation of drinkers. In temperance fiction, readers are morally elevated, while drinkers are morally tainted. Drinkers and readers became binary opposites. By exploiting the popular trope of Demon Rum, temperance fiction of the 1840s and 1850s externalized the slavery of drinking and internalized the freedom of reading, all in very personal terms. Temperance and publishing worked in tandem to denounce the consumption of a self-evidently evil commodity, drink, by promoting the consumption of an ostensibly moral one, books.

The classic temperance novel of the nineteenth century was Arthur's *Ten Nights in a Bar-Room, and What I Saw There*. Published in 1854, the novel exploited two quite different enthusiasms. One was the phenomenal success of Harriet Beecher Stowe's *Uncle Tom's Cabin*, the 1852 antislavery novel on which Arthur's work was loosely modeled. The other was the controversial implementation of statewide prohibition legislation, called Maine Laws, throughout most of the northern United States during the early 1850s.

T. S. ARTHUR AND THE LITERATURE OF MORAL UPLIFT

Temperance fiction was not Arthur's only claim to fame. By the time *Ten Nights* was published, T. S. Arthur was an established popular writer. Temperance fit neatly into his already formulated symbolic universe. His didactic tales, in the form of either short stories or novels, invariably took place at the intersection of the personal and the monetary. At the center of his morally uplifting world was the home, a sanctuary from the commercial world but also a resource for the forces that would cleanse and perfect that world. In Arthur's fiction, the self did not exist in isolation. Neither the self-made man nor the self-made woman was alone. A young person's journey through life depended on familial and communal relationships, but the trip was dangerous. The happy reconstruction of violently shattered families and communities concluded almost all his tales. Arthur's utopian vision of domestic comfort required men to have the sense to make financially sound decisions and the sensibility to avoid the heartlessness that might accompany those decisions. For women, respectability meant carefully steering men in moral directions, all in the name of protecting the sacred home. And nothing was more dangerous to the home than alcoholic drink.[2]

The temperance message attracted Arthur because of its commercial popularity and adaptability. He had never been a drunkard. Unlike the renowned Washingtonian speaker John Gough, Arthur left no carefully crafted narrative of his redemption from the bottle. Apparently, he never felt ensnared by the allure of the deceiving cup and the grog shop. He never referred to a magical conversion to temperance because, in terms of the persona he projected, there was no need. The moral authority of a John Gough rested on his personal experience of escape from the thralldom of a common drunkard and his liberation by the Washingtonians. Gough's life story was thus the product he presented to the public. Arthur, on the other hand, did not obtain his moral authority from an inward temperance miracle but rather by his manifest ability to play the emotions of his readers, to "pull their heartstrings," to become a vehicle for middlebrow sentimental release. His personal experiences mattered little, and he felt no need to outline them in detail for the public. Persona, on the other hand, mattered a great deal.[3]

Arthur did publish an account of his life in a "Brief Autobiography" as an introduction to a collection of his stories titled *The Lights and Shadows of Real Life*, first appearing in 1851. Even this he presented with "reluctance." Revealing

the contradictory demands of the literary marketplace for both artistic authenticity and commercial viability, Arthur confessed how "before the public" he
was despite his own natural shyness. He also admitted the "necessity to write as
means of livelihood, and to write a great deal." He felt a "natural sensitiveness"
about publicity, adding, perhaps disingenuously, "I have lost none of that
shrinking from notoriety and observation which made me timid and retiring
when a boy." The demands of publicity may have been the underlying meaning
of an unattributed poem that appeared in the first edition of *Arthur's Magazine*
in 1844 titled "The Poet's Lot":

> His lot may be a heavy lot,
>   His thrall a heavy thrall,
> And cares and griefs the crowd knows not,
>   His heart may know them all.[4]

The tortured artist, enslaved by his faith in beauty, was a romantic icon but
hardly an accurate reflection of the career of a man such as T. S. Arthur. Despite romanticism's idealization of the lonely artist smitten by his own genius,
Arthur had to cater to popular tastes and may have felt ensnared by the demands of commerce.[5]

Arthur's "Brief Autobiography" illustrated his persona without providing a
sense of the person he really was. Born in Newburgh, New York, in 1809, Arthur
moved with his family to Baltimore in 1817. He received little formal education,
finding math difficult and grammar "completely unintelligible." Instead of the
tender nurturing his mind required, he was "scolded and whipped" by harsh
teachers. The repeated self-denigration of his intellect emphasized the intensity
of his feelings. Heart mattered more than mind. After an apprenticeship, Arthur
worked briefly as a tailor, curiously—given his later career—abandoning the
trade because of defective eyesight. He then became a clerk in a countinghouse.

Economic instability steered Arthur in a new direction. In search of a larger
income, he gained a position as a traveling agent for the Susquehanna Bridge
and Banking Company. His employers suddenly went bankrupt in 1833 while
he was somewhere in the "West." The event was pivotal. Jobless, Arthur returned to Baltimore.

Arthur turned to writing for a livelihood, and his stories frequently stressed
financial insecurity and its moral implications. As he later explained, "During

all this time, I was devoting my leisure moments to writing, not that I looked forward to authorship as a trade—nothing could have been more foreign to my thoughts;—I continued to write, as I had begun, prompted by an impulse that I felt little inclination to resist." Whether because of the irresistible muse within or because of the prodding market without, he became the coeditor of one of Baltimore's numerous and ephemeral literary journals, the *Athenaeum*. Arthur joined a small literary group that included Edgar Allan Poe, meeting in an establishment called the Seven Stars Tavern. Whether he was touched by any sort of immoral miasma there and how much he drank he never intimated. By 1836, he was editing the *Baltimore Monument*, a "weekly journal, devoted to polite literature, science, and the fine arts."[6]

As early as 1838, Arthur wrote stories with clear temperance themes. His interest in the literary potential of the reform thus pre-dated his introduction to Washingtonianism. For example, for the *Baltimore Literary Monument*, now a monthly that he both published and edited, Arthur wrote "The Orphan," a story about a young girl's suffering. The narrator, returning from a business trip in the West, overheard the story of an orphan girl of six put to work in a grog shop. Her mistress pitilessly beat her, but the orphan only responded with prayer. Eventually, the brutal woman's heart softens. She becomes motherly and allows the orphan to go to church and learn to read. The theme of the transformative, redemptive, even miraculous powers of suffering girls exposed to the intemperate, a dominant theme in *Ten Nights*, thus appears quite early in Arthur's career as a writer.[7]

Arthur entered the world of publishing through magazines. His first efforts in magazines during the early 1830s seem more expressions of literary pomposity than of lachrymose and lurid melodrama, hinting little of future works such as *Ten Nights*. As might be expected, his first magazines were commercial failures. One chronicler of Baltimore's cultural life in the mid-nineteenth century wrote, "No strictly literary journal published in the city of Baltimore will pay." Slowly, he was drawn into the vortex of commerce, ably rode the wave of literary fashion, and became "an indefatigable contributor" to the increasingly popular domestic magazines of the antebellum period.[8]

His stories appeared frequently in the most popular antebellum domestic magazine, *Godey's Lady's Book*, and he enjoyed a close friendship with its editor, Sarah Josepha Hale. In the early 1840s, Arthur wrote didactic tales for women with such titles as "Hiring a Servant," "Marrying a Merchant," and

"Paying the Doctor." Between July 1840 and December 1844, a total of thirty-three stories appeared in *Godey's* under Arthur's name.

If Arthur's collaboration with Hale was by design, his association with the temperance movement was almost accidental. As he wrote in his "Brief Autobiography,"

> My choice of temperance themes has not arisen from any experience in my own person of the evils of intemperance, but from having been an eye and ear witness to some of the first results of Washingtonianism, and seeing, in the cause, one worthy the best efforts of my pen.

He happened to be in Baltimore when the first Washingtonian meetings were noticed by the local press. Though nominally a member of a temperance society as early as 1833, Arthur was less a temperance zealot than a literary entrepreneur whose espousal of domestic morality was inseparable from the pursuit of commercial success. For his efforts, he gained an exceptionally large readership, especially among middle-class women.[9]

By the time he published *Ten Nights in a Bar-Room*, Arthur's readers were familiar with his stance on temperance. *Six Nights with the Washingtonians*, a collection of temperance tales published in 1842, was his first best-selling volume. Washingtonianism and the emotionally expressive experience meetings proved a fertile source of material for Arthur's rapidly expanding imaginary world of good and evil, male and female. *Six Nights* was a collection of fictionalized accounts of Washingtonian travails and redemptions. The book presaged much of *Ten Nights in a Bar-Room*. Even the prefaces of the two temperance volumes were similar. Both happily accepted commercial success while denying that commercial gain was Arthur's motive in writing them. In *Six Nights*, the preface asserted the importance of stories as "powerful auxiliaries in that noble cause," temperance, while denying that the tales were really creations of Arthur's mind, "not mere fictions of his own imagination." Instead, the temperance tales in *Six Nights* revealed the underlying truths of Washingtonianism. The author's unique faculties of description and sympathy on observing Washingtonian meetings made the writings possible. Suggested the preface to *Six Nights*, "At every step of his progress in these tales, the writer has felt with the actors—sympathising with them in their heart-aching sorrow, and rejoicing with them the morning after a long night of affliction." Arthur's works fit neatly with a literary marketplace where sorrow, affliction, and rejoicing were valuable commodities. He gave readers what they wanted. He also blew with the winds of change in the publishing industry. In the name of success, Arthur was willing to publish in any profitable format.[10]

Six Nights appeared at a time when the American book trade was in a state of both self-destructive disarray and unprecedented promise. The depression that swamped the American economy between 1837 and 1843 was a decisive turning point in the history of American publishing. As one historian writes of the period, "A mania for cheapness had descended upon the trade, and things would never be the same." Plummeting prices allowed more readers access to literature but threatened established publishing houses. In New York City, a virtual war over the twin issues of cheapness and copyright infringement erupted between *Harper's* and upstarts such as *The New World* and *Brother Jonathan*, periodicals that serialized pirated novels or published "mammoth" supplements of entire novels for a mere six cents. During the 1820s, books on average cost two dollars. By the early 1840s, in a counterattack against the cheap periodicals, older publishing firms had lowered their prices to around fifty cents per book. Meanwhile, established publishers such as Harper of New York City and Ticknor of Boston urged a sharp increase in postal rates as a powerful and ultimately successful weapon against the new competitors.[11]

To protect his "cheap" realm, Park Benjamin, editor of *The New World*, argued against legal protections for intellectual property. For Benjamin, copyrights delayed perfection by obstructing the people's access to moral instruction. Moral uplift required the widest possible dissemination of moral literature. About the same time *Six Nights* appeared, Benjamin wrote that he was "sorry" about the animosity from book publishers, "but the milk is spilled and there is no use crying about it." The community could only benefit, posited Benjamin, from the reduced prices of literature. Thus began "a great literary revolution, which will result in enlarging the understandings of the masses. It is truly democratic—utterly subversive of that intellectual aristocracy which has hitherto controlled the energies of the nation."[12]

Benjamin similarly argued that authors should sacrifice personal gain in the name of a more moral society. It might be financially "hard" on authors, wrote Benjamin,

but when we see the mechanic and the laborer hurrying home to his family after daily toil, with a bundle of publications which would otherwise have cost

him a month's wages, we feel that the injustice done the individual, is merged in
the benefit done thousands.

He then explicitly linked the augmentation of readership made possible by
lower prices with the promise of the temperance movement:

> Besides, this influence of the press is a powerful auxiliary to the great temperance
> movement. Joined with them, it is fast robbing the rum-palace of its victims; it
> renders the neglected home pleasant; restores to the dejected inebriate a true
> sense of his own real worth; and is, in fact, the very essence of civilization. The
> seed thus unwittingly scattered by the way-side, will bring forth a thousand fold,
> and the harvest will be—*the human mind redeemed, regenerated, disenthralled!*[13]

The ministry saw matters differently. The Congregationalist *Boston Recorder*
condemned the cheap press as a purveyor of immorality and competitor to the
religious press, the true guardian of society. In 1844, the *Recorder* wrote,

> A cheap press, if not a positive evil, is at least an equivocal blessing. A vast ma-
> jority of its productions are of a vicious character. It is the depraved appetite
> which is so craving as to create the demand which a cheap press is designed to
> supply. . . . What a torrent of contaminating influences is now flowing over the
> land from the fountain of the cheap press. We are almost tempted sometimes to
> wish that a censorship of the press could be established, or that it were the
> province of some Pope to anathematize and annihilate the worthless and cor-
> rupting issues which are pouring like a continual rain from the cheap press.

The *Recorder* added that the religious press "affords ready and efficient means
of counteracting these pernicious influences, of creating a healthful literary
ta[s]te, of enlightening the mass of mind, and of promoting sound morality
and true religion." The Baptist *Christian Secretary* similarly rued the popularity of light reading and indecent pictures and stories, including in *Brother
Jonathan*. Especially disheartening was the appearance of the same stories,
published "to satisfy the morbid appetite of their readers," in "literary" or
"family" journals read by the religious. Some readers were even pleading
poverty and refusing to buy religious papers.[14]

Arthur positioned himself in the literary marketplace somewhere between
the *Boston Recorder* and *Brother Jonathan*. Even though Park Benjamin applauded Arthur as someone who "writes with singular force and skill," Arthur

found Benjamin's views on cheap publishing and copyright laws troubling. After all, Arthur's financial well-being rested on the reputation of his works as promoting society's moral well-being, and he did not want the cheap press hoarding profits he felt were his. He was horrified by the lack of an international copyright agreement and the "international freebooting" of British publishers who reproduced his works on the other side of the Atlantic. Arthur wanted to ensure the financial position of the primary producer of literature, the author. Benjamin's efforts to spread cheap moral literature as widely as possible damaged Arthur's career interests. Benjamin wanted no copyright protection for authors because copyrights infringed on society's need for moral instruction. Arthur's own argument to legitimize the reading of fiction was rebounding against him.[15]

On the issues of both cheapness and copyright, Arthur occupied a middle position. One could gain readers through cheapness but protect the author's interests by enforcing copyright laws. Ultimately, Arthur offered his books in multiple formats to maximize profits. He seemed to understand that the book trade was in the process of market segmentation and that books as material possessions could be put to different uses. Thus, his writings appeared in various guises, from the dime novel to the gilded gift book.

Just prior to the publication of *Six Nights*, Arthur and his family moved to Philadelphia, a desirable move for an ambitious literary entrepreneur. By the early 1840s, Philadelphia, Boston, and New York City were rapidly consolidating their positions as the leading entrepôts of literary distribution. Baltimore's cachet as a center for letters was in eclipse. In Philadelphia, Arthur continued his prodigious production of bound fiction but also launched his own domestic magazine, an imitation of *Godey's Lady's Book*. *Arthur's Ladies Magazine* first appeared in 1845 and lasted three years. Arthur's own reputation as a didactic moralist was the primary marketing tool for the magazine. As a way to induce gift subscriptions for women, one notice implored men with assurances of propriety:

> Parents, brothers, guardians, and others may introduce our Magazine to those whose interests lie near their hearts, with perfect confidence. We pledge ourselves, on the faith of our Editor, to its moral purity. No improper sentiment— no insidious assault upon virtue—no immodest allusion will ever be found upon its pages. But, instead, every incentive to virtuous actions.

Arthur's Ladies Magazine, at two dollars per year, tried to undersell *Godey's*, but the venture ultimately failed.[16]

Arthur's next attempt at magazine publishing was more durable. *Arthur's Home Gazette* commenced publication in 1850 as a weekly and was transformed into *Arthur's Home Magazine*, a monthly, in 1852. The *Home Magazine* outlived Arthur himself, who died in 1885. He used his magazine to press for an international copyright agreement and to condemn those journals that procured foreign literature at no cost. Arthur argued that "the public mind cannot be satisfied with such [foreign] mental aliment, and will come back to more genial home repasts." In launching his *Home Magazine*, Arthur again stressed his moral reputation. The magazine would enter the home "as a valued friend and pleasant visitor, and leave the minds of all who read refreshed and strengthened." Parents need not have feared a subversive home intruder in print. When he turned from magazines to novels, Arthur was established as a safe author among morally obsessed middle-class women.[17]

TEN NIGHTS IN A BAR-ROOM

While Arthur was promoting his new magazine venture, he was writing his first full-length temperance novel. According to the "Publisher's Preface" to the first edition of *Ten Nights in a Bar-Room*,

> This new temperance volume, by Mr. Arthur, comes in just at the right time, when the subject of restrictive laws is agitating the whole country, and good and true men everywhere are gathering up their strength for a prolonged and unflinching contest. It will prove a powerful auxiliary to the cause.
>
> "Ten Nights in a Bar-Room" gives a series of sharply drawn sketches, some of them touching in the extreme, and some dark and terrible. Step by step the author traces the downward course of the tempting vender and his infatuated victims, until both are involved in hopeless ruin. The book is marred by no exaggeration, but exhibits the actualities of bar-room life, and the consequences flowing therefrom, with a severe simplicity, and adherence to truth, that gives to every picture a Daguerrean vividness.

The preface renders the novel, ostensibly a work of fiction and thus to be read for pleasure, more acceptable and utilitarian by promoting a political program, the prohibition of alcohol in the various states of the Union. Unlike the pro-Washingtonian *Six Nights*, *Ten Nights* advocated state intervention to achieve social perfection. Political mobilization and pleasurable reading were not necessarily mutually reinforcing. The result was a novel structurally bifurcated between political advocacy and emotionally evocative imagery, particularly of familial and communal suffering, violence, and insanity, "some touching" and "some dark and terrible." The last scene of the book, in which the men of Cedarville gather to pass a resolution calling for the prohibition of alcohol within their town, lacks the sensitivity and "heart" so dominant in the earlier, tear-drenched pages decrying the community's moral and physical devastation. In other words, the conclusion replaces the invisible institutionalism of sentimental fiction with the "overt institutionalism" of law. But first comes a besotted apocalypse.[18]

Warding off the potential criticism that *Ten Nights* was a prurient work of voyeuristic excess, the "Publisher's Preface" further protected the novel from attack by asserting that it realistically described life in the taverns. That drinkers were embarked on a "downward course," presented so vividly in the Currier and Ives lithograph of "The Drunkard's Progress" and repeated so often by various temperance media, seemed a stark truth. The novel contains "sketches," a common literary device in antebellum literature, that accurately portray reality with "a Daguerrean vividness." The work connected the literary with the visual arts and thus made a bald assertion of truth. Just as the daguerreotype captured a sort of hyperreality, so would the novel.

For antebellum middle-class readers, the barroom was a morally poisonous place, and the author faced a dilemma similar to that faced by many moral reformers. How does one bear witness to immorality without being contaminated by the lethal miasma of degradation? T. S. Arthur's narrator, some sort of philanthropic traveler and businessman, spends time, ten nights spread out over several years, in the barroom only as a by-product of his need for lodging. Arthur's narrator attempts to elude the double bind of gazing on irresistible immorality while asserting his own moral cleanliness by periodically passing through the village of Cedarville, not participating in its sordid events. At times, he even literally peers over a shielding newspaper as events unfold. Arthur's narrator is a spectator in a forum of drunken folly. He passes moral judgment but does little else. He is also a voyeur, as the subtitle—"and What I Saw There"—makes clear.[19]

In his observations, the narrator scans faces for hints of character. He notes the commercial surroundings with an eye to immoral influences and provides an almost phrenological reading of the entire community of Cedarville. Cedarville, its name nostalgically suggestive of agrarian solidity, has been besmirched by the construction of a tavern, the aptly named "Sickle and Sheaf." By the conclusion of the novel, it is clear what this particular institution harvests. The "man-trap" harvests souls. Even as it wistfully recalls traditional relationships, the novel studiously ignores the role drinking played in fostering premarket communal solidarity. And while nostalgic for aspects of the past, the novel never rejects modernity and its bourgeois norms. At the heart of the novel lies the conflict between two characters, Simon Slade, the proprietor of the "Sickle and Sheaf," and Joe Morgan, erstwhile miller who has slowly but inexorably descended into a life of habitual drunkenness. Over their lives rule spiritual forces of good and evil. Alcohol guides the two men on a downward path, Slade as a purveyor and tempter, Morgan as a consumer and victim. Evil "resides" in the tavern, a commercialized male space that flourishes under the protection of darkness.

With the separation of drink and labor during the antebellum period, the consumption of alcohol was increasingly associated with nocturnal pleasures, a relationship that exists to this day. As sociologist Joseph Gusfield writes, alcohol in America consistently "exists as a sign. Already segregated and separated from work, it is an index to the appearance of a nighttime attitude." A great deal of antebellum reform literature sought to reveal the hidden activities of the night. Good, unlike night and alcohol, "resides" in the middle-class home, a private female space lighted and enlightened by womanly morality. The collision of these forces, in the context and peculiar understandings of antebellum American culture, drives the novel's plot.[20]

Ten Nights in a Bar-Room tells two parallel tales, one following Joe Morgan and the other tracing Cedarville. Both require apocalyptic violence and the sacrifice of young people in order to achieve regeneration. Both body and body politic require the same cure, the elimination of alcohol and thus of evil, from their boundaries. With the banishment of drink comes a reconfigured outlook and appearance—stable, prosperous, and domesticated. Out of the cleansing fire comes a new community, not a return to simplicity and tradition but a new chastened community centered on moral capitalism and civic virtue, represented by prohibition.

The tale opens with the arrival of the narrator at the "Sickle and Sheaf," welcomed by "the good-natured face of Simon Slade," whose handshake is "like that of a true friend." His children Frank and Flora, twelve and sixteen years old, work in the tavern. The narrator worries that Frank may lose his earnest honesty and Flora may somehow be deflowered. Slade dismisses such concerns. His primary concern is his standard of living. Although a successful miller of flour, he launched the tavern as a more profitable enterprise, "thus materially advancing the interests of Cedarville."

At the bar sits Joe Morgan, "a poor, broken-down inebriate, with the inward power of resistance gone." After spending his last few pennies on drink, Joe is retrieved by his daughter, Little Mary. Morgan worked for Slade at the mill but slipped into the life of a ragged drunkard after Slade opened the tavern. At his side remained Fanny, who has never "been any thing but a loving, forbearing, self-denying wife." After a year, the narrator returns to the Sickle and Sheaf. Slade's flour mill is to be converted into a distillery. The moral threats to Frank and Flora have increased in the intervening year. Frank exhibits the heightened ruddiness of the tippler, while Flora's work exposes her to the familiar banter and sexual innuendo of malicious characters. During this "second" night, Slade and Morgan get into a ferocious argument, in which Morgan declares, "As if it were any more decent to sell rum than to drink it." This climactic scene continues,

> There was so much of biting contempt in the tones, as well as the words of the half intoxicated man, that Slade, who had himself been drinking rather more freely than usual, was angered beyond self-control. Catching up an empty glass from the counter, he hurled it with all his strength at the head of Joe Morgan. The missive just grazed one of his temples, and flew by on its dangerous course. The quick sharp cry of a child startled the air, followed by exclamations of alarm and horror from many voices.

Little Mary, in the doorway to once again retrieve her father from the scene of his degradation, lay unconscious on the floor. Carried home, she makes her father promise not to go out again until she gets well, then whispers in his ear, "I shall not get well father; I'm going to die." Before she dies, however, she shelters her father in her bed from the hallucinated monsters brought forth by his delirium tremens. Mary has become Joe's protector. She relates a dream in which Joe Morgan becomes "Mr. Morgan," the owner of "a store full of goods" that has replaced the Sickle and Sheaf. Immediately after securing from her father a pledge never again to drink, Mary dies.[21]

Five years intervene before the narrator's next visit to Cedarville. Slade was indicted for manslaughter, but an influential friend succeeded in having the indictment quashed. Slade is now "a rotund, coarse, red-faced man." The Sickle and Sheaf "had grown coarser in growing larger." Two "greasy-looking Irish girls" work at the tavern, and an overpowering stench leaves the narrator with little appetite for his dinner. The narrator sums up the effects of the Sickle and Sheaf upon the village:

> An eating cancer was on the community, and so far as the eye could mark its de-
> structive progress, the ravages were fearful. That its roots were striking deep,
> and penetrating, concealed from view, in many unsuspected directions, there
> could be no doubt. What appeared on the surface was but a milder form of the
> disease, compared with its hidden, more vital, and more dangerous advances.

During an argument over a card game, a young man is stabbed and then dies in his mother's arms. She immediately dies from grief on the corpse of her son. The assailant is arrested for murder but is killed by a besotted mob, who then turns its fury on the Sickle and Sheaf and its proprietor, Simon Slade. In act of frontier ruffianism, someone gouges out Slade's eye.[22]

Two years later, the narrator returns to the Sickle and Sheaf to witness a vi-olent culmination that brings an end to both the tavern and the tavern keeper. Slade's wife has long since been a resident of an insane asylum and is assisted by her now almost monastic daughter, Flora. The son, Frank, is a habitual ine-briate. During an argument with his father, Frank kills him with a decanter. After a failed attempt at suicide, Frank is hauled off to the county jail.

On the tenth night, ten years after the first, the townsmen of Cedarville come together and decide to close down the Sickle and Sheaf. As he boarded the stage from Cedarville, the narrator sees a man take an ax to the sign that advertised the tavern, "and just as the driver gave word to his horses, the false emblem which had invited so many to enter the way of destruction, fell crash-ing to the earth." The community was saved. The traditional community of Cedarville, unhinged by a witches brew of greed, violence, and sin, would be reconfigured by a rational citizenry and a moral economy. Cedarville, despite the fearful costs, thus traversed the market revolution. Joe Morgan would get his dry-goods store, and the Sickle and Sheaf would be no more.[23]

In the context of nineteenth-century America, what did this tale mean? By the conventions of temperance discourse, both the conversion of Joe Morgan and the destruction of the Sickle and Sheaf represented utopian alternatives to a degraded present. If, as Karl Mannheim asserted, utopias are profoundly delegitimizing, what was being delegitimized by *Ten Nights in a Bar-Room* and its fictional account of an individual and a communal conversion to sobriety? How does one interpret this popular novel in a way that makes it historically meaningful? Jane Tompkins suggests that literary texts are "attempts to redefine the social order" and that readers obtain from texts ways "of ordering the world." What kind of new order was Arthur proffering in *Ten Nights in a Bar-Room*? What did characters such as Joe Morgan, Simon Slade, and Little Mary mean to antebellum American readers? How did this didactic, sentimental temperance novel operate in nineteenth-century American culture? The historian needs to resuscitate a moribund cultural product.[24]

As author, Arthur usurped the minister's traditional role of interpreting and inculcating morality. As Unitarian minister William Ellery Channing admitted in 1841, "The press is a mightier power than the pulpit."[25] As a purveyor of a particular kind of print, the novelist attempted "to redefine the social order" by dictating that leisure be enjoyed at home. Arthur was no ascetic—he offered no "puritanical" rejection of all pleasure. Nor was he a social Darwinist who advocated unrestrained fulfillment through unlimited accumulation. His values were petit bourgeois. Arthur's characters craved middle-class respectability, but even the drive for a modicum of economic security was fraught with moral land mines. Little Mary's utopian vision for her father, seen during a dream, was a dry-goods store. Alcohol, ragged clothes, and Simon Slade's spurious prosperity marked her father's dystopian present.

Slade was irredeemable because he was maddened not just by drink but also by greed. Slade's greed would send an entire community to a violent, anarchic netherworld of cutthroats and scam artists. Slade strove for respectability and, like an upstanding member of the community, believed in the merits of economic development. But the Sickle and Sheaf provided no safe passage through the market revolution. At the other side of an attempt at economic development lay the mayhem of frontier murder, dissipation, and insanity. Slade's unrestrained efforts to climb the social ladder brought both him and his family to destruction. His desire for wealth, unencumbered by morality and effective feminine influences, was as addictive and vile as his patrons' thirst for rum. Slade experienced a change in identity, but it was one that ruined him.

Historian Jackson Lears explains the antebellum obsession with transformations of identity in terms of economic unease over periodic downturns and the unreliability of paper money. The notion of magical self-transformation, long a feature of "animistic modes of thought," itself became a marketable commodity. T. S. Arthur was a particularly adept purveyor of images of self-transformation. Like the evangelical revival and the medicine show, the temperance novel offered a world of second chances. Reform meant more than tinkering with the rules of society; it meant the radical transformation of self. In Cedarville, stability was elusive but attained ultimately through temperance principles. Morgan became a man; he was no longer torn apart by the monster. According to Lears, the bourgeoisie "created an ideal of unified, controlled, sincere selfhood—a bourgeois self—as a counterweight to the centrifugal tendencies unleashed by market exchange." *Ten Nights in a Bar-Room* outlined the creation of that self.[26]

The novel offered more. Because the plot creates a clear parallel between Joe Morgan and Cedarville, between body and body politic, individual goodness and social goodness are achieved in the same way. Both self and community strive for stability, a stability undermined by the intertwined economic and moral dangers of the market revolution. In the grip of the twin monsters, Mammon and Bacchus, Cedarville is itself a drunkard, hurtling toward destruction and chaos. Salvation comes by what Joseph Gusfield terms "benevolent repression," the cleansing of the community through prohibition. But a Maine Law is enacted only after apocalyptic fires engulfed Cedarville, just as intense suffering cleansed Joe Morgan. Conversion follows mayhem, and mayhem makes for a good story.[27]

Joe was at heart a good man. In antebellum America, Demon Rum was the ultimate trickster, the quintessential confidence man. There could be no rational argument with the forces of the rum power conspiracy. A Manichean struggle brooked no compromise. Drunkenness was a direct attack on the unified male self, a Jekyll-and-Hyde nightmare of the most fearful sort. In a pre-Freudian world devoid of id, ego, and superego, a unitary self became a refuge from a dangerously unstable world, especially the dangers and uncertainties of market exchange. The Sickle and Sheaf was evil because it introduced into Cedarville the means by which individual men would be torn asunder and destroyed. Alcohol itself held a magical, diabolical, magnetic attraction—men did not seek it from genetic predisposition or some other medical reason. *It* actively sought them with demonic power. Evil, here defined as bifurcated selfhood, entered the community through market relations, the buying and selling of drink. The temperance novel was thus a powerful indictment of illegitimate forms of capitalism and especially the greed of traffickers in "sin." Traditional communities of colonial America had assumed the right to regulate morality. But the temperance novel introduced a new way of inducing people to choose right, one that was deeply internalized and emotional yet simultaneously spread by an impersonal market in books. The result was a commercialized community of heightened feeling, united by a sense of its own moral superiority.[28]

In *Ten Nights*, as in so much antebellum melodrama, while men contested with evil, women suffered. In domestic fiction, women, often through the flaws of the men in their families, were especially vulnerable to wasting diseases. The consumptive female became a stock character in nineteenth-century popular fiction, and her appeal, according to Roy Porter, suggests that tuberculosis acted as a metaphor for the cultural, intellectual, and moral wasting that accompanied the consumption of goods. The nineteenth-century literary focus on tuberculosis in women may have had a male equivalent. The image of the reeling drunkard parallels concerns with a society and an economy out of control. For single men left adrift by social and geographical mobility, the excessive excitement of drink rendered their systems debilitated and enervated. Similarly, the stimulation of rapid economic expansion might leave society weakened and prey to social diseases such as crime, prostitution, and penury. To successfully transit the market revolution, Americans would need to somehow overcome these threats and become consumers of morality.[29] The readers of *Ten Nights in a Bar-Room*, members of a new community of literary feeling and reassured that the forces of chaos would not prevail, were such consumers.

TEMPERANCE, LITERATURE, AND THE MARKET REVOLUTION

Temperance, as exemplified by *Ten Nights in a Bar-Room*, helped make possible the growth of modern consumerism even as it condemned the excesses of unrestrained capitalism. At first glance, the temperance movement and consumer culture seem contradictory. Temperance is usually associated with Victorian repression. The movement certainly rejected the classical hedonistic practices of Bacchanalian revelry, and the modern pleasures of consumption are usually considered hedonistic. But temperance exalted one type of hedonistic excess, the pleasures of projected emotion. That novels were pleasurable made them morally suspect. Reading a novel is an exercise in the manipulation of emotion and imagination, a helpful skill if one is to attach pleasurable meanings to consumer goods. The pleasure comes from emotional response, not direct sensation as in classical hedonism. Temperance writers exploited the enshrinement of emotion by evangelical Protestantism, repackaged it, and sold it as books. Temperance themes, morally safe, were particularly effective tools in making novels legitimate objects to buy, own, and pine over.[30]

Novels taught readers how to behave. For antebellum Americans passing through the market revolution, the lessons of generations past seemed increasingly inappropriate. Didactic writers such as T. S. Arthur made livings dispensing new truths to help the young make their way through this transformed and uncertain world. Merged with social instability was the theological instability of the era. The "democratization of American Christianity" made theology not the inherited preserve of an educated elite but rather something to be sold to an audience. Rejecting the predestination of their Puritan forbears, Americans in the antebellum North gave credence to a veritable cornucopia of theological systems. With the banishment of Calvinistic gloom and doom came a profound dilemma about the nature of evil. According to vociferous advocates of perfectionism such as Charles Grandison Finney, every individual could be saved through free acts of goodness. Given such theological optimism, what was evil? The answer of T. S. Arthur was clear—it was drink.[31]

T. S. Arthur was a prominent member of the Swedenborgian Church in Philadelphia. He popularized the views of Immanuel Swedenborg, an eighteenth-century Swedish mystic who believed the material world "corresponds" to the spiritual realm. This theological perspective appealed to many antebellum reformers, such as Ralph Waldo Emerson. Since good and evil have their physical manifestations, perfection could be attained by ridding the world of the various embodiments of evil. The bottle of the drunkard and the chains of the slave conducted evil into the world. Bordering on a Manichean outlook, the temperance of Arthur rejected the Augustinian definition of evil as a negation. It would not be a great leap for a reader to believe that goodness was also active in the world and made manifest by the temperance novel. The physical book could bring literally bring good into the world.[32]

The world of *Ten Nights* was textual, not real in any conventional sense. What was real was a printer using stereotype plates to produce innumerable copies of text, a bookbinder collecting those pages inside a machine-produced binding of apparent luxury and artisanal skill, a bookseller exchanging the book for seventy-five cents, a reader sitting in an armchair poring over its pages, and a volume gathering dust on a shelf. How did the textual world of *Ten Nights* connect to the "real" world of production, exchange, and consumption?

Arthur offered his own understanding how books were consumed in one of his earlier stories written for *Godey's* titled "That Vile Book." The story encapsulated the fetishism surrounding book ownership among the emerging American middle class. For the protagonist, the ideal book is "not only beautiful without, but, like a casket, contains precious jewels within." The woman loans the books to "a narrow-minded, sectarian bigot" who figures to discern the character and religious affiliation of the book's owner. Finding "vile and miserable heresy" rather than "precious truth," the sectarian exclaims, "Why this book is enough to corrupt a whole community. . . . The floodgates of infidelity might just as well be opened at once." She is outraged that the book's owner "should not only imbibe such horrible doctrines, but present them to others in the hope of corrupting them likewise." Like a copy editor gone mad, she defaces the book with scrawled condemnations in the margins and even rips out parts of several pages. The book, a cherished gift from a sister in England, is "rendered utterly valueless." The owner is appalled and reduced to tears. For Arthur, the "sectarian" is guilty of an unforgivable crime. Clerical debates over specific religious tenets are irrelevant in this milieu. What matters are the meanings of the little volume as a gift from a loved one and the personal relationship between the author and the reader. The "sectarian" is shown to be lacking in any sense of propriety and respectability. With the story, Arthur cultivates among his readers a faith in the sanctity of books and places them at the very center of middle-class existence.[33]

His sentiments seemed to resonate with middle-class readers. *Godey's* in 1853 described Arthur as "a good man":

He puts no idea upon paper, he adopts no precept, he advocates no maxim, he favors no theory that may not safely be connected with the highest and purest interest of society.[34]

Earlier, in 1844, *Godey's* had published a "sketch" of Arthur, including a full-page etching of his almost boyish likeness. Lauding Arthur as a moral proselytizer,

Godey's emphasized his ability to spread the gospel of domesticity. The magazine did not mention his temperance themes even though he had already published *Six Nights with the Washingtonians*. Instead, *Godey's* alluded to "a number of nouvelettes which were published in the cheap form and diffused over every part of the country, greatly to the advantage of social happiness and the cultivation of elevated moral feeling in the people." The article concluded, "It is fortunate that, in the present instance, the feelings appealed to are the best which belong to our nature, and the popular favorite is one who will never abuse his advantages to the detriment of human virtue and happiness."[35]

Godey's would never have suggested that Arthur's popularity may have rested on prurient interest, on the conventions of what Karen Haltunnen calls "the pornography of pain" and David Reynolds calls "immoral reform." Both *Godey's* and Arthur himself carefully cultivated the image of moral guardian. Despite the violence and voyeuristic excesses of much of Arthur's fiction, his moral message made him a "safe" writer, especially for middle-class women. Reviews often described Arthur's stories as "unexceptionable."

Competitors in the literary marketplace could be less kind. For example, Poe, who probably resented Arthur's commercial success the way Hawthorne resented the popularity of "the damn'd scribbling mob," wrote in "A Chapter on Autography" for *Graham's Magazine* in 1841,

> Mr. ARTHUR is not without a rich talent for description of scenes in low life, but is uneducated, and too fond of mere vulgarities to please a refined taste.... His hand is common-place clerk's hand, such as we might expect him to write. The signature is much better than the general MS.

Poe, who benefited from Arthur's assistance in getting some of his stories published, simply saw Arthur as a hack.[36]

On the publication of *Ten Nights*, *Godey's* offered more ebullient praise for T. S. Arthur. The "practical teachings" of Arthur's many works "have restored so many erring hearts and wandering footsteps to the sanctities and comforts of desecrated and deserted homes." According to the editor of *Godey's*, Sarah Josepha Hale, the novel was "written in the author's best vein" and "abounds in vivid portraiture and scenes of powerful and touching interest." Hale was sure a temperance novel by Arthur while the controversy over Maine Laws roared would "create a sensation." Hale predicted that *Ten Nights* would be a best-seller, with six thousand copies of the book ordered within two weeks of its announcement, even before it had gone to press. If sales failed to reach fifty thousand within six months, wrote Hale, "we shall be very much mistaken." Two months later, she exclaimed what a "wonderful . . . sale there is for every work emanating from the pen of this gifted author. The sale of the last of his productions has far exceeded the most sanguine hopes of the publisher." Meanwhile, *Godey's* acted as an agent for Arthur's books, selling sixteen of his titles by mail, including *Ten Nights* for seventy-five cents. The following year, *Godey's* was also offering combined subscriptions to *The Lady's Book* and Arthur's own domestic literary magazine.[37]

Ten Nights enjoyed hearty sales, but according to Frank Luther Mott, assertions that the book enjoyed sales approaching those of *Uncle Tom's Cabin* were "exaggerations." Still, Mott lists the novel as one of the top thirty-two sellers of the 1850s, with at least 225,000 copies sold by the end of the decade. Sales during the 1850s were certainly aided by the "puffing" of *Godey's*. Many more were sold after the Civil War; cheap editions proliferated after the copyright expired in the 1890s.[38]

Hale found it a "pleasure to publish anything favorable to this just man," adding that she had "never seen anything unfavorable to him yet in print." *Godey's* published excerpts from various positive reviews of *Ten Nights*. For example, the *Germantown Telegraph* called Arthur "one of the most successful writers in the United States" and asserted that

in every one of the numerous productions emanating from his pen, there is a vein of elevating, refreshing thought running through it, that fastens itself upon the heart of the reader, producing an impression which, in many instances has no doubt been the groundwork of many a permanent ennobling moral structure.[39]

Arthur's writings explained the moral implications of the new market economy for a large audience of young men and women, many of whom lacked effective parental guidance. Between Arthur's readers and their parents lay a gaping generational divide, and consumers of domestic literature replaced parents with books. Alongside the economic prosperity of the antebellum decades came unprecedented instability, in terms of both economic fluctuations and the uncertainty of identity itself. According to prescriptive literature such as that of Arthur, only a consciously refashioned identity could cope with the vagaries of social and economic change.

Arthur gave lessons in the cultivation of character. His fiction explored the self as it was assaulted by invisible influences. Both the magnetic pull of Demon Rum and the invisible hand of market relations merged material and spiritual forces. For Arthur, influences that eroded spiritual health impacted on one's financial well-being. Even unrestrained greed, a character flaw, would ultimately result in penury—of self, family, and community. The most inward questions of moral essence thus had enormous social consequences. Books became active agents for moral improvement.

Arthur and temperance writers like him presented the book as the antithesis of alcohol. The temperance novel was a talisman against Demon Rum. Illustrations accompanying temperance fiction often represented the miracle of temperance conversion in terms of material possessions, the most important of which were books. Prior to an acceptance of temperance principles, the husband was violent, clothed in tattered rags, and clutching—and in the clutches of—a bottle, glass, or cask. With temperance comes a new life. The man, now placid and dressed respectably, pores over the pages of a book. Contentment replaces fear on the faces of his wife and children.

Books were a new kind of product. The illusion that the author was speaking directly and privately with the reader was carefully cultivated by the conventions of sentimental fiction. Thus, books maintained an aura of marketlessness even as they were more intensely marketed. In fact, books were marketed *by* the aura of marketlessness. The democratization of reading did not come about solely through cheapness, availability, and mass production. Resistance to printed works other than the Bible needed to be overcome, and the re-creation of feelings of community through books was a powerful tool in that effort.

For middling readers, books seemed to make possible self-actualization without dependence. Liberating rather than confining, encouraging rather than disheartening, books became the perfect teacher and parent for the new American middle class, uneasy about, yet materially benefiting from, market forces.

The novel was a commodity that denied its own commodification. It was consumed in the privacy of one's own home long after an exchange of money had been made. It pretended to be a friend. A reform novel asked only to do good, not to be a good. But in the years prior to the Civil War, the book *was* an increasingly popular commodity, and temperance fed that hidden commodification. By the time *Ten Nights* was published, the American book trade was stable and prosperous. The price wars of the early 1840s had destabilized the publishing industry, but the efforts of the cheap press opened a huge and relatively unexploited market for the established firms. The period between 1845 and 1857 has been called "the greatest boom the book business had ever witnessed." A new cohort of readers had been introduced to fiction in the days of the cheap press. Along with the new nationalistic appetite for American authors, the increasing popularity of fiction reading made Arthur especially successful. With the middle-class home as the target of publishers in the 1850s, Arthur was well-positioned to thrive. He was particularly adept at maintaining control of the financial benefits from his writing. For example, he personally held the copyright to *Ten Nights* and initially offered the novel through three separate publishers.[40]

Arthur's temperance fiction was popular at a time when much of cultural life was being commodified. Its appeal rested on how it dealt with the issues raised by the market revolution. Within works of temperance fiction were vigorous debates on the legitimacy of leisure, production, consumption, public spaces, and social relationships. In such works, alcohol itself became part of those debates. A storehouse of semiotic messages, Demon Rum was truly loaded with meaning, and the manner in which fictionalized accounts of drinking incorporated those messages increased the commercial viability of temperance literature.[41]

During the antebellum temperance movement, Americans published not just their first "high" literature—later called the American Renaissance—but also their first flood of middlebrow books. After the Civil War, publishing and the older temperance movement fused. In 1865, the American Temperance Union became the National Temperance Society and Publication House and resembled a publishing firm more than a moral reform society. During the 1840s and 1850s, the temperance movement's emphasis on reading was meant to displace alcohol with print. Books, signifiers of respectability, would subsume drinks, markers of degradation. For some Americans, the ploy was successful. The consumption of spirits fell as the consumption of books exploded. As that happened, temperance accelerated the commodification of culture. Arthur and others like him railed against the trickster that was Demon Rum.

Ultimately, Timothy Shay Arthur, who so carefully and craftily cultivated the illusion of literary marketlessness, was the more successful businessman.

The confusing cup or the illuminating volume, the deluding siren or the goddess of truth, T. S. Arthur told the consumer to choose. The "real" drunkard of the street, the man whom the Washingtonians sought to save, disappeared in a flurry of print as imaginary brethren such as Joe Morgan struggled onward into bourgeois respectability. The conflation between the literary drunkard and the urban underworld became so pronounced that William Sanger could cite as evidence for the link between prostitution and the rum trade a passage from a temperance novel.[42] Books became a sign of an increasing cultural gulf between drinkers and nondrinkers, a chasm that widened as new waves of imbibing immigrants washed on American shores. Arthur was clearly on one side of that divide.

On the evening of September 27, 1855, the Book Publishers' Association of New York City celebrated the rise of American publishing with a banquet. Arthur, along with seven hundred authors and booksellers, attended this "Complimentary Fruit Festival." Held in the Crystal Palace and illuminated by gaslight, the festivities included toasts to Benjamin Franklin, technological progress, and the newfound international respect for American literature. The president of the Publishers' Association proudly asserted that the publishing industry had "done more for our country than a dozen societies for the suppression of vice and immorality can ever do" by allowing "genius, guided by virtue and sanctified by religion, to struggle into the sunshine of public favor."

Newspaper accounts of the dinner emphasized two things—the presence of women and the absence of alcohol. As a teetotal toast by the Reverend Dr. Osgood announced,

> Let us have a truer festivity that shall alike rebuke churlish selfishness and degrading dissipation. Banishing strong drink and welcoming ladies with less gormandizing and more good taste, our festive entertainments may be cheering as well as elevating and help the social education of the people.

With the banquet, the temperance reform and the publishing industry were wed.[43]

Arthur must have especially applauded the toast. His own career depended on the banishment of alcohol and the welcoming of middle-class women. He discussed the celebration at length in his own publication, *Arthur's Home Magazine*. For Arthur, the banquet affirmed the artistic and reformatory powers of American writers, himself included. He must have been flattered by the marble statue of Clio, the muse of history, and the words above her, written in gas flame, "HONOR TO GENIUS." But what most struck Arthur was his membership in a special but strangely invisible community of authors. Arthur relished the "brilliant affair" and found it "tantalizing to be moving among friends and compeers, and yet seeing all as strangers." Literary production made possible a community of interests but one lacking in direct human contact, and he desired a return to the face-to-face contacts of traditional life:

> How much better will it be for authors and publishers to meet, now and then, on a different plain from that of business, and in pleasant, social intercourse, come to know each other more intimately, and have the feelings stirred with a mutual, personal interest.[44]

Recognized as a literary celebrity, Arthur expressed deep satisfaction that he was at last counted among the renowned writers of American fiction, but he also was uneasily aware that the production of books was a business. For Arthur, books and their creators had mystic connections and communal sympathy. If books had transcendent meaning, authors must also emerge from the mire of quotidian market exchanges. Despite the impersonal nature of the publishing industry, he imagined a real community of book producers. Cold financial calculations sullied aspirations to an ethereal "genius," ironically celebrated by the businessmen present.

Nonetheless, Arthur *was* a commercial success, especially when his pen turned to the world of temperance. In his career, he ably fused bourgeois domesticity, the mass production of print, and the conventions of the temperance movement. Arthur used what today would be called "synergisms" between an expanding publishing industry and a popular crusade against liquor. Arthur's desire for a community of authors mirrored the temperance movement's search for new forms of community modeled on a nonexistent premarket past. Like the larger temperance movement, Arthur was romantically nostalgic for communal connections no longer possible or even desirable from an economic point of view. The market revolution dissolved community, and despite tremendous efforts, new forms of community in the real world were difficult to maintain. A year after the publication of *Ten Nights in a Bar-Room*, Timothy Shay Arthur was still searching for his Cedarville.

NOTES

1. Charles Sellers, *The Market Revolution: Jacksonian America, 1815–1846* (New York: Oxford University Press, 1991), 372; Renato Rosaldo, *Culture and Truth: The Remaking of Social Analysis* (Boston: Beacon Press, 1993).

2. One dissertation credits Arthur as a founder of genre termed the "marketplace romance" and places him at the center of a study of the literary implications of anxieties over political economy and identity. See Francis Timothy Ruppel, "Marketplace Romances: Elusive Ambitions in the Fiction of T. S. Arthur, Edgar Allan Poe, and Nathaniel Hawthorne" (Ph.D. diss., University of Maryland, College Park, 1997).

3. John Bartholomew Gough, *An Autobiography* (Boston, 1845). On authorial person and persona, see R. Jackson Wilson, *Figures of Speech: American Writers and the Literary Marketplace, from Benjamin Franklin to Emily Dickinson* (Baltimore: Johns Hopkins University Press, 1989).

4. "The Poet's Lot," *Arthur's Magazine*, January 1844.

5. The outline of his life is suspiciously similar to that presented in *Godey's Lady's Book* in 1844, suggesting that he also wrote the 1844 "Sketch" as well as an example of his frequent recycling of written material.

6. T. S. Arthur, "Brief Autobiography," in *The Lights and Shadows of Real Life* (Boston: L. P. Crown), 7–8. For more on Arthur's early life, see Warren Graham French, "Timothy Shay Arthur Views His Times," (Ph.D. diss., University of Texas, Austin, 1954), 3–5, and Donald A. Koch, introduction to T. S. Arthur, *Ten Nights in a Bar-Room, and What I Saw There*, ed. Donald A. Koch (Cambridge, Mass.: Belknap Press, 1964), xii–xviii. On how Edgar Allan Poe may have been touched by the conventions of dark temperance, see David S. Reynolds, *Beneath the American Renaissance: The Subversive Imagination in the Age of Emerson and Melville* (New York: Knopf, 1988) and "Black Cats and Delirium Tremens: Temperance and the American Renaissance," in *The Serpent in the Cup: Temperance in American Literature*, ed. David Reynolds and Debra J. Rosenthal (Amherst: University of Massachusetts Press, 1997), 32–35. For a somewhat different interpretation of the relationship between temperance, especially Arthur's view that evil resides in drink itself rather than in the individual, and Poe's writings, see T. J. Matheson, "Poe's 'The Black Cat' as a Critique of Temperance Literature," *Mosaic* 19 (summer 1986): 69–81.

7. T. S. Arthur, "The Orphan," *Baltimore Literary Monument*, November 1838. French, "Timothy Shay Arthur Views His Times," 85, considers "The Orphan" the first condemnation of the sale of alcohol in his writings.

8. John H. Hewitt, *Shadows on the Wall, or Glimpses of the Past* (Baltimore: Turnbull Brothers, 1877), 56. Frank Luther Mott, *A History of American Magazines, 1741–1850* (Cambridge, Mass.: Harvard University Press, 1930), 499. Mott called Arthur "one of the most prolific authors in the history of American literature."

9. Arthur, "Brief Autobiography," 9. "Only three men before the Civil War enjoyed widespread success with women—Timothy Shay Arthur, Nathaniel P. Willis, and George

Mitchell," writes Nina Baym (*Woman's Fiction: A Guide to Novels by and about Women in America, 1820–1870* [Ithaca, N.Y.: Cornell University Press, 1978], 13).

10. Frank Luther Mott, *Golden Multitudes: The Story of Best Sellers in the United States* (New York: Macmillan, 1947), 319 (Mott places *Six Nights* among the second tier of best-sellers during the 1840s); preface to T. S. Arthur, *Six Nights with the Washingtonians* (Philadelphia: L. A. Godey and Morton McMichael, 1842); see also note "To the Reader" in a twenty-five-cent edition of *Six Nights* in which the author is described as writing "without any aim at artificial effect, but simply with a view to let truth and nature speak forth in their legitimate power and pathos," and T. S. Arthur, *Six Nights with the Washingtonians: A Series of Temperance Tales* (Philadelphia: R. G. Berford, 1843).

11. James J. Barnes, *Authors, Publishers and Politicians: The Quest for an Anglo-American Copyright Agreement 1815–1854* (London: Routledge & Kegan Paul, 1974), 1–29; John Tebbel, *Between Covers: The Rise and Transformation of Book Publishing in America* (New York: Oxford University Press, 1987), 64–76.

12. *The New World,* August 13, 1843.

13. *The New World,* August 6, 1842.

14. *Boston Recorder,* July 11, 1844; *Christian Secretary,* August 19, 1842.

15. *Boston Recorder,* December 31, 1842.

16. *Arthur's Ladies Magazine,* January 1845.

17. *Arthur's Home Magazine,* December 1852, September 1852, November 1852.

18. The term "overt institutionalism" to describe Arthur's support for the Maine Law in *Ten Nights* is from Francis Lauricella Jr., "The Devil in Drink: Swedenborgianism in T. S. Arthur's *Ten Nights in a Bar-Room* (1854)," *Perspectives in American History* 12 (1979): 377.

19. Karen Haltunnen, "Humanitarianism and the Pornography of Pain in Anglo-American Culture," *American Historical Review* 100 (April 1995): 303–34.

20. On the cultural tendency to equate night, commercial leisure, and alcohol, see Joseph Gusfield, *Contested Meanings: The Construction of Alcohol Problems* (Madison: University of Wisconsin Press, 1996), 57–74.

21. Indicative of the disdain some historians have held for temperance novels, one history of the role of women in the temperance movement has Joe die along with Mary in *Ten Nights in a Bar-Room.* Had he died, the entire meaning of the novel changes from one of purging transformation through feminine sacrifice to the inevitable death of drunkards. See Barbara Leslie Epstein, *The Politics of Domesticity: Women, Evangelism, and Temperance in Nineteenth-Century America* (Middletown, Conn.: Wesleyan University Press, 1981): 105–6.

22. Arthur was at times a virulent nativist. In *Arthur's Home Magazine* (November 1853), for example, he wrote, "We offer Europeans an asylum, and they turn our country into a common sewer."

23. The conclusion encapsulates Frederic Jameson's view of mass culture and modernism working together to "repress" social problems. According to Jameson, mass culture compensated for the costs of modernity by providing "imaginary resolutions and by the projection of an optical illusion of social harmony." Temperance novels such as *Ten Nights in a Bar-Room,* coming at the birth of modernity, created a utopian space for the restoration of community by

destroying the evil of alcoholic drink, albeit at a fearful cost. Frederic Jameson, "Reification and Utopia in Mass Culture," *Social Text* 1 (winter 1979): 141.

24. Karl Mannheim, *Ideology and Utopia: An Introduction to the Sociology of Knowledge* (New York: Harcourt Brace Jovanovich, 1936), 192–93; Jane Tompkins, *Sensational Designs: The Cultural Work of American Fiction* (New York: Oxford University Press, 1987), xiii–xvi, 123. Herbert Ross Brown wrote that "the temperance novel is dead, and, unlike John Barleycorn, whose demise they so confidently anticipated, these doubly dry pages are without that lusty gentleman's surprising power of resurrection" (*The Sentimental Novel in America 1789–1860* [Durham: University of North Carolina Press, 1940], 240).

25. William Ellery Channing, "The Present Age," in *The Works of William Ellery Channing* (Boston: American Unitarian Association, 1903), 6:162.

26. Jackson Lears, *Fables of Abundance: A Cultural History of Advertising in America* (New York: Basic Books, 1994), 54–75.

27. Gusfield, *Contested Meanings*, 75–100.

28. A theory of addiction was discernible as early as the writings on alcohol by Benjamin Rush, but the antebellum understanding of addiction was in one respect very different from the thoroughly medicalized modern one. Temperance advocates understood addiction as originating in alcohol itself rather than in some genetic predisposition in the individual. The drink and drinker were thus *mutually* attractive. See Harry Gene Levine, "The Discovery of Addiction: Changing Concepts of Habitual Drunkenness in America," *Journal of Studies on Alcohol* 39 (1978): 159. On the impact of the market revolution on how Americans rejected Calvinist dogma and changed their thinking on the relationship between self and evil, see Andrew Delbanco, *The Death of Satan: How Americans Have Lost the Sense of Evil* (New York: Farrar, Straus & Giroux, 1995).

29. Roy Porter, "Consumption: Disease of the Consumer Society," in *Consumption and the World of Goods*, ed. John Brewer and Roy Porter (New York: Routledge, 1993), 58–81; Stephen Nissenbaum, *Sex, Diet, and Debility in Jacksonian America: Sylvester Graham and Health Reform* (Westport, Conn.: Greenwood Press, 1980).

30. Colin Campbell links the creation of modern consumerism with a "romantic ethic" by which material goods acquired almost mystical powers of reverence and transcendence. Campbell argues that "materialism" of the culture of consumption is ironically deeply antimaterialist, that what counts to a consumer is not the good itself but rather symbolically loaded meanings attached to a good. Colin Campbell, *The Romantic Ethic and the Spirit of Modern Consumerism* (New York: Basil Blackwell, 1987).

31. See, for example, Nathan Hatch, *The Democratization of American Christianity* (New York: Yale University Press, 1989), and R. Laurence Moore, *Selling God: American Religion in the Marketplace of Culture* (New York: Oxford University Press, 1994).

32. For a detailed exposition on the relationship of Swedenborgian and *Ten Nights*, see Lauricella, "The Devil in Drink." In Arthur's *Baltimore Literary Monument* for February 1839 appeared an article titled "Swedenborg," which included "propriety of behavior" and social usefulness as among the mystic's tenets.

33. T. S. Arthur, "That Vile Book; or, By Their Fruits Ye Shall Know Them," *Godey's Lady's Book*, October 1842. Historians have recently explored the importance of books as gifts in maintaining social bonds among antebellum Americans. See, for example, Ronald J. Zboray and Mary Saracino Zboray, "Books, Reading, and the World of Goods," *American Quarterly* 48 (December 1996): 595–98, and Stephen Nissenbaum, *The Battle for Christmas* (New York: Vintage Books, 1996), 140–50.

34. *Godey's Lady's Book*, March 1853, quoted in Nina Baym, *Novels, Readers, and Reviewers: Responses to Fiction in Antebellum America* (Ithaca, N.Y.: Cornell University Press, 1984), 193.

35. *Godey's Lady's Book*, November 1844.

36. *Graham's Magazine*, December 1841; Koch, xxv–xxxi.

37. *Godey's Magazine and Lady's Book*, August 1854.

38. Mott, *Golden Multitudes*, 129–30, 308. In the *Dictionary of American Biography*, (New York: Charles Scribner's Sons, 1928), 1:378, the sales for *Ten Nights* during the 1850s is described as second only to *Uncle Tom's Cabin*.

39. *Godey's Magazine and Lady's Book*, November 1854.

40. Tebbel, *Between Covers*, 71. Mott, *Golden Multitudes*, 122, 129; Barnes, *Authors, Publishers and Politicians*, 29.

41. In its ability to absorb, organize, and reorganize various meaning-laden social anxieties, the discursive "alcohol" is similar to Jameson's readings of the novel *Moby Dick* and the film *Jaws*. Of course, in terms of its commercial successes, *Ten Nights in a Bar-Room* more closely parallels the latter than the former.

42. Sanger, whose book is filled with statistical analysis and at least the appearance of scientific rigor, quotes the novel *Mary Barton* by a Mrs. Gaskell (London, 1848) to illustrate the connection between drinking and prostitution: "'If I go without food and without shelter, I must have my dram. Oh! what awful nights I have had in prison for want of it.' She glared round with terrifies eyes as if dreading to see some supernatural creature near her" (William W. Sanger, *The History of Prostitution* [New York: Harper & Brothers, 1859], 542–43).

43. *American Publishers' Circular and Literary Gazette*, September 29, 1855. The banquet is discussed in Ronald J. Zboray, "Antebellum Reading and the Ironies of Technological Innovation," *American Quarterly* 40 (March 1988): 65–82. Zboray examines the publishers whose self-image embodied traditional relationships but whose technological innovations radically transformed the printing trade. Similarly, Arthur nostalgically harkens back to a community of letters while taking part in a restructuring and commercialization of literary production.

44. *Arthur's Home Magazine*, November 1855.

10

Interpreting *Metamora*: Nationalism, Theater, and Jacksonian Indian Policy

SCOTT C. MARTIN

John Augustus Stone's 1829 Indian play *Metamora, or, The Last of the Wampanoags* deserves a place in American cultural history for several reasons. It was the most popular Indian drama of the nineteenth century and one of the first successful plays written by an American playwright. *Metamora* also merits attention as the signature role of the first native-born American star, Edwin Forrest. The tragedian, who became the highest-paid and most celebrated American actor of the 1830s and 1840s, owed much of his success to the perennial appeal of the noble but ill-fated Indian chief Metamora. As one scholar has noted, Forrest's later triumphs "were extensions of his stage Indian, Metamora transplanted to another time and place, but still the proud, doomed individual."[1]

In the past decade, literary scholars and theater historians have suggested other reasons for regarding Stone's play as a significant text. *Metamora*, they argue, justified and promoted the federal government's emerging policy of Indian removal. Southeastern tribes, especially the Cherokee, Creek, Choctaw, Chickasaw, and Seminole, occupied millions of acres of fertile farming land, and white settlers and speculators wanted it. With the passage of the Indian Removal Act in 1830, Washington initiated a conscious and determined effort to aid state governments to abrogate treaties, expropriate tribal lands, and relocate Indians—by force if necessary—to trans-Mississippi reservations.[2]

This chapter is reprinted from Scott C. Martin, "Interpreting *Metamora*: Nationalism, Theater, and Jacksonian Indian Policy," *Journal of the Early Republic* 19, no. 1 (spring 1999): 73–101. Copyright © 1999, Society of Historians of the Early American Republic.

Recent interpretations insist that Stone's play and Forrest's personation of the title character, coming as they did when the fate of the southeastern tribes emerged as an urgent issue in congressional debate and the public mind, represented more than a mere coincidence in the realm of popular culture. Rather, these readings emphasize *Metamora*'s usefulness as a "political instrument" in the Democratic Party's pursuit of its Indian removal policies. While diverging on some of the details, B. Donald Grose, Mark E. Mallett, Jeffrey Mason, Sally L. Jones, and most recently Jill Lepore, who have all written on *Metamora*, concur that the play supported Jacksonian policy.[3]

Compelling as these perspectives sometimes are, they ultimately supply at best a partial explanation of *Metamora*'s place in antebellum culture. Frequently relying on selective readings of the script, interpretations that highlight the Indian drama's political implications make implicit contentions about Jacksonian audiences' reception of the play while offering little evidence to support them.[4] Assuming the operation of Jacksonian racial ideology in popular culture, they beg the question of exactly *how* the play accomplished its putatively political work. What did audiences find appealing, and why? Were alternate readings of *Metamora* possible? Considering the importance of race and Indian policy in Jacksonian society, the dynamics of this intersection between politics and popular culture merits closer study.

This chapter argues that an examination of the emerging mass market for popular entertainment and the nascent theatrical star system it engendered can shed new light on the political and racial aspects of *Metamora*. Central to the discussion will be Edwin Forrest and his audience. Forrest's self-promoting patriotism, growing celebrity, and canny exploitation of an expanding market for popular entertainment are closely linked to *Metamora*'s ability to function as a prop for Jacksonian Indian policy. At the same time, the Jacksonian audience's enthusiasm for the Indian tragedy, even years after other political issues eclipsed removal policy in the public eye, suggests that more than partisan appeal drew *Metamora*'s patrons to the theater. To set the stage, we will begin with some background on the play's creation and then proceed to a critical discussion of its recent interpretations. Finally, we will turn to the broader context of the Jacksonian theater to illustrate how the expanding market in popular culture both furthered and muted *Metamora*'s political and racial messages.

Metamora originated in response to the first of Edwin Forrest's nine playwriting contests. In the process of developing a uniquely "American" school of acting, Forrest sought parts suited to his athletic physique and bold, physical dramatic style. Motivated both by patriotism and by a self-interested search for roles suited to his singular histrionic talents, Forrest decided early in his career to promote American playwriting. In November 1828, Forrest wrote to his friend William Leggett, then the editor of *The Critic*, a New York weekly. As Forrest put it,

> Feeling extremely desirous that dramatic letters should be more cultivated in my native country, and believing that the dearth of writers in this department is rather the result of a want of the proper incentive than of any deficiency of the requisite talents, I [tender] the following offer. To the author of the best Tragedy, in five acts, of which the hero or principal character shall be an aboriginal of this country, the sum of five hundred dollars, and half of the proceeds of the third representation, with my own gratuitous services on that occasion.[5]

Leggett obliged his friend by printing the offer, and by the following summer fourteen plays had been submitted for the judges' consideration. Of these, one stood out. *Metamora; or The Last of the Wampanoags*, by John Augustus Stone, won the prize and was first performed at the prestigious Park Theater in New York on December 15, 1829. An immediate hit, *Metamora* became the mainstay of Forrest's repertoire, earning him tens of thousands of dollars over the next few decades.

Based loosely on the historical Metacomet, or King Philip, as the English called him, *Metamora* recounted the struggles of an Indian chief attempting to protect his family and tribe against Puritan expansion and aggression in seventeenth-century New England. Stone drew extensively on romantic notions of the "noble savage" to depict Metamora as loyal, patriotic, brave, and virtuous despite his lack of civilization. Though Stone and Forrest portrayed the character as immutably different from the English, their treatment bordered on cultural relativism. An exchange early in the play between Oceana and Walter, two young lovers who befriend the chief, highlights this aspect of the character:

Oceana: Teach him, Walter; make him like to us.

Walter: 'Twould cost him half his native virtue. Is justice goodly? Metamora's just. Is bravery virtue? Metamora's brave. If love of country, child and wife and home, be to deserve them all—he merits them.

Oceana: Yet he is a heathen.

Walter: True, Oceana, but his worship though untaught and rude flows from his heart, and Heaven alone must judge of it.[6]

Though initially friendly toward the English, Metamora eventually loses patience with their haughty demeanor, incessant demands, and arrogant treatment of the Wampanoags. Vowing to avenge the wrongs committed against his people, Metamora proceeds to make war on the Puritans, engaging in a number of savagely violent acts. At one point, for example, Metamora commands his braves to enter "the white man's dwelling and drag him to me that my eye can look upon his torture and his scalp may tell Metamora's triumph to the tribe." This is far from the simple creation of a barbaric caricature, however, for Stone and Forrest temper images of Indian brutality and savagery with assertions that white violence and expansion, not innate Indian brutishness, produced the bloodletting:

Mordaunt: Mercy! Mercy!

Oceana: My father! Spare my father!

Metamora: He must die! Drag him away to the fire of the sacrifice that my ear may drink the music of his dying groans.

Oceana: Fiends and murderers!

Metamora: The white man has made us such. Prepare.[7]

After initial military successes, the Wampanoag forces are exterminated by more numerous and better-armed English troops. Metamora retreats to a mountain stronghold with his wife, Nahmeokee, and the body of his infant son, who had been slain by an English soldier. To prevent Nahmeokee from being captured and sold into slavery, Metamora kills her. Defiant to the end, the chief confronts the approaching English troops and offers to fight them all individually, armed only with a knife. The craven English soldiers fire on Metamora en masse, wounding him mortally, but the proud chieftain dies unconquered, cursing the English.[8]

As noted previously, the timing of *Metamora* and Forrest's desire for an Indian play have caused some scholars to detect either sinister motives on the part of author and star or the operation of racist ideology in popular culture.

Certainly, the play's opening a year before the passage of the Indian Removal Act does raise questions, especially considering Forrest's later identification with the Democratic Party. Did Forrest sense emerging political trends and jump on the Democratic bandwagon with a cultural expression of Jacksonian policy?[9] Does the text offer evidence of evil intent or racist proselytizing? What of the response of Jacksonian audiences to *Metamora*? Might the play have evoked white racism and support for removal regardless of the intentions of author or star?

Interpretations that answer in the affirmative incorporate one of two somewhat overlapping claims. The first identifies Stone and Forrest as agents of a racist agenda promoting morally repugnant treatment of Indians and portrays *Metamora* as a fairly straightforward political vehicle for Jacksonian policy. B. Donald Grose, for example, cites Metamora's warlike and barbarous actions in the latter part of the play to argue that Stone and Forrest discard the image of the "noble savage" in favor of the "red devil" stereotype: the Indian as "a sub-human animal who thrives in an environment of rape, murder, violence, torture, and trickery toward well-meaning whites." This reconfiguration of the character—the revelation of his true colors, so to speak—presumably justified the policy of removal and harsh treatment of Indians as mere matters of justice and self-defense. The "timeliness of the script in relation to contemporary white-Indian affairs cannot be disallowed," Grose avers, for "Forrest as Metamora continually reaffirmed to white audiences the irrefutable inevitability of white progress and Indian extinction." Mark E. Mallett focused on the links between Stone, Forrest, and the Democratic Party to argue that *Metamora* supported Jacksonian Indian policy. "Forrest's plays," Mallet contends, "brought the Democrat's message back into the theatre, mirroring the drama staged by politicians. . . . Forrest's *Metamora* effectively distracted public attention from the horrors of the government's Indian removal campaign." Even the more sophisticated arguments of Sally L. Jones, Jeffrey Mason, and Jill Lepore, discussed later in this chapter, partake of this exercise in finger pointing. Jones remarks on Stone's artistry in adhering "to the Jacksonian's party line" while killing off the admirable and sympathetic Metamora, and Mason asserts that Forrest and "Stone appropriated the poetic Indian in order to promote whites' inaccurate concept of themselves as free, lonesome hunters," ultimately vindicating "both nostalgia and removal." Even Jill Lepore's nuanced examination of *Metamora*'s "ambiguities" lapses into denunciation, charging that the federal government "sought support" for removal "partly by invoking images like those popularized in Indian plays and Indian fiction. . . . Metamora was just one of dozens if not hundreds of literary productions by which the fate of the Cherokees, Choctaws, Seminoles, Creeks, and Chickasaws was made acceptable to the American public by virtue of its very inevitability."[10]

The second, more sophisticated rendition of this argument casts *Metamora* as a theatrical imagining of the "other" tailored by Stone and Forrest for Jacksonian audiences. By deploying the noble-but-doomed-savage motif, the play supported removal by making Indian decline and demise appear inevitable and thus no cause for guilt or further debate. *Metamora*, Jeffrey Mason contends, was

> a political instrument, a means of delicately balancing several components of the American sensibility, projecting the passionate nationalism of the new nation by incorporating, incongruously, an emblematic Native American into white narrative, presenting him as an idealized hero who embodied sentimental values—but without suggesting any inconsistency with Andrew Jackson's policy of Indian removal.[11]

Depicting Metamora as a romantic warrior, he urges, allowed white Americans to respect the fictional Indian of the past and mourn his inevitable but "luxuriously melancholy demise." Similarly, Sally L. Jones contends that Stone's Indian is vanquished by the "ineluctable 'march of civilization' and his own intractable nature" but manages to "kill an evil English lord, foil an exiled regicide's devious plans, and befriend the honest, plainspoken Walter and the warm-hearted Oceana, who signify the 'new world order'" before he marches dutifully off into oblivion. Jill Lepore strikes a similar note, arguing that during the 1830s and 1840s, "Edwin Forrest's *Metamora* served as an important vehicle by which white Americans came to understand Indian removal as inevitable, and Philip, newly heroized, became a central figure in the search for an American identity and an American past."[12]

The first claim cited above, and the question of baneful motives can be dismissed relatively quickly. Forrest was but twenty-three years old when *Metamora* opened and had not yet developed his close connection with the Democratic Party. Nor had he acquired the Bowery Boy following that in 1849 would precipitate the Astor Place riot on the pretext of defending Forrest's honor and American dignity against the alleged insults of the aristocratic English actor William Macready.[13] Forrest did not possess a specific constituency at this point, and there is little reason to suppose that he intended to use an Indian character to gain Democratic support. Nor can we infer such intentions from the text, despite the assertions of some scholars.

Though Stone does have Metamora killing the English, he also allows the chief to retain the nobility that made him attractive early in the play. In the first act, Metamora gives Oceana an eagle plume for her hair, telling her that it will protect the wearer from Wampanoag violence in the event of war. Later, in act 3, Oceana gives the plume to her father to prevent his death, offering Metamora her life instead:

> Metamora: Old man, I cannot let the tomahawk descend upon thy head, or bear thee to the place of sacrifice; but here is that shall appease the red man's wrath. [*seizes Oceana; flames seen in house.*] The fire is kindled in the dwelling, and I will plunge her in the hot fury of the flames.
>
> Mordaunt: No, no, thou wilt not harm her.
>
> Oceana: Father, farewell! Thy nation savage, will repent this act of thine.
>
> Metamora: If thou art just, it will not. Old man, take thy child. Metamora cannot forth with the maiden of the eagle plume; and he disdains a victim who has no color in his face nor fire in his eye.[14]

Grose regards this exchange as a "puzzling reversal," but it is puzzling only if one hopes to find the character transition for which he argues. Clearly, Stone and Forrest took pains to portray Metamora in a decidedly favorable light.[15]

Nor can the argument that *Metamora* promoted removal by justifying Indian demise as a product of the inevitable march of civilization be easily sustained by reference to the play script. At several points, Stone's script makes clear that it is not progress that destroys Metamora and the Wampanoags but English perfidy, cruelty, and aggression. In a number of scenes, Stone pricks the audience's conscience by making Metamora seem *more* civilized than his English enemies. In act 2, scene 3, Metamora appears before the English council to answer charges of treachery and hostile intent. The chief, his English interrogator complains, sheltered a religious dissident who had been banished by the holy synod and thus raised questions about the Wampanoag's honesty. Metamora quickly points out the hypocrisy inherent in such a charge:

Why was that man sent away from the home of his joy? Because the Great Spirit did not speak to him as he had spoken to you? Did you not come across the great waters and leave the smoke of your fathers' hearth because the iron hand was held out against you, and your hearts were sorrowful in the high places of prayer. Why do you that have just plucked the red knife from your own wounded sides strive to stab your brother?[16]

Metamora goes on to condemn English aggression, hunger for land, trickery of Indians, and ingratitude for the help his people had given the first English settlers fifty years earlier. Later in the play, Stone juxtaposes Metamora's sparing of Oceana with the treatment the chief's own child received at the hands of the English, who first plan to sell the boy into slavery and later shoot him as he and Nahmeokee attempt to flee. Metamora perishes not because he is an obstacle to white progress but merely, in the character's own words, because "numbers overpower me and treachery surround[s] me." If one does not approach the play looking for evidence of how the text "disempowers"[17] Indians, it becomes clear that Stone wrote and Forrest enacted a version of white–Indian relations much more complimentary to the Wampanoags than to the English.

But if the case for viewing *Metamora* as a conscious attempt by Forrest and Stone to promote Indian removal fails, what of the second interpretation, which emphasizes the participation in and contribution to a larger cultural discourse of white racism, independent of individual motive? Certainly, the work of Alexander Saxton, David Roediger, Eric Lott, and others has demonstrated the capacity of antebellum popular culture to incorporate a variety of images of an ethnocentrically defined other, some sympathetic, into a larger narrative of white superiority and dominance. Leaving aside the question of motive, did the mere deployment of a noble but doomed savage on the Jacksonian stage "instill a sense of the exotic and of 'otherness,' while at the same time retaining attributes with which the audience would identify," thereby combining "both the 'pesky injuns' and 'noble savages,'" to advance the "ideology of a necessarily vanishing race"? Was the Indian drama another species of love and theft and Forrest's noble chief an interlocutor in redface?[18]

Forrest's personation of the chief does appear to have resonated with the same kind of homosocial relation between actor, audience, and character that Eric Lott detected in minstrel shows. The "homosexual-homosocial pattern persisted all through minstrelsy's antebellum tenure," Lott argues, "structuring in white men's 'imaginary' relation to black men a dialectic of romance and repulsion." A similar process seems to have been at work in Forrest's conception and execution of Metamora. The tragedian based his portrayal of Metamora on observation of a Choctaw chief, Push-Ma-Ta-Ha, whom the young actor had met in New Orleans during the 1825 theatrical season. Forrest gained a genuine admiration for the chief's moral and physical endowments while taking careful note of his gait, movements, and bearing. He believed that Push-Ma-Ta-Ha embodied the finest qualities of masculine physical development and that his nobility of character reflected values that Americans could easily and justifiably applaud. Richard Moody recounts Forrest's "vivid recollection" in later life of the "symmetry and grace of the young Indian's figure":

> Forrest shared the ancient Greeks' delight in the beauty of the naked human form. He maintained that fashionable clothes degraded and obscured the beauty that God had created. One evening he asked the Chief to strip and walk back and forth before him between the moonlight and the firelight so that he might feast his eyes and soul on so complete a physical type of what man should be. The Chief obliged. Forrest said that it was as if a living statue of Apollo in glowing bronze had come to life.[19]

White audiences responded to Forrest's histrionic paean to the male form, particularly appreciating the physicality of his performance. As Montrose Moses noted, Forrest wanted not "subtle art" but a "*forensic* pose" that "would hold—and did hold—the masses":

> Forrest wanted characters of a combative nature, which admitted the grace of taut body, and the music of conflicting emotion—sarcasm, pride, hate, love, inspiration, ecstasy. "Metamora" was teeming with these qualities. . . . It gave Forrest an opportunity to stand forth as a gorgeous figure of the red man, whom he had loved in Push-Ma-Ta-Ha, and he conjured into being all he had seen during his sojourn among the Louisiana Indians.[20]

Descriptions of Forrest and his characters often crackled with homoerotic intensity, perhaps pointing to another instance of a process Lott detects in minstrelsy, "in which homosexual desire is deflected by identifying with potent male heterosexuality." Certainly, this approach would explain much of the appeal of the character to white working-class audiences who adopted Forrest as their hero. It could also incorporate and support elements of existing interpretations of *Metamora*. Forrest created an exotic male "other," as Sally L. Jones has suggested, and any anxiety generated by homoerotic attraction to Forrest's body could be assuaged by focusing on the image of a natural man who had long ago passed away, rather than the actor's robust physique, as the object of guilty desire. The adulation of this bygone romantic warrior would allow white male audiences to distance themselves from their homosocial yearnings and, as Jeffrey Mason contends, leave "only contempt for the disappointingly real natives of the present, who, if mere relics, probably deserved to melt away." Whatever Forrest's intentions, then, one might persuasively argue that *Metamora* presented audiences with racial and sexual dynamics analogous to those of blackface minstrelsy, which, in conjunction with the vanishing noble savage theme, served to promote the Jacksonian removal policy.[21]

Yet even here we must tread with caution to avoid an overdetermined explanation supported by little data. Certainly, the smoke of *Metamora*'s timing and content seems to point to the fire of racist ideology and support for removal. But statements about the appeal and effect of *Metamora* are implicit arguments about audience reception. While it seems incontestable that antebellum audiences enthusiastically embraced the play, few contemporary accounts specify exactly *what* about it they liked. In fact, the only anecdote detailing audience response concerns a southern audience who reacted much differently than what might be expected. In 1831, an Augusta, Georgia, audience who witnessed Forrest's performance took the play as an indictment of white treatment of Indians. If Indians were as brave, noble, and virtuous as Forrest's character suggested, how could one interpret the expropriation of tribal land as anything other than theft? "Forrest believes in that d———d Indian speech," one Georgian remarked indignantly, "and it is an insult to the whole community." Sally L. Jones uses the existence of "only one anecdote" of this type to argue confidently that while "some viewers may have squirmed in response to the condemnation of white society's motives and treatment of the Indian, most probably did not." Fair enough, but since no specific evidence exists of antebellum audiences interpreting *Metamora* as a proremoval vehicle, the relative scarcity of antiremoval anecdotes is hardly an indication of audience support for Jacksonian policy.[22]

Given the paucity of data on audience reception, two possible avenues by which Forrest and the play might have promoted removal and racist ideology present themselves. First, the mere deployment of the noble-but-doomed-savage motif may have operated in Jacksonian society as a cultural code for anti-Indian sentiment and thus the support of removal. One can locate abundant evidence for a position of this sort in the works of James Fenimore Cooper and others. But it is also the case that authors sympathetic to the Indian's plight employed similar general themes, the story of King Philip in particular. Washington Irving's "Philip of Pokanoket" offers one example, though it might be argued that Irving's reconceptualization of Philip as a tragic patriot only served to heighten white America's belief in the inevitability of Indian demise. Such an argument works less well for William Apess's "Eulogy on King Philip." Apess, a Pequot, used Philip's story to portray Indian bravery, honesty, and patriotism overwhelmed not by progress but by white treachery, brutality, and hypocrisy. Apess's "Eulogy," which highlights many themes touched on in Stone's play, can hardly be considered support for racism and removal, covert or otherwise. While this does not eliminate the possibility that the noble savage theme may have operated in the white mind to support removal and racist ideology in some circumstances, it does problematize the notion that it invariably did so or that it must have done so in *Metamora*.[23]

The second possibility is that a white actor's portrayal in redface of a noble savage would tap into racist assumptions and support removal in much the same way that white entertainers in blackface pandered to and promoted antiblack feeling. But even locating the appeal of Forrest's Metamora to Jacksonian audiences in its invocation of an exotic, doomed other, both desired and despised, risks overstatement and distortion, for we do not know that this was the specific source of popularity of *this* character. Most of the characters Forrest won fame playing were tragic heroes who could be portrayed in bold, physical style, just like Stone's Indian chief. In fact, two of Forrest's other prize plays, Robert Montgomery Bird's *The Gladiator* and Robert T. Conrad's *Jack Cade*, contain plot structures and noble but doomed leading characters similar to those in *Metamora*.[24] These plays also incorporated opportunities to strut, posture, and flex his undraped muscles, but they did not rely on a racially defined other to generate audience interest. How then can we confidently assert that *Metamora*'s appeal and political importance lay in its message of Indian decline and white progress when other of Forrest's dramatic vehicles used similar character types and plot structures?

Even if we put aside doubts raised by scanty evidence and accept the proposition that *Metamora* promoted the notion of inevitable Indian decline in the face of white progress, questions remain. Who in Jacksonian society needed to be convinced that white America would ultimately supplant, if not destroy, the continent's Indian population? Despite the bare majorities by which the Indian Removal Act passed in both houses of Congress, the overwhelming majority of white Americans shared the conviction of Native American inferiority and eventual extinction in the face of "civilized" society, and many shed no tears on this count. At best, Stone and Forrest were, in effect, preaching to the choir.

In addition, the problem persists of connecting this message of inevitable decline to Jacksonian removal policy. Did the belief of white Americans in the inescapable demise of Indian peoples automatically translate to or equal support for removal? Lepore, Mason, Jones, and others seem to believe so. But juxtaposing *Metamora* with the political and social debates surrounding removal suggests other possibilities. As Sherry Sullivan noted of Indian fiction, "Acceptance of the inevitable end of White civilization's triumph does not mean accepting, or even condoning, the cruel means by which that end is accomplished." The significant opposition that Jackson's removal policy elicited from political opponents and social reformers stemmed from exactly such a distinction. In this context, *Metamora* appears as an obstacle to rather than facilitator of Democratic plans for removal. If anything, the play's negative depiction of the English and Forrest's sympathetic portrayal of the Indian chief suggests that white mistreatment and treachery were especially reprehensible in dealings with this admirable if unfortunate people. But this position does not support the contention that Forrest hoped to court Democratic support, for he would have been rendering the party the dubious service of articulating the National Republican and, later, the Whig position on removal.[25]

There are other reasons for questioning the argument that *Metamora* piqued audience interest through a narrow partisan appeal or even a more diffuse invocation of white racism. Evidence suggests that these tactics simply did not draw spectators. Theatrical managers, perhaps the canniest and most knowledgeable students of audience taste, realized the danger of using plays as political vehicles: paying customers who were offended by the message might be driven away, threatening further the always precarious financial position of theater companies. David Grimsted noted the pitfalls involved in politicizing drama by eliciting emotional responses to sympathetic or loathsome characters that represented ideological positions:

> *Uncle Tom's Cabin* was the first play to use these techniques successfully in a really controversial cause, and it probably would have failed, as it did at first, had not the novel readied the public for its message. Even farces like *The Bank Monster; or, Specie and Shin-Plaster,* "an excellent hit at the time," had to keep "free from political allusions." [Actor James] Hackett understood the situation when he asked an author to write a play "spiced with some pungent glances at the present state of affairs without going deep enough to offend any party."[26]

If political themes proved risky, were racial allusions any better as crowd-pleasers? Exaggerated vernacular dialogue and stereotypical characters might fill houses, but racist images could hardly be subtly drawn. If actors and playwrights appealed to Jacksonian audiences' racist assumptions and predilections, they did so in the broadest possible strokes to evoke the maximum approval. Audiences might miss references to noble savages as derogatory to Indians; they were less likely to mistake the meaning, for instance, of *The Lion of the West*'s Nimrod Wildfire contemptuously commanding an African American servant to "skulk, you black snake" and observing to an English visitor that the "Niggers [are] such lazy varmints. I had one once myself, he caught the fever and ague—the fever he kept, but the ague wouldn't stay with him, for he was too lazy to shake!" To attract Jacksonian audiences, playwrights had to mute politics and foreground racism. Thus, those scholars who claim that *Metamora*'s popularity rested on a complex racial argument in support of a blatantly partisan cause flout contemporary wisdom about the financial viability of topical subjects.[27]

Further, assuming that *Metamora*'s significance depends solely on the identification of its racial or partisan elements threatens to blind us to what the play can reveal about larger cultural, economic, and political currents in Jacksonian society. In the past fifteen years, U.S. historians have become increasingly interested in the notion of a "market revolution" in the early nineteenth-century United States as a way to conceptualize and understand the turbulence of that era's political, economic, and cultural change. Supplementing theoretical approaches to the operation of power relations with detailed historical research into the impact of market forces, historians have generated new insights into the antebellum United States and established the importance of the expanding market as a context for analysis. Broadening the analytical horizons to include the market in mass entertainment and popular culture brings Forrest's involvement with *Metamora*, the play's relation to Indian policy, and audience response into clearer focus.[28]

Metamora's larger significance rests in its reflection of broad developments in American artistic, cultural, and economic life during the early nineteenth century, not in a narrow quest for partisan support or political influence. With the shift from elite to popular patronage as the dominant form of artistic economic support, Americans often eschewed what many artists and critics considered to be uplifting and refined entertainments in favor of sensational or pedestrian amusements. Artists, authors, playwrights, and actors responded in a variety of ways. Some bemoaned the average American's lack of taste. Others attempted to find methods of attracting popular support while retaining artistic standards, and some budding entrepreneurs exploited the economic possibilities of a mass audience.[29] Edwin Forrest embodied this third group as well as any member of his generation.

Early in his career, Forrest realized that in the expanding Jacksonian market for popular entertainment, artistic productions, as well as performers themselves, were valuable commodities that could be exploited economically. In 1826, Forrest earned $40 a week as a stock player. Even at this amount, Forrest's wages compared favorably to those of skilled workers, who earned approximately $1 a day. But Forrest recognized that he could earn far more, especially as his celebrity grew. His physical, "American" acting style became so popular that his manager, James Gilfert, "loaned" him to other theaters for $200 a night. When his contract with Gilfert expired and the manager approached him about a renewal, the young actor "replied that he would willingly remain for the valuation which Gilfert himself had placed upon him." Forrest's first essay in self-commodification proved successful. Gilfert engaged him for eighty performances at $200 a night, thereby establishing Forrest as one of the biggest stars of the American stage.[30]

The emergence of a star system in the American theater, which Forrest's talent for self-promotion illustrates, provides a context for addressing the question of why Jacksonian audiences thronged theaters to see an Indian play.

Evidence suggests that in large measure it was not the play's content or political implications but rather the star that attracted them. Though Indian characters had appeared in American plays prior to 1829, there had been no "wild enthusiasm" for them before. Forrest's charismatic performance changed that, but not because Americans suddenly wanted plays about Indians to justify government policy or endorse racist notions of white superiority. Most contemporaries recognized that *Metamora*'s success sprang from Forrest, not the play itself, which they considered inferior. Journalist Charles Congdon, for example, called the play a "farrago of bombast and bad rhetoric," wondering why Forrest did not abandon it for superior material such as Shakespeare but rather "went on playing those parts written for his private legs and larynx, to the end." James Rees, Forrest's biographer, remarked that the drama owed its success "almost entirely to the actor, as its literary merits were feeble." Likewise, for Francis C. Wemyss, it was the actor and not the play that drew crowds. Wemyss observed that it "is a very indifferent play, devoid of interest; but the character of Metamora is beautifully conceived, and will continue to attract, so long as Mr. E. Forrest is his representative; it was written for him, and will, in all probability, die with him." As it turned out, Wemyss was right.[31]

Modern scholars support the opinions of Forrest's contemporaries. Theater historian Bruce McConachie, for instance, contended that Forrest's prize plays were designed to focus audience attention on him, not on the dialogue or plot structure. McConachie argues that the "rhetoric of Forrest's heroic melodramas encouraged generalized hero worship, not attention to specific political concerns of the day." Thus, *Metamora* represented a venue for the adulation of Forrest, not the endorsement of Jacksonian Indian policy. Richard Moody's account of *Metamora*'s reception in Natchez, Mississippi, in 1839 supports this interpretation nicely. Despite atrocious supporting actors, inadequate props, technical mishaps, and onstage interference by local ruffians, Forrest nonetheless received tremendous applause when he finally abandoned efforts to salvage the performance and "squeezed a small bag of red paint upon his dauntless countenance, turned to the audience, fell and expired." Comparable episodes occurred elsewhere during Forrest's touring engagements, with similar results, suggesting that audiences paid little attention to the content and quality of the play and much to the performance of the star.[32]

The financial opportunities presented to cultural entrepreneurs by the emerging star system offer another vantage point from which to interpret both *Metamora*'s and Edwin Forrest's relation to Jacksonian politics. One might assume that Forrest's championing of Democratic initiatives would win him theatrical patronage from the party's adherents, thereby furthering both his financial interests and Jacksonian policy. But a closer look reveals that in many ways, the imperatives of marketplace and voting booth conflicted rather than coalesced. Whether one argues that author and star intended to promote removal policy with *Metamora* or that the play fostered anti-Indian sentiment by participating in a larger racist discourse, examination of Forrest's relation to Democratic politics indicates that his determined pursuit of the main chance diminished the play's viability as a vehicle for disseminating a political message. Though he often courted the Democratic Party and its working-class supporters with public effusions of strident masculinity and chauvinistic patriotism, Forrest's commitment to exploiting the new market for American plays and actors led him to pursue economic gain to the detriment of political service throughout his career. The tragedian frequently employed nationalistic rhetoric to enhance his image, but his patriotic enthusiasm usually benefited him more than the American public or the Democratic Party. The playwriting contests in general and *Metamora* in particular illustrate this point.

Forrest and his supporters often depicted his sponsorship of the playwriting contests that produced *Metamora* as an act of unmitigated patriotism, but his treatment of the prize winners appears to have had a chilling rather than a stimulating effect on American drama. After paying out the prize money and the proceeds from a benefit performance, Forrest considered his responsibility to the playwrights completely discharged. Certainly, the direct payment of an author for a script was an accepted and traditional method for compensating playwrights. But Forrest could hardly claim as unvarnished patriotism his recourse to a policy that discouraged American authors and produced reactions ranging from hard feelings to, quite possibly, suicide. John Augustus Stone did not benefit from the prosperity *Metamora* generated for Forrest. While the actor apparently lent Stone money and paid his hotel bills from time to time, he did not share the windfall profits he garnered from performances of the Indian drama. Stone's continuing financial problems may have contributed to what one commentator called his "symptoms of incipient insanity." Stone committed suicide by drowning himself in the Schuylkill River in June 1834. Forrest, feeling a "sentimental pang," made the "grand gesture" of paying for a tombstone over the author's grave. It read, "By his friend, Edwin Forrest."[33]

Nor were Forrest's relations with Robert M. Bird, another prize winner, much happier. Bird authored three prize plays and revised Stone's *Metamora* for use on the English stage. Disputes over finances strained communications between actor and author, as each claimed the other owed him money. Forrest had lent Bird money, but Bird believed he was due a much greater share of the profits from his enormously successful *Gladiator* and *Broker of Bogota*. Forrest refused to pay Bird any more than the prize money and proceeds from one benefit and demanded repayment of a $2,000 loan. Bird refused, broke off relations with the actor, and gave up playwriting entirely, thereby denying the fledgling American drama a promising author. In his treatment of both playwrights and dramatic literature, Forrest demonstrated clearly his proclivity to place his own interests in exploiting an expanding market in popular entertainment before those of party or nation.[34]

Highlighting the tension between market exploitation and political proselytization also sheds light on the sympathetic aspects of the character Metamora. Forrest's primary purpose was to create a character that would produce large box office receipts, not to contribute to a cultural discourse emphasizing Indian decline. Indeed, his commitment to the former goal effectively compromised *Metamora*'s usefulness, consciously intended or otherwise, to serving the latter. To use the character to its best effect, Forrest depicted Metamora as noble and virtuous, not base and treacherous. Hence, Forrest could not enact an Indian character sure to garner white antipathy, such as the brutish, bloodthirsty savages created by Robert Montgomery Bird in *Nick o' the Woods*, though such caricatures might have generated more overt support for removal. Villains were simply not Forrest's forte, and Metamora was no exception to the rule.

Though obviously savage by "civilized" American standards, Metamora was written to be an admirable, attractive character that would advance Forrest's heroic image and theatrical career. Available evidence suggests that Forrest played Metamora sympathetically and, by the standards of the time, realistically. One perhaps apocryphal story relates that a delegation of western Indians who viewed the play were so convinced by Forrest's performance that they chanted a dirge after the death scene to honor the fallen chief. From a very different perspective, no less a discerning critic than Margaret Fuller praised Forrest's realistic portrayal of the role, if not the literary quality of the play.[35] If an admirable Metamora raised questions about the morality and justice of white treatment of Indians, so be it, as long as performances produced heavy gates. Whatever the political exigencies of Jacksonian Indian policy, Forrest perceived clearly that a noble savage was a much more salable commodity than a murderous brute. In effect, the demands of the market and the star system it created muted whatever racism the deployment of an Indian character might otherwise have engendered.

Attention to Forrest's dedication to market rather than political imperatives also illuminates his monopolization of the character he commissioned. If Forrest wanted *Metamora* to be effective either as proremoval propaganda or as a stimulus to American playwriting, the play would have to be disseminated reasonably widely through performance or publication and the author suitably rewarded. Such was not the case. After paying Stone for the manuscript, Forrest considered the play to be his personal property, which, in the absence of a copyright law protecting plays, it probably was. He refused to allow anyone else to play the title role, so that it truly would be a signature piece. Nor would he permit it to be published, lest other actors perform it without his knowledge. Forrest guarded the manuscript so jealously that for decades the play was lost. Only in the mid-twentieth century did scholars uncover complete copies, and then in England, not in the United States.[36] Though Forrest performed *Metamora* widely, he could be in only one theater at a time, effectively diminishing the possibility of saturating a mass audience with proremoval propaganda. Possibly, Forrest had multiple motives or conflicting intentions for the play, but his actions bespoke greater devotion to personal than to partisan concerns. In both his tailoring of the role to his particular talents and his restriction of its performance, Forrest heeded the siren song of the market, not the huzzahs of a political party or patriotic cause.[37]

No incident illustrates Forrest's priorities better than his brush with electoral politics. In 1838, New York City Democrats invited Forrest to deliver an oration at the party's Fourth of July celebration. For an hour and a half, Forrest thrilled the large Democratic crowd that filled the Broadway Tabernacle with his patriotic rhetoric and charismatic declamation. As he did on stage, the tragedian took particular pains to praise and please the common man. "Here at last," he thundered, "is discovered the grand political truth, that in the simplicity of government consists the strength and majesty of the people."

By "what principle, accordant with equal rights," Forrest demanded, "are the penal interdictions of the law thrown across my path, to shut me from a direction which another may pursue without fear or hindrance?" The overwhelming acclaim that greeted Forrest's speech produced a favorable notice in the September 1839 issue of the *Democratic Review*. Forrest's stirring oration demonstrated, the editors trumpeted, that the "power of wealth has not had sufficient strength to draw the literature of the country wholly into its sordid grasp."[38]

Forrest's oratorical triumph, along with his celebrity, persuaded New York's Democratic nominating committee to solicit the actor as a candidate for the House of Representatives in the next election. Considering Forrest's visibility, popularity, and reputation for spread-eagle patriotism, "it was the general opinion," fellow actor Francis Wemyss observed, "[that] had he entered the contest, he would have been elected." Still, he declined to run. In a letter to the nominating committee, Forrest explained his reluctant refusal. The "duties of Legislation," he asserted, "could not be adequately discharged without more preparatory study and reflection" than he had time to bestow on them. Staunch Democrat to the end, however, Forrest promised to return to New York despite "a very considerable pecuniary sacrifice" so that his "ballot may swell the majority."[39]

To be sure, talk of nominating Forrest raised eyebrows. Philip Hone, who had enjoyed Forrest's performance as Othello a year earlier (Hone observed that Desdemona never had "so good an excuse for her misplaced affections"), fulminated in 1838 that the actor had

> no claim, that I ever heard of, to the honor of representing the people of New York in Congress but that of exciting the pit of the Bowery Theater to raise their shirt sleeves high in the air and shout Hurrah for Forrest! He may be the leader of the Pitt party [that is, the Bowery's patrons], but no statesman.[40]

Other critics questioned Forrest's intelligence, suggesting that if the actor won a seat in Congress, William Leggett, his friend and adviser, would have to be given a stool beside him.[41]

Considering this type of criticism and the reasons Forrest gave to the nominating committee for his refusal to run (insufficient "preparatory study and reflection"), one might conclude that Forrest declined for altruistic reasons. Patriotism demanded that he step aside in favor of a more qualified candidate;

flattering his vanity by accepting an undeserved honor courted injury to both his reputation and that of the Democratic party, especially if he proved to be an incompetent legislator. In private, however, Forrest told a very different tale. A friend asked him why he declined to run, considering the honor the nomination had conferred on the otherwise questionable profession of acting. Forrest responded, "I want no further honor, and can't afford to give my time for $8 a day, when I can make $200 out of it."[42] As with the playwriting contests, Forrest recognized the marketability of cultural commodities, whether human or literary, and exploited them to the utmost. Political and partisan considerations ran a distant second.

Where, then, does this leave us? Did Stone's play and Forrest's performance resonate with Jacksonian audiences because of their cultural proximity to the unfolding political discussion of Indian removal? Probably. It would be a mistake, though, to overemphasize the relationship between *Metamora* and Indian removal, if only for the lack of evidence supporting a close connection between the two. Were Jacksonian audiences more interested in Forrest than the plays in which he appeared? Undeniably. But this still begs the question of *Metamora*'s unparalleled popularity and durability and brings us back to the problem of audience reception. If support for removal was not the play's primary draw, then why did Jacksonian audiences pack theaters to see it? What made *Metamora* more popular than Forrest's other prize plays and the doomed chief his most memorable and successful character?

In the absence of data on audience reaction, the most satisfactory answer, I believe, lies not in narrowing the scope of cultural analysis to a search for the mechanisms of political or racial domination. Rather, we must broaden it with the recognition that, taken together, the play and Forrest's portrayal of the main character constitute a symbolic field whose density and complexity encompasses but also surpasses that of the noble savage. In this regard, it will be useful to remember what the late anthropologist Victor Turner termed the "multivocality" of symbols. The varying meanings with which observers invest symbols, Turner demonstrated, depends not just on the temporal and cultural contexts in which they are deployed but also on their proximity to other symbols. Thus, identical images might convey something quite different, depending on how they are displayed.[43]

From this perspective, *Metamora* and Forrest's portrayal of the title role comprise a rich fabric of interwoven and interacting symbols. On one level, the noble savage theme did, as the previously cited scholars suggest, play into white America's notions of progress, race, and territorial expansion. If it did not directly promote removal, it may well have pandered to the racist ideology that underpinned the policy and made it acceptable to white Americans. Still, this does not exhaust its symbolic possibilities. Stone's and Forrest's images of a heroic son of the forest also evoked the long European tradition of primitivism, the "belief that other, simpler societies were somehow happier than one's own." Though most eighteenth- and nineteenth-century theorizing on primitive societies and the "savages" that populated them predicted and approved their ultimate destruction by the progress of civilization, this smugness coexisted with a less confident element of the tradition. As Roy Harvey Pearce has pointed out, implicit in Euro-American primitivism was a critique of the corruption and decadence of civilized life that conceived the Indian "as the paradoxical man who was civilized because he was uncorrupted by civilization."[44]

This aspect of primitivism emerges in Stone's script when he depicts Metamora as more just and humane than his English enemies despite his savagery and their civilization. This invocation of a critical primitivism influences the meaning of the Indian as symbol. In the context of the play's English–Indian rivalry, the virtuous and brave Metamora points to America's claim of moral superiority to the Old World. Here the Indian symbolizes a distinctively American character, a product of the unsullied natural environment of the New World, superior physically and morally to the arrogant and treacherous English.

On the most basic level, Forrest's conception of the play as a tragedy, not a melodrama, as subsequent critics have termed it, had important cultural ramifications for Jacksonian audiences. Forrest and Stone imparted American history with dignity and importance by deriving tragedy from it. *Metamora* asserted that American characters, situations, and actors provided eminently suitable material for tragedy, a genre previously the sole province of aristocracy.[45] In an era when Americans still smarted from the recognition of their cultural inferiority to England and Europe, Stone and Forrest affirmed the worthiness and value of American civilization by deploying the Indian as symbol of American virtue against English decadence. In this reading, the Indian functions as inspiration for, rather than obstacle to, true national progress. Only by incorporating natural virtue into American civilization could the United States escape the decay and corruption that characterized the Old World. *Metamora's* nationalism, then, may have leveled a confident gaze westward across a continent awaiting settlement by white Americans, but it also glanced anxiously eastward, across the Atlantic to an England that still cast a long cultural shadow on the new republic.[46]

The meaning of primitivism and the Indian as American were further shaped by their proximity to another potent symbol: Edwin Forrest himself. Philip J. Deloria has explored how many white American men during the Jacksonian era joined clubs, such as the Order of Red Men, that emphasized Indian dress and themes. Playing Indian, Deloria argues cogently, allowed white men to imagine new American identities, "meaningful in relation to the successful Revolution, the emerging market economy, and the new governments and political parties busy consolidating and distributing power across the landscape." But Forrest was hardly comparable to these legions of fraternal Indians. The tragedian self-consciously promoted himself as the quintessential product of American democracy, a common man whose irrepressible vitality, untutored talent, and natural virtue made him a fitting representative of the new nation's promise of greatness. As David Grimsted observed, "Forrest pictured himself as a knight-errant of American democracy and lost no chance to draw attention to his love of country and love of the people."[47] By the time he premiered in *Metamora*, Forrest's creation of his patriotic image was well under way, and audiences had already begun to embrace him as a symbol of vibrant American culture unfettered from the stultifying aristocratic influence of the Old World. Thus, we cannot interpret Edwin Forrest and Metamora separately, for the appeal of the play rested on Edwin Forrest *as* Metamora, a uniquely American actor portraying a uniquely American character.

Here again it is useful to reflect on how the juxtaposition of symbols functioned. Forrest's identification with the common man allowed Jacksonian audiences to see themselves in him, vying successfully with classically trained and highly educated English actors for dramatic laurels. At the same time, they could also claim Metamora's virility, heroism, and nobility, qualities Forrest sought to exemplify, on- and offstage, as their own. This process mirrors what Rosemarie K. Bank has identified, in slightly different contexts, as a transformation "in which the history of the 'native' became the native history," whereby white Americans "could see the Native American next door as alien yet treat him or her as a symbol of mediated self."[48]

What made *Metamora* more popular than Forrest's other prize plays or Shakespearean productions, which also offered physically imposing heroes battling tyranny, was its use of a distinctively American primitivism to address the nationalist and class interests of its audience. If *Metamora* demonstrated the superiority of democratic America to aristocratic England, did it not also follow that American democrats surpassed the nation's would-be aristocrats in virtue and worth? Forrest's increasing identification with the Jacksonian common man gave *Metamora*'s primitivism a class as well as a nationalist tenor and helps account for the play's popularity even after Indian removal faded as an urgent public issue. The fusion of actor and character asserted that the common man could aspire to the heights of civilization while retaining the primitive virtues that defined America's superiority to the Old World.[49] And best of all, this affirmation of self, class, and nation could be had for the price of a theater ticket.

Moreover, Forrest's robust acting and muscular physique offered his working-class audience the same kind of overbearing masculinity and homoerotic allure that Eric Lott has detected in minstrelsy. Here again, Forrest demonstrated enormous perspicacity in packaging himself and a dramatic vehicle to suit the needs and desires of an increasingly assertive working-class audience. In essence, *Metamora* exploited the market in mass entertainment by providing Jacksonian audiences with a commodified patriotism that affirmed (and to some extent linked) self-confident nationalism and working-class pride.

The foregoing suggests that overemphasis of political and racial ideology as the preeminent analytical context may cloud rather than clarify the relationship between *Metamora* and Jacksonian Indian policy. There is little evidence that the author or star intended the play to drum up support for removal or that antebellum audiences perceived it as an apology for the Democrat's anti-Indian policy. Partisan politics may be one context for interpreting *Metamora*, but the expansion of the market in popular entertainment during the early decades of the nineteenth century is another. Forrest understood well the value of artistic productions and of himself as valuable commodities in that market.

Metamora fulfilled several of Forrest's requirements: it provided a vehicle for his theatrical ambitions, a chance to demonstrate his physical prowess, and an opportunity for self-promotion as a patriotic supporter of American culture. To Jacksonian audiences, *Metamora* offered the opportunity to celebrate their national and class identities while temporarily forsaking their everyday lives for "a stage reality reflecting their ideas of what life should or might be— all charged with excitement and transcendent fantasy."[50] The play may indeed have owed most of its popularity to the Indian theme, but any connection to Jacksonian policy must be viewed as subsidiary or indirect. Certainly, the expansion of the market produced a number of results, among which were both the commercialization of art and the expropriation of Indian lands. But a close consideration of *Metamora*'s place in antebellum culture and the contexts in which it can be interpreted should give pause to scholars who are quick to detect efforts to engineer political advantage in every corner of art and popular culture.

NOTES

1. Donald Grose, "Edwin Forrest, *Metamora*, and the Indian Removal Act of 1830," *Theater Journal* 37 (May 1985): 185.

2. Among the most useful treatments of Jacksonian Indian policy are Ronald Satz, *American Indian Policy in the Jacksonian Era* (Lincoln: University of Nebraska Press, 1975); Anthony F. C. Wallace, *The Long Bitter Trail: Andrew Jackson and the Indians* (New York: Hill & Wang, 1993); and Francis Paul Prucha, *American Indian Policy in the Formative Years: The Indian Trade and Intercourse Acts, 1790–1834* (Cambridge, Mass.: Harvard University Press, 1962).

3. The term "political instrument" comes from Jeffrey D. Mason, "The Politics of Metamora," in *The Performance of Power: Theatrical Discourse and Politics*, ed. Sue-Ellen Case and Janelle Reinelt (Iowa City: University of Iowa Press, 1991), 93. In addition to Mason's and Grose's work, already cited, see Mark E. Mallett, "'The Game of Politics': Edwin Forrest and the Jacksonian Democrats," *Journal of American Drama and Theatre* 5 (spring 1993): 31–46; Sally L. Jones, "The First but Not the Last of the 'Vanishing Indians': Edwin Forrest and Mythic Re-Creations of the Native Population," in *Dressing in Feathers: The Construction of the Indian in American Popular Culture*, ed. S. Elizabeth Bird (Boulder, Colo.: Westview Press, 1996), 13–27; and Jill Lepore, *The Name of War: King Philip's War and the Origins of American Identity* (New York: Knopf, 1998), esp. 191–226.

4. Throughout this chapter, I will use the both "Jacksonian audience" and "working-class audience" to describe those who attended *Metamora* and Forrest's other productions. Some imprecision is unavoidable, as definitive studies of audience composition are not available. For our purposes here, "Jacksonian audiences" refers to anyone who attended the theater during the years of the Jacksonian Democrats' ascendancy, while "working-class audience" designates a specific subset of the former group that became the most loyal and vociferous element of Forrest's supporters during the 1830s and 1840s. In general, I have taken Forrest's audiences to be predominantly male or at least representing the tastes and proclivities of men more than women. On the analytical problems posed by nineteenth-century audiences, see David Grimsted, *Melodrama Unveiled: Theater and Culture, 1800–1850* (Berkeley: University of

California Press, 1987), esp. 46–75; Bruce A. McConachie, *Melodramatic Formations: American Theatre and Society, 1820–1870* (Iowa City: University of Iowa Press, 1992); Lawrence W. Levine, *Highbrow/Lowbrow: The Emergence of Cultural Hierarchy in America* (Cambridge, Mass.: Harvard University Press, 1988); and Rosemarie K. Bank, *Theatre Culture in America, 1825–1860* (New York: Cambridge University Press, 1997), esp. 82–87, 113–14.

5. Quoted in Richard Moody, *Edwin Forrest: First Star of the American Stage* (New York: Knopf, 1960), 88.

6. John August Stone, *Metamora, or The Last of the Wampanoags,* act 1, scene 2 (p. 208 in Richard Moody, ed., *Dramas from the American Theatre, 1762–1909* [Cleveland: World Publishing, 1966]). On King Philip's War, see Russell Bourne, *The Red King's Rebellion: Racial Politics in New England, 1675–1678* (New York: Atheneum, 1990).

7. *Metamora,* act 3, scene 4 (p. 217 in Moody, *Dramas*).

8. For an interpretation of the significance of Metamora's curse, see Lepore, *The Name of War,* 191–92, 210–20.

9. Mark E. Mallett suggests that Forrest cultivated ties with the Jacksonian Democrats to further his career. See Mallett, "'The Game of Politics,'" 32, 36–42.

10. Grose, "Edwin Forrest," 187, 185; Mallett, "'The Game of Politics,'" 38; Jones, "The First but Not the Last of the 'Vanishing Indians,'" 17; Mason, "The Politics of Metamora," 105, 106; Lepore, *The Name of War,* 193, 211. Ethnohistorian Sherry Sullivan claims, in contrast to Lepore, that the overwhelming majority of novels and short stories about Indians published in the United States between 1820 and 1850 were sympathetic to Indians and at least implicitly critical of white actions toward them. See her "Indians in American Fiction, 1820–1850: An Ethnohistorical Perspective," *Clio* 15, no. 3 (1986): 243–44.

11. Mason, "The Politics of Metamora," 93. Mason discusses *Metamora* at somewhat greater length, though with the same emphasis and argument in his *Melodrama and the Myth of America* (Bloomington: Indiana University Press, 1993), 23–59.

12. Mason, "The Politics of Metamora," 105, 106; Jones, "The First but Not the Last of the 'Vanishing Indians,'" 16; Lepore, *The Name of War,* 224. For a view sympathetic to the foregoing, see Philip J. Deloria, *Playing Indian* (New Haven, Conn.: Yale University Press, 1998), 64–65.

13. On the Astor Place riot, see Richard Moody, *The Astor Place Riot* (Bloomington: Indiana University Press, 1958).

14. *Metamora,* act 3, scene 4 (p. 217 in Moody, *Dramas*).

15. Grose, "Edwin Forrest," 189. On authors' attempts to portray Indians in a positive light in fiction, see Sullivan, "Indians in American Fiction," 243–47.

16. *Metamora,* act 2, scene 3 (p. 213 in Moody, *Dramas*).

17. The term is Jeffrey Mason's. See "Politics of Metamora," 105.

18. Quotes are from Jones, "The First but Not the Last of the 'Vanishing Indians,'" 16, 22. On race and Jacksonian popular culture and theater, see Alexander Saxton, *The Rise and Fall of the White Republic: Class Politics and Mass Culture in Nineteenth-Century America* (London: Verso, 1990); David Roediger, *The Wages of Whiteness: Race and the Making of the American Working Class* (London: Verso, 1991); and Eric Lott, *Love and Theft: Blackface Minstrelsy and the American Working Class* (New York: Oxford University Press, 1995). On white representations of Native

Americans, see Robert F. Berkhofer Jr., *The White Man's Indian: Images of the American Indian from Columbus to the Present* (New York: Knopf, 1978), esp. 72–96; Eugene H. Jones, *Native Americans as Shown on the Stage, 1753–1916* (Metuchen, N.J.: Scarecrow Press, 1988); Marilyn J. Anderson, "The Image of the Indian in American Drama during the Jacksonian Era, 1829–1845," *Journal of American Culture* 1 (winter 1978): 800–810; and Rosemarie K. Bank, "Staging the 'Native': Making History in American Theatre Culture, 1828–1838," *Theatre Journal* 45 (December 1993): 46–86. For a fascinating discussion of a related theme, the ideological and performative uses to which white men put the practice of Indian masquerade, see Deloria, *Playing Indian*, esp. 38–70.

19. Lott, *Love and Theft*, 86; Moody, *Edwin Forrest*, 47–48. Moody speculated that, though Forrest recalled this story frequently, "he might have hesitated to repeat [it] today" (47). For more on Forrest's relationship with Push-Ma-Ta-Ha, see Lepore, *The Name of War*, 201.

20. Montrose J. Moses, *The Fabulous Forrest: The Record of an American Actor* (Boston: Little, Brown, 1929), 100.

21. Lott, *Love and Theft*, 54; Jones, "The First but Not the Last of the 'Vanishing Indians,'" 16; Mason, "The Politics of Metamora," 105, 106.

22. James E. Murdoch, *The Stage; or, Recollections of Actors and Acting* (Philadelphia: J. M. Stoddart and Co., 1880), 298–300; Jones, "The First but Not the Last of the 'Vanishing Indians,'" 17. There is some question about the accuracy of the Murdoch anecdote. See Mason, "The Politics of Metamora," esp. 41ff., 109. For more on this incident, see Jones, *Native Americans*, 67–68, and Lepore, *The Name of War*, 203–4. Lepore acknowledges that Forrest's performance may have "insulted Georgians in 1831" but that this does "[n]ot necessarily" render the play "an indictment of Indian removal" (204).

23. On Irving, see Jones, "The First but Not the Last of the 'Vanishing Indians,'" 13, 15. Apess's "Eulogy on King Philip, as Pronounced at the Odeon, in Federal Street, Boston" (1838), appears in Barry O'Connell, ed., *On Our Own Ground: The Complete Writings of William Apess, A Pequot* (Amherst: University of Massachusetts Press, 1992), 275–310. Jill Lepore emphasizes the malleability of the story of King Philip's War during the antebellum era but concludes nonetheless that *Metamora* "intensified and accelerated" the "pursuit of Indian removal" (*The Name of War*, 192–93). For an interpretation of the popularity of another retelling of King Philip's War during the early national period, see Philip Gould, "Reinventing Benjamin Church: Virtue, Citizenship and the History of King Philip's War in Early National America," *Journal of the Early Republic* 16 (winter 1996): 645–57. Rather than focusing on early national enthusiasm for King Philip's War as a reflection of racism, Gould emphasizes the usefulness of Church, a participant in the war, as a link between the Puritan past and new visions of citizenship.

24. McConachie's *Melodramatic Formations* (91–118) contains a useful discussion of the plot and dramatic structure of *Metamora* in the context of the period's dramatic literature. Richard Moody also noted the similarity between the characters of Metamora and Jack Cade and the appeal of Spartacus as an opportunity for Forrest to display his physique, just as he did in *Metamora*. See his *Edwin Forrest*, 104, 197.

25. Sullivan, "Indians in American Fiction," 247. The Indian Removal Act passed in the Senate by 28 to 17 and by 102 to 97 in the House. For an account of the debate, see Wallace, *The*

Long Bitter Trail, 65–72. On the differing ideological positions of the parties and the deployment of the "noble savage" in political discourse, see Saxton, *The Rise and Fall of the White Republic*. For more on the noble savage theme in nineteenth-century U.S. thought and culture, consult Berkhofer, *The White Man's Indian*, 88–96; Jones, *Native Americans*, 63–83; Don B. Wilmeth, "Noble or Ruthless Savage? The American Indian on Stage and in the Drama," *Journal of American Drama and Theater* 1 (1989): 39–78; and Brian W. Dippie, *The Vanishing American: White Attitudes and U.S. Indian Policy* (Middletown, Conn.: Wesleyan University Press, 1982).

26. Grimsted, *Melodrama Unveiled*, 161.

27. James Kirke Paulding, *The Lion of the West* (1831; reprint, Stanford, Calif.: Stanford University Press, 1954), 1:2, 37.

28. Several excellent discussions of the market revolution are Charles Sellers, *The Market Revolution: Jacksonian America, 1815–1846* (New York: Oxford University Press, 1991); Sean Wilentz, "Society, Politics, and the Market Revolution, 1815–1848," in *The New American History*, ed. Eric Foner (Philadelphia: Temple University Press, 1990), 51–71; Paul E. Johnson, "The Market Revolution," in *Encyclopedia of American Social History*, 3 vols., ed. Mary K. Cayton, Elliott J. Gorn, and Peter W. Williams (New York: Scribner, 1993), 1, 545–60; and Melvyn Stokes and Stephen Conway, *The Market Revolution in America: Social, Political, and Religious Expressions, 1800–1880* (Charlottesville: University Press of Virginia, 1996).

29. On these points, see Joseph J. Ellis, *After the Revolution: Profiles of Early American Culture* (New York: Norton, 1979); Steven Watts, "Masks, Morals, and the Market: American Literature and Early Capitalist Culture, 1790–1820," *Journal of the Early Republic* 6 (summer 1986): 127–49; McConachie, *Melodramatic Formations*, 5–28, 74–82; and Neil Harris, *Humbug: The Art of P. T. Barnum* (Chicago: University of Chicago Press, 1973).

30. Lawrence Barrett, *Edwin Forrest* (London, 1881; reprint, New York: B. Blom, 1969), American Actor Series, 42–43. Forrest's recognition of the commodity value and marketability of stardom presaged later developments in the entertainment industry. For a suggestive interpretation of the star system and its relationship to law and capitalism in the twentieth century, see Jane M. Gaines, *Contested Culture: The Image, the Voice, and the Law* (Chapel Hill: University of North Carolina Press, 1991).

31. Moody, *Edwin Forrest*, 89; Congdon, from "Reminiscences of a Journalist (1880)," quoted in Barrett, *Edwin Forrest*, 136; James Rees (Colley Cibber), *Life of Edwin Forrest with Reminiscences and Personal Recollections* (Philadelphia: T. B. Peterson, 1874), 97; Francis C. Wemyss, *Twenty Six Years in the Life of an Actor and Manager* (New York: Burgess and Stringer, 1847), 175. Congdon thought that *Metamora* was such a bad play that he sarcastically attributed its author's suicide to "atone[ment] for the injury which he had inflicted upon the world by the production of this play." Congdon added graciously that the world would "accept this presumptive apology" (136).

32. McConachie, *Melodramatic Formations*; Moody, *Edwin Forrest*, 181.

33. Rees, *Life of Edwin Forrest*, 98; Moses, *The Fabulous Forrest*, 95; Moody, *Edwin Forrest*, 171; Walter J. Meserve, *Heralds of Promise: The Drama of the American People during the Age of Jackson, 1828–1849* (New York: Greenwood Press, 1986), 51–52.

34. Moody, *Edwin Forrest*, 168–70; Moses, *The Fabulous Forrest*, 105–12. Bird later aired his grievances in an unpublished manuscript entitled "Dramatic Authors and Their Profits."

35. For the Indian story, see Garff B. Wilson, *A History of American Acting* (Bloomington: Indiana University Press, 1966), 24. Rosemarie K. Bank was unable to find any reference to this incident in Boston newspapers; see her "Staging the 'Native,'" 481, 21ff. Jill Lepore explores the meaning of the dirge incident in *The Name of War*, 212–13. Fuller noted in an essay called "The Modern Drama" that even if the play had "no other merit, [it] yields something that belongs to the region, Forrest having studied for his part the Indian's gait and expression with some success." Quoted in Meserve, *Heralds of Promise*, 48. On Forrest's realism, see also Moody, *Edwin Forrest*, 96.

36. Richard Moody discovered the missing fourth act among the Lord Chamberlain's plays in the British Museum. When Forrest performed the play in England, he had to deposit a copy with government censors before the opening. See Moody's introduction to *Metamora* in his *Dramas*, 204.

37. This is not to suggest that Forrest's actions arose from sheer cynicism and self-promotion, for there is some reason to believe that he identified, in his own mind, his interests with those of his country. At the very least, Forrest's irrepressible blend of self-interest and civic duty allowed him to blur the line between profit and patriotism. For instance, David Grimsted noted that when "the Bowery [Theatre] refused to give some money to William Leggett, at the time editor of a magazine devoting much space to the drama, Forrest personally donated $50, less to relieve 'a necessitous, virtuous friend' than to 'exalt our national drama.'" Quoted in Grimsted, *Melodrama Unveiled*, 43.

38. Edwin Forrest, *Fourth of July Oration, 1838* (New York: Jared W. Bell, 1838), 15, 21; "Mr. Forrest's Oration," *United States Magazine and Democratic Review* 2 (September 1839): 53.

39. William R. Alger, *Life of Edwin Forrest, the American Tragedian* (1877; reprint, New York: Arno Press, 1977), 350.

40. Alan Nevins, ed., *The Diary of Philip Hone* (New York: Dodd, Mead, 1927), 275, 347.

41. Moses, *The Fabulous Forrest*, 177. These critics apparently rejected the proposition that an actor who was ignorant of national affairs would make a good public servant if only he chose the right advisers.

42. Wemyss, *Twenty Six Years*, 324.

43. On these points, see Victor Turner, *The Ritual Process: Structure and Antistructure* (Chicago: Aldine Publishing, 1969); *The Forest of Symbols: Aspects of Ndembu Ritual* (Ithaca, N.Y.: Cornell University Press, 1967); and *Dramas, Fields, and Metaphors: Symbolic Action in Human Society* (Ithaca, N.Y.: Cornell University Press, 1974). Useful here too is Rosemarie K. Bank's recent work on what she terms "theatre culture," which she argues is "constitutive of multiple, simultaneous relationships." See her *Theatre Culture in America*, 4.

44. Roy Harvey Pearce, *Savagism and Civilization: A Study of the Indian and the American Mind* (Baltimore: Johns Hopkins University Press, 1965), 138.

45. I differ with Jill Lepore on the significance of Metamora's death at the conclusion of the play. She asserts that "in the end, and especially in its ending, *Metamora* made Indian removal palatable to the American public by insisting that Indians look best from a distance" (*The Name of War*, 224). Here Lepore finds far-reaching and sinister implications in a tragic hero perishing

at the end of a tragedy. In contrast, I argue that the tragic ending created not distance but proximity. By using the noble chief to claim that Americans provided appropriate material for tragedy, *Metamora* intertwined white and Indian identities in the present as well as the past. Thus, the primary distinction was not between white Americans and Indians but between the virtuous American New World and the corrupt English Old World.

46. On the symbolic importance of nature to the Jacksonian image, see John William Ward's classic *Andrew Jackson: Symbol for an Age* (New York: Oxford University Press, 1955), esp. 13–97. On American cultural inferiority, see Ellis, *After the Revolution*. Murry H. Nelligan discusses the Indian as nationalistic symbol in "American Nationalism on the Stage: The Plays of George Washington Parke Custis (1781–1857)", *Virginia Magazine of History and Biography* 58 (July 1950): 299–324, esp. 307–8. For further reflections on the use of Indians by white Americans in constructing a national identity, see Sullivan, "Indians in American Fiction," 248–54.

47. Deloria, *Playing Indian*, 40; Grimsted, *Melodrama Unveiled*, 70–71For a discussion of Forrest's role in defining and creating American identity, see also Lepore, *The Name of War*, 198–200. Lepore is correct that Forrest's "theatrical performance were, in a sense, at the vanguard of establishing what it meant to be an American" (199). Her attempts to link the identity Forrest helped to create to support for Indian removal are less persuasive.

48. Bank, "Staging the 'Native,'" 486, and *Theatre Culture in America*, 70.

49. Sullivan, "Indians in American Fiction," 240, 249–50, discusses this theme in antebellum novels and short stories.

50. Grimsted, *Melodrama Unveiled*, 233–34.

Index

About the Contributors

James Taylor Carson is associate professor of history at Queen's University, Ontario, Canada. He is the author of *Searching for the Bright Path: The Mississippi Choctaws from Prehistory to Removal* (University of Nebraska Press, 1999).

Catherine E. Kelly is associate professor of history at the University of Oklahoma. She is the author of *In the New England Fashion: Reshaping Women's Lives in the Nineteenth Century* (Cornell University Press, 2002).

Scott C. Martin is associate professor of history and American Culture Studies at Bowling Green State University. He is the author of *Killing Time: Leisure and Culture in Southwestern Pennsylvania, 1800–1850* (University of Pittsburgh Press, 1995) and is currently at work on a study of women, gender, and temperance before the Civil War.

Brett Mizelle is assistant professor of history and director of the American studies program at California State University Long Beach. He is currently completing a book on the cultural work of exhibitions of exotic and performing animals in early national and antebellum America.

Jeffrey A. Mullins is assistant professor of history at St. Cloud State University. He is currently completing a book on race, reform, and human nature in antebellum America.

Patrick Rael is associate professor of History at Bowdoin College in Brunswick, Maine. He earned his Ph.D. at the University of California, Berkeley in 1995 and the author of *Black Identity and Black Protest in the Antebellum North* (University of North Carolina Press, 2002).

Joseph T. Rainer received his B.A. in history from Georgetown University, and his Ph.D. in American studies from the College of William and Mary. The title of his doctoral dissertation is: "The Honorable Fraternity of Moving Merchants: Yankee Peddlers in the Old South, 1800–1860."

Kevin Thornton holds a Ph.D. from the University of Michigan and teaches at the University of Vermont. He grew up in Charlotte.

Graham Warder received a Ph.D. in History from the University of Massachusetts, Amherst. He teaches at Keene State College in New Hampshire and works as the library catalog and acquisitions director of the Disability History Museum website.